The New Direction
in American Politics

JOHN E. CHUBB AND PAUL E. PETERSON

Editors

The New Direction in American Politics

THE BROOKINGS INSTITUTION

Washington, D.C.

Copyright © 1985 by

THE BROOKINGS INSTITUTION

1775 Massachusetts Avenue, N.W., Washington, D.C. 20036

Library of Congress Cataloging in Publication data:

Main entry under title:

The New direction in American politics.

Includes bibliographical references and index.
1. United States—Politics and government—
1945–   —Addresses, essays, lectures.
I. Cavanagh, Thomas E.   II. Chubb, John E.
III. Peterson, Paul E.
JK271.N44   1985   320.973   85-71272

ISBN 0-8157-1406-8
ISBN 0-8157-1405-X (pbk.)

4 5 6 7 8 9

THE BROOKINGS INSTITUTION is an independent organization devoted to nonpartisan research, education, and publication in economics, government, foreign policy, and the social sciences generally. Its principal purposes are to aid in the development of sound public policies and to promote public understanding of issues of national importance.

The Institution was founded on December 8, 1927, to merge the activities of the Institute for Government Research, founded in 1916, the Institute of Economics, founded in 1922, and the Robert Brookings Graduate School of Economics and Government, founded in 1924.

The Board of Trustees is responsible for the general administration of the Institution, while the immediate direction of the policies, program, and staff is vested in the President, assisted by an advisory committee of the officers and staff. The by-laws of the Institution state: "It is the function of the Trustees to make possible the conduct of scientific research, and publication, under the most favorable conditions, and to safeguard the independence of the research staff in the pursuit of their studies and in the publication of the results of such studies. It is not a part of their function to determine, control, or influence the conduct of particular investigations or the conclusions reached."

The President bears final responsibility for the decision to publish a manuscript as a Brookings book. In reaching his judgment on the competence, accuracy, and objectivity of each study, the President is advised by the director of the appropriate research program and weighs the views of a panel of expert outside readers who report to him in confidence on the quality of the work. Publication of a work signifies that it is deemed a competent treatment worthy of public consideration but does not imply endorsement of conclusions or recommendations.

The Institution maintains its position of neutrality on issues of public policy in order to safeguard the intellectual freedom of the staff. Hence interpretations or conclusions in Brookings publications should be understood to be solely those of the authors and should not be attributed to the Institution, to its trustees, officers, or other staff members, or to the organizations that support its research.

Foreword

THE LANDSLIDE victories of President Ronald Reagan in the 1980 and 1984 elections have raised once again the question that has stymied election analysts for the last twenty years: is the United States undergoing a major electoral realignment? The country has experienced five realignments before, most recently during the New Deal. Given the sequence of erroneous realignment predictions in the 1960s and 1970s, the safe answer is that it is too early to tell. But perhaps the question is itself erroneous. The important issue, this volume suggests, is not whether current voting patterns will remain intact over the long run, but whether the electoral change that has already occurred has set in course a series of institutional and policy changes that have shifted the terms of political debate. Is government now being moved in a new direction that is unlikely to be reversed by subsequent elections?

Taking the more comprehensive view of realignment implied by this question, this book analyzes the principal components of the political system—from voting and elections to institutions and major policies. Each essay compares developments during the 1980s to trends that were in place before President Reagan took office. The findings reported in these essays show the forces for change to be preponderant, though they have encountered strong stabilizing institutions. Change has been most evident in voter loyalties, party organization, campaign finance, senatorial elections, and presidential politics. Indeed, with the increasing capacity of the executive branch to dominate the policy agenda, and with a president and a governing party holding a clear vision of what goals and policies to place on that agenda, the changes have been extensive, and the consequences profound. Even though continuity is strong in the House of Representatives and state government, these institutions have been unable to block transformations in domestic spending, entitlement programs, defense capacity, and fiscal policy. The editors of this volume conclude that together these changes represent a new direction in American politics, substantially different from that established during the New Deal.

This conclusion is based on analyses that grew out of two conferences held at the Brookings Institution in which the authors of the essays participated. The first, held shortly after the 1984 elections, was devoted to placing the results of the election in longer-term perspective and to identifying the issues around which the essays would be organized. Drafts of these essays were critiqued at the second conference, which was held in February 1985, and were then revised for inclusion in this volume.

The editors, John E. Chubb and Paul E. Peterson, wish to thank the many people who assisted in the volume's preparation. Nancy D. Davidson, Venka Macintyre, Caroline Lalire, James R. Schneider, and Theresa B. Walker edited the manuscript; Ellen Garshick, Claire D. Lincoln, and Jeanette Morrison did the proofreading; and Ward & Silvan prepared the index. Vickie L. Corey and Chisolm B. Hamilton prepared the manuscript for typesetting. Alan G. Hoden, Alice G. Keck, and Paul M. Wright verified the factual statements and citations in the papers. They were assisted by Lynn Cassidy, John A. Clark, Michael F. Flanagan, and Steven J. Levine. Pamela D. Harris, Janet A. Hathaway, Debra M. Johanson, Julie Bailes Legg, and Judith H. Newman provided secretarial assistance.

The authors include the following Brookings staff members: Paul E. Peterson, director of the Governmental Studies program; John D. Steinbruner, director of the Foreign Policy Studies program; John E. Chubb, Samuel Kernell, Terry M. Moe, A. James Reichley, Steven S. Smith, and James L. Sundquist, senior fellows; and R. Kent Weaver, research associate. The other authors are Thomas E. Cavanagh, senior research associate at the National Academy of Sciences; John A. Ferejohn, professor of political science at Stanford University and senior research fellow at the Hoover Institution at Stanford; Morris P. Fiorina, professor of government at Harvard University; Gary C. Jacobson, professor of political science at the University of California, San Diego; D. Roderick Kiewiet, associate professor of political science at the California Institute of Technology; and Douglas Rivers, assistant professor of political science at the California Institute of Technology.

The interpretations and conclusions presented here are solely those of the authors and should not be ascribed to the persons whose assistance is acknowledged above, to any agency that funded research reported herein, or to the trustees, officers, or other staff members of the Brookings Institution.

BRUCE K. MAC LAURY
President

May 1985
Washington, D.C.

Contents

Tables

Figures

The New Direction
in American Politics

CHAPTER ONE

Realignment and Institutionalization

JOHN E. CHUBB AND PAUL E. PETERSON

THE AMERICAN political system, during the presidency of Ronald Reagan, has been transformed to an extent unknown since the days of Franklin Delano Roosevelt. The terms of political debate, the course of domestic and foreign policy, and the dominant line of partisan cleavage have all been fundamentally changed. Only rarely in American history has the political system broken as sharply with governing customs to address festering national problems or to confront social and economic issues head-on.

Electorally, the president won smashing victories in 1980 and 1984, and the Republicans in the Senate, after years in the political wilderness, have been the majority party since 1981. More voters consider themselves Republicans than at any time in the last twenty years, and the Republican party treasury has never been so well endowed. In policy terms the Reagan administration has reduced entitlements, curtailed or eliminated other domestic programs, boosted national defense, slashed taxes, and incurred unprecedented fiscal deficits. Most recently, President Reagan has advocated a strategic defense initiative and proposed a wholesale revision of the U.S. tax code. Institutionally, he has centralized and politicized the executive branch, built a conservative majority in support of his program in Congress, altered the shape of American federalism, and used the public relations power of the presidency with extraordinary effectiveness.

These kinds of electoral, institutional, and policy changes are quite outside the usual scope of American politics. Characteristically, the

1

workings of American government are resistant to all but modestly incremental changes. Most of the time Americans do not change their party identification. And even if their opinions on issues change, policy consequences are slow to follow. Agreements must be made among executive departments, bargains must be struck with relevant committees in Congress, and the complexities of the intergovernmental system must usually be traversed. No aphorism seems more true of the American republic than the one affixed to the ancien régime in France: the more things change, the more they remain the same.

Yet at five junctures in American history—1800, 1828, 1860, 1896, and 1932—leaders moved the political system decisively in a new direction. If a politics of incrementalism was eventually restored, it took place on a new plane that had previously been obscure to all but the most farsighted. On each occasion, government was brought up to date, revitalized, and prepared to address more innovatively the issues that had plagued the preceding generation.[1] In each instance a major political realignment is generally believed to have occurred.

The Reagan years, many observers believe, do not yet qualify as a major realignment. The House of Representatives and a sizable majority of state governments remain solidly Democratic. Partisan loyalties still leave Republicans in the minority, and public opinion has not moved unambiguously in a conservative direction. Reagan's first landslide victory may have been as much a rejection of the Carter years as an endorsement of Reagan. Were it not for the fact that the turn of the business cycle worked to Reagan's advantage in 1984, he might not have become the dominant political personality of the 1980s. Because such a concatenation of circumstances could be undone with equal swiftness, the Reagan revolution may have little of the sweep and permanence of the New Deal realignment. Some of the authors of the ensuing essays voice these doubts and show ways in which the innovations of the Reagan years may be limited and transitory.

But to the editors of this volume these doubts understate the significance of contemporary developments. Major political and policy changes need not occur today in the same fashion as during the Civil War, the 1890s, or the New Deal years. While the American political system is still organized by many of the same constitutional rules and its institutions

---

1. Much the same conceptualization is advanced by Walter Dean Burnham in "Into the 1980s with Ronald Reagan," in Walter Dean Burnham, ed., *The Current Crisis in American Politics* (Oxford University Press, 1982), pp. 268–320.

governed by much the same formal powers, the relationships among voters, institutions, and public policy have changed significantly. Shifts in voting behavior have different effects on the composition of political institutions today than they did in the past, and changes in the composition of institutions have different effects on public policy. Any evaluation of political change must therefore be more than a simple, straightforward comparison with past electoral or governmental changes. Only by adopting a broader perspective that incorporates all the political system's major elements can we assess contemporary developments accurately.

Broadening the Perspective

Notwithstanding the profound and far-reaching consequences that major realignments have had on American government, the analysis of them has emphasized their electoral elements.[2] The main drawback of this focus is that it overlooks the way in which political leaders, the policies they formulate, and the institutions they create also shape and reshape political life, turning it in new directions that the electorate then endorses.[3] Perhaps the greatest lesson of past realignments is that major political change involves equal parts of voter unrest and governmental

2. The seminal article in electorally based realignment research is V. O. Key, "A Theory of Critical Elections," *Journal of Politics,* vol. 17 (February 1955), pp. 3–18. It was followed by a series of studies in that vein, including Angus Campbell, "A Classification of Presidential Elections," in Angus Campbell and others, eds., *Elections and the Political Order* (Wiley, 1967), chap. 4; Gerald M. Pomper, *Elections in America: Control and Influence in Democratic Politics* (Dodd, Mead, 1968); Walter Dean Burnham, *Critical Elections and the Mainsprings of American Politics* (Norton, 1970); and James L. Sundquist, *Dynamics of the Party System: Alignment and Realignment of Political Parties in the United States,* rev. ed. (Brookings, 1983).

3. While other aspects of realignment have been examined in detail, they have never been integrated into a coherent perspective on realignment. See Barbara Deckard Sinclair, "Party Realignment and the Transformation of the Political Agenda," *American Political Science Review,* vol. 71 (September 1977), pp. 940–53; David Brady with Joseph Stewart, Jr., "Congressional Party Realignment and Transformations of Public Policy in Three Realignment Eras," *American Journal of Political Science,* vol. 26 (May 1982); Stephen Skowronek, "Presidential Leadership in Political Time," in Michael Nelson, ed., *The Presidency and the Political System* (CQ Press, 1984), pp. 84–132. The notable exception is Jerome M. Clubb, William H. Flanagan, and Nancy H. Zingale, *Partisan Realignment: Voters, Parties, and Government in American History,* Sage Library of Social Research (Beverly Hills, Calif.: Sage Publications, 1980), chap. 6.

action.[4] Electoral protests that produce presidential landslides and sizable congressional turnover are fairly common, but the party that benefits seldom finds the wherewithal to reinforce the protest, to convert voters permanently to its side. Major transformations seem to require a special reciprocal relationship between the people and their government: the voters must indicate their support for change in a way that transfers effective institutional control from one party to the other while the new government, for its part, must somehow use that control to inspire new voters to swear allegiance. Until this is understood—that is, until the electoral side of realignment that has been thoroughly analyzed is connected to the governing side that provides realignment with its historical significance—the meaning of contemporary political change will remain unclear.

Plainly, each realignment has derived its identity as much from the new direction in which institutions and policy were taken as from the new majority established in the electorate. When American politics was restructured for the first time with the election of Thomas Jefferson in 1800, the Federalists were replaced by Republicans, and Bostonian men of commerce were superseded by Virginia farmers. In the subsequent consolidation of this first party system, as it has been called, the growth of national institutions was checked, the first Bank of the United States was disestablished, Anglophobia gained ascendancy and led in 1812 to a disastrous war with Britain, and the Louisiana Purchase preserved an agrarian republic for more than a century.[5] When the second party system was created by Andrew Jackson's election in 1828, the sociopolitical elite that had established the Republic was swept from power by rough-hewn frontiersmen from west of the Appalachians. The new majority also made indelible marks on American government. The administration of public service became riddled with the "spoils system," suffrage was extended to virtually the entire white male population, party conventions replaced the congressional caucus as the mechanism for selecting presidents, and, once again, established institutions, as symbolized this time by the Second Bank of the United States, were dismantled.

4. For illustrations see Burnham, *Critical Elections and the Mainsprings of American Politics,* chap. 1; Sundquist, *Dynamics,* chap. 2; and Clubb and others, *Partisan Realignment,* chap. 1.

5. The concept of party systems is introduced in Walter Dean Burnham and William Nisbet Chambers, eds., *The American Party Systems* (Oxford University Press, 1967).

The third party system, which took shape amid talk of secession and ultimately war, went well beyond electoral change in its effects on the political system. Indeed, the Civil War represented, in the view of Abraham Lincoln, a second founding of the Republic. In its aftermath slavery was abolished, the semisovereignty of the states was curtailed, and a national program of economic development (including the Homestead Act, land grants for railroads, and the establishment of land grant colleges) was initiated. The third party system was, of course, also characterized by major electoral change inasmuch as the Republicans not only replaced the Whigs as the second major party but also controlled Congress and the presidency for more than a decade.

With William McKinley's landslide victory over William Jennings Bryan in 1896, the Republican ascendance was complete. Republican policies repudiated the "easy money, low tariff" platform of the Populists and Bryan Democrats, and the success of the policies destroyed the potential for a farm-labor coalition not unlike the left-wing alliances that were forming in Europe. The economic depression of 1893 that had precipitated voter unrest was addressed with tariff and monetary policies that affirmed a modern industrial path rather than with measures that would have sustained an agrarian one.

It was also a major depression that in 1932 ended the Republican-dominated alignment, swept Democrats into office, and divided the electorate along class lines. But the fifth party system would not have been initiated at this juncture had Franklin Roosevelt and the Democrats not turned government policy dramatically in a direction that promised relief. The Democratic coalition consolidated its position by means of policies that aided trade unions, created the welfare state, and sustained economic growth.

Institutionalization and Realignment

Electoral realignments have thus been held together by institutional and policy changes. But the ways in which policies and institutions have reinforced realigning elections have not been the same throughout American history. While it is true that each realignment altered the dominant line of political cleavage, brought new issues to the top of the political agenda, modernized the terms of political debate, broke governmental deadlocks, and established the popular basis for effective government for the generation to come, realignments have differed in one crucial respect: namely, in the moderating effects that existing institutions have increasingly placed upon realigning forces. In assessing whether American politics is experiencing major change today—that is, moving in a new direction— attention must be paid to this institutional difference.

As the Republic has matured, its government has become further established and resistant to change. Citizens and groups have become increasingly attached to established practices, and officeholders have been ever more successful at insulating themselves—and their organizations—from external political pressures. These increments in complexity, autonomy, and constituent loyalties have occurred slowly, and their cumulative impact has become fully apparent only when political institutions have been confronted by external demands for breaks with past practice that characteristically accompany realignments.

In the early years of the Republic the institutions created by the Constitution were so weakly established that realignments threatened their very existence. Even the relatively modest shift in power from Federalists to Republicans in 1800 threatened the foundations of government. Cries of treason surrounded the XYZ affair, and the powers of the Alien and Sedition acts were used to quell dissent. The Electoral College mechanism was so poorly designed it turned a landslide election for Thomas Jefferson into a cliff-hanger decided in the House of Representatives by one vote. The loser, Aaron Burr, was himself accused of treasonous activities a few years later.

The Jacksonian revolution was in many ways more profound, for it brought to power a distinctly new social class. But American institutions were by now a good deal more resilient: this time there was no question of the legitimacy of political opposition, no Hartford Convention with its talk of secession, and no doubt about the electoral outcome. Yet institutionalization had not progressed so far that Andrew Jackson could not dramatically alter political practice.

While the Republic was probably even more institutionalized by 1860, the antislavery movement unleashed such a powerful set of political forces that the government was unable to contain the passions that led to civil war. Had the federal government in the 1840s been better able to assert itself in a national program of economic development, had the doctrine of state's rights not become an entrenched component of Democratic party doctrine, and had the presidential office been given more distinguished leadership in the 1850s, secession and war might have been avoided. But it is more likely that Lincoln was correct when he observed that every drop of blood drawn by the slavemaster's lash would have to be paid by blood drawn by swords in battle before a house divided against itself could be reunited. A realigning force so powerful that it provoked secession and prolonged civil war could have been buffered only by the most well entrenched governmental institutions.

Fortunately, American political institutions have not been challenged by a political movement of comparable force in the century and a quarter since the Civil War. By now the constituent components of the American government have become so institutionalized that they could probably withstand a shock of even such dramatic proportions. Certainly, they were not challenged in any fundamental sense either by the realignment of 1896 or by the New Deal, though both constituted major turning points in American political history.

Significantly, the New Deal realignment was electorally the more profound, but its immediate effect on key governing institutions was more modest. Voting in congressional elections, for example, shifted toward the Democrats by 9.6 percentage points in the 1930s, compared with only a 3.9 percent shift toward the Republicans in the 1890s.[6] The Democrats' extraordinary electoral gains during the New Deal enabled them to double their seats in the House of Representatives, but that achievement, though substantial, was actually considerably less than what the Republicans had accomplished between 1890 and 1894, when they nearly tripled their representation in the House.[7] Institutional changes were also slower at the state level in the 1930s than they were in the 1890s. Republican gains in gubernatorial voting in 1896 were comparable to the party's presidential gains, but Democratic gains in gubernatorial voting in 1932 lagged well behind presidential gains.[8]

6. David Brady, "A Reevaluation of Realignments in American Politics: Evidence from the House of Representatives," *American Political Science Review*, vol. 79 (March 1985), p. 39.

7. Norman J. Ornstein and others, *Vital Statistics on Congress, 1982*, American Enterprise Institute Studies in Political and Social Processes (Washington, D.C.: AEI, 1982), pp. 28–29. It is well known, of course, that legislatures elected from single-member districts reward the majority party with a higher percentage of seats than its share of the national vote—a bias often expressed by the cube law. But as Brady in "A Reevaluation of Realignments" has shown, the bias in favor of the victorious party in 1860 and 1894 exceeded the cube law prediction while the bias in 1932 fell far short of it.

8. Clubb and others, *Partisan Realignment*, p. 194.

The parties also divided less sharply on the issues in 1932 than during the earlier realignment. Presidential party platforms became polarized during the campaign of 1896, but party differences changed little in 1932.[9] Voting along party lines increased in Congress after each electoral realignment but once again to a lesser degree during the New Deal.[10]

These differences between the New Deal and the realignment of the 1890s indicate an increasing institutional resistance to even sweeping social and political change. A moderate shift in voting behavior during the 1890s was accompanied by major institutional change. The much more dramatic swing in voting in the 1930s took longer to have its institutional impact. Congress, the executive bureaucracy, state governments, even public policy—all were growing more resistant to change. Political officials with a stake in maintaining their institutions were finding ways to insulate them from the voters. Government at all levels and in all branches was employing more people divided into more departments, agencies, and committees; following more rules; and adhering more closely to established norms of behavior. Restrained internally by extensive commitments to the status quo, the political system, though responding to the rising demands of a country experiencing rapid growth and modernization, was containing these demands within increasingly well-entrenched organizations. The system was, in other words, becoming institutionalized.

When comparing the Reagan realignment with those of the past, one must keep in mind both the elements that earlier realignments had in common and the crucial ways in which they differed. On the one hand, each realignment has established a new direction for American voters, institutions, and policies that continued for years. On the other hand, realignments differed in the degree of political institutionalization that they encountered. In this regard the Reagan realignment has its own distinctive characteristics. Like past realignments it has capitalized on voter unrest, altered the focus of domestic and foreign policy, and changed the balance of power among political institutions. But even more than the New Deal realignment, the Reagan policy change is circumscribed by the increasingly institutionalized context within which innovation is occurring. The engine of change is ever more limited to the

9. B. Ginsburg, "Critical Elections and the Substance of Party Conflict, 1844–1968," *Midwest Journal of Political Science,* vol. 16 (November 1972), p. 612.

10. Brady with Stewart, "Congressional Party Realignment"; Sinclair, "Party Realignment"; Clubb and others, *Partisan Realignment,* pp. 228–46.

executive branch, the national political parties, and, to a lesser extent, the U.S. Senate. The House of Representatives, state governments, and networks of interest groups are mainly conservators of past practices. Even the institutional structure of public policy itself becomes an element that resists political innovation. Programs are so complex, associated interests are so entrenched, and procedural protections are so extensive that the rate of change is inevitably slowed. But though the capacity for change has become attenuated, this does not depreciate the significance of realigning periods. Once the groups impelling a new direction have surmounted the institutional barriers, their policies, too, will be difficult to dislodge.

Voters and Elections

That major political change in a highly institutionalized political system ultimately depends on governmental action does not diminish the significance of elections. Although the newly dominant party must find appropriate policies or improve economic conditions in order to reinforce a partisan change, the shift in the first instance is initiated by voter unrest. Because voters initiate a realignment, the essays in the first part of this volume examine both the circumstances moving voters toward the Republican party, especially in presidential and senatorial politics, and the ways in which House and state elections have been insulated from this presidential shift.

Partisanship

American voters have a long-standing tendency to identify with one of the major parties—to think of themselves as Democrats or Republicans—and to vote for that party in most elections for most offices. Although shifts in allegiance from one party to another and back again occur with greater frequency among the public at large than among the politically active elite, ordinary voters who pay little attention to politics tend to remain wedded to their parties, even when their opinions on specific issues wander erratically.[11] Stable political eras are to a consid-

11. Philip E. Converse, "The Concept of a Normal Vote," in Angus Campbell and others, *Elections and the Political Order* (Wiley, 1967); and Morris P. Fiorina, *Retrospective Voting in American National Elections* (Yale University Press, 1981).

erable extent founded upon such enduring partisan attachments. Indeed, without them it is difficult to conceive of lasting political alignments.

During the 1960s and 1970s, however, partisanship appeared to be vanishing from the American political scene. The proportion of the electorate identifying with either of the major parties fell steadily from 1964 to 1974 and for nearly a decade failed to recover.[12] At first many observers believed that the "decay" phase of an electoral cycle was occurring and that the political system was ripening for realignment. But as the years went by and one prediction of impending change after another proved wrong, skepticism that partisanship would ever revive began to spread. Young people, at the vanguard of the movement toward independence, were not becoming more partisan as they aged in the way that previous generations had.[13] New issues were arising—energy, the environment, Vietnam, Watergate, inflation—that did not divide voters along readily identifiable party lines. Political party labels had become little more than banners flown by independent-minded candidates who often succeeded in primaries by running against traditional partisan and group attachments.[14] Partisanship was not being reinforced, and with increasing levels of education and seemingly direct access to candidates via television, voters seemed to feel they were getting along fine without identifying with a party.[15]

12. The decline is analyzed in Norman H. Nie, Sidney Verba, and John R. Petrocik, *The Changing American Voter* (Harvard University Press, 1979), chaps. 4, 20; its persistence is discussed in David B. Hill and Norman R. Luttbeg, *Trends in American Electoral Behavior* (Itasca, Ill.: F. E. Peacock, 1983).

13. The studies pointing to the weakening relationship between experience and partisanship strength are numerous. For example, see Paul R. Abramson, "Generational Change and the Decline of Party Identification in America, 1952–1974," *American Political Science Review,* vol. 70 (June 1976), pp. 469–78; Norval D. Glenn, "Sources of Shift to Political Independence: Some Evidence from a Cohort Analysis," *Social Science Quarterly,* vol. 53 (December 1972), pp. 494–519; and Kent Jennings and Richard G. Niemi, "Continuity and Change in Political Orientations: A Longitudinal Study of Two Generations," *American Political Science Review,* vol. 69 (December 1975), pp. 1316–35.

14. Generally, see Burnham, *Critical Elections.* The weak control of parties over presidential nominations is underlined in Nelson W. Polsby, *Consequences of Party Reform* (Oxford University Press, 1983), and in congressional elections before the 1980s in Gary C. Jacobson and Samuel Kernell, *Strategy and Choice in Congressional Elections* (Yale University Press, 1981).

15. The possibility of party identification eroding permanently with increasing levels of education is explored in W. Phillips Shively, "The Development of Party Identification among Adults: Exploration of a Functional Model," *American Political Science Review,* vol. 73 (December 1979), pp. 1039–54.

In 1984, however, partisanship—specifically, Republican partisanship—made a comeback. As the proportion of the electorate calling themselves independent fell and the proportion declaring themselves Democratic plummeted, the Republican proportion soared. After years of trailing the Democrats by a three-to-two margin, the Republicans drew nearly even. As Thomas Cavanagh and James Sundquist report (chapter 2), the Republicans' one-year gain of 7 percentage points is larger than any surge in a party's stable core of supporters occurring in previous presidential elections.[16] And in the spring of 1985 most of the Republican gains remain intact.

Except for Jews, blacks, and the unemployed, nearly every demographic and geographic group has moved toward the Republican party. In fact, the Republicans now have a plurality among white voters and are ahead of or tied with the Democrats in at least seven of the nine largest states.[17] Equally important, Republican gains occurred among groups of voters where partisan change is most likely to occur and where the change may have the greatest political significance. Persons under thirty years old, who have the least well entrenched partisan identifications but the most future opportunity to influence electoral outcomes, shifted away from the Democrats and toward the Republicans by a combined 22 percentage points. Southerners, long subject to the cross-pressures of Democratic traditions and conservative beliefs, shifted equally sharply in the same direction. These changes in the South raise the prospect of still more Republican success in local, state, and congressional elections within what had been a traditional bastion of Democratic strength.

There are, of course, reasons to question how permanently the Republicans have narrowed the Democratic lead in partisanship. A similar Republican gain in 1980 and 1981 fell back somewhat when the economy entered a recession. The resurgence of Republican partisanship in 1984 may be little more than the result of the economic boom that, as D. Roderick Kiewiet and Douglas Rivers (chapter 3) demonstrate,

16. Lyndon B. Johnson's landslide in 1964 was associated with nearly as large a surge toward the Democrats; however, by 1966, a bad election year for the Democrats, those gains had completely disappeared. The 1986 elections could be as costly to the Republicans, but the 1982 elections suggest they will not be. Despite unfavorable off-year conditions, the Republicans narrowed the Democratic lead in partisanship between 1980 and 1982.

17. Laurily K. Epstein, "The Changing Structure of Party Identification," *PS*, vol. 18 (Winter 1985), pp. 48–52.

rejuvenated Ronald Reagan's approval ratings. Public opinion has not shifted substantially in a conservative direction, and Republican leaders remain ideologically to the right of their supporters.[18] Young voters especially will feel this tension because on the so-called social issues—abortion and school prayer, for example—many hold opinions that differ from those espoused by Republican leaders. But these reasons for skepticism should not be exaggerated. The current growth in Republican partisanship is twice the size of the 1980 increase and has lasted twice as long. There is also no evidence that partisanship varies with short-term changes in economic conditions. To the contrary, between 1978 and 1982 the Republicans steadily reduced the Democratic lead in partisanship, despite the 1981 recession. The Republican comeback in partisanship is more than an artifact of the 1984 election.[19]

Political Parties

However large and durable, Republican gains in partisanship do not necessarily portend a sustained new direction in American politics. They may merely mean that as Republicans become more evenly competitive with Democrats, control of political institutions will alternate regularly between the parties. If the two parties still stand for the same principles as in the past, contest the same bundle of issues, derive popular support from traditional supporters, and find it equally difficult to dominate the national agenda, then electoral politics will have changed, but one could hardly claim a major realignment.

If the Republican electoral resurgence does not by itself signify a new

18. Seymour Martin Lipset, "The Elections, The Economy, and Public Opinion, 1984," *PS*, vol. 18 (Winter 1985), pp. 28–38.

19. Some have argued (for example, Lipset, "The Elections") that party identification has grown so volatile that it has lost its traditional meaning. But it now appears that even among the unusually independent 1960s generation, party identification began to stabilize as voters passed their thirtieth birthdays. Partisanship also continued even when voters defected to the opposition in a particular election. A national sample of high school seniors surveyed in 1965 and resurveyed in 1973 and 1982 showed that people were more consistent in their partisanship between 1973 and 1982 than they had been in the preceding period. Even four consecutive votes for candidates outside their party changed voters' partisanship just one unit on a seven-point scale—for example, from independent Republican to weak Republican. When partisanship did change, moreover, it shifted toward the Republican party. These findings are reported in M. Kent Jennings and Gregory B. Markus, "Partisan Orientations over the Long Haul: Results from the Three-Wave Political Socialization Panel Study," *American Political Science Review*, vol. 78 (December 1984), pp. 1000–18.

direction, however, comparable changes among political elites give it a special meaning. Electoral change has coincided with a redefinition of the central issues political leaders are debating. The national parties no longer debate questions of public policy in the same categories that characterized public rhetoric from the New Deal through the early 1970s. Admittedly, the appropriate degree of national governmental intervention in the economy remains a focus of disputation. But the imagery with which this question is addressed has evolved considerably. Stagflation— the combination of a stagnant, low-growth economy and high inflation— began to change the nature of the economic debate in the mid-1970s. The issue was transformed from one of the balance between unemployment and inflation to one of competent political management to restore stable economic growth. With the inflationary debacle at the end of the Carter administration and the sustained recovery at the end of Reagan's first administration, the Republicans acquired a new image on the economic issue.

The 1984 presidential election campaign crystallized these changes. As Ronald Reagan took credit for the best two years of economic performance in more than a decade, Walter Mondale attempted to discredit the recovery as heavily mortgaged to the future. Mondale proposed tax increases, fiscal responsibility, and cautious growth. Just as Herbert Hoover had opposed federal relief during the Depression, thereby giving Franklin Roosevelt the popular side of the key issue, so Mondale identified the Democratic party with a painful policy, leaving Republicans the popular alternative—cutting deficits through economic growth and the elimination of wasteful spending. As Cavanagh and Sundquist report in chapter 2, the effects of these positions and others on the images of the parties have been profound. "The Democratic party [is] not seen as the traditional defender of the middle class but as the tax collector of the welfare state, the Republican party not as the tool of Wall Street and the rich but as the instrument to bring about widespread economic growth and opportunity."

For young people, especially, the differences between Democratic and Republican philosophies have been defined by the Carter and Reagan years. As they acquire their partisan identities they will not be thinking of the parties in the same terms as the preceding generation, and certainly not in terms defined in the 1930s. Carter has replaced Hoover as the negative symbol; Reagan can serve as a Republican party hero for decades to come. Stagflation, not depression, is the past evil to be avoided at all costs; budget cuts and tax reductions have become identified with rising economic prosperity.

Barring an economic reverse sufficient to tarnish this Republican image, these changing party identities will be reinforced during Reagan's second term. In the long run, reinforcement of the new direction has always depended on demonstrably effective policies for the problems that caused the electoral revolt. But in the short run (upon which longer-term developments crucially depend), the appearance of success is also critical. The new majority party must communicate to the public a confidence that it has the ability to sustain current accomplishments into the future.

The Republicans in the 1980s have excelled at giving this impression and in the process have increased their prospects for future policy success. Reagan's own self-confidence and unclouded vision of the future is of paramount importance, of course, but other factors are also present. For one thing, the Republican National Committee has an institutional presence that easily surpasses that of its competitors. With a permanent staff exceeding 500 and revenue of more than $200 million for each election cycle (see chapter 6), the committee is marketing the party in ways that are almost bound to reinforce Republican partisanship. The Democratic National Committee, with half the staff and only 15 percent of the resources, cannot match this effort and will require years to catch up—if it ever does. As James Reichley (chapter 7) points out, the Republican National Committee is aggressively selling a singular Republican image to the public. Television advertising conveys a coherent Republican philosophy; candidate training schools, together with centrally prepared position papers, enable Republican congressional candidates to bring similar messages to the voters; and campaign contributions, especially to promising challengers of Democratic incumbents, ensure that Republican candidates have the resources to communicate effectively. In the process, they establish before the public a fairly consistent image of the Republican party, distinct from hundreds of disparate images created in individual campaigns, and reinforce the partisan themes articulated by the president.[20] To the extent that the process leads to the election of like-minded (or simply indebted) Republicans to Congress, it also increases the probability of policy victories in government.

20. The elections of 1860, 1896, and 1932 also evidenced a substantial weakening of local forces in congressional elections. See Brady, "A Reevaluation of Realignments."

The future role of the Republican National Committee in the emerging political alignment could differ significantly from the role of such institutions in the past. In no previous redirection of American politics did the triumphant party have a national organization at its disposal; the impact of parties was mainly local and limited to affecting the rate at which particular cities and counties followed national trends. But today's political parties operate in a significantly altered legal and social context. Reforms in campaign financing have breathed new life into national party organizations, and technological developments have facilitated mass-mail fund-raising on a nationwide scale. Together these developments have enabled the Republican party, weary of its minority status, to centralize its operations and create an institution unknown in either 1896 or 1932. As the party strives to provide voters with reasons to maintain their support, the image of accomplishment can be sustained by that revived institution, the Republican National Committee.

Presidential Elections

The growing strength of the national Republican party is reinforced by repeated Republican successes in presidential politics. Republicans have won six of the nine presidential elections since Dwight Eisenhower first overcame the New Deal coalition. By 1988 they will have held the presidency for sixteen of the preceding twenty years. Although each victory is explained in part by circumstances particular to that election, more general and enduring factors have also affected the outcome. In fact it can be said that the presidential election system that has evolved favors the Republican party.

First, the Electoral College has a Republican bias. Because every state receives a minimum of three electoral votes regardless of its population, each electoral vote in smaller states is won with fewer popular votes than each electoral vote in larger states. If a party's strength is concentrated in less populous states, as is the Republicans', it can win an Electoral College victory with fewer popular votes than can its opponent.[21]

21. It is estimated that between 1964 and 1984 the Republicans benefited from such a bias: on the average, Democrats are said to have needed over 52 percent of the popular vote for an Electoral College victory; the Republicans needed less than 48 percent. Steven J. Rosenstone, "Explaining the 1984 Presidential Elections," *The Brookings Review*, vol. 3 (Winter 1985), pp. 25–32.

The Electoral College also favors the Republicans because they have established a large block of states—including most of the territory west of the Mississippi River—that is "safe" for the Republican party. With the realignment of southern partisanship, the South may also become safe. The Democrats have little beyond the District of Columbia. Until the Democrats find a candidate who can appeal to the South or the West, the Republicans will begin each election with a substantial base that Democrats will be able to challenge only with an especially strong candidate or a compelling set of issues. In most circumstances Republican resources may then be concentrated on the remaining states in which a competitive contest is usually waged. The Democrats can forsake the West or the South and concentrate their resources too, but there is a difference. The Republicans need to win only a few of these close contests; the Democrats need to win almost all of them.

Contemporary presidential selection rules handicap the Democrats in another important way. As Samuel Kernell (chapter 5) explains, the elaborate primary and caucus process that precedes the general election has demanded a new style of campaigning—one that not only reaches the public at large through endless face-to-face encounters that require multiyear primary campaigns but also communicates effectively with a national audience through the media. Nominations are seldom won by negotiating with party leaders or winning endorsements from major interest groups. Even if a candidate manages to win the nomination in this old-fashioned way, the nomination threatens to be tainted, as was Walter Mondale's, by its association with "special interests." Endorsements before the primaries also inhibit efforts during the general election to strike a broad theme that transcends attachments to particular groups.

Both parties, of course, have special interests that must be appeased in the course of securing a presidential nomination. Republicans must consider the competing interests of farmers and consumers, of small-town midwesterners and aspiring members of the urban professions, of Catholics and fundamentalist Protestants, of southerners and western-ers, of business and a white ethnic working class. But even with such diversity, they still seem more homogeneous than the fragmented coalition once known as the Democratic party. The Democrats' supporters—union members, blacks, Hispanics, the unemployed, affluent liberals, the elderly, environmentalists—not only constitute a diverse set but one that is organized into identifiable, competing, politically active groups. Each is represented by an association ready to work hard for a presidential candidate but eager to exact a promise in return. Their endorsements are difficult for someone in pursuit of the party nomination to ignore, yet campaigns built around explicit interest-group coalitions are at a disadvantage in the sort of presidential campaign that the rules and technology of the 1980s demand.

Congressional and State Elections

None of this discussion of partisan change is meant to deny the mixed success Republicans are having in nonpresidential elections. In 1980 Republicans won a majority of Senate seats for the first time in twenty-eight years and in 1984 they captured the presidency for the fourth time in the past five elections, but the Republican minority in the House of Representatives is smaller today than in 1981 and the party's strength at the state level is weaker too. These limits to Republican success, however, are more a sign of the extent to which the House and state governments have insulated themselves from emerging political forces than an indication that the Republican surge is of only marginal significance.

In the House the insulation from electoral tides has been growing for more than a century. For one thing, members have been reelected for longer and longer periods. Before the Civil War realignment the average number of terms served by House members was less than two; before the New Deal realignment the average was more than twice that.[22] In 1980, when Ronald Reagan first contested the presidency, incumbents had an average tenure of five terms.[23] Tenure has also increasingly been the basis for rewarding members of Congress. By the 1910s a seniority system was established that allocated House leadership positions on the basis of service, and even though the practice was slightly modified in the 1970s, it remains a norm that is seldom violated. The few occasions when a more junior member of Congress edges out a more senior member for a leadership position (the success of Wisconsin Democrat Les Aspin in securing the chair of the Armed Services Committee is the most recent example) win so much attention and comment simply because they remain extraordinary events.

22. The average tenure before the Civil War was 1.81 terms; before the 1890s, 2.65 terms; and before the New Deal realignment, 4.49 terms. Nelson W. Polsby, "The Institutionalization of the U.S. House of Representatives," *American Political Science Review*, vol. 62 (March 1968), pp. 144–68.
23. Ornstein and others, *Vital Statistics*, p. 17.

As members of Congress have increased their time of service in Washington and as the reward system has been structured to benefit those who have succeeded, the makeup of the House has grown less responsive to electoral changes. From 1868 to 1970 a 1 percentage point change in the total vote for the majority party produced a 2.39 percentage point change in the share of House seats held by that party. But over time this so-called swing ratio has been declining.[24] Between 1972 and 1982 it was a mere 1.47.[25]

Politicians in state governments have also buffered themselves against national tides of change. As John Chubb reports in chapter 10, the proportion of states giving a plurality to presidential and gubernatorial candidates of the same party fell from more than 90 percent in the late 1800s to 61 percent since 1960. This trend is accentuated by the increasing tendency to schedule gubernatorial elections at times other than when a president is being chosen.[26] Presidents in the 1980s are forced to build support at the state level in off-year elections, which are generally less favorable to them. In fact, the president's party has not increased its share of governorships, state houses, or state senates in any off-year election since 1954.[27]

The speed and magnitude of historical realignments are thus lessened considerably by the greater institutionalization of much of the electoral system. The election results of the Reagan years are in many ways consistent with this generalization. As John Ferejohn and Morris Fiorina report (chapter 4), the House elections of 1980–84 convincingly demonstrate that the many advantages incumbency confers on candidates were not seriously undermined by the force of the Reagan candidacy or the national swing to the Republican party. When the Republicans picked up thirty-three seats in the House in 1980, they defeated twenty-seven Democratic incumbents. Still, 90 percent of all Democrats survived (as compared to the 1964 Democratic landslide, when only 75 percent of all Republican incumbents survived). Reagan's coattails were even less

---

24. Edward R. Tufte, "The Relationship between Seats and Votes in Two-Party Systems," *American Political Science Review*, vol. 67 (June 1973), p. 543. The swing ratio from 1900 to 1970 was 2.09, and from 1948 to 1970, 1.83.

25. Calculated from data in Ornstein and others, *Vital Statistics*.

26. Today only thirteen states elect governors during presidential election years; thirty-five did so when Franklin Roosevelt was consolidating his realignment.

27. In addition, the average length of a governor's term doubled from the 1960s to the 1970s, and the average number of state legislative bodies changing control at each election was cut in half.

strong in his 1984 reelection bid. Even though he campaigned vigorously on behalf of Republican challengers, over 95 percent of all House incumbents won reelection, and the Republicans netted an increase of only fourteen seats—barely half of what they had lost in 1982. His coattails have not been noticeably longer than those of other recent presidents, and they have had little effect on the states.[28]

The increasing insulation of political institutions from changing popular opinion is hardly a contemporary phenomenon. By the time of the New Deal, institutionalization was well advanced, and officeholders were quite insulated from political tides. While only half of the House incumbents managed to survive the election of 1894, two-thirds survived the election of 1932.[29] Likewise, three times as many state governments shifted to unified and enduring Republican control in the 1890s as shifted to the Democrats in the 1930s.[30] Since the 1930s these processes have continued, and House and state elections have become substantially insulated from presidential politics.

Institutional development has not, however, entirely buffered Congress from broad electoral change. The Senate, despite its institutional development, is subject to many of the same tides of opinion that have such impact on presidential politics. Incumbent senators are only slightly better bets for reelection today than they were during the New Deal, and their 72 percent reelection rate during the 1970s is well below the House rate of 93 percent.[31] The 1980 election reflected these differences clearly. The Republicans defeated nine incumbent Democratic senators and won three open seats that had previously been Democratic. The magnitude of this swing may have been accentuated by special circumstances (see chapter 4), but it was nonetheless consistent with the general tendency of senatorial elections—well-financed, highly publicized, often nationally oriented contests—to be competitive two-party events that can produce surprising changes in the institution's composition.

28. Unless the 1982 election is taken as evidence of "negative" coattails. Their losses in governorships and statehouses in 1982 were twice as large as their gains in 1980.

29. The 1933 Congress had 37.2 percent freshmen, the 1895 Congress 48.6 percent. Polsby, "Institutionalization of the U.S. House," p. 146.

30. The 1930s shift was 14 percent of the states; the 1890s shift 39 percent of the states. Clubb and others, *Partisan Realignment*, p. 210.

31. Likewise, only about 40 percent of all senators typically win "safe" victories of 60 percent or better, while three-fourths of all House members typically do so. Ornstein and others, *Vital Statistics*, p. 48.

In 1982 the element of surprise was present again. With the economy mired in its worst recession since the 1930s, the elections could have proved disastrous for Republicans. Yet House losses were held to only twenty-six and Republicans gained a Senate seat. The reason, as Gary Jacobson explains (chapter 6), is a combination of aggressive candidate recruitment by the Republican party and a shrewd strategy of campaign financing by the party and allied political action committees. Vulnerable Republican incumbents were shored up financially, and fifty-two open House seats were pursued with an unusual effort that produced twenty-one victories.[32] These investments helped protect the Republican Senate majority in 1982, and similar expenditures promise to pay comparable dividends in the future.

The financial advantage Republican candidates enjoy shows no sign of diminishing. It is true that Democratic candidates for Congress currently receive a share of total political action committee contributions roughly equal to that received by Republican candidates. But the Democratic recipients who receive a disproportionately large share of these contributions are incumbents who can translate key committee assignments into campaign revenue. Challengers, who benefit more from extra campaign dollars than incumbents do, are more likely to receive ample financial support if they are Republican than if they are Democratic. In the not-too-distant future the nationalization of campaign finance—through parties and political action committees—may turn congressional elections into less localized affairs.[33] If this happens, the Republican party might not only secure its Senate majority but move toward installing one in the House as well.

Institutions

Each historical realignment was consolidated through swift and substantial policy actions that demonstrated the victorious party's capacity to govern and reinforced the loyalty of its new supporters. Each

32. Data on 1982 election results are taken from Richard E. Cohen, "A Coalition of Moderates Is Likely to Call the Tune in the 98th Congress," *National Journal*, vol. 14 (November 6, 1982), p. 1881.

33. But see Richard E. Cohen, "Taking the Very Long View: The Parties Begin Planning for 1992 House Elections," *National Journal*, vol. 17 (April 13, 1985), pp. 794–97.

time, the process was facilitated by unified party control of the national government. In 1860, 1896, and 1932 one party captured the presidency, the House, and the Senate, and held them without interruption for fourteen years.[34] If 1980 comes to be viewed as a major turning point in American politics, it will be the first to have occurred when the dominant party controlled only the executive branch and the Senate.

A closer look at previous realignments suggests, however, that partisan control of the legislative branch has been of diminishing significance for some time. Admittedly, both in the 1860s and the 1890s, cohesive House and Senate majority parties voted down cohesive minority parties to carry out the new mandate. But by the 1930s the mechanisms had begun to change. The driving force was now more clearly centered in the White House, with the president defining the program and mobilizing the requisite popular and institutional support. Although both houses of Congress were of the same party as the president, the Democrats were not nearly as cohesive as dominant parties had been in the past.[35] Roosevelt had to put together specific coalitions for each of his programmatic innovations, and in his second term he found it increasingly difficult to realize his objectives. A new direction was no longer synonymous with unified political control by a single political party. Something more—but also something less—was needed. In recent years this has been demonstrated convincingly by the legislative failures of Jimmy Carter when the Democrats supposedly controlled the government and the successes of Ronald Reagan when the Republicans supposedly did not.

Before Reagan, many thought that institutional complexity had advanced to such an extent that a new direction in American politics was no longer possible. Congress was so fragmented, parties were so weak, and political relationships were so ad hoc and individualized that a coherent program of action could simply not be sustained. Yet in 1981 the national government made decisions that sharply changed the direction of domestic and foreign policy. Major pieces of legislation reversed the course of domestic social spending, initiated the largest sustained peacetime increase in defense spending, and by creating an unprecedented budget deficit, constrained federal policymaking for years to come. These innovations (to be discussed in the next section)

34. Clubb and others, *Partisan Realignment*, p. 164.
35. Brady with Stewart, "Congressional Party Realignment"; and Clubb and others, *Partisan Realignment*, chap. 7.

are likely to be equal in their long-term significance to any associated with previous realignments. They are also clear Republican victories. The manner in which they were achieved, however, suggests the need to rethink conventional conceptions of governmental control.

The Republican triumphs were realized through two devices: presidential control of the policy agenda and extraordinary party cohesion in the House and the Senate. Operating with a widely perceived election mandate, President Reagan set a simple and focused agenda for the Congress. Although his proposals to cut popular programs might have been derailed in the Democratic House and even in the Republican Senate, he managed through direct appeals to the public and through centralization of the congressional budget process (by means of the reconciliation procedure) to keep the agenda focused on the broad issue of excessive government spending. Those members of Congress who wanted to shift discussion to the merits of individual programs were prevented from doing so. The House was limited to a single vote on a package of budget reductions (and defense increases), which the President won. The White House then had little difficulty in placing the other half of its economic program—a major tax cut with broad public appeal— at the top of the congressional agenda. Once on the agenda, both the Omnibus Budget and Reconciliation Act and the Economic Recovery Tax Act were supported almost unanimously by House and Senate Republicans.[36] With these levels of cohesion, effective control of the national government became a matter of convincing a few House Democrats to vote with the president.[37]

On key issues the Republicans ran the national government in 1981 as assuredly as if they had controlled all three instead of just two of its major institutions. But what is the significance of these accomplishments? Why might they indicate more than isolated triumphs of a popular president during his honeymoon? One reason, to be discussed later, is their profound and enduring effects on public policy. The other is their

36. In the Senate the Republicans suffered no defections on the budget bill and only one on the tax bill. In the House the defections were only five and one respectively. For vote tallies, see *Congressional Quarterly Almanac,* vol. 37 (1981), pp. 33–35, 42– 43, 40-H, 42-H.

37. The president, on the strength and clarity of his electoral mandate, persuaded the Democrats' more conservative members that the political costs of opposition were simply too high. With 47 House Democrats supporting the budget bill and 103 the tax bill, both passed handily. Ibid., p. 62-H.

connection to the long-term development of national political institutions.

The agenda control that President Reagan exercised so effectively in 1981 is a presidential power that has been developing over the last several decades and promises to increase in importance. Since the presidency of Harry S Truman, Congress has expected the White House to formulate a legislative program, and every president has followed suit. This in itself does not ensure presidential control of the policy agenda, because Congress may decide to pursue its own initiatives (as it frequently did while Dwight D. Eisenhower was president). Moreover, the executive apparatus known as the institutionalized presidency has not always given presidents the influence over their own bureaucracy that they need to exercise effective leadership. Yet as Terry Moe explains (chapter 9), modern presidents have increased their capacity for leadership by expanding, centralizing, and politicizing the institutional presidency. These changes provide a foundation for more effective control of the executive branch of government and an enhanced probability of success in Congress. Recent presidents have also relied increasingly on direct appeals to the public—skills they honed during their successful, media-oriented campaigns (see chapter 5).

President Reagan exploited the capacity of the institutional presidency better than any of his predecessors, especially on matters pertaining to the federal budget. For example, by appointing David Stockman, a congressionally grown expert on the budgetary process, head of the Office of Management and Budget and by supporting Stockman's austere budgetary program, the president was able to shape decisively congressional action. He also demonstrated the way in which carefully designed appeals to the public can influence congressional decisions. Future presidents, attempting to live up to public expectations Reagan has heightened, will build on the institutional arrangements he has devised and learn from his ability to mobilize public support.

Congress has become the perfect foil for this strategy because as an institution it has substantially lost the ability to establish an agenda for itself. Over the last two decades, as Congress has insulated itself against national electoral swings, it has decentralized collective power into more than 200 subcommittees, which enjoy considerable policy autonomy within their respective spheres of interest. At the same time, representatives and senators alike have also grown dissatisfied with the limited policy influence that decentralization provides. Partly because they represent a new breed of legislator and partly out of an old-fashioned desire for electoral security, members of Congress today are trying to influence not only the committee decisions in which they participate but legislative items as they appear on the floor of Congress itself. The crescendo of member demands for participation—what Steven Smith (chapter 8) calls collegialism—does create opportunities for broader discussions of the issues. Still, members have powerful, constituency-related incentives to guard jealously the prerogatives that the decentralized and fragmented system provides them and little incentive to make the sacrifices that broad compromises might entail. As a result, Congress is hampered by tensions between an orderly but highly fragmented process dominated by committees and a disorderly but potentially more comprehensive one that originates in party caucuses or on the floors of the House and Senate. Party leaders are criticized for failing to resolve these tensions, but their task cannot be accomplished with the limited powers members have granted them. As former Senate leader Howard Baker observed recently from his retirement perch, "It's only a highly developed sense of decency that kept me, when I read the paper every morning, from laughing out loud."[38] Congress simply lacks the mechanisms to formulate a coherent agenda to counter that of a strong president.

In the long run the significance of congressional politics in the early 1980s is not that the Republican party was cohesive but that congressional parties, whether in the majority or the minority, are no longer able to effect substantial policy changes on their own. To be sure, individual members of Congress now more than ever before have the freedom to initiate policy innovations. Representative Jack Kemp and Senator Bill Bradley, for example, played important roles in promoting discussion of tax reform. But their power to establish the agenda of Congress is circumscribed in a way the president's is not. Congress as an institution simply lacks the capacity to compete with a president intent on focusing the agenda on issues of broad national significance (see chapter 13).

Policy

Among the major elements of the political system—voters, parties, institutions, and policy—examined in this chapter, policy has changed

38. Martin Tolchin, "Ex-G.O.P. Leader Finds There's Life After Senate," *New York Times*, April 29, 1985.

in the manner most reminiscent of past political realignments. This is important for two reasons. First, policy itself has become institutionalized inasmuch as the government is now constrained by long-standing commitments to serve major domestic constituencies such as the elderly, the poor, or military retirees and to meet international and security obligations. This is more true today than during any other realigning period and lends added significance and permanence to such nonincremental policy changes as the government manages to bring about. Second, without changes in policy it would be difficult to attach significance to even sharp and durable changes in voter alignments. In fact, it is hard to imagine how large permanent changes in voter alignments could have come about without policy changes to reinforce them.

Past major shifts in policy had several characteristics in common: they responded decisively to a major crisis, they offered innovative approaches to long-standing problems, and they established a new agenda of issues for years to come.[39] Developments under the Reagan administration have followed the same pattern. By 1980 a decade of stagflation had crystallized an economic issue—the trade-off between economic and governmental growth—that the welfare state had come to pose. While the Democratic party floundered in search of an answer, the Republican party offered a decisive one. As a consequence the basic domestic issue of the 1970s and indeed of the entire New Deal era has been superseded. The main issue is no longer by how much the federal government's economic role—in taxing, spending, and regulating—will expand but where, when, and by how much it will be curtailed. That this is a new policy direction and, equally important, that it will be sustained are evident when national policy is broken down into several conventional categories of analysis: federalism, entitlements, national security, and fiscal policy.

Federalism

The Reagan administration has first of all reversed an important component of the trend toward increasingly centralized policy control within the federal system. For forty years (see chapter 10) intergovernmental relations had become increasingly complex and subject to direc-

39. These policy transformations are discussed in Walter Dean Burnham, "Party Systems and the Political Process," in Chambers and Burnham, eds., *The American Party Systems*, pp. 277–307.

tion and control from Washington. The national government increased its contributions to state and local governments from less than 2 percent of those governments' revenues in 1929 to more than 26 percent in 1978. It did so through more than 500 categorical grant programs that profoundly influenced lower government objectives and activities. But with Reagan's election these patterns have been shattered. Federal expenditures for intergovernmental programs have fallen in real dollar terms; the share of the GNP these expenditures represent has shrunk by one-fourth, their contribution to state and local budgets has dropped by one-fifth, and the number of programs has declined to around 400. Power over and responsibility for many domestic programs has shifted to state and local governments.

Yet the change in direction has been limited by the complex, institutionalized, intergovernmental system that evolved over the preceding decades. While expenditures have been cut, the categorical programs themselves remain largely intact, supported by bipartisan congressional coalitions responsive to the pressures of interest groups and the demands of state and local officials. Most of the dramatic policy change has been confined to expenditure levels. The institutionalized framework of the federal system is responding to the Reagan revolution much more slowly. Once again one sees the way the contemporary realignment's impact is shaped and limited by the institutional bedrock upon which it is occurring. But "mere" expenditure cuts can have their own lasting consequence, especially if the political support for a reversal of the trend does not emerge. Institutions impede political responses to external pressures for change, but they cannot prevent them indefinitely. As long as the climate of budget austerity continues, intergovernmental programs will continue to dwindle, deteriorate, lose their constituency connections, and in some cases simply disappear.

Entitlements

The second major change in domestic policy has been the curtailment of entitlement programs such as social security, unemployment compensation, medicare, and food stamps. These programs are of central importance to domestic policy because they are the major vehicle by which the federal government meets the income and health needs of large portions of the American public. They can also generate costs that are difficult to control. Expenditures escalate not only with legislative increases in benefit levels and extensions of eligibility requirements but also with demographically or economically induced changes in the size of eligible populations. By 1979 they represented over 60 percent of the domestic budget and consumed roughly 9 percent of GNP.

The establishment and development of these programs since the New Deal is well known. For decades, as R. Kent Weaver explains in chapter 11, powerful interest groups and voting blocs provided political protection for entitlement programs. Exclusion from the annual appropriations process meant that Congress would have to enact new authorizing legislation to modify expenditure levels, a requirement that gave these programs vital procedural protection. The widely endorsed concept of social insurance justified these protective mechanisms and further legitimized entitlement expansion.

It is thus significant that the Reagan administration has been able to restrict even these entrenched components of the welfare state. Entitlement spending as a proportion of the federal budget and as a percentage of the gross national product has leveled off (see chapter 11). While the legislative changes behind this new direction began in the mid-1970s, the most substantial ones have occurred since Reagan took office—the most important being contained in the 1981 Omnibus Budget and Reconciliation Act. By tying together a multitude of benefit and eligibility changes in a single package that rewrote authorizing legislation, the legislation transformed a host of entitlement issues into a single issue of excessive government spending. Similarly, in 1983 the administration accomplished significant cost containment in social security by means of a bipartisan commission operating outside of the constraints that ordinarily protect entitlements from change. In both cases presidential leadership overcame formidable obstacles to policy innovation even in as controversial an area as entitlement policy.

Again policy change is to be understood within the institutional context in which it occurs. Social security, medicare, medicaid, food stamps, unemployment insurance, and disability benefits are so well entrenched a part of the American political system that it is inconceivable any political movement could fundamentally restructure their operations. The changes wrought by the Reagan administration are necessarily limited by the choices that are already embedded in American political life. If the Reagan administration has only limited the expansion of entitlement programs and not eliminated or even significantly reduced their size, that does not detract from the magnitude of its accomplishment. Policies that were exploding have been contained; the expansionary pace at which they were once growing is unlikely to be resumed for the foreseeable future.

Security Policy

Under President Reagan America has undergone the largest sustained peacetime buildup of its military forces in history (see chapter 12). It has taken a tough stance in arms control negotiations that has made Richard Nixon's and Henry Kissinger's assessment of Soviet intentions seem restrained by comparison. And it has enhanced a process of technical modernization, exemplified by the strategic defense initiative, that may well dominate defense policy debates for a generation to come. Along the way President Reagan has transformed the budgetary politics of defense. For five budget cycles debate has been restricted to the size of defense increases; that expenditures might return to their late-1970s level has barely been discussed. While continued growth will probably not keep pace with that of recent years, modifications in current policy are unlikely in the near term to undo the administration's program.

Yet in defense policy, too, there are limits to change imposed by the institutional context in which foreign policy decisions are taken. In large part these constraints are external, dictated by relations with the Soviet Union, Europe, and the third world. The United States is not free to alter its external alliances with a change in partisan control of the presidency, as was the case in 1800. Indeed, President Reagan continues to pursue strategic arms limitations despite the much greater commitment his administration has made to new missiles and defense systems. As John Steinbruner explains (chapter 12), the Soviet Union, especially under a new generation of leaders symbolized by Mikhail Gorbachev's ascension to power, has the capacity to challenge the United States with a major technical modernization of its own, a hard line in arms control negotiations, or aggressive military action.

Domestic circumstances also limit the magnitude of the new emphasis on military capability in foreign policy contests. The memory of Vietnam has eclipsed Munich as a symbol of what must be avoided. American troop commitments in the third world must be for short durations with high prospects of victory. Even as modest an effort as the token presence of American troops in Lebanon proved politically infeasible over the long run. Similar constraints limit the Reagan administration's options in Central America.

Constraints on policy innovations are in fact so great that apart from security policy it is difficult to identify any clear new direction that the Reagan administration has taken in foreign affairs. Little effort has been made to remove the iron curtain from Eastern Europe, the tilt toward Israel has hardly altered the boiling Middle East cauldron, South Africa is more threatened economically and politically than it was during the Carter administration (in part because the price of gold, South Africa's main export, has collapsed under the weight of the Reagan administration's anti-inflation policies), and Taiwan remains even more isolated than when Reagan assumed office (in part because of the British-Chinese agreement with respect to Hong Kong). Only in Latin America has the Reagan administration aggressively pursued an anticommunist policy that is sharply distinguished from that of its predecessors.

Fiscal Policy and the Deficit

The Reagan administration's fiscal policies are at once the most politically problematic and substantively significant policy elements of the new direction in American politics. Running now in excess of $200 billion per year and costing the federal government $130 billion in annual interest payments, the budget deficit looms as the major threat to all the Reagan administration has accomplished. The next serious recession could well be attributed to the size of the deficit, and if Reagan is still in office when it strikes, Republicans may suffer unusual electoral losses. The president will have difficulty convincing the public that he and his party are not to blame for a problem that originated with his administration (see chapter 13).

But the deficit is by no means an unambiguous political liability. To the contrary, it is the president's major weapon for enforcing control over government spending. With Republicans and Democrats alike becoming concerned that the deficit is affecting interest rates, export industries, and business investment, increases in expenditures for domestic programs no longer appear on any political leader's agenda. As long as the deficit remains a problem, the nation's spending priorities, as established by the Reagan administration in its first term, will not be altered more than incrementally. Those portions of the budget that are difficult to control in the short term—entitlements, defense commit-

ments, and interest payments—will absorb the majority of the budget
while those portions that are relatively easy to control will compete for
the diminishing remainder. Even if a tax increase provides the government with additional revenue, constraints on spending will probably not
weaken. New revenues will go to deficit reduction, not to real spending
growth. If the deficit produces an economic crisis with electoral consequences detrimental to the dominant party, these deficits are the insurance that the new direction in public policy will be sustained.

Conclusion

One cautionary word needs to be said in conclusion so that our
analysis will not be interpreted in ways we do not intend. It would be
incorrect to predict on the basis of our analysis that the Republican party
will necessarily rise to a position of national dominance comparable to
the achievement of majority parties in past realignments. It is true that
the Republicans have decided advantages in party organization, campaign financing, and presidential politics, and they are winning southerners and young people to their side. It is also true that the Democratic
party's residual strengths in state government and the House are a far
less promising base upon which to build a resurgent political force. But
the point of this essay would be missed if attention were focused solely
on the electoral issues it has addressed. A new direction has already
been taken in American government that is comparable in basic respects
to realignments of the past. The terms of political debate and the course
of public policy have been fundamentally transformed. The forces of
institutionalization that had to be overcome in the course of bringing
these innovations about not only indicate the political strength underlying
them but ensure that they, like the policy transformations of past
realignments, will be sustained for a long time to come. There is little
likelihood of an immediate return to the policies of the Great Society
era. An economic downturn or a foreign policy reverse may rejuvenate
the Democrats, but the policies they once espoused will not be as
resilient. Big deficits, strong defense commitments, and doubts about
the welfare state will shape the political and policy future—whatever the
fate of parties or presidents in particular elections.

PART ONE

Voters and Elections

CHAPTER TWO

The New Two-Party System

THOMAS E. CAVANAGH AND JAMES L. SUNDQUIST

EACH TIME a Republican president has been elected or reelected by a landslide in the years since World War II—and that has happened five times in the last nine elections—Republicans have jubilantly proclaimed the final collapse of the modern era of Democratic dominance. After the first four of those victories—in 1952, 1956, 1972, and 1980—they were disappointed. When things settled down, the Democrats remained dominant everywhere but in the White House. They continued to hold most of the seats in Congress and the state legislatures and to elect most of the governors and big-city mayors most of the time. And after two of those landslides, 1956 and 1972, they snapped back to win the White House at the next election.

From a reading of the election returns alone, one might quickly add 1984 to the list of Republican disappointments. GOP strength was not strikingly evident below the presidential level on Ronald Reagan's reelection day. The Democrats posted a net gain of two seats in the Senate, and they lost only fifteen or sixteen in the House (depending on a recount in Indiana), one governorship, and five of the nation's ninety-eight state legislative houses that are chosen through partisan competition.[1] These modest setbacks were not enough to wipe out their gains in the midterm election of 1982. The Democrats are actually stronger by a couple of seats in the Senate, a dozen in the House, and half a dozen

The authors would like to thank Diane Colasanto of the Gallup organization, Lois Timms of the Roper Center for Public Opinion Research, and Kathleen Frankovic of CBS News for their assistance in providing unpublished data.

1. The Republicans gained four houses while one, in New Mexico, reverted to a tie. The New Mexico legislature is effectively controlled by a conservative coalition of Republicans and boll weevil Democrats, however. Nebraska's unicameral legislature is nonpartisan and hence excluded from the total.

governorships than they were when President Reagan was first inaugurated. Though still outnumbered fifty-three to forty-seven in the Senate, they hold thirty-four of the fifty governorships, sixty-six of the ninety-eight partisan state legislative houses, and 58 percent of the U.S. House of Representatives.

Nevertheless, if one looks beyond the election returns to a more fundamental indicator of basic party strength, 1984 does differ from the earlier Republican landslide years. That indicator is party identification, the number of people who consider themselves to be members of a party. When a voter tells a pollster, "I am a Republican" or "I am a Democrat," he or she is expressing a commitment far deeper than that of one who merely says, "I voted for the Republican [or Democratic] presidential candidate this year." Party identification structures an individual's voting choices over time and over the various levels of office; it represents what the voter professes to be his normal political behavior.

By the measure of party identification, the Republican gains during the 1984 campaign season were impressive. The GOP did not replace the Democrats as a new majority party in the nation, but it appears to have drawn almost even. For the first time since 1934 the country may now have a well-balanced, competitive two-party system at the national level instead of the one-and-one-half-party system it has known since the great realignment of the New Deal era. If the Republicans can solidify most of their gains, American politics will have entered an era quite distinct from that of the half century that separated Franklin Roosevelt from Ronald Reagan.

Contours of a New Alignment

A new political era is marked by a new structure of party competition, and the passage from an old era to a new is usually called a realignment. But that term has acquired a variety of meanings, frequently vague and sometimes contradictory, as it has passed from the realm of political science into common usage. Before the shape of a new era can be sketched, the word *realignment* and some concepts related to it need to be defined—not necessarily for others, but at least as they will be used in this discussion.[2]

2. For a more extended discussion of the realignment concept, see James L. Sundquist, *Dynamics of the Party System,* rev. ed. (Brookings, 1983), pp. 3–14.

For our purposes the *strength* of a party is measured not by the number of people who vote for it in any given election but by the number of people who feel they belong to it. The *alignment* of the party system reflects the composition of the strength of each competing party in terms of identifiable groups—demographic, occupational, religious, ethnic, ideological, or whatever—to which individuals belong. The *line of cleavage* between the parties is created by the combination of issues and circumstances that have generated the partisan attachments. A *realignment* denotes a relocation of the line of cleavage, with a redistribution— enduring rather than transitory—of some members of some voting groups on opposite sides of the line, resulting in reconstitution of the parties' strengths.

Realignments occur when a change in the agenda of politics causes established voters to reconsider and alter the party affiliations they had formed on the basis of the previously prevailing agenda and causes new voters to form party affiliations different from those that persons of like origin and circumstances formed in the preceding generation. In other words, a realignment occurs if, and only if, the parties quarrel over a new set of issues, and the displacement of one set of conflicts by another leads to a lasting shift in the parties' electoral bases of support. If the shift is massive, as when a major party is supplanted by a new party, or when a minority party becomes the majority party, a major realignment has occurred. If the restructuring is on a lesser scale, the realignment is a minor one. To complicate matters further, separate realigning forces can be operating simultaneously, set in motion by different issues that cleave the electorate along different lines.

Historians and political scientists have identified five successive systems of party competition in the country's history, each so distinct from its predecessor that the realignment that brought it into being could clearly be classified as major. Each era was ushered in by one or more critical elections that centered on a set of issues hotly contested between the parties and that resulted in extraordinary and lasting alterations in the composition and strength of the two major parties. The first party system, which pitted the Federalists against the Jeffersonian Republicans (and which succeeded a brief period without parties after the Constitution was adopted), was established in the Adams-Jefferson presidential contests of 1796 and 1800. After the slow disappearance of the Federalists, the Jacksonian victory of 1828 ushered in a new era of competition between Democrats (descended from the Jeffersonian Republicans) and

Whigs. As the slavery issue came to the fore, a new Republican party eclipsed the Whigs in the 1850s and enjoyed a narrow edge over the Democrats for the next four decades. The election of 1896, fought between a conservative GOP and a Democratic party radicalized by the absorption of the Populist movement, resulted in a regionally based party system with a solid Republican majority entrenched everywhere outside the Deep South and the border states. Finally, in the turmoil of the Great Depression, Franklin D. Roosevelt assembled a new majority Democratic coalition of blue-collar ethnics in the northern cities, liberal activists, southern whites, and blacks.[3] Though frayed and tattered in the following decades, the Democratic majority remained—at least until the 1980s—as the recognizable lineal descendant of the Roosevelt coalition, united by the same ideological approach to government and confronting the Republicans along the line of cleavage defined by the issues of the Depression era.

On the basis of historical experience, then, a major realignment is overdue. Yet applying to the circumstances of the 1980s the conceptual apparatus derived from the study of major realignments of the past yields considerable ambiguity. The line of cleavage established in the 1930s has not been superseded by a new one cutting across the electorate in a different direction, carved by a fresh and powerful issue that arose to dominate political discussion—as the issue of slavery did in the 1850s, free silver in the 1890s, and relief of Depression hardship in the 1930s. The quarrel between the parties in 1984 centered on the same set of issues that impelled the New Deal realignment: What is the proper role of government? How big, how active, and how expensive should it be? How much should the haves be taxed for the benefit of the have-nots? How activist should the government be in redistributing wealth and income and opportunity from the more to the less favored and in protecting citizens against the hazards of life?

To some extent the debate has been carried on in the familiar language of the past half century. When the Republicans appear to threaten broadly based social security and medicare and the Democrats spring to the defense of those creations of their golden years, the New Deal alignment is reinforced. The arguments of 1981 over how the benefits of tax reduction should be distributed found the parties in their accustomed roles, the Democrats striving to appear more solicitous of working men

3. William Nisbet Chambers and Walter Dean Burnham, eds., *The American Party Systems: Stages of Political Development,* 2d ed. (Oxford University Press, 1975).

and women and painting the GOP as partial to the corporations and the rich. Of late the advantage in this debate appears to have gone to the Republicans as skepticism toward governmental intervention has grown, particularly when that intervention has concentrated its benefits on minorities and the poor. Many Democrats have edged away from the liberal activism that the party has traditionally espoused, and some have moved so far as to cross the old line of party cleavage and declare themselves Republicans. This is not a realignment in our usage of the word as long as the line of cleavage remains as originally defined; it is simply a shift in the party balance within the existing alignment.

Yet the debate between the parties on the old role-of-government and economic policy issues has been placed in such a new ideological context in the 1980s by the radicalized Republican party of Ronald Reagan that the distinction between the parties may have taken on quite new meanings, especially for young people whose political awareness does not go back to New Deal days or even to the era of the Great Society. To that extent the line of party cleavage can be seen as having shifted, with much the same impact on the party system that a new line born of wholly new issues might hypothetically have had. The Republican party is no longer the party of austerity, the party of balanced budgets and tight money that, in its obsession with inflation, produced recessions under Presidents Eisenhower, Nixon, and Ford. The adoption of supply-side economics has given it a new rhetoric of growth and opportunity, and its policies have given priority to tax reduction for both individuals and corporations with an almost casual disregard for deficits far larger than those for which it used to castigate the Democrats. Meanwhile, Walter Mondale chose to seize the mantle of austerity for his party, proclaiming the virtues of fiscal responsibility and tax increases. By election day of 1984 it seemed clear that substantial numbers of voters were forming or reforming their party identities on the basis of new party images. The Democratic party was seen not as the traditional defender of the middle class but as tax collector for the welfare state, the Republican party not as the tool of Wall Street and the rich but as the instrument to bring about widespread economic growth and opportunity. To the extent that the pattern of allegiances was being redrawn in response to new perceptions of the parties, a realignment can be said to have been taking place, whether or not the Republicans emerged as the majority party when the process was complete.

In addition, two new clusters of issues have arisen during the past

two decades that cut across the traditional economic alignment altogether, and on these issues the two parties have taken distinguishable
stands. In the past when such new crosscutting issues have been of
sufficient power to dominate the country's politics, they have produced
major realignments. The crosscutting issues of the 1980s have not
possessed that magnitude of impact, but they have undoubtedly contributed to the party choices of some voters and hence can be classed as
minor realigning forces.

The first of these sets of issues concerns the relative weight to be
accorded military strength and negotiation in dealing with the Soviet
Union and the third world. The bitter conflict between hawks and doves
over the Vietnam War led to the capture of the Democratic presidential
nomination by the antiwar McGovern insurgency in 1972. The American
withdrawal removed much of the intensity from the dispute, but the
same players have generally lined up on the same sides in subsequent
fights over détente, the Panama Canal treaty, President Carter's human
rights policy, the SALT II treaty, and the Reagan military buildup.

The second cluster of new issues, often given the catchall label "the
social issue," has arisen from conservative objections to liberal federal
policy (especially on the part of the courts) on such questions of values
and morals as school prayer, abortion, women's rights, busing, affirmative action, crime, gun control, pornography, and homosexual rights.
While the Republicans have staked out increasingly conservative—or,
literally, reactionary—positions on these concerns, the Democrats have
blunted the realignment potential of some issues, especially the racially
tinged ones of busing and affirmative action, by straddling them. But in
other cases, such as the equal rights amendment, clear policy differences
between the parties have emerged, and probably in every case a
difference in the degree of fervor and commitment is evident to the
single-issue or religiously motivated voter who looks to some aspect of
the social issue as the basis for political decisions.

Measuring Party Attachments

A realignment implies a lasting change in partisanship, and to endure,
such a change must be attitudinal as well as behavioral. Merely voting
for one or more of a party's candidates is not in itself sufficient proof of

partisanship, because a member of one party may cross the party line in a particular election without in any sense belonging to the opposition party. If the defection is motivated by the characteristics of the candidate rather than of the opposition party, then the defector's underlying partisanship remains essentially undisturbed. And of course a true independent can vote for years without feeling attached to any party at all.

Political affiliation is much like church affiliation. Being a Democrat or a Republican, like being a Catholic or a Baptist or a Presbyterian, is a part of one's identity. Once acquired, the affiliation is not quickly and easily changed. One may not go to services regularly—may even go to another church on occasion—but will still remain a member of one's denomination. Similarly, a party member may visit another political church on election day, attracted by the music or the sermon or the charisma of the preacher, without undergoing conversion and gaining a new political identity.

Much has been written about the process whereby individuals acquire a partisan identity. In its infancy this literature drew heavily upon the discipline of social psychology and tended to emphasize the influence of parental socialization in the development of partisanship. Because it was assumed to be extremely stable, partisanship was considered the primary determinant in the attitudinal "funnel of causality" leading up to the choice to support a given candidate in a given election.[4] In *The Responsible Electorate*, V. O. Key, Jr., described partisanship as a standing commitment on the part of the voter, a judgment that one or the other major party was preferable on most of the important issues most of the time. Key believed that this standing commitment would be honored at each election unless some intervening factor, a new issue or a specific candidate, induced a reevaluation.[5] The application to an analysis of realignment is straightforward: if a series of issues consistently deflects a voter away from a standing commitment, then at some point the voter will realize that his commitment has changed. More recent treatments have demonstrated in a variety of ways that party identification can indeed be a consequence of a voter's reactions to issues and candidates at successive points in time. In other words, party

4. Angus Campbell and others, *The American Voter* (Wiley, 1960).
5. *The Responsible Electorate: Rationality in Presidential Voting, 1936–1960* (Harvard University Press, 1966).

clearly affects the choice of candidates, but candidates and issues also affect the choice of party.[6]

In recent years the debate over the causes and effects of partisanship has been partially superseded by a debate over whether partisanship can be said to exist any longer in any meaningful way. Proponents of the theory of dealignment argue that the electorate contains fewer partisans and more independents than formerly, that the remaining partisans are less firmly attached to their parties, making them more likely to defect or split their tickets, and that the decline of party attachments makes a realignment in the traditional sense virtually impossible. According to this view, shifts in the party vote are largely issue- and candidate-specific. They are therefore unlikely to carry over from one election to the next and structure an individual's voting behavior along party lines in a lasting way.[7]

A third point of view, associated with conservative analyst Kevin Phillips, holds that a "split-level realignment" has already taken place and that the country now has a normal Republican majority at the presidential level, a competitive system in the Senate, and a system that favors the Democrats in the House of Representatives and below the federal level. A voter might therefore consider himself a Republican in national politics and a Democrat in state and local politics.[8] Such a hypothesis implies a certain stability in the ticket-splitting behavior of

6. Several models have been specified to test the assumption of an interactive relationship among party identification, issue positions, and candidate choice, both at a given point in time and across time. See, for example, Morris P. Fiorina, *Retrospective Voting in American National Elections* (Yale University Press, 1981); John E. Jackson, "Issues, Party Choices, and Presidential Votes," *American Journal of Political Science,* vol. 19 (May 1975), pp. 161–85; Gregory B. Markus and Philip E. Converse, "A Dynamic Simultaneous Equation Model of Electoral Choice," *American Political Science Review,* vol. 73 (December 1979), pp. 1055–70; and Benjamin I. Page and Calvin C. Jones, "Reciprocal Effects of Policy Preferences, Party Loyalties and the Vote," *American Political Science Review,* vol. 73 (December 1979), pp. 1071–89. While there are significant differences in the conceptualizations and findings of these analysts, these differences are less fundamental than the broad agreement that party identification can function as a dependent as well as an independent variable in the process of electoral choice.

7. Typical statements of this position can be found in Walter Dean Burnham, "American Politics in the 1970's: Beyond Party?" in Chambers and Burnham, eds., *The American Party Systems,* pp. 308–57; and Everett Carll Ladd, "The Brittle Mandate: Electoral Dealignment and the 1980 Presidential Election," *Political Science Quarterly,* vol. 96 (Spring 1981), pp. 1–25.

8. See the discussion in Phillips's biweekly newsletter, *The American Political Report,* vol. 14 (January 11, 1985).

individuals and the electorate as a whole, as well as a lengthy period of divided party control of government in Washington.

Measuring party attachment in order to sketch the contours of an existing alignment and detect and analyze any realignment that may be going on is a rather more formidable task than defining it. Democrats and Republicans do not pay dues or carry membership cards, so one must proceed by indirection, diagnosing the inward attitudes by cataloging the outward symptoms. The nineteenth century has left us few indications, beyond election returns themselves, of the party attachments of the many sectors of the electorate. In this century, with the introduction of voter registration, a new body of evidence became available, but it is limited to states that require voters to declare a party affiliation in order to vote in primary elections. Even for these states, registration data must be interpreted with caution. The majority party's registration is usually inflated, partly because that is the party whose primaries are significant and partly because the governing party can offer rewards to those who identify with it and threaten penalties for those who do not. Moreover, a particularly exciting primary contest among contenders for the presidency or for state office may stimulate a flurry of registration changes that have little or no relationship to underlying partisanship.

The invention of public opinion polling has opened new opportunities to probe directly into party affiliation and the attitudes that may underlie and determine it. The voter can simply be asked, "Do you think of yourself as a Republican, a Democrat, or an independent?" The Gallup poll has asked this question in the same wording more or less regularly since 1937. Many organizations now competing with Gallup ask some version of the question as well. The resulting data have become the most important measure of the trends in party strength and in the alignment of the party system and are a rich source of inferences as to the causes of political change.

Yet party identification data have their weaknesses too. During the heat of a presidential campaign, a respondent's party identification may simply reflect the party of the presidential candidate he has decided to support. This is especially likely in the case of the Gallup poll, which prefaces its question with the words "as of today" rather than a phrase such as "generally speaking" that most other polls use in order to divert the respondent's attention from current preferences among candidates.

Given these weaknesses, whatever shifts in party identification the polls reveal may have to be discounted, at least until later polls confirm their durability. One can, however, invert the logic of the argument and search for the phenomena one would expect to find if a realignment of significant magnitude were occurring. While the existence of those phenomena would not be sufficient to prove the existence of such a realignment, they would at least establish a hypothesis to be tested through continuing observation of political behavior and more sophisticated analysis of attitudes. The measurements employed can be considered a series of leading indicators, but the direction and scale of any realignment would not be confirmed until the changes in the leading indicators demonstrated staying power instead of vanishing at the next election.

To the extent that a realignment of the party system may be under way, it should be reflected in some departures from the historical norm in the patterns of party identification. Moreover, one would expect to find new patterns of partisanship most dramatically evident among groups possessing the most tentatively developed party attachments, because the newly emergent partisan cleavages would operate most strongly upon such voters. Thus a distinctive pattern of partisanship among younger voters and newly registered voters should appear, as should a consistent pattern of issue-based party defections, which may extend over several successive elections. In the aggregate there should be a tendency for many individuals, constituting definable electoral groups, to shift their party attachments to accord with shifts in their voting behavior. And because realignment is by definition a partisan phenomenon, the proportion of independents in the affected segments of the electorate should decline, and the share of partisans should rise.

Taken at their face value, party identification data suggest that all these criteria were indeed met in 1984. The Republican gains were most notable among young and first-time voters; there was an issue-based consistency to the pattern of defections to the GOP; and one important voting bloc (white southerners) has clearly been in the process of adapting its aggregate partisanship to its aggregate preferences in the last several presidential elections. There is even evidence that the long-lived trend toward political independence may have reached a plateau in the mid-1970s and begun to reverse. In short the data show exactly the pattern that would appear if a substantial partisan realignment were in progress. All that is in question is the durability of the changes. If the current trends persist into 1988, one would probably be justified in declaring that

Figure 2-1. *Political Party Identification, 1937–85*
Percentage

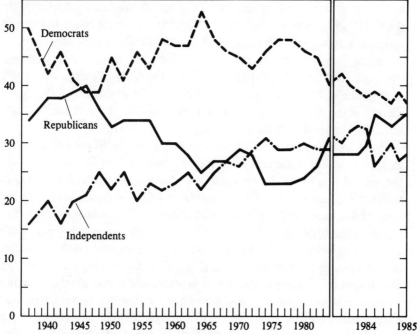

Source: *Gallup Report*, nos. 228, 229 (August, September, 1984), p. 33.

a realignment—not one as decisive as that of the 1930s but one of a
second order of magnitude—had occurred.

Trends in Party Identification

From 1950 until the summer of 1984, Gallup polls showed a consistent
and substantial Democratic advantage over the Republicans in party
identification (figure 2-1). In the nation as a whole the Democrats always
claimed more than 40 percent of the electorate, and usually 45 to 48
percent, while Republican identification was always below 35 percent
and, for the last quarter of a century, 29 percent or less. But this long-
standing, one-and-one-half-party relationship gave way during the fall
campaign when all the major polling organizations found the GOP nearing
parity with the Democrats.

Surprisingly, the movement toward the Republicans as measured by successive Gallup polls was not gradual; it took place in a single ten-week period. Until then the election and inauguration of Ronald Reagan and the first three and one-half years of his administration had brought the GOP no accretion of strength above its historical base. In his first campaign, Reagan had brought the Republicans some new adherents, as a winning presidential candidate usually does, but they were only enough to recoup the losses the party had suffered during the Watergate scandals and President Nixon's resignation. Through the first half of 1984, party identification figures still displayed the familiar three-to-two ratio—virtually identical with the pre-Watergate 1972 figures.

But a shift in strength from the Democrats to the Republicans began to appear in late June and continued through Labor Day—essentially the period spanning the two party conventions (figure 2-1). Reagan pollster Richard Wirthlin has stated that the Democratic convention did substantial harm to the party's standing with the electorate, notwithstanding the brief surge of support for Mondale toward the end of the convention week. The Republican tracking surveys found that "a lot of Americans applauded selecting a woman as the running mate. But we also found that because she was a woman and a liberal, the decision strengthened our position in the southern states," a pattern that was reinforced by the controversy over dismissing Georgia Democratic party chairman Bert Lance from the chairmanship of the Mondale campaign. Wirthlin also felt that the Democratic candidate's pledge to raise taxes enabled the Republicans "to link Walter Mondale to the most negative aspects of the past" at a time when most voters were reasonably satisfied with the present.[9] One may speculate whether other negative factors may have impelled Democrats to leave their party—the prominence of Jesse Jackson at the convention, perhaps, or the alienation of supporters of Gary Hart. Whatever the causes, by early September the partisan balance had shifted to 39 percent Democratic, 35 percent Republican, and 26 percent independent, where it remained essentially unchanged for the rest of the campaign and through the first three months of 1985.[10]

What remained of the Democratic advantage by then was entirely accounted for by the overwhelming commitment of blacks to the Dem-

9. Ben J. Wattenburg, "Moving Right Along? Campaign '84's Lessons for 1988," *Public Opinion*, vol. 7 (December 1984/January 1985), p. 60.

10. Given the margin of error in each of the successive Gallup polls (about 3 percent), some doubt must remain as to the exact timing of the shift in voter sentiment. The CBS/*New York Times* polls found the traditional Democratic margin among party identifiers continued until October. See *Public Opinion*, vol. 7 (December 1984/January 1985), p. 39.

ocratic party, a preference that appears to have strengthened somewhat during the Reagan years. According to the CBS News/*New York Times* exit polls, 73 percent of black voters identified themselves as Democrats and 10 percent as Republicans in 1980; four years later, the margin was an even more massive 77 to 7 percent (table 2-1). Reagan initiatives on civil rights and social spending cutbacks have threatened programs considered vitally important by many blacks. Moreover, the economic recovery has largely bypassed the black community, leaving blacks distinctly unimpressed by Reaganomics.[11]

A smaller minority, the Hispanics, moved strongly in the opposite direction; their preference shrank from 67 percent Democratic and 15 percent Republican in 1980 (a difference of 52 percentage points) to a more modest 56 and 27 percent, or 29 points, in 1984. This change of 23 points represents one of the strongest pro-Republican shifts among any group in the electorate. But the movement should not be surprising, because the GOP has vigorously courted Hispanics for several years in the belief that the party needs to offset the heavily Democratic propensity of the black vote.

Table 2-1 also compares the 1980 and 1984 CBS/*New York Times* exit poll data on party identification among white subgroups to identify those in which the Republican tide was running most strongly. The most dramatic shifts in partisanship occurred among younger voters and southerners. (In fact, southern whites under the age of thirty exactly reversed their partisan allegiance in the four-year period from a 45–33 percent Democratic plurality to a 45–32 percent edge for the Republicans.) The unemployed were the only major white subgroup to strengthen their Democratic allegiance, no doubt because of the severity of the 1982 recession. Some other white constituencies displayed continuing Democratic loyalties: union households, residents of large cities, northeasterners, and Jews, groups that overlap substantially. While Jewish allegiance to the Democratic party may have been briefly shaken by Jesse Jackson's anti-Semitic remarks and by his association with Louis Farrakhan of the Nation of Islam, the allegiance appears to have been strongly reinforced by the prominence of the Reverend Jerry Falwell and other Christian fundamentalists in the Reagan campaign.

The recent Republican gains have produced the narrowest gap in the parties' strengths since the 1940s. Some of the changes of the past year may ultimately prove to be short-lived—merely part of an election year

11. Thomas E. Cavanagh, *Inside Black America* (Joint Center for Political Studies, forthcoming).

Table 2-1. *Changes in Party Identification, by Demographic Categories, 1980–84*
Percentages of eligible voters

Category	1980			1984			Change in Democratic margin
	D	R	I[a]	D	R	I[a]	
Blacks	73	10	17	77	7	16	+7
Hispanics	67	15	18	56	27	17	−23
Whites	42	32	26	34	39	27	−15
White subgroups							
Men	39	33	28	32	38	30	−12
Women	44	31	25	36	39	25	−16
Age 18–29	40	32	28	30	42	27	−20
Age 30–44	38	30	32	33	35	32	−10
Age 45–59	44	32	25	34	37	29	−15
Age 60 and over	45	37	18	38	42	19	−12
Northeast	41	30	29	36	33	30	−8
Midwest	38	33	29	32	41	28	−14
South	46	30	24	33	39	28	−22
West	41	36	23	34	44	22	−15
Professional/managerial	36	34	30	31	40	29	−11
Other white collar	41	32	27	34	36	30	−11
Blue collar	48	25	27	38	30	32	−15
Agricultural	41	38	21	35	49	16	−17
Unemployed	37	37	26	42	26	32	+16
Union household	50	24	26	46	26	28	−6
Less than high school education	52	29	19	47	35	18	−11
High school graduate	47	29	24	37	37	26	−18
Some college	37	33	30	30	41	29	−15
College graduate	35	34	31	31	39	30	−9
Protestant	35	41	24	28	47	26	−13
Catholic	48	23	29	43	28	29	−10
Jewish	63	15	22	61	15	23	−2
Born-again Christian	40	37	23	29	45	26	−19
Large city	49	26	25	46	28	26	−5
Small city	43	27	30	35	37	28	−18
Suburban	37	35	28	33	41	26	−10
Rural	42	34	24	32	40	28	−16

Source: CBS News/*New York Times* exit polls.
a. D = Democratic; R = Republican; I = independent.

surge to the winning party such as has appeared on occasion previously in Gallup polls. The Johnson landslide of 1964, for instance, was accompanied by a gain of 6 percentage points in Democratic identification that vanished shortly thereafter. But if party identification stabilizes at or near current levels, a major equalization of the two-party competitive balance will have occurred.

The data in figure 2-1 show 1974 as the high-water mark of political independents. After a steady increase since the dawn of public opinion polling and a burst beginning in the mid-1960s, the share of the electorate outside the two parties has remained more or less constant for the past decade and may even be starting to decline. It is especially striking that only 27 percent of whites under the age of thirty now consider themselves independent compared with 32 percent of those thirty to forty-four (table 2-1). Because the tendency of the youngest voters to be most independent has been one of the most reliable constants in all studies of political attitudes and voting behavior,[12] the sudden appearance of a curvilinear relationship is startling. It may suggest that the generation of the 1960s was socialized into independence while the newer generation is developing a stronger sense of partisanship.[13] As noted earlier, an increase in the partisanship of the youngest voters is precisely one of the patterns that typify a realignment period.

Voter registration data confirm the pro-Republican direction of the trend, although they are of little use in gauging its magnitude. Relatively few people have gone to their courthouses to change registration from one party to the other—as many did in the New Deal era—but new voters, most of them young, appear to have given the Republicans the edge. The Committee for the Study of the American Electorate found GOP registration gains exceeding those of the Democrats in ten states, compared to four with a better Democratic showing. A *Washington Post*

12. Campbell and others, *The American Voter*, pp. 146–67. The tendency of the youngest voters to be the most independent appears in every Survey Research Center study between 1956 and 1974; note the table in Norman H. Nie, Sidney Verba, and John R. Petrocik, *The Changing American Voter* (Harvard University Press, 1979), p. 60.

13. The new curvilinear relationship between age and independence is especially striking in the NBC News exit poll data from the last two elections. In 1980 the level of independents ranged from 21 percent among those aged eighteen to twenty-four to a peak of 29 percent among those thirty-five to forty-nine and a trough of 19 percent among voters sixty-five and older. The corresponding figures for 1984 were 22, 32, and 21 percent. See Laurily K. Epstein, "1984—A Realigning Election?" *Election Politics*, vol. 2 (Winter 1984–85), p. 4.

survey gave the Republicans the lead in nine states and the Democrats in five, with three even.[14]

The GOP's Youth Movement

The dramatic rise in the turnout among minorities, the aged, and the unemployed in the 1982 midterm election encouraged many Democrats to believe that get-out-the-vote drives concentrated on groups disadvantaged by Reagan's policies could yield the margin of victory in 1984. In some respects the strategy was successful; the Census Bureau found that black turnout increased by 5.3 percentage points over its 1980 level.[15] The CBS/*New York Times* exit poll likewise found that 11 percent of black voters and 13 percent of Hispanic voters were first-time registrants, as opposed to 7 percent of white voters.

What threw the Democrats' assumptions awry was a remarkable countermobilization of younger, more conservative whites by the Republicans. To some extent the GOP registration surge was spontaneous and self-generating; a postelection survey by the Committee for the Study of the American Electorate found that only 33 percent of newly registered whites had been signed up by organizations, as opposed to 47 percent of newly registered blacks. Nonetheless, the targeting of such groups as born-again Christians, recently transferred business executives, military personnel, college students, and suburban women provided such a boost for the Republicans that they emerged as the victors in the registration war. The CBS/*New York Times* exit poll found new voters supporting Reagan by a margin of 61 to 38 percent—the same proportions as established voters—but they were identifying with the Republicans in greater numbers, giving the GOP a margin of 38 to 35 percent over the Democrats while the electorate as a whole maintained a Democratic plurality. An upscale and therefore conservative and Republican bias is especially apparent if one isolates first-time white voters, 75 percent of whom were under thirty years of age. Of this group,

14. Mike Feinsilber, "Tuesday's Voters," United Press, press release, November 1, 1984; and Thomas B. Edsall, "New Voter Sign-Ups May Favor the GOP," *Washington Post*, November 2, 1984.

15. U.S. Bureau of the Census, *Current Population Reports*, Series P-20, no. 397, "Voting and Registration in the Election of November 1984" (Advance Report) (Government Printing Office, 1985), Table A.

Table 2-2. *Deviation from Democratic Presidential Vote, by Age,*
1936–84
Percent

Year	Democratic percentage, all ages	21–29	30–49	50 and over
1936	62	+6	+3	−6
1940	55	+5	+1	−4
1944	54	+4	−1	−3
1948	53	+4	+2	−4
1952	45	+6	+2	−6
1956	42	+1	+3	−3
1960	50	+4	+4	−4
1964	61	+3	+2	−2
1968	43	+4	+1	−2
1972	38	+10	−5	−2
1976	50	+3	−2	+2
1980	41	+6	−3	0
1984	41	−1	−1	0

Sources: *The Gallup Political Almanac for 1946* (Manchester, N.H.: Clarke Press, 1946), p. 204; *Gallup Reports*, November, 1984, pp. 8–9; and Gallup study no. 432, made available by the Roper Center, University of Connecticut.

47 percent were college educated, and 40 percent had incomes greater than $25,000, which is above the national median income of $24,600 in 1983. Fully 71 percent supported Reagan, and they gave the Republicans the edge over the Democrats in party identification by 44 to 28 percent.

The significance of the GOP's youth movement becomes clear when one recalls that the surge of new voters and young voters toward the Democratic party was one of the most important factors in the rise to dominance of the New Deal coalition during the 1930s.[16] The tendency of voters under thirty to favor the Democrats disproportionately has been one of the most durable of all of the legacies of the Roosevelt-era realignment (table 2-2). It may be considered the most important as well because it has ensured a constant replenishment of the supply of Democrats as previous generations of the party faithful died. Thus the abrupt departure from this tendency in 1984 is perhaps the most momentous of all the leading indicators suggesting that the Democrats' status as the majority party may no longer be secure.

16. Kristi Andersen, *The Creation of a Democratic Party Majority, 1928–1936* (University of Chicago Press, 1979).

Policy Issues and Party Images

As the movement of younger voters toward the Republicans began to attract attention during the autumn of 1984, commentators speculated that young people's perceptions of the two parties had been almost wholly shaped by their reactions to the two most recent administrations. Whatever one's own policy predilections, one must concede the stark difference between the leadership and managerial images projected by Jimmy Carter and Ronald Reagan—the one seemingly overwhelmed by events and forces outside his or the nation's control, the other confidently articulating and pursuing a vision of national restoration. When asked the single most important reason for their presidential choice by the ABC News exit poll, 28 percent of the sample said, "He's a strong leader," more than cited any other reason; and Reagan carried these voters by an extraordinary margin of 83 to 17 percent.

It is not surprising that the perceived success of the Reagan administration, coming so close on the heels of an administration widely regarded as a failure, would make such a vivid impression on the young. But there is considerable evidence that an image of Republican competence in coping with the nation's problems has also caused partisan shifts among older sectors of the electorate. In January 1984 the ABC poll of registered voters found the Democrats favored by 42 to 37 percent over the Republicans as the party best able to handle the nation's "most important problem" (as each respondent defined it). The two parties were essentially tied on this measure as late as July. In September, however, the Republicans had moved ahead of the Democrats by 49 to 39 percent, and they outpointed the Democrats by 56 to 44 percent among the voters in the ABC election day exit poll. Of the 44 percent who thought the Democrats were the better managers of the country's affairs, 90 percent had supported Mondale. Of those who preferred the Republicans, 95 per cent had voted for Reagan.

The image of Republican competence is primarily due to the party's recent record of economic management. In a CBS/*New York Times* postelection survey, 30 percent of the respondents said they had formed a better opinion of the Republican party during the past five years, while only 11 percent had a worse opinion. When those with an improved opinion were asked why, 25 percent said the economy, far more than specified any other single reason.

The contribution of Reaganomics to the Republican surge was fore-shadowed in a Gallup poll of early April that found 44 percent of the nation identifying the GOP as the party that "will do a better job of keeping the country prosperous"—the highest figure recorded for the Republicans since the question was first asked in 1951. Whites, south-erners, westerners, and young people preferred the Republicans as the party of prosperity in this survey, even though each group was still showing a Democratic edge in partisan allegiance as late as June.[17] The crystallization of the economy as an issue evidently drew these groups into the Republican fold during the campaign, for by November, plural-ities of these groups had come to consider themselves Republicans outright. The salience of the relationship is confirmed by the fact that blacks, labor union families, and low-income households, who had more confidence in the Democrats as the party of prosperity in April, still retained their Democratic party allegiance in November. The correlation suggests that a seemingly detached, "objective," and perhaps tentative judgment in the spring on the parties' comparative merits as economic managers was becoming internalized as a change in self-definition for sizable numbers of voters by the fall.

The defense issue also aided the Republicans. For most of the public, Reagan's tough posture vis-à-vis foreign powers contrasted favorably with an impression of indecisiveness and drift during the Carter years that seemed confirmed by the humiliation of the Iranian hostage crisis. The October CBS/*New York Times* survey found the Republicans favored over the Democrats by 64 to 18 percent as the party "more likely to make sure U.S. military defenses are strong." The fear of conflict acts as a partial counterweight to the GOP advantage on this issue, however; the Republicans were seen as the party "more likely to keep us out of war" by a much more narrow margin of 37 to 34 percent.[18] Evidently, military strength is popular as long as it is unlikely to be used. This public schizophrenia also carried over into candidate preference. According to ABC, 84 percent of voters whose top priority was to "keep America strong militarily" supported Reagan. But voters whose top priority was to "keep us out of war" went for Mondale by a mirror-image 85 percent. There were more of the former (14 percent of the

17. *Gallup Report,* May 1984, pp. 17–18, August–September 1984, pp. 31–32.
18. David E. Rosenbaum, "Growing Support for Republicans Found in Survey," *New York Times,* October 7, 1984.

voters) than of the latter (9 percent), so the issue of war and peace in toto worked to the net advantage of the Republicans.

While the Republicans polished their image, the Democrats managed to tarnish theirs. The CBS/*New York Times* postelection poll found 23 percent of voters saying they had a worse opinion of the Democrats than they had had five years before, while only 7 percent of voters had a better opinion. Remarkably, even among Democrats 18 percent had a worse opinion of their party and only 9 percent a better opinion, which may presage further erosion in the party base. When asked why they had lost faith in the Democrats, the poll's respondents gave a wide range of answers with no single reason dominant.

When Democratic defections to Reagan indicated by the CBS/*New York Times* exit poll data are analyzed, however, the economy and America's military posture appear to have been the key issues. Reagan carried a comfortable 59 percent majority of the Democrats who believed the economy had improved during his first term. He also won 48 percent of the Democrats who considered stronger defenses a higher priority than a nuclear freeze. These issues were bound to exert an even stronger pull among independents. Self-declared independents who perceived economic progress cast 85 percent of their votes for Reagan, as did 84 percent of those preferring military strength to a nuclear freeze. With over half of the independents falling into each of these categories, a large group of Reagan supporters is perhaps edging toward identification with the Republican party.

To be sure, the Republicans have their liabilities. In the CBS/*New York Times* postelection survey, among those who had developed a worse opinion of the Republicans, 10 percent gave the economy as a reason (undoubtedly a reference to the 1982 recession), 6 percent cited unemployment, 5 percent resented cutting back social programs, 6 percent dismissed the GOP as the party of big business or the rich, and 5 percent found it unrepresentative.

The Democrats were favored over the Republicans by 46 to 36 percent as the party more "concerned with the needs and problems of people like yourself," by 43 to 34 percent in running "a government that is fair to all people," and by a wide 54 to 24 percent when it came to preserving social security and medicare.[19] The 1982 recession had brought the fairness issue to the fore in the elections of that year; in tandem with

19. Ibid.

concerns over Reagan's confrontational foreign policy style, it was responsible for the prominence of the gender gap. And the fairness question is still with us; it was, along with fear of war, Mondale's most potent issue in the 1984 campaign.[20] In the midst of a general economic boom, however, it was overshadowed by approval of the Reagan administration's economic performance: the economy was considered a priority issue by 40 percent of the voters, exactly double the share concerned about fairness toward the poor. This shift in the relative salience of the two issues should raise a cautionary flag: the very success of the Reagan administration's economic program in winning support for the Republican party has left the GOP hostage to the performance of the economy over the next several years. Should the recovery continue, the Republicans are well positioned to claim a large share of the credit, but another slowdown would almost certainly revive the fairness issue once again.

The social issues may also impede the efforts of Republicans to solidify their new party strength. Controversies over abortion, gun control, school prayer, and the equal rights amendment (ERA) cut across the current economic alignment in ways that are not necessarily helpful to the GOP in the long term. The ABC News exit poll found that 63 percent of the voters especially concerned about abortion voted for Reagan, but 76 percent of those keying on the ERA voted for Mondale, and 58 percent of self-described environmentalists voted for him. Those saying "the Moral Majority's backing of Reagan" was "very important" in their presidential choice voted for Reagan over Mondale by only 55 to 44 percent, less than Reagan's aggregate margin. From various polling data we know that young voters are especially cross-pressured by their economic and cultural preferences. Reagan's economic performance is most popular with those under thirty, yet the young are also more supportive of abortion rights, women's rights, racial tolerance, and environmentalism and less supportive of the Moral Majority than any other age group. Should the prominence accorded the religious right in Republican circles begin to overshadow the attractiveness of the Republican economic package, young voters might well revert to the independent column or even shift to the Democrats.

Despite these caveats, however, the emerging lines of conflict between

20. In the ABC/*Washington Post* exit poll, Mondale carried the 22 percent of the voters who said fairness was the most important issue by 90 to 9 percent, and the 9 percent most concerned with peace by 85 to 14 percent.

the two parties are currently working to the net advantage of the Republicans. The GOP is coming to be seen as the party of economic prosperity, military strength, and ultraconservative social views; the Democrats as the party of peace, fairness, and cultural diversity. In the aggregate the former package is currently more attractive to the electorate than the latter. In the CBS/*New York Times* postelection survey, 60 percent of the voters had a favorable image of the Republican party in general, but only 47 percent had a favorable image of the Democrats. More ominously for the Democrats, these divergent party images were highly correlated with the 1984 presidential balloting. Those with a favorable image of the Republican party voted for Reagan by 87 to 12 percent, according to the same postelection survey; those with an unfavorable opinion of his party rejected Reagan by 85 to 13 percent. These lopsided margins are comparable to those cited earlier among the voters who perceived one or the other party as best able to handle the nation's problems. The voters' perception of a party's competence and their image of the party in general are necessarily interdependent. One may argue that the election was a referendum not merely on Reagan's first term but also on the relative attractiveness of the two parties, and it was largely the Republican party's perceived success in office that enhanced its general appeal.

The Republican Tide in the South

Along with Hispanics and whites younger than thirty, white southerners showed the largest swing toward the Republicans (table 2-1). Similarly, the Gallup poll found the GOP claiming the loyalties of 40 percent of whites in the South at election time—the largest Republican share of the white electorate in any region—compared with 28 percent just four months earlier. The ABC News exit poll found that 61 percent of all southern voters thought the Republicans would better cope with the nation's problems than the Democrats, again the best Republican showing in any region.

The election returns confirm the clear impression from the polling data that a Republican party tide was running in the South, as distinct from idiosyncratic support for a popular president. Half the party's gains in the House of Representatives came in the South: Republicans captured four Democratic seats in Texas, three in North Carolina, and one in

Georgia, while losing one in Arkansas. The GOP picked up one gover-norship, in North Carolina. It returned every one of its four incumbent senators seeking reelection—in the erstwhile unshakably Democratic states of Virginia, North Carolina, South Carolina, and Mississippi—while holding the seat of retiring Republican John Tower in Texas. The GOP defeated an incumbent Democratic senator in a border state, Kentucky, while losing the seat held by retiring Majority Leader Howard Baker in neighboring Tennessee.

In some states at least, the Republican surge extended to lesser offices. In Texas, Republicans increased their share of the 150-member state house of representatives from 37 to 53 seats, the highest level ever, and gained more than a hundred county offices. In a postelection statewide poll, 49 percent of Texans identified themselves as Republicans or Republican-leaning independents compared with only 33 percent on the Democratic side. If that poll is accurate, Texas alone could account for more than a million new Republicans.[21] In North Carolina the GOP gained 25 state legislative seats.

That the Republican party should be rising spectacularly in the South should not surprise anyone. The wonder is that its ascent has been delayed so long. Ever since the Democratic party committed itself in the 1930s to an activist, interventionist economic and social policy, con-servatives have not had a congenial home in it. But changing party loyalties is like changing churches; people do not do so easily. Moreover, the South had always seen its one-party system as the bulwark of white supremacy. So the movement of southern conservatives to the Repub-lican party was slow. The region remained the solid South for nearly two decades before the first ripples of the coming GOP tide could be observed.

Two events in the early post–World War II period shattered the South's solidity: the Democratic party's embrace of civil rights and the Republican nomination of Dwight D. Eisenhower, a war hero and native Texan. The one cost the Democratic party its standing as the defender of southern traditions; the other made the GOP, stigmatized for nearly a

21. The Texas poll, conducted by Harte-Hanks Communications, Inc., was cited in David S. Broder, "A Republican Texas," *Washington Post*, December 12, 1984. The growth of voting for Republicans for local offices in urban Texas has been extraordinarily rapid. The number of Republican judges in Dallas County has zoomed from none in 1978 to sixty-one of sixty-eight in 1984. See Paul Taylor, "3 Dallas County Judges Switch to GOP Ranks," *Washington Post*, February 9, 1985.

century as the party of the carpetbaggers, respectable at last. In the Eisenhower era, metropolitan areas in the Rim South (as opposed to the Deep South) conformed their presidential voting to the national pattern, dividing on class lines; upper-income voters preferred the Republicans and those of lower income the Democrats. On this beachhead zealous Republican organizations could be built, and the GOP could begin to compete effectively for local and, after that, state offices. But in the Deep South and in most rural areas throughout the region, white voters found themselves adrift. They were severed from the national Democratic party, but they were not yet ready to embrace a Republican party whose president had sent troops to enforce school desegregation in Little Rock. Eventually, however, the Republican leadership passed from Eisenhower to a man who sent white southerners an unmistakable message that he was on their side—Barry Goldwater. As one of the few nonsouthern senators who had voted against the Civil Rights Act of 1964, he was the first Republican nominee who spoke the states' rights language that segregationist southerners wanted to hear. Goldwater turned the political map upside down. He lost ignominiously in the North, but five of the six states he carried were in the Deep South.[22]

The Watergate scandal set the Republicans back everywhere, including the South, and their revival in that region was stalled further when the Democrats chose a native son, Jimmy Carter, as their leader. But Reagan was able to pick up where Goldwater had left off. Indeed, his achievement was even greater than Goldwater's, for once in office he could send a clear signal that not just the presidential candidate as an individual but the Republican party as an institution was sympathetic to southern views on social questions. Under Reagan, the Justice Department's stance on mandatory busing for school desegregation switched from support to opposition. The administration's proposed tuition tax credits for private schools would aid the "segregation academies" set up by whites who had found desegregated public schools intolerable. Moreover, Reagan arrayed the GOP with southern conservatism on some potent new issues thrust into the political arena by court decisions— school prayer, abortion, and the teaching of evolution in public schools. In so doing he mobilized millions of Christian fundamentalists, led by their pastors, as a virtual adjunct of the Republican party in his campaign for reelection.[23]

22. Sundquist, *Dynamics of the Party System*, rev. ed., pp. 277–97, 352–75.
23. Among southern whites, those who claimed to be born-again Christians had

The dramatic racial polarization of the vote in the South has led some observers to express concern over white flight out of the Democratic party in response to the highly visible role of Jesse Jackson and other black leaders in the party's affairs. None of the exit polls included questions that directly tapped racial sentiments, making the proposition difficult to test directly. However, the mid-1984 Gallup study of black and white opinion commissioned by the Joint Center for Political Studies included some questions designed to measure racial backlash. Not surprisingly, antiblack sentiments were more common among southern whites than among other sectors of the electorate. Thirty percent of southern whites said blacks had too much influence in national politics, as opposed to 16 percent of whites nationally. Surprisingly perhaps, southern hostility to Jackson did not appear especially intense. Nineteen percent of southern whites said they were less likely to vote for Mondale because of Jackson's endorsement, while 8 percent said they were more likely to vote for Mondale. (The figures for whites nationally were 17 percent less likely and 10 percent more likely.) By way of contrast, as Harold Stanley has noted, "in 1956 and 1960, between one-third and a majority of southern whites claimed a Negro group's endorsement of a candidate would make them less likely to vote for the candidate."[24] Given that Mondale lost the southern white vote by 71 to 29 percent, the net loss of 11 percentage points on the Jackson question seems relatively modest, particularly because many of the anti-Jackson voters would probably have voted against Mondale for other reasons.

Indeed, one of the most striking aspects of southern white voting patterns is the extent to which they can be explained without reference to racial issues. As we have seen, approval of the nation's economic performance and a strong defense posture were key predictors of a preference for Reagan. These views were especially prevalent among southern whites. In the CBS/*New York Times* exit poll, fully 68 percent of southern whites felt the economy had improved, and 86 percent of this group voted for Reagan. Fifty-eight percent of southern whites preferred strong defenses to a nuclear freeze, and 72 percent of this

---

been somewhat more Democratic in 1980 than the group as a whole, according to the CBS/*New York Times* exit poll, but in 1984 they moved to the Republican party in disproportionate numbers, bringing their support to the level of the region's white population as a whole.

24. Harold W. Stanley, "The 1984 Presidential Election in the South: Race and Realignment," in Robert P. Steed, Lawrence W. Moreland, and Tod A. Baker, eds., *The 1984 Presidential Election in the South* (Praeger, forthcoming).

group voted for Reagan. The president received the votes of a massive 93 percent of southern whites who considered a strong military one of their two highest-priority issues and 85 percent of the votes of those who considered the economy most important. On these two issues conservative Republican policies are striking a very responsive chord in the South.

Democrats can take some comfort that the full fury of southern resentment against them is still limited to the national party. State and local Democratic candidates and leaders have been able to hold the allegiance of enough traditional Democrats to retain most state and local offices so far in every southern state. Before the 1984 election, ten of the eleven governors of the region were Democrats; afterward there are still nine. Democrats control both legislative bodies in all the states, most of them by overwhelming margins. Except in metropolitan areas and in mountain counties whose tradition goes back to the Civil War, the GOP has made little progress in local politics.

Yet Southern Democratic leaders walk a tightrope; they have to speak and act progressively enough to retain the allegiance of blacks, whose votes are crucial to their election, while not speaking or acting so boldly liberal as to earn the antipathy reserved for northerners. As of 1984 they were maintaining their balance, but it is difficult to see how they can do so much longer.

The experience of the last three decades suggests that conservatives who become accustomed to voting regularly for Republican presidential nominees find it easier every year to accept GOP candidates for other offices. The 1984 shift in the party identification of white southerners simply brought their expressed partisanship into line with their recent presidential voting history (table 2-3). Southerners have already extended their presidential Republicanism into U.S. Senate races, with ten of the region's twenty-two senators now representing the GOP, and into a steadily rising number of congressional districts. As the news from Texas indicates, many are now thinking of themselves as Republicans and voting that way for offices from the top to the bottom of the ticket. It is only a matter of time until the South too is finally realigned on the national pattern, with conservatives firmly ensconced in the party in which they have belonged for fifty years.

This does not mean that the solid Democratic South will become a solid Republican South. The GOP's failure to make headway with the black vote will prove a serious obstacle to attaining majority status in

Table 2-3. *Republican and Democratic Party Identification and Presidential Preference for Southern Whites, 1960–84*
Percentages of eligible voters

Year	Republican presidential preference	Republican party identification	Democratic presidential preference	Democratic party identification
1960	43	21	45	60
1964	38	22	52	55
1968	36	21	20	46
1972	75	25	20	40
1976	45	24	48	45
1980	45	25	40	48
1984	69	40	26	31

Source: Gallup final preelection surveys.

the region. The 1982 experience also suggests that an economic downturn could revive a potent populist coalition of blacks and lower-income whites in many parts of the South. But at the least the entire region will see a reasonably balanced two-party competition. And Republican gains in the South should be sufficient to bring the party into a fairly even balance with the Democrats nationally.

If a New Direction, Which?

Before his reelection, President Reagan suggested hopefully that his anticipated triumph might bring about the historical political realignment that Republicans had vainly heralded whenever the Democrats showed signs of slipping from the peaks to which Franklin Roosevelt had carried them. The public opinion data summarized above fall short of confirming the president's aspirations, but they do support the thesis that something historic is indeed happening to the party system. The Republicans have approached parity with the Democrats, finally establishing a genuine two-party system. What that portends, however, is far from clear. Will the Republicans continue their triumphal march and supplant the Democrats as the country's majority party and its normal party of government? Or did their tide crest on Inauguration Day? Analysis of past cycles of party domination can illuminate the possibilities, but it cannot provide sure answers. Divergent scenarios of what may lie ahead can be sketched, and each can find support in aspects of American party history.

One scenario, wishfully propounded these days by the Republicans and dreaded by their opposition, rests on the premise that the Democratic collapse of 1984 revealed weaknesses that are beyond repair. On the morrow of the election, that did not seem a farfetched conclusion. Clearly, the New Deal coalition of labor, white ethnics, racial minorities, and southerners had become hopelessly uncompetitive at the presidential level. The Democrats had lost four of the last five elections—three of them by landslides. Their electoral college base had shrunk to an undependable hard core of Frost Belt industrial states (which can be defined as those states that Mondale lost in 1984 by margins of fewer than 10 percentage points). The Republican base was far more formidable and far more consistent, anchored by a solid wall of Great Plains and Rocky Mountain states that had become as staunchly Republican in presidential voting (though they still chose a fair share of Democratic governors, senators, and representatives) as the South used to be unswervingly Democratic. Add just a few states from either the industrial belt or the South, plus California, and the Republicans could count on a comfortable majority. The continuing flow of population to the South and West would be likely to increase the Republican advantage in the electoral college following the post-1990 reapportionment.

True, the Republicans had not done as well below the presidential level, but in this scenario that would change. The split-level realignment discerned by Kevin Phillips was the result of two passing phenomena: the unnatural lag in Republican progress in the rural South and the power of incumbency. But "yellow dog" southern Democrats had had their day; party supremacy built on tradition alone could not much longer survive the nationalization of politics in the age of television, and the extension of Republicanism to lesser offices was only a matter of time. The presence of ten southerners in the Republican Senate majority where there were none at all as recently as 1960 seemed proof of that. Where the South could once count a hundred safe Democratic House districts, hardly twenty could be numbered now. And even that number would decline, for every southern district had by now given a majority at least once to a Republican presidential candidate. As entrenched Democratic incumbents in the House retired, Republicans would pour their limitless campaign funds into those districts and win them one by one. After that, to vote Republican for both House and Senate candidates would be normal too. Then would come the races for state legislatures and county court houses. It might take some time because the GOP's organizational base was still virtually nonexistent in many areas, but—so goes the argument—it was bound to come.

Meanwhile, in national politics the Republicans had the tremendous advantage of possessing a vision for the future and a program, while the Democrats were squabbling and groping for philosophy and direction. They had no coherent national agenda. In their post-Watergate revival they had enacted most of their unfinished legislative program, including consumer and environmental protection legislation and the creation of federal departments of energy and education. That left only such high-expenditure items as a federal takeover of welfare payments and adoption of national health insurance. But the political appeal of such proposals was overwhelmed in the late 1970s by the growing concerns over inflation, taxes, and diminishing American influence in the world. The coincidence of high unemployment and high inflation soured many policymakers on the Keynesian model for managing the public economy, but it caught the Democrats bereft of an alternative. In 1981 enough congressional Democrats followed Reagan's lead to drain the federal revenue stream for years to come, vitiating any aspirations for new social programs and leaving the party with precious little to talk about.

By 1984 the Republican vision of national prosperity and military strength contrasted with a Democratic image of intellectual and institutional exhaustion. Even to those who saw Mondale as the last in the New Deal lineage of Democratic party leaders, it was far from clear just where a party revitalization could spring from. The Democrats could mimic the Republicans in pledging governmental shrinkage and low taxes—Walter Mondale had tried the alternative, to the party's sorrow—while promising greater fairness in distributing the pain of budget cuts. But that would only emphasize that the Republicans had redefined the terms of policy debate. Indeed, the GOP was beginning to sound and act like the normal party of government, the Democrats like a party resigned to opposition. Even with their big majority in the House, Democratic leaders were advancing no program of their own. They waited for the president to take the lead, then fretted and complained; but they avoided confrontation.

Some analysts saw in all this the beginning of a new era. In their reading of history, one party was always dominant, outshining its opposition as the sun outshines the moon, in Samuel Lubell's felicitous simile.[25] Since 1800 the parties have reversed positions every half century or so: the Democrats were the sun, the Federalists and Whigs the moon, from Jefferson to Lincoln; the Republicans were dominant from Lincoln

25. *The Future of American Politics*, 2d ed. (Doubleday, 1956).

to Franklin Roosevelt, the Democrats since. Tracing parallels among these periods, A. James Reichley, for one, finds portents of a new era of Republican hegemony beginning in 1980. In his view the GOP supremacy would be sustained by a congruity of the party's philosophy with contemporary national beliefs: conservatism in world affairs, confidence in the market as the director of economic life, and a renewal of traditional moral and religious values.[26]

The second scenario is pressed nowadays by Democrats, albeit with more anxiety than confidence. In brief, it sees an early revival of their party. Their present agony of soul-searching, in this view, is mostly an overreaction to the election, something a losing party always goes through. One need but recall the Republican party's identity crisis after its searing defeat in the Lyndon Johnson landslide twenty years ago. Yet the GOP won the very next presidential election, not because it had a systematic philosophy and program but because it was the alternative when Johnson, puffed with reelection hubris, led his party into fatal errors. Sooner or later, Reagan or his successor will do likewise, the Democratic optimists argue, and the Democratic party need only show that it has heeded the lesson taught by its recent defeats—and be available.

Indeed, the spring of 1985 found the Reagan administration taking intransigent and unpopular stands on a variety of issues. To rein in federal spending, the White House proposed significant reductions in federal assistance to farmers, many of whom were in severe distress, and to middle-income college students. So many other constituencies were threatened with cutbacks that even the Senate Republican majority treated the President's budget as dead on arrival in Congress. In particular, many of the twenty-two incumbent Republicans facing re-election in 1986 were distancing themselves from Reagan's more unpopular policies.

Just as the Republicans emphasize their strength at the presidential level, the Democrats point to their own power bases: the House of Representatives, the governorships (currently thirty-four of fifty), the state legislatures, the major city halls. The split-level realignment, they contend, can be resolved in two ways. While the Republicans may be able to extend their presidential voting strength to balloting for lesser

26. "Religion and Political Realignment," *Brookings Review*, vol. 3 (Fall 1984), pp. 34–35.

offices, it is also possible for the Democrats to parlay their local power into presidential victory.

Even the optimists concede, however, that the task is formidable. Almost from its founding but particularly in this century, the Democratic party has been riven between its northern and southern wings—the one urban, Catholic, liberal, and allied with labor, the other rural, Protestant, conservative, and cool or even hostile to union influence. The northern wing has dominated the presidential nominating conventions by force of numbers, but that has served the party well, because Democrats could take the South for granted and needed candidates who could add the necessary electoral votes from the North and West. With the breakup of the solid South, however, the party's problem is quite different. It must now find presidential candidates with appeal across the whole Democratic spectrum. But what southerner will stir a mass response in the cities of the North? And what northerner will not be so liberal, so urban, so ethnic, so beholden to organized labor as to antagonize large elements of the party's southern wing?

The distinctiveness of the various party factions was outlined with unusual clarity during the 1984 nomination campaign. The party's structural and ideological center (labor and party officials) supported Mondale, blacks supported Jackson, yuppies (young urban professionals) backed Gary Hart, and conservative southern whites preferred John Glenn and stopped voting in the presidential primaries after he was knocked out of the race in the early going. Dissatisfaction with Mondale was so intense among the latter two groups that large portions of each defected to Reagan in the fall.

The crosscurrents within the Democratic party are less ideological than generational. Surely this is one of the portents of the Hart campaign. While the Hart constituency is somewhat more conservative than the Democratic norm on economic issues, the senator's call for new ideas was not so much a programmatic manifesto as a simple rejection of the shopworn style of leadership exemplified by Mondale. This spirit also fueled much of the impetus behind the Jackson insurgency, which became the vehicle in many communities for the emergence of a new cadre of black political leadership less wedded to traditional (white-dominated) party organizations.

The difference in styles also helps explain the prominence of the issue of "special interests" in Democratic party circles. For many voters the party appears to be dominated by the concerns of distinctive groups—

minorities, women, labor unions, homosexuals—to the exclusion of a broader vision of the national interest. Yet these special interests are by no means equally unpopular. When the Joint Center for Political Studies/Gallup study asked respondents whether a variety of groups had "too much influence over national policies and programs," the economic interests were the main targets of resentment: 62 percent of whites and 43 percent of blacks singled out labor leaders, while 51 percent of whites and 58 percent of blacks mentioned business leaders. By comparison, the groups Jackson hoped to include in his Rainbow Coalition finished well down the list. Sixteen percent of whites thought blacks had too much influence; well below 10 percent considered women, Hispanics, poor people, and the elderly too influential. These data suggest that the damage inflicted on the party by its association with the special interests other than labor may be overemphasized in the party's self-examination. And while the Democrats' alliance with labor may be a problem, it is not significantly more troublesome for them than the public opprobrium for business interests can become for the Republicans, particularly if the economic climate becomes less favorable.

Democrats can also take comfort from the GOP's internal schisms. The Republican party may be somewhat more homogeneous in composition than the Democrats can ever claim to be, but its divisions are nevertheless apparent and will become more so as the next nominating convention approaches. Centered in the South and Southwest is an ultraconservative, New Right wing, uncompromising in foreign policy, libertarian in economic policy, fundamentalist in social policy, and crusading in its style. Arrayed against the New Right are the inheritors of the older strain of conservatism that was for a long time the party's mainstream. They are more moderate now in foreign, economic, and social policies alike, and more pragmatic in exercising governmental responsibility. As the struggle over the succession to Reagan waxes, the internal strain will be intensified, and at the point where one group defeats the other the Reagan coalition of 1984 could well come unglued.

The two key swing groups are white southerners and yuppies. Both were important contributors to the Republican surge of 1984, yet they were attracted to the party for contrasting reasons. White southerners fear hard times and dislike the GOP's country club image, but they admire Reagan's foreign policy toughness and his social conservatism. Yuppies' preferences are almost precisely reversed: they are attracted by Reagan's free market philosophy and his promises of economic growth and affluence but are relatively progressive on social issues and dovish on foreign policy. To get both groups, along with big business and the Moral Majority, to enter the Republican tent for a single revival meeting is one thing; to maintain them as a happy congregation is quite another. Should attempts to legislate morality come to dominate the political agenda, the Republican gains among young people could vanish as quickly as they emerged.

Underlying the Democratic scenario is a different reading of historical political cycles. While the sun-moon simile may accurately depict most of the country's history, no theoretical reason has been advanced to explain why a highly competitive two-party system is not equally possible. Indeed, there have been a number of periods (the 1840s, the 1880s, the 1910s) when the two major parties have been about evenly balanced nationally. Many periods of one-party dominance can be explained by traumatic national events—the Civil War, the Great Depression—that destroyed the standing of one of the major parties in much of the country. In the absence of such an event, as at present, there appears to be no compelling reason why one party must of necessity maintain a lasting advantage over the other.

In the Democratic scenario, then, control of the national government is likely to swing back and forth between the parties in much shorter cycles. Recent history seems to support this view. While the Republicans can boast of their four victories in the last five presidential elections, that claim embodies the statistical trick of choosing the most advantageous base date. To say that the Republicans won four of the last seven or six of the last fourteen would be less impressive but no less accurate.

The interpretation of the modern party system as one normally characterized by short-term alternations has a solid theoretical foundation. It is based on the fact that most voters are neither pure liberals nor pure conservatives but exhibit a bundle of attitudes that incorporate elements of both and tend to be equivocal, changeable, muddled, and often contradictory. The typical voter is suspicious of both political extremes; he may be labeled centrist (accounting for the normal-curve distribution of the electorate across the ideological spectrum), but the middle position is not so much a rational and fixed centrism as the product of ambivalence. The modal voter looks both ways on almost any issue: in favor of a strong defense but against militarism; for a tough stance against communism but against another Vietnam; for helping the deserving poor but not the undeserving; for increased spending for education, health, and a variety of other services but against increased taxes; for economic development but without damage to the environment; for cutting budgets but not services; for the right to abortion in some circumstances but against complete freedom of choice; for progress by blacks but not at the expense of whites; for regulating the economy but not stifling enterprise with regulatory burdens.

The political party in power can be ambivalent, too, but only for a while; on most issues it must ultimately take a stand, and when it does, it comes down on one side of the voters' ambivalence. So it is either to the left or the right of the "centrist" electorate. In either case it is out of sync. In a two-party system, then, the liberal party is always more liberal than the voting public, the conservative party more conservative. Whichever party is in power, grievances accumulate as time passes. The gap widens between what the governing party offers and what the people expect and want—and think they voted for. At some point the electorate expresses its dissatisfaction in the only way it can: by turning to the other party. That party takes office, reverses the policies and satisfies the old grievances, but at once introduces its own set. When it in turn has worn out its welcome, the pendulum swings once more.

Even within periods of one-party dominance, the short-term cycle is evident. The country was in a conservative mood and elected conservative presidents in the 1890s, the 1920s, the 1950s, and now the 1980s. But it was in a liberal mood and backed liberal presidential candidates in the 1910s, the 1930s, and the 1960s. There is no reason to believe that it is any more permanently attuned to the Reagan-Republican philosophy now than it was immovable in its support of the credo of Lyndon Johnson's Great Society twenty years ago. This interpretation is supported by a wealth of data showing a wide gap now exists between the electorate's policy preferences and the Reagan policies. To cite only a few examples: in contrast to the Republican position, most of the electorate supports the equal rights amendment, is opposed to prohibiting abortion altogether, strongly favors arms control (here the resumption of negotiations has now brought the GOP closer to the majority position), believes military spending should be increased no further, and is opposed to further reductions in spending for almost every enumerated domestic social purpose.

Finally, one cannot omit recognizing the elements of skill, and serendipity, in coping with events. Just as the recent rise of the Republican party has come in large part from the achievements of Reaganomics in the president's first term, so is it dependent on the continuing success of economic policy in his second. The president has staked his party's fate on a gamble—not supported by all the economists of even his own party—that the current enormous deficits in the national budget can be overcome through economic growth alone before they precipitate a new inflationary crisis or a breakdown of the international trading and monetary systems. Foreign affairs always presents risks to any president, as Jimmy Carter learned when the Tehran embassy was sacked. In Reagan's case a breakdown in arms negotiation, a deeper involvement in Central America, a new flare-up in the Middle East, or any of a dozen other dangers could shatter the confidence of many voters in the Republican competence in foreign policy. The poll responses to the question, "Which party do you think would do the best job of . . . ?" have always been volatile. Of late those answers have moved strongly in favor of the Republicans, but they reflect the day's headlines, and they can go down as well as up.

The two scenarios sketched above are by no means mutually exclusive. Even if the Republicans prove correct in their anticipation of a new long-term cycle of GOP dominance, there will still be a short-term alternation of control of the presidency and probably of the Congress, as there has been throughout much of U.S. history. Elections will still be decided by the fluid multitudes of voters who are independents or weakly attached to a party. While some of the Republican gains of recent months may not survive the Reagan presidency, at least those in the South appear to be the durable product of longer-term trends. It would require only a small—and likely—increment of additional permanent strength from the party's new adherents elsewhere, particularly from its generation of young recruits, for 1984 to take its place as the critical election year that gave the country a new, balanced, and highly competitive two-party system.

CHAPTER THREE

The Economic Basis of Reagan's Appeal

D. RODERICK KIEWIET AND DOUGLAS RIVERS

AT THE END of his 1980 debate with Jimmy Carter, Ronald Reagan suggested that when people vote, "It might be well if you would ask yourself: Are you better off than you were four years ago? Is it easier for you to go and buy things in the stores than it was four years ago? Is there more or less unemployment in the country than there was four years ago?"[1] Because Reagan defeated Carter by a wide margin, it is assumed that many Americans answered these questions negatively. If voters were asked the same question in 1984, then by the same logic they must have answered them positively and the result was Reagan's landslide victory over Walter Mondale.

There is but one problem with this interpretation of the 1980 and 1984 elections: if these were in fact the criteria voters used to choose between presidential candidates in the two elections, Ronald Reagan probably would never have been elected president and certainly would not have been reelected by such a large margin. The reality is that between the time Carter entered office and the time Reagan asked Americans whether it was easier "to buy things in the stores," consumer purchasing power (as measured by personal disposable income in constant dollars) grew by 11.6 percent. Although the unemployment rate in October 1980 stood at the same 7.5 percent level as in January 1977, for most of the Carter years the rate was below 7 percent (and fell to as low as 5.6 percent).

The authors wish to thank the National Science Foundation, which provided research support under grant SES83-09994.
1. Elizabeth Drew, *Portrait of an Election* (Simon and Schuster, 1981), p. 325.

Table 3-1. *Four-Year Comparisons of Economic Performance,*
1961–64 to 1981–84
Percentages

Period[a]	Change in real disposable income	Change in inflation rate (CPI)	Average unemployment rate	Change in unemployment rate
1961–64	+ 19.9	+ 4.5	5.8	– 1.5
1965–68	+ 17.7	+ 12.9	3.9	– 1.5
1969–72	+ 17.0	+ 18.7	5.0	+ 2.2
1973–76	+ 7.5	+ 35.7	6.8	+ 2.8
1977–80	+ 11.6	+ 45.0	6.5	0
1981–84	+ 14.0	+ 19.8	8.7	– 0.2

Sources: U.S. Department of Commerce, Bureau of Economic Analysis, *Business Statistics, 1982* (Government Printing Office, 1983); "Current Business Statistics," *Survey of Current Business,* vol. 65 (January 1985).
a. Period from January following the presidential election until October before the next presidential election.

The record of the Reagan administration, as measured by the standards Reagan himself suggested, is roughly comparable to that of the Carter administration. Real income grew by a slightly higher 14.0 percent during Reagan's first forty-five months in office (see table 3-1). The unemployment rate started and ended at about the same level (7.5 percent in January 1981 and 7.3 percent in October 1984), but the average monthly unemployment rate was much higher (8.7 percent as compared to 6.5 percent under Carter). The rate of inflation did fall under Reagan while it rose under Carter, but inflation alone does not affect purchasing power, nor does it appear to count for much of Reagan's popularity.[2] Why, then, was Ronald Reagan able to win reelection—and to win handily—while Jimmy Carter, in apparently similar circumstances, was defeated so decisively?

One explanation for Reagan's success is a shift in public opinion and party allegiances. Both the 1980 and 1984 elections, it could be argued, were manifestations of a long-run trend toward conservatism that has benefited the Republicans. Opinion surveys find more voters classifying themselves as conservatives and taking conservative positions on national defense and social welfare issues.[3] By turning the course of public

2. William C. Adams, "Recent Fables about Ronald Reagan," *Public Opinion,* vol. 7 (October–November 1984), pp. 6–9. We do not mean to imply that voters are insensitive to nominal fluctuations in price levels but that opinions about inflation are more complicated than is generally supposed. We deal with these issues at length in a forthcoming paper. See also D. Roderick Kiewiet, *Macroeconomics and Micropolitics* (University of Chicago Press, 1983).
3. See, for example, *Gallup Report,* November 1984, p. 23.

Table 3-2. *One-Year Comparisons of Economic Performance,*
Selected Years, 1963–64 to 1983–84
Percentages

Period[a]	Change in real disposable income	Change in inflation rate (CPI)	Average unemployment rate	Change in unemployment rate
1963–64	+6.9	+1.2	5.3	-0.4
1967–68	+4.4	+4.7	3.6	-0.6
1971–72	+6.1	+3.4	5.7	-0.2
1975–76	+2.7	+5.3	7.8	-0.7
1979–80	+0.7	+12.6	6.9	+1.5
1983–84	+5.8	+3.6	7.8	-1.5

Sources: U.S. Department of Commerce, Bureau of Economic Analysis, *Business Statistics, 1982* (GPO, 1983); "Current Business Statistics," *Survey of Current Business,* vol. 64 (December 1984) and vol. 65 (January 1985).
a. Period from October preceding the presidential election until October of the election year.

policy away from big government and the welfare state, Ronald Reagan succeeded in converting conservative sentiment into Republican votes. Several analysts, including Thomas Cavanagh and James Sundquist, cite an increase in the number of self-identified Republicans as evidence for the possible permanence of this movement (see chapter 2).

Alternatively, both the 1980 and 1984 elections could be viewed as reflecting the personal strength of Reagan as a candidate and the particular liabilities of his Democratic opponents. Perhaps what really mattered on November 6, 1980, was that it was "day 365" of the Iranian hostage crisis. Four years later, America was "standing tall." If Ronald Reagan had restored the nation's confidence in itself and its leader, his reelection was, as Elizabeth Drew wrote, "above all a testimonial to the man as a political phenomenon."[4]

But neither explanation—of fundamental partisan change or of short-term deviations caused by the candidates' personalities—is really necessary. Both the 1980 and 1984 election results are consistent with past patterns of economic voting. The difference between Carter and Reagan that explains their varying electoral fortunes is not really *how much* they increased consumer purchasing power or reduced unemployment but *when.* If economic performance during the twelve months preceding the 1980 and 1984 presidential elections is compared, performance under Reagan is far superior to that under Carter (table 3-2). Real disposable income grew by 5.8 percent in the year before the 1984 election but by

4. Elizabeth Drew, "A Political Journal," *New Yorker,* December 3, 1984, p. 100.

only 0.7 percent in the year before the 1980 election. Though the average unemployment rate was higher in the last year of Reagan's first term than in the comparable period of the Carter administration (7.8 percent versus 6.9 percent), the trend was downward (− 1.5 percent) in 1983–84 and upward (+ 1.5 percent) in 1979–80. Reagan's timing was much better than Carter's.

Reagan's reelection-year performance was also better by historical standards. The growth rate for real income during 1983–84 was slightly lower than that during 1971–72. The unemployment rate was somewhat lower in 1963–64 and 1971–72 than in 1983–84, though the trend was more favorable in 1983–84 than in the earlier years. Is it any surprise then that Reagan's reelection margin in 1984 was about the same as Johnson's in 1964 or Nixon's in 1972?

This chapter demonstrates that it should be no surprise. First we show that Reagan's growing lead over Walter Mondale in public opinion polls during 1984 is what would be predicted by the economic voting model, but it is also consistent with many other explanations. Subsequently we analyze the evolution of public support for presidents from John F. Kennedy through Reagan. For President Reagan as well as for his predecessors, most of the variance in presidential popularity can be accounted for by economic conditions. We next suggest that the timing of economic conditions under Reagan was nearly optimal from the standpoint of his chances of reelection. Finally, we briefly consider some of the issues of presidential accountability for economic changes and whether economic expansions could be timed to coincide with elections.

What Happened during the 1984 Presidential Campaign?

What one sees in a political campaign is largely a matter of perspective. Journalists and campaign activists see the day-to-day decisions that a candidate makes about where to go, what to say, and what to do. A campaign is composed of countless such decisions and these are not unimportant. As weak a showing by Ronald Reagan in the second presidential debate as in the first, for instance, might have changed the course of the campaign and led voters to question the advisability of having a president who would be in his late seventies before the end of his term. This, however, is highly speculative, and the evidence supporting the allegedly decisive role of other campaign events is often not much better.

The effects of the economy are not the sort of thing one sees clearly or easily in the midst of an electoral campaign. Candidates talk about the economy, but it is doubtful what they say has much impact. Mondale could not convince the country that the economic recovery was illusory; Reagan could not convince those adversely affected by his economic policies that the policies were good for them. Mondale tried to argue that the recovery was purchased at the cost of enormous budget deficits and could not be sustained, while Reagan claimed that those hurt by his policies would be better off in the long run. However, these arguments were a poor match for the reality of economic conditions, and for most voters in 1984 that reality was an economic boom. Although Walter Mondale was probably not an ideal candidate for the Democrats, there is little reason to believe any Democrat had much chance to defeat Ronald Reagan in 1984. This is not to say that campaigns are unimportant, but simply that in 1984, as in many other elections, the pluses and minuses for each side tended to even out. Mondale and Reagan each ran campaigns about as effectively as could be expected. Each made mistakes that in retrospect they may have wished they had not made, but it is difficult to identify any major blunders that dramatically changed the course of the campaign. Mondale lost because the economy was booming, unemployment was falling, inflation was under control, and Ronald Reagan was president.

To see that no further explanation is required, consider the trial heats that polling organizations conducted on an almost weekly basis throughout 1984 to determine what would happen if Ronald Reagan faced Walter Mondale in an election. These trial heats were reported and analyzed by the press with great frequency, and small and large variations in their outcomes were attributed to the campaign actions of Mondale or Reagan. Undoubtedly these actions were responsible for some of the variation in the polling results. But how much?

It should first be noted that differences of 5 percent or more may be nothing more than survey noise. Different polling organizations ask questions slightly differently, order questions differently, and draw their samples differently. The consequences of such seemingly minor variations can be substantial, and none is taken into account when the polling organizations calculate confidence intervals for their results.[5]

5. The "design effect" can also reduce the variance of sample moments if there are heterogeneous clusters. See Leslie Kish, *Survey Sampling* (Wiley, 1965), pp. 257–63.

Table 3-3. *Reagan Lead in Trial Heats with Mondale*[a]

Variable	(1)	(2)
Polling Agency		
Harris	0.98	−0.201
	(1.37)	(1.480)
ABC	−1.44	−0.776
	(1.44)	(1.55)
Penn/Schoen	3.82	4.36
	(3.00)	(3.16)
CBS	5.22	6.16
	(1.81)	(1.44)
Roper	−3.53	−3.12
	(1.81)	(1.97)
Los Angeles Times	2.95	3.34
	(2.00)	(2.12)
Time	5.68	6.94
	(2.18)	(2.32)
USA Today	8.43	9.96
	(1.49)	(1.59)
Newsweek	−2.91	−2.74
	(1.97)	(2.12)
NBC	11.70	12.57
	(1.83)	(1.98)
Month		
February	2.36	...
	(2.43)	
March	5.94	...
	(2.30)	
April	2.60	...
	(2.52)	
May	1.59	...
	(2.93)	
June	5.88	...
	(2.48)	
July	3.25	...
	(2.29)	
August	6.36	...
	(2.49)	
September	10.76	...
	(2.26)	
October	9.58	...
	(2.11)	
November	9.41	...
	(2.43)	
Constant	6.56	54.61
	(1.99)	(7.54)
Unemployment	...	−5.38
		(.94)
R^2	.73	.64
N	101	101

Sources: Basic data from various polls are from *Public Opinion*, vol. 7 (October–November 1984), pp. 38–40; and *Gallup Report*, various editions.

a. Entries are regression coefficients. Standard errors are in parentheses.

Variations in Reagan's lead over Mondale in the polls can arise from at least three different sources. First, all polling involves sampling error, which is what the press is referring to when the range of "statistical error" associated with some poll is said to be "plus or minus 3 percent." This language is inexact, and in any event a proper 95 percent confidence interval is probably somewhat larger for most polls. Second, differences in procedures between polling organizations can cause two seemingly identical questions to produce divergent results. Finally, opinion can change over time, but in 1984 relatively little of the week-to-week or month-to-month variation in poll results actually reflected true change.

A rough picture of the 1984 campaign can be gleaned from examining the set of trial heats conducted by different polling organizations during the 1980 campaign. Table 3-3 shows regression estimates for the trial heat data using a model that incorporates the month the survey was taken and the polling organization that conducted the survey. There are significant differences between the polling organizations. Using the Gallup poll as a point of comparison, table 3-3 shows that the ABC, Newsweek, and Roper polls came in with percentages that were somewhat more pro-Mondale (between 1 percent and 4 percent less support for Reagan). The Gordon Black/USA Today and NBC polls showed between 3 percent and 5 percent more support for Reagan than the Gallup poll did.[6]

Beyond these differences, we observe that the coefficients associated with the month variables fluctuate in a narrow interval between February and July and then increase sharply through the fall campaign. What remains to be explained after differences between polling organizations and trends have been taken into account has a standard deviation of 2.18—well within what could be attributed to sampling variation in each poll. The steady increase in Reagan's support between July and November 1984 is therefore all that needs explanation.

It could be argued that this increase was caused by effective campaigning or by Mondale's mistakes. But economic factors alone can account for the trend. To show this, we constructed a second model, which

---

Some commercial polling organizations using complex survey designs even assume random sampling in calculating standard errors, despite the fact that cluster sampling typically produces less precise estimates.

6. An F-test on the set of ten polling organization dummies yields a test statistic of 3.52, which is significant for $p < 0.01$.

Figure 3-1. *Reagan Lead in 1984 Reagan-Mondale Trial Heats*

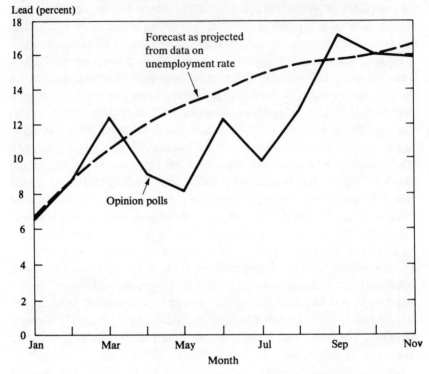

estimated outcomes of trial heats on the basis of unemployment rates averaged over the preceding six months. One economic variable would not be expected to account for all the variation in Reagan's lead over Mondale, but in fact almost all of the growth in Reagan's lead can be accounted for by fluctuations in the unemployment rate alone. Figure 3–1 shows Reagan's lead as estimated by one of the equations used to derive table 3-3 (which controls for differences between polling organizations). Also displayed in figure 3-1 is Reagan's lead as forecast from another equation used to derive table 3-3. This forecast also controls for differences between polling organizations, but otherwise the only predictor is the unemployment rate. Reagan's lead does not exactly follow the prediction based on unemployment, but the overall trend in support for him is well accounted for by the improvement in the unemployment rate.

Sources of Reagan's Support

Though the increase in support for Reagan over the course of the 1984 campaign is consistent with an explanation based on an improving economy, other factors may also be invoked. The analysis in the previous section can be strengthened by examining the evolution of public support for Reagan and previous presidents during their terms in office. The Gallup poll tracks public approval of the incumbent president's performance on a frequent basis (sometimes sampling as often as once a week). The advantage in using presidential popularity rather than voter intentions or actual voting data rests primarily in the length of the available time series and the frequency with which it is recorded. Our interest, of course, is mainly in accounting for election outcomes, but presidential popularity is still relevant for this purpose because responses appear to be good surrogates for voters' intentions.[7]

The dynamic relation between the state of the economy and public support for the president will be analyzed using the quarterly Gallup popularity series. Our analysis builds on several studies, which have tried to estimate models of presidential popularity with different lag structures that allow the effects of economic performance to be distributed over several time periods. From these results, it is clear that the effect of economic performance on voter evaluations of the incumbent president does not occur instantaneously, but the exact form of the lag between economic performance and presidential popularity is difficult to determine.[8]

---

7. The most important distinction between support for the president in a trial heat and approval of the president's job performance is that the former is influenced more by the strength of the challenger facing the president. In the midst of an election campaign, the Gallup popularity item appears to reflect an implicit comparison between the incumbent and his challenger; for this reason the Gallup organization stops asking the question during the fall campaign.

8. See Douglas A. Hibbs, Jr., R. Douglas Rivers, and Nicholas Vasilatos, "On the Demand for Economic Outcomes: Macroeconomic Performance and Mass Political Support in the United States, Great Britain, and Germany," *Journal of Politics*, vol. 42 (May 1982), pp. 426–62; and Douglas A. Hibbs, Jr., and Nicholas Vasilatos, "Macroeconomic Performance and Mass Political Support in the United States and Great Britain," in Douglas A. Hibbs, Jr., Heino Fassbender, and R. Douglas Rivers, eds. *Contemporary Political Economy* (Amsterdam: North Holland, 1981). Hibbs, Rivers, and Vasilatos and Hibbs and Vasilatos estimated complicated geometric

To obtain a more precise understanding of how voters discount past economic conditions, we estimated presidential popularity with three indicators of macroeconomic activity (the unemployment rate and the rates of growth of real personal disposable income per capita and of the consumer price index). Economic variables do not necessarily affect presidential popularity immediately, so we also included in our analysis measures of economic activity that preceded (or lagged) by one and two quarters the date presidential popularity was measured. We included lagged values of presidential popularity to capture more complex forms of dynamic response to economic conditions. This allowed popularity to exhibit considerable habit persistence or stability over time.[9]

In addition to the three macroeconomic indicators, we also included a variable intended to capture the effects of international crises. Involvement in an international crisis that enables the president to exercise national leadership almost invariably generates a "rally-round-the-flag"

---

distributed lag models and obtained good results (the model fit the data well, the parameter estimates seemed plausible, and the model produced accurate out-of-sample predictions). The geometric lag structure imposed by Hibbs and his co-workers implies that the largest effect of changing any variable is felt in the current period, with smaller declining effects for later periods. All variables shared the same lag structure. Golden and Poterba and Monroe estimated separate polynomial distributed lags for each of the variables in their models; see David G. Golden and James M. Poterba, "The Price of Popularity: The Political Business Cycle Reexamined," *American Journal of Political Science*, vol. 24 (November 1980), pp. 696–714; and Kristen Monroe, "Presidential Popularity: An Almon Distributed Lag Model," *Political Methodology*, vol. 7 (1981), pp. 43–70. This procedure allows different variables to have different lagged response effects. In most cases, contrary to geometric lag assumption, the peak impact of the economic variables occurred after a one- or two-period lag. The estimated distributed lags, however, sometimes had implausible shapes, and it was difficult to distinguish between different lag structures.

9. Data on presidential popularity were taken from the 1961–84 Gallup poll series on presidential approval, which asks the question, "Do you approve or disapprove of the way ——— is handling his job as president?"

Our approach differed somewhat from previous efforts because our goal (essentially prediction) was slightly different. Current econometric thinking is to avoid imposing ad hoc restrictions on lag structures and instead to estimate unrestricted vector autoregressions. See Christopher Sims, "Macroeconomics and Reality," *Econometrica*, vol. 48 (January 1980), pp. 1–48. See also Sims, "Distributed Lags," in Michael D. Intrilligator and David A. Kendrick, eds., *Frontiers of Quantitative Economics*, vol. 2 (Amsterdam: North Holland, 1974), pp. 289–332.

An arbitrary lag function can be approximated to any desired degree of accuracy by selecting sufficiently high-order lag polynomials. See Dale W. Jorgenson, "Rational Distributed Lag Functions," *Econometrica*, vol. 34 (January 1966), pp. 135–49.

effect, which appears to hold whether or not the crisis is resolved favorably. Jimmy Carter's approval rating, for example, stood at 32 percent before the American hostages were seized in Tehran in November 1979. Four weeks later, his popularity had risen to 61 percent, and as it started to fall later in December, the Soviet invasion of Afghanistan gave him another boost of 3 percent or 4 percent.[10] Our measure of "rally events" was just the number of such events in each quarter. The coding included only events that were international, involved the president directly, and were "specific, dramatic, and sharply focused."[11]

Estimates of the popularity model are presented in table 3-4 and are based on quarterly data from the first quarter of 1961 to the fourth quarter of 1984, with observations deleted where lagged variables would cross over partisan administrations.[12] Three specifications are reported with different combinations of lags of the variables. The estimates of the different versions of the popularity equation do not differ much, and we will concentrate on the model with the least restricted lag structure, which is reported in the last column of table 3-4. The estimated coefficients of the economic variables are relatively insensitive to the form of the lag structure. Though the estimated unemployment effects are statistically insignificant at conventional significance levels, they are reasonably stable and relatively large. The final technical point to be noted is that a logistic transformation was applied to the Gallup percentages. To assist readers in interpreting these estimates, the accompanying discussion refers to the changes in the percentage approving the president's performance (rather than changes in the logit) caused by variables in the model.

The claim that Reagan's popularity is primarily personal and not linked to economic conditions under his administration receives little support in table 3-4. In all the specifications tried, higher levels of unemployment and inflation lower presidential popularity while real

10. *Gallup Opinion Index,* August 1980, pp. 24–26.

11. John E. Mueller, *War, Presidents and Public Opinion* (Wiley, 1973), pp. 208–13. Douglas Hibbs kindly provided his updated coding of the rally variable. The coding was originally the work of John Mueller and was extended by Douglas Hibbs.

12. The use of the logit transformation as well as the varying number of observations on which the popularity variable is based generally induces heteroskedasticity. The reported standard errors permit robust inferences to be drawn in the presence of heteroskedasticity. See Halbert White, "A Heteroskedasticity-Consistent Covariance Matrix Estimator and a Direct Test for Heteroskedasticity," *Econometrica,* vol. 48 (May 1980), pp. 817–38.

Table 3-4. *Reagan Popularity*[a]

Variable	(1)	(2)	(3)
Inflation	−0.007	−0.12	−0.12
	(0.007)	(0.007)	(0.007)
Inflation t-1	...	−0.022	−0.024
		(.007)	(0.007)
Unemployment	−0.17	−0.010	...
	(0.025)	(0.059)	
Unemployment t-1	...	−0.021	−0.030
		(0.058)	(0.024)
Change in real income	0.016	0.012	0.012
	(0.005)	(0.005)	(0.005)
Change in real income t-1	...	0.003	...
		(0.005)	
Rally	0.134	0.138	0.139
	(0.031)	(0.029)	(0.029)
Rally t-1	...	0.063	0.059
		(0.031)	(0.030)
Approval t-1	0.862	0.846	0.869
	(0.047)	(0.100)	(0.095)
Approval t-2	...	−0.068	−0.080
		(0.103)	(0.099)
Johnson	−0.144	−0.154	−0.139
	(0.086)	(0.082)	(0.079)
Nixon	−0.100	−0.033	−0.020
	(0.080)	(0.079)	(0.074)
Ford	0.021	0.179	0.196
	(0.114)	(0.125)	(0.116)
Carter	−0.134	−0.035	0.056
	(0.099)	(0.105)	(0.098)
Reagan	−0.012	0.044	0.058
	(0.110)	(0.118)	(0.109)
Constant	0.086	0.229	0.230
	(0.173)	(0.176)	(0.172)
t (number of observations)	90	84	84
R^2	.91	.93	.93

Sources: Basic data from various polls are from *Public Opinion*, vol. 7 (October–November 1984), pp. 38–40; and *Gallup Report*, various editions.
a. Entries are regression coefficients. Standard errors are in parentheses.

income growth adds to popularity. A tendency to rally around the president in times of crisis is also evident, with each rally point generating an immediate boost of 3 percent to 4 percent in the approval rating and smaller gains in later periods. After controlling for economic performance, we discovered that Johnson and Nixon are less popular than Kennedy, Ford, Carter, and Reagan, but none of these differences, except in the case of Johnson (which could be accounted for by the Vietnam War), is very large. In none of the models, for instance, are the Carter and Reagan terms significantly different from one another. Put another way, differences between Carter's and Reagan's levels of popularity are satisfactorily explained by the differences between the respective economic records and rally points of the two administrations.

In interpreting the estimates in table 3-4, it is helpful to simulate the effects of a temporary 1 percent change in each of the economic variables on presidential popularity. The response of the president's popularity to a 1 percent reduction in the inflation rate followed immediately in the next quarter by a 1 percent increase in the inflation rate (returning inflation to its initial level) was simulated. Such innovations in an initial period will of course influence future popularity scores by affecting the values of the lagged popularity variables. The same procedure was then applied to a temporary 1 percent decrease in the unemployment rate and a temporary 1 percent increase in the real income growth rate. Results of these simulations are shown in figure 3-2.[13]

The first point to notice is that the lagged response effects differ from one variable to another. For both inflation and unemployment the peak impact occurs with a one-period lag, while for real income growth the entire effect of a 1 percent change in the variable occurs in the current quarter and remains stable for one quarter before starting to decline. Second, for all practical purposes presidential popularity has returned to its equilibrium level eight quarters after a temporary change in any of the variables. This means that performance during the first half of an administration need not adversely affect its levels of public support in its second half. Thus the Reagan administration suffered no lasting harm from presiding over the deepest recession since the 1930s during its first two years. Reagan's popularity at reelection was almost solely a function

13. Assuming that each variable initially stands at its mean level during the estimation period (5.3 percent for inflation, 6.0 percent for unemployment, and 2.6 percent for real income growth), the second-order difference equation (3) was solved for the equilibrium-level popularity (approximately 50.1 percent).

Figure 3-2. *Lagged Effects of Economic Variables on Presidential Popularity*

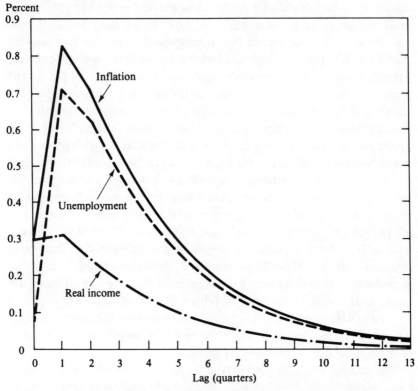

of the performance of the economy after the 1982 midterm elections. Finally, the magnitude of the estimated effects varies. Changes in the unemployment and inflation rates initially cause almost point-for-point changes in presidential popularity, while the effect for real income is much smaller (almost a 3 percentage point increase in the rate of real income growth is required to increase presidential popularity by 1 percent). These calculations, of course, pertain only to temporary changes in each variable; permanent changes would have a correspondingly larger impact. The long-run effect of any variable is obtained by summing all its lagged effects. A percentage decrease in unemployment or inflation, if sustained, increases presidential popularity by over 3 percent.

The final point to be established is how well the economy accounts for Reagan's popularity. The models reported in table 3-4 use past values of the president's popularity as well as macroeconomic indicators to predict his level of public support. This enables us to obtain a close fit to the popularity series, but because the lagged popularity values incorporate the effects of past noneconomic (as well as economic) events, the variation that we have explained ($R^2 = 0.94$) may exaggerate the predictive power of economic conditions. Instead, we have produced an unconditional forecast of Reagan's popularity using the coefficients in the second column of table 3-4. That is, given Reagan's popularity in the first two quarters of 1981 (which were used as starting values), a forecast was produced for each period of the Reagan administration with lagged values of presidential popularity replaced by their forecast values. This simulation is displayed in figure 3-3. The forecast tracks Reagan's popularity remarkably well, with a forecast error of less than 5 percent in most periods. The simulation was repeated assuming no rally events occurred during the Reagan administration. Of course, all presidents have some rally events, but the simulation shows that even if Reagan had never benefited from any rally effect, his popularity would have remained at high levels.

The Political Business Cycle in 1980 and 1984

As described in most textbooks, macroeconomic policy is geared toward stabilization. The role of government policy is to encourage steady growth by stimulating aggregate demand during recessions and to moderate spending when inflationary pressures rise. How, or even whether, effective demand management is possible is a matter debated by macroeconomists. But what is usually ignored in such debates is why policymakers follow macroeconomic advice—whenever their macroeconomic advisers agree among themselves as to which policies are desirable.

If presidents are judged by the performance of the economy under their administrations, they can be expected to choose macroeconomic policies that will serve their political interests. William Nordhaus and others have suggested that electoral incentives generate a "political business cycle" in which economic expansions are timed to coincide with elections. Nordhaus has analyzed optimal government behavior in a simple macroeconomic model in which policymakers control the

Figure 3-3. *Estimated Popularity of Ronald Reagan, Third Quarter 1981 to Second Quarter 1984*

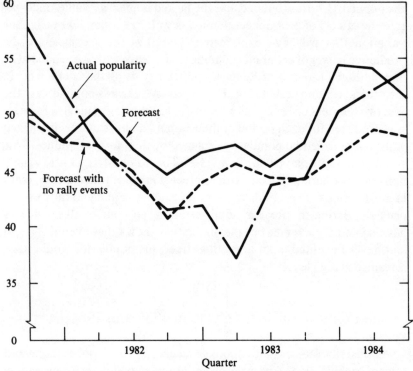

Percent approving performance

Sources: Data on actual popularity from *Gallup Report*, various monthly issues.

unemployment rate while the inflation rate is determined by a shifting Phillips curve.[14] The existence of different short- and long-run Phillips curves provides policymakers with an opportunity to manipulate the economy for political advantage. Nordhaus assumes that voters evaluate

14. Nordhaus's treatment of the Phillips curve is standard. The supply and demand of labor in various markets is subject to random shocks. Excess labor demand increases wage rates, which in turn affect prices for commodities. Price expectations are also incorporated in wage demands and affect general price levels. If expectations are formed adaptively or if higher employment levels do not immediately result in higher prices, unemployment can be reduced in the short run without much inflation. In equilibrium, however, the expected inflation rate will be the same as the actual rate and unemployment will reach some equilibrium level, called the "natural rate." The long-run trade-off between inflation and unemployment is very steep or even vertical (for example, long-

incumbents retrospectively; that is, voters base their evaluations of incumbents upon their memory of past performance and give greatest weight to recent events.[15] Engineering a boom as the election nears, the incumbent party could take credit for reducing unemployment by a policy whose inflationary effect will only be felt after the election. Moreover, the rate of time preference implied by retrospective voting is negative: policymakers could also win votes by absorbing poor performance early in an administration.

Although Nordhaus's model suggests that presidents have strong incentives to manage the economy to their political advantage, there are still a number of reasons why political business cycles might not occur. The model requires the assumption that policymakers can choose a level of unemployment and rate of inflation on a Phillips curve. The president, of course, does not directly control employment and price levels, and it is not clear that the tools of demand management at his disposal give him even short-term control over these variables. Robert E. Lucas was able to generate a short-run Phillips curve in a model embodying rational expectations, but policies that attempt to exploit the trade-off between unemployment and inflation appear only to worsen that trade-off by shifting the curve outward.[16] Few economists currently would argue that there is any usable long-run trade-off between unemployment and inflation, and Milton Friedman has even argued that the long-run Phillips curve is positively sloped.[17]

Nordhaus's model also lacks any significant institutional detail. Parties have no internal structure, and the party that wins the presidential election does not have to contend with Congress, the Federal Reserve Board, or any other competitors for control over policymaking. Even if

run unemployment is independent of the price level). See William Nordhaus, "The Political Business Cycle," *Review of Economic Studies,* vol. 42 (April 1975), pp. 169–90. Some empirical studies along similar lines are Ray C. Fair, "The Effect of Economic Events on Votes for President," *Review of Economics and Statistics,* vol. 60 (May 1978), pp. 159–73; and Bruno S. Frey and Friedrich Schneider, "An Empirical Study of Politico-Economic Interaction in the U.S.," *Review of Economics and Statistics,* vol. 60 (May 1978), pp. 174–83. See also C. Duncan MacRae, "A Political Model of the Business Cycle," *Journal of Political Economy,* vol. 85 (April 1977), pp. 239–63.

15. For a summary of empirical evidence on this point, see D. Roderick Kiewiet and Douglas Rivers, "A Retrospective on Retrospective Voting," *Political Behavior* (forthcoming).

16. "Some International Evidence on Output-Inflation Tradeoffs," *American Economic Review,* vol. 63 (June 1973), pp. 326–34.

17. "Inflation and Unemployment," *Journal of Political Economy,* vol. 85 (June 1977), pp. 451–72.

one accepts the logic of the model, very large manipulations would seem necessary to benefit the incumbent in any significant way.[18] An attempt by the president to create a substantial political business cycle would draw a great deal of attention and probably encounter serious opposition from forces in and out of government who do not share the president's political interests.

These caveats aside, however, it is still an interesting exercise to evaluate the economic record of the Carter and Reagan administrations in terms of what a vote-maximizing policymaker following a political business cycle strategy would have produced. Our simulations indicate that such a president would be well advised to have the economy in good shape before the election quarter. Because the response patterns for unemployment and inflation are similar, a president could potentially try to stimulate employment with the hope that any inflationary response would not be fully realized until after the election. Changes in real income do not have to occur as early to have their maximum electoral impact, but because real income is highly correlated with the employment level and its independent effect is small, this possibility is of little interest.

We do not have any evidence that the Reagan administration either consciously or otherwise attempted to time the 1983–84 recovery for political advantage. Yet if it had tried to do so, it is hard to see how it could have created a business cycle with better political consequences. Figure 3-4 simulates Reagan's level of popularity for the five quarters surrounding the 1984 election. The figure is designed to answer the hypothetical question of what would have happened in the election if the same economic performance as actually realized had been shifted forward or backward one or two quarters. It is clear that economic events were timed almost perfectly to maximize the president's popularity during the election quarter; a two-quarter shift, either forward or backward, would have lowered Reagan's popularity between 0.6 percent and 2.0 percent.

The same simulation can be carried out for the 1980 election (see figure 3-4). The contrast is striking. The 1980 election occurred at nearly the bottom of the economic cycle. If Carter could have run for reelection with the economy as it stood either two quarters before or after the election, his popularity would have been over 3 percent higher than it was in the election quarter. Even with these shifts, of course, Carter

18. Golden and Poterba, "The Price of Popularity," pp. 696–714.

Figure 3-4. *Simulations of Popularity of Presidents Carter and Reagan for Two Quarters before and after an Election*

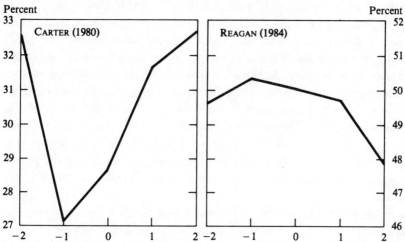

remains less popular than Reagan, but a well-timed political business cycle would have greatly improved his reelection chances. The economy under Reagan followed a pattern that was, in terms of the president's political interests, nearly optimal. The economy under Carter, in contrast, looks like a political business cycle run backwards.

Carter's inability to manipulate the macroeconomy for political advantage should make us suspicious of claims that political control over economic policies inevitably leads to electoral economic cycles. Much of recent macroeconomic theory casts doubt on the government's ability to fine tune the economy. Nonetheless, the experiences of Carter and Reagan indicate very clearly how economic performance determines who will hold political power. One unexplored feature of the political business cycle is the possibility that voters will hold presidents responsible for events over which they have relatively little control.

Conclusions

Many observers of the American political scene have sensed that there is something special about the appeal of Ronald Reagan. Some believe that he must be coated with the political equivalent of Teflon that enables him to avoid blame for political and policy failures. Others attribute his impressive popular appeal to a mastery of the spoken word and visual image. Still others say he wins voters by a nostalgic invocation of the small-town virtues of a simpler, more innocent past.[19]

But President Reagan's electoral strength has much less mysterious sources. The patterns of public support for him can be largely accounted for by short-run fluctuations in prices, income, and employment. Although there is some degree of inertia in the public's linkage of the economy with presidential job performance, the economic conditions of the previous few years are what really matter. Because of the public's rapid discounting of economic performance, comparisons of how well the economy performed during entire presidential administrations are not informative as to how different presidents have fared at the polls. Reagan's four-year record, for example, was roughly comparable to Carter's.

Because of the retrospective nature of political evaluations, an incumbent president's reelection prospects depend in no small part upon the conjunction of the electoral calendar and the business cycle. Without taking a position on the inclination or ability of incumbent presidents to engineer political business cycles, we do find that from the point of view of Reagan's reelection in 1984 the economy peaked at nearly the best possible time. But for Carter in 1980 the course of the economy was nearly as bad as it could have been in its effect on the election.

It has generally been assumed that retrospective voting ensures citizen control of government because it makes politicians accountable for their behavior.[20] However, the expectation that retrospective voting produces responsive government can be questioned on two grounds. First, if presidents can control the course the economy takes, the propensity of voters to choose on the basis of recent economic conditions gives presidents an incentive to create a political business cycle, which may in fact impede longer-term economic growth. Second, if presidents do not control economic events, then retrospective voters will hold them responsible for events out of their control. The economic record of President Reagan's first term looks suspiciously like a political business cycle, but the second possibility—that he benefited in part from events not under his control—is at least as plausible. This possibility also affects

19. Robert Dallek, *Ronald Reagan: The Politics of Symbolism* (Harvard University Press, 1984).

20. See especially Morris P. Fiorina, *Retrospective Voting in American National Elections* (Yale University Press, 1981).

how the 1984 election should be interpreted and what its long-run implications are likely to be.

Whatever the merits of Reagan's policies, the economy clearly benefited from some good fortune that was notably missing during the Carter years. The economic expansion of 1983–84, for example, was aided by the collapse of OPEC, which had managed nearly to double the value of U.S. petroleum imports between 1978 and 1980.[21] It does not seem reasonable to hold President Carter entirely responsible for the actions of OPEC or to credit President Reagan for its demise. Reagan's policies may have had a favorable impact, although any fair evaluation of them will depend on the performance of the economy during his second term.

In 1984, of course, voters could base their evaluations of Reagan's policies only on the record of his first term. The effects of incomplete information on retrospective voting decisions are not well understood, but some simple conclusions can be drawn by analyzing policymaking in a simplified setting. Consider, for example, two presidents of equal skill. If the macroeconomy is subject to random shocks outside the control of the presidents, each will produce a range of outcomes. But because each has the same skill, the expected or average outcome will be the same for both. Now suppose voters use a simple decision rule: if economic performance since the last election has been relatively high, the president is reelected; if economic performance is unacceptable, the president is replaced. If the state of the economy is actually beyond presidential control, good performance during a first term does not in any way imply equally good performance during a second term. Good performance only indicates that the incumbent was lucky; any president with the same skill could have done as well under the same conditions. Thus in good economic times the president is rewarded for something beyond his control.

In such a situation an incumbent president returned to office because of good performance can be expected to perform, on average, less well during a second term. Similarly, replacing an incumbent who performs poorly will, on average, lead to better performance by a successor. Under such conditions, voters could easily conclude that punishing poor performance is more effective than rewarding good performance. More-

21. Petroleum and petroleum product imports increased from $39.1 billion in 1978 to $73 billion in 1980. These figures represent 1.8 percent and 2.8 percent of GNP, respectively.

over, none of this analysis really depends on the policymakers' having the same levels of skill.[22] As long as economic performance is not completely under the control of the president, voters will incorrectly attribute responsibility to the president for events he did not cause. The result will be that occasionally presidents of greater skill will be replaced by ones of lesser skill. Voters are therefore well advised to seek more information than the nation's economic performance over the previous twelve months in deciding which candidate to vote for. Whether voters will take such advice is another matter.

Without stretching the argument too far, this description of the consequences of retrospective voting does appear to correspond with recent American political experience. The second terms of incumbents reelected by landslides (Franklin Roosevelt in 1936, Lyndon Johnson in 1964, and Richard Nixon in 1972) have not been notably successful. On the other hand, turning failed incumbents out of office (Herbert Hoover in 1932 and Jimmy Carter in 1980, to cite two examples) has produced apparently satisfying results. V. O. Key described the public in this role as a "rational god of vengeance and reward" and observed that it "can express itself with greatest clarity when it speaks in disapprobation of the past policy of performance of an administration."[23] If economic outcomes are not within the control of policymakers, however, one wonders about the effectiveness of negative voting.

These concerns need not worry Ronald Reagan, except for the possibility that the approval the public expressed for him and his policies in the 1984 election can, if the economy falters, easily turn into disapproval. Winning office in 1980 gave Reagan and the Republicans the chance to implement policies different from those pursued before. To the extent that those policies were successful—the 1984 election outcome showed that a large fraction of the electorate judged them to be successful—Reagan has strengthened the Republican position. But neither the 1980 nor 1984 election outcome has decisively changed party competition. We are witnessing a political debate over economic policy that is likely to continue for many years to come.

---

22. The effect is a "regression toward the mean." Some psychological literature indicates that regression effects are not well understood. See Amos Tversky and Daniel Kahneman, "Judgment under Uncertainty: Heuristics and Biases," *Science*, vol. 185 (September 27, 1974), pp. 1124–31.

23. The quotations are from *Politics, Parties, and Pressure Groups*, 5th ed. (Crowell, 1964), p. 568; and *Public Opinion and American Democracy* (Knopf, 1961), p. 473.

CHAPTER FOUR

Incumbency and Realignment in Congressional Elections

JOHN A. FEREJOHN AND MORRIS P. FIORINA

As THE 1984 campaign reached its final months, political commentators speculated about the magnitude of Republican congressional gains likely to accompany President Reagan's reelection. Given his apparent coattails in 1980 and the strong economic recovery of 1984, the prospects for Republican congressional candidates looked rosy. Writing in mid-September, for example, Alan Ehrenhalt of *Congressional Quarterly* observed that "it will not be as easy to stay out of presidential politics as it was in 1972. . . . If the Republicans succeed in making 1984 an election of party, rather than of personality, the potential for damage to Congressional Democrats is greater than many of them now seem to believe."[1] Democratic candidates for Congress in 1972 treated George McGovern as if he carried a serious communicable disease. Most of them had not attended the party's national convention and could legitimately deny any close association with the national ticket. But in the spring of 1984 congressional Democrats publicly embraced Walter Mondale. Could they credibly disavow the top of the ticket in the fall?

As the election drew near, the electoral situation took an even more pronounced tilt in favor of the Republicans. By October it was apparent that President Reagan would win reelection by a wide margin; aides began to speculate about a "fifty-state sweep." Late polls even showed an erosion of identification with the Democratic party. In the final CBS News/*New York Times* poll a majority of those in the "probable elec-

---

1. "House Democrats: Reason for Concern?" *Congressional Quarterly Weekly Report*, vol. 42 (September 15, 1984), p. 2287.

torate" who reported leaning or identifying with one of the two major parties chose the Republicans (see chapter 2). The same poll also reported the seldom-expressed intention of more voters to support Republican House candidates than Democrats.

If the 1980 election had been largely a referendum on the performance of the Carter administration,[2] so the 1984 choice similarly would contain a large element of retrospective judgment. In this instance, it could hardly fail to benefit the party in power. Inflation had fallen to its lowest level in seventeen years, and after a severe recession the economy was growing at a rate of nearly 7 percent per year, the best since 1951. True, unemployment remained above 7 percent and deficits were at an all-time high, but there was a general sense in the land that the economy was improving and that the Republicans were better able to manage it. On the world scene, too, the American voter judged the administration favorably.[3] Not only had decisive action by the administration averted a possible communist takeover in Grenada, but the allies seemed to show renewed respect for American resolve in dealing with the Soviets. True, the administration had suffered an embarrassing defeat in Lebanon, but the president had quickly cut his losses and the electoral damage seemed minimal.[4] The poorly understood situation in Central America and heightened concern about nuclear war created some generalized anxiety, but there were no problems so concrete as Americans being held hostage in Tehran.

Over and above national conditions, the issues, and the candidates, still other factors favored the Republicans. Beginning with the chairmanship of William Brock, the national Republican party had accumulated an impressive stock of campaign resources and organizational skills (see chapter 7). Compared with the Democrats, the Republicans had a superior capacity to raise money, recruit and train candidates, and

2. See William Schneider, "The November 4 Vote for President: What Did It Mean?" in Austin Ranney, ed., *The American Elections of 1980* (Washington, D.C.: American Enterprise Institute, 1981), pp. 212–62; and Arthur Miller and Martin Wattenberg, "Policy and Performance Voting in the 1980 Election," paper prepared for the 1981 annual meeting of the American Political Science Association. More generally, see Morris Fiorina, *Retrospective Voting in American National Elections* (Yale University Press, 1981).

3. *Public Opinion*, vol. 7 (December–January 1985), pp. 36–37.

4. Everett C. Ladd, "Is Election '84 Really a Class Struggle?" *Public Opinion*, vol. 7 (April–May 1984), p. 45.

facilitate the movement of money and other resources to races where they were most valuable (see chapter 6).

Thus, in the period leading up to the 1984 election, conditions seemed ripe for a long-awaited realignment of party strengths. Republicans could dream of achieving what the Democrats had done in 1932 and 1936: first, capture the presidency through the voters' rejection of the way the previous administration had handled serious problems, and then manage a successful response to those problems—so that a grateful electorate would reward it with an even broader mandate. Voters would support not only Reagan but Republicans in general, and a new electoral era would be at hand.

At least with respect to Congress, reality threw cold water on such dreams. The Republican party made only modest gains in the House and lost two seats in the Senate.[5] Despite a forty-nine-state victory for the president, Democrats remained in solid control of the House and were poised to recapture the Senate in 1986. Why did Republican congressional candidates fail to make substantial inroads on the Democratic congressional forces? Why did a party with superior organization, an edge on the issues, and, above all, a successful and popular president not gain solid majorities in Congress?

No one can be sure of the answers at this time—detailed data on the 1984 election are not yet available. But the results of that election resemble those of most recent elections closely enough that we think the same factors were at work as in previous elections. Put simply, the 1984 election provides still more evidence of the continued importance of incumbency in congressional elections, the limited effect of presidential coattails, and therefore the limited capacity of national elections to impose a programmatic vision on a constituency-minded Congress. In all but the most extraordinary circumstances the varied advantages of sitting congressmen are sufficient to overcome superior party organization, national party records, and presidential coattails. Cavanagh and Sundquist have analyzed data on party identification and found indications of party realignment. Our look at the elections of the 1980s reveals that if these historic shifts are occurring, they have yet to have an impact on the congressional level.

5. Republican gains also were modest at lower levels of the federal system. See chapter 10.

Congressional Elections: Insulation versus Responsiveness

Despite the omens in the waning days of the campaign, the failure of the 1984 Reagan landslide to sweep in a large number of new Republicans on Capitol Hill came as no surprise to those who study congressional elections closely.[6] The literature on recent elections speaks with unanimity on one point: during the course of the past generation congressional contests have increasingly become local, candidate-centered affairs. As Mann puts it, "Congressional elections are local, not national events: in deciding how to cast their ballots, voters are influenced not by the President, the national parties, or the state of the economy, but by the local candidates."[7]

Statistically, party identification remains the single most important factor in the popular voting, but the influence of such attachment has declined.[8] And to a considerable degree voting in congressional elections has become detached from broad national currents reflecting reactions to the president and national issues and problems.[9] Such factors still exert some effects, but they do so less systematically and less strongly than in earlier periods of electoral history. They have been displaced by reactions to the individual candidates, especially the incumbents. No matter who runs for president, or what happens to the economy or the world order, the great majority of congressional incumbents will survive. To do so they deemphasize the platform of their party and their allegiance to the president and emphasize instead their personal relationship with their constituents.[10] By developing a reputation with a minimal amount

6. From our informal contacts with colleagues, we would guess that the median prediction among the experts was a net Republican gain in the House of fewer than twenty seats. Without naming names, one of us stood steadfast on his own work and predicted fifteen in his department pool. The other allowed himself to be seduced by poll data and made an embarrassing overprediction.

7. Thomas E. Mann, *Unsafe at Any Margin* (American Enterprise Institute, 1978), p. 1.

8. Morris Fiorina, "Congressmen and Their Constituents: 1958 and 1978," in Dennis Hale, ed., *The United States Congress* (Boston: Eusey Press, 1982), pp. 33–64; and Bruce Cain, John Ferejohn, and Morris Fiorina, *The House Is Not a Home,* forthcoming, chap. 11.

9. Gary Jacobson, *The Politics of Congressional Elections* (Little, Brown, 1983), chaps. 5, 6; and Fiorina, *Retrospective Voting,* chap. 8.

10. Richard Fenno, *Home Style: House Members in Their Districts* (Little, Brown, 1978).

of partisan or ideological content, members of Congress induce constituents to evaluate them separately from the state of the nation and the performance of parties and administrations.

There are numerous mechanisms by which they accomplish this separation. Members of Congress receive generous allocations of staff and other resources, and direct much of these to constituency affairs.[11] They visit their districts frequently and broker the relationships between individual constituents, groups, and local governments and the federal agencies who regulate and disburse projects, programs, and individual benefits.[12] In speeches, bill introductions, and other ways they faithfully articulate the particularistic interests of their constituents. Consequently, most incumbents are judged to be sensitive to the interests of their districts and accessible to constituents in need of assistance. Research shows that citizens hold a relatively negative view of the collective Congress, but most think highly of their individual congressmen.[13]

Because most incumbents are popular and viewed as likely to win reelection, credible challengers are loath to take them on. For an attractive candidate already holding a lower office and planning a career, prudence suggests waiting for a seat to open up, for the incumbent to make a serious error in political judgment or personal behavior, or for the incumbent to "lose touch" with the district.[14] Thus the typical House election finds a popular incumbent facing a little-known, inexperienced, and poorly financed challenger, and sometimes none at all—the Republicans allowed forty-one Democratic incumbents a free ride in 1984. More than 90 percent of those incumbents who sought reelection have met with success in recent years.[15]

11. Austin Ranney, "The Working Conditions of Members of Congress and Parliament," in Norman J. Ornstein, ed., *The Role of the Legislature in Western Democracies* (American Enterprise Institute, 1981), pp. 67–76; and Cain, Ferejohn, and Fiorina, *The House,* chap. 5.

12. Cain, Ferejohn, and Fiorina, *The House*; and John R. Johannes, *To Serve the People* (University of Nebraska Press, 1984).

13. Glenn R. Parker and Roger H. Davidson, "Why Do Americans Love Their Congressmen So Much More Than Their Congress?" *Legislative Studies Quarterly,* vol. 4 (February 1979), pp. 53–62.

14. Gary Jacobson and Samuel Kernell, *Strategy and Choice in Congressional Elections,* 2d ed. (Yale University Press, 1983).

15. Norman J. Ornstein and others, *Vital Statistics on Congress: 1984–1985 Edition* (American Enterprise Institute, 1984), pp. 49, 50.

Differences and Similarities in Senate Races

This portrait is especially apt for understanding House elections. For Senate elections, however, some amendments are necessary. On average, Senate races are more competitive than House races. Senate seats are fewer in number and come up less frequently—33 or 34 every two years versus 435 in the House. Senate seats serve as a principal source of presidential hopefuls. For these and other reasons they are more prestigious and more newsworthy than House seats. As a result, Senate races typically attract experienced challengers who have the financing to make credible races. Whereas recent House reelection rates have generally remained higher than 90 percent, Senate reelection rates have fluctuated widely, and at least until 1982 appeared to be declining from a high in the 1960s.[16]

However, Senate contests are no less idiosyncratic than House contests. That is, although senatorial campaigns are frequently more controversial and ideological than House contests, there is little evidence that national issues and conditions exert any more of an across-the-board effect in Senate campaigns than in House campaigns—the 1980 outcomes notwithstanding. What happens to senator A in one state bears no more relation to what happens to senator B in another than what happens to incumbent representatives in different districts.

Historic Patterns of Competition

The change in the shape of competition for House seats appears most graphically in the sorts of diagrams displayed in figure 4-1.[17] It shows the distribution of House reelection attempts over the range of the percentage of the two-party vote received by the Democratic candidates. As shown, the pattern of competition in the early postwar period was concentrated around the 50 percent point of the distribution, as most races were highly competitive. But a generation later this unimodal distribution had evolved into a strikingly bimodal distribution that shows Democrats either winning or losing by substantial margins. The increasing margins by which members have been returned to office has produced troughs of

16. Ibid., p. 51.
17. See David Mayhew, "Congressional Elections: The Case of the Vanishing Marginals," *Polity*, vol. 6 (Spring 1974), pp. 295–317.

Figure 4-1. *Patterns of Competitiveness in Congressional Elections,*
by Percentage of Two-Party Vote Received by Democratic
Candidates, Selected Years, 1948–84

Percent of races

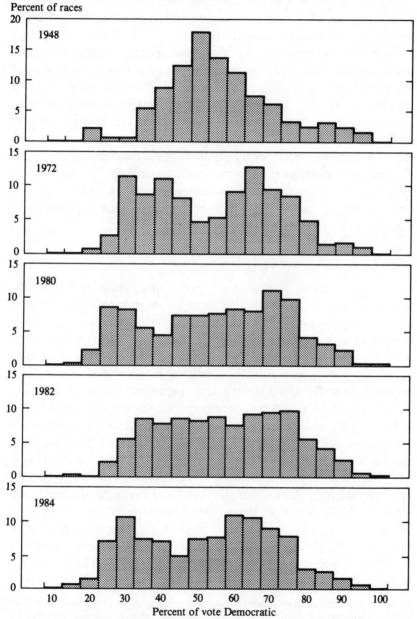

Percent of vote Democratic

Sources: Authors' estimates, based on data in Gary Jacobson, *The Politics of Congressional Elections* (Little, Brown, 1983); data tape provided by Gary Jacobson; and *Congressional Quarterly Weekly Report,* vol. 42 (November 10, 1984), pp. 2923–30.

varying depths in the middle, competitive range of the distribution. This simple fact is fraught with political consequences. For our purposes the most important of these arises from the effects of presidential coattails on varying patterns of competitiveness.

Suppose that approval of a successful, popular president leads 5 percent of the electorate to vote also for the congressional candidate of the president's party—a 5 percent coattail effect, in other words. If distributed uniformly across districts, such a 5 percent swing would tip far more districts to the president's party given the 1948 structure of competition than that in 1972. Thus one reason presidential coattails are less noticeable in contemporary elections lies in the altered shape of the distribution of electoral margins in congressional races. Richard Nixon's 1972 landslide reelection would not have appeared to have been a purely personal victory had there been as many competitive congressional races that year as there were in 1948.

Ticket Splitting and Shorter Coattails

A second reason contemporary presidents appear to have short coattails, however, is simply that today's American voter is less likely to cast a vote for presidential and congressional candidates of the same party than were the voters of earlier periods. This decline is the reverse side of the increasingly local and candidate-centered nature of congressional elections. Party affiliation, national issues and conditions, and presidential performance show a declining impact on the votes cast in congressional elections. As a result, coattail voting has declined. This shortening of presidential coattails is evident in table 4-1, which presents coefficients from statistical models that predict the vote for congressional candidates as a function of party affiliation, vote for president, and, where applicable, House incumbency. As shown, the association between presidential vote and congressional vote has dropped dramatically since the 1950s, while the impact of incumbency has risen even more dramatically. In open seats the estimated effects of presidential coattails fluctuate more—partly because the relatively small number of elections in which no incumbent is running makes any estimation less reliable—but a decline appears there as well.[18]

18. Other analyses that incorporate detailed evaluations of presidential candidates provide additional statistical estimates of the magnitude of coattail voting for the period from 1956 to 1980. These too show a general decline in the size of the coattail vote, accompanied by a rise in the incumbency effect. John Ferejohn and Randall Calvert,

Table 4-1. *The Effect of Presidential Vote and Congressional Incumbency on Vote for Congressional Candidates, 1956–80*

| | Seats with incumbents[a] | | Open seats[b] |
| | Presidential | Congressional | Presidential |
Year	vote	incumbency	vote
1956	0.38	0.09	0.45
1960	0.47	0.13	0.69
1964	0.47	0.15	0.91
1968	0.50	0.17	0.49
1972	0.31	0.24	0.28
1976	0.24	0.34	0.42
1980	0.24	0.34	0.19

Source: Data from the American National Election Studies (University of Michigan, Center for Political Studies). All coefficients are significant at the 5 percent level or beyond.

a. Regression coefficients of congressional vote report on presidential vote report and incumbency, controlling for respondent party identification, contested races only.

b. Regression coefficients of congressional vote report on presidential vote report, controlling for respondent party identification, contested races only.

Another way of showing the decreased association between presidential and congressional voting is to look at the frequency with which voters report that they split their tickets. As can be seen in table 4-2, in the most recent elections about one-fourth of the electorate reports voting for the presidential candidate of one party and the congressional candidate of the other. Again, there is a significant rise from the elections of a generation ago. Ticket splitting is related to both congressional incumbency and the attraction of the presidential candidates: in the 1964 election, for example, the split-voting rate was much higher in the districts of Republican incumbents (whose supporters in many cases could not abide Goldwater); the reverse happened in 1972 with Democratic incumbents whose supporters rejected McGovern. The rate of split-ticket voting appears to be marginally smaller in contests for open seats than in those contested by incumbents.

The increased importance of congressional incumbency and declining importance of presidential coattails not only produce increased ticket splitting on the individual level, but naturally enough lead to a greater frequency of split outcomes at the congressional district level. As shown below, in recent elections almost one-third of the congressional districts in the country were carried by presidential and congressional candidates of different parties.[19] Obviously, the typical pattern finds a congressional

"Presidential Coattails in Historical Perspective," *American Journal of Political Science*, vol. 28 (February 1984), pp. 127–46.

19. Ornstein and others, *Vital Statistics on Congress*, p. 56.

incumbent of one party winning a district carried by the victorious presidential candidate of the other. How do congressmen interpret their mandates in such cases? Should they accept the leadership of the president their districts supported or should they emphasize the personal independence their districts approved? Typically, one-third of the members of Congress have wrestled with that question after recent elections, and following the 1984 election, a near-record number faced this issue.

| | Districts choosing candidates of different parties |
Year	(percent)
1952	19.3
1956	29.9
1960	26.1
1964	33.3
1968	32.0
1972	44.1
1976	28.5
1980	32.8
1984	43.7

In sum, research carried out during the mid- to late 1970s reported a central finding that presidential and congressional elections increasingly were going their separate ways. The bonds that had served to tie them together in the past—party identification and presidential coattails—were on the decline, while the fragmenting force of individual incumbency was on the rise. On the basis of this scholarly portrait, few students of congressional elections anticipated a Republican congressional landslide in 1984.

Table 4-2. *Voters Reporting Ticket Splitting between Presidential and Congressional Races, 1956–80*
Percent

| | Status of congressional district seat | | | |
Year	Democratic incumbent	Republican incumbent	Open seat	Total
1956	17.6	12.1	14.1	14.5
1960	14.4	12.3	7.4	13.2
1964	10.9	20.0	9.4	14.7
1968	18.4	16.6	15.7	17.2
1972	30.1	18.2	22.1	25.1
1976	26.0	26.7	14.9	24.2
1980	29.1	23.6	24.4	26.7

Source: Data from the American National Election Studies.

But the impatient reader might interrupt here with a simple query: what about the 1980 outcomes? Did not Republicans ride Reagan's coattails to make impressive congressional gains in 1980? Did the first election of the new decade not prove that the old knowledge was outdated? Upon first consideration these questions suggest that Reagan may have introduced a new electoral era with altered possibilities.

Congressional Elections in the 1980s: A New Era?

Objectively, the 1980 elections had a great impact on American politics. The Republicans captured control of a chamber of Congress for the first time in more than thirty years. In the House the elections produced a "working conservative majority," which along with a Republican majority in the Senate enabled President Reagan to push through major policy initiatives that reversed the thrust of at least a generation of national legislation. Psychologically, the elections had at least as great an impact. In their aftermath congressional Democrats adopted a low profile, and for a few brief months Republicans dreamed about capturing the House in 1982.

Yet as various analysts have pointed out, subjective interpretations of the elections exaggerated what the voting actually represented—most citizens were rejecting Carter more than endorsing Reagan.[20] Moreover, the upheavals in Congress occurred in the absence of major changes in the patterns of voting: small vote shifts made dramatic differences in the results.

The House in 1980

In the House, Republicans gained thirty-three seats, defeating twenty-seven Democratic incumbents and taking ten Democratic open seats, while losing only three incumbents and one open seat. If judged against 1976, when only twelve incumbents were defeated, and 1972, when only nine lost, the defeat of thirty incumbents in 1980 seems like a major departure from the past. On the other hand, in 1964, before the significant rise in the advantage of incumbency, forty-four incumbents were de-

20. That is, the great majority of citizens made retrospective, performance-based decisions, rather than prospective, ideology-based decisions. See Schneider, "The November 4 Vote for President"; Miller and Wattenberg, "Policy and Performance Voting in the 1980 Election"; and Fiorina, *Retrospective Voting.*

feated.[21] When all was said and done, 90 percent of the unindicted Democratic congressmen who sought reelection in 1980 succeeded (six members were under indictment for Abscam involvement). In contrast, only 75 percent of the Republican members who sought reelection in 1964 survived the Johnson tide. The short-term forces at work during the 1980 election created greater difficulties for Democratic incumbents than they had experienced in 1976 or 1972, but by no means did 1980 recall the elections before the era of the strong incumbency advantage.

As figure 4-1 shows, the pattern of competition in 1980 (74 districts in the 45–55 percent marginal range) was different from the 1972 low point (60 marginal districts) but still a far cry from a high point like 1948 (120 marginals). Similarly, table 4-1 shows that the estimated association between the vote for Reagan and the vote for congressional candidates in 1980 was lower than in Nixon's "personal victory" in 1972, and the estimate of incumbency was higher. Because these findings conflict with so much of the conventional wisdom, they deserve some elaboration.

The coattail estimates reported in table 4-1 represent the marginal effect of voting for a presidential candidate of a given party on the probability of voting for a congressional candidate of that party. Stated another way, the figures in the table indicate the proportion of each incremental vote for a presidential candidate that carries over to his party's candidates for Congress. Journalists and other political commentators commonly base their estimates of coattail effects on shifts in seats. But the shift in seats depends on two factors—the coattail effect measured in votes, as in table 4-1, and the pattern of competition, as depicted in figure 4-1. Our analyses show that Nixon in 1972 had longer coattails than Reagan in 1980, in the sense of increasing the vote for Republican congressional candidates, but he faced a seat distribution much less sensitive to any given vote shift than the seat distribution faced by Reagan (contrast the 1972 distribution with that for 1980).

All in all, then, the 1980 House elections proved more trying for incumbents than the rather uneventful elections of 1972 and 1976. But there is little in the results to suggest that voting behavior in the 1980 congressional elections had returned to the pre-1960s pattern. As we will discuss below, the results do provide some evidence that the efforts of the national Republican party apparatus had some impact, but that impact was small relative to the basic fact of individual incumbency, which remained as prominent as ever.

21. Ornstein and others, *Vital Statistics on Congress*, p. 45.

The Senate in 1980

And what of the Senate? Nine Democratic senators lost their seats to Republican challengers and three Democratic open seats shifted to Republican control. Given the visibility of some of the losers, the consequences of their defeats, and the preelection activities and post-election credit claiming of ideological political action committees (PACs), it was easy to believe that a new era had dawned, in which general ideology and national organization would extend downward into subnational contests. But here too the reality was less noteworthy than the appearance.

In the first place, as numerous observers have detailed, the Republican Senate victory was fashioned by winning the close contests in small states. A switch of 50,000 votes in seven states would have allowed the Democrats to retain control of the Senate.[22] The Democrats actually outpolled the Republicans nationwide by a margin of approximately 30 million to 27 million. Democratic candidates ran up large majorities in some big states such as California, while losing narrowly in a number of small states.

But of course Senate elections take place within their individual states. One reason the margins of Alan Cranston of California and other big-state senators were so great is precisely because the Republicans and their associated PACs used their resources efficiently, concentrating on states where prospects were good and the money productive and deemphasizing states where chances were slim. Thus those who discount the election results because of the consequences of a few votes in small states miss the point, which was exactly to shift a few votes in small states. This rejoinder has some validity, but it does weaken the interpretation of the Senate results as an ideology-based ground swell for Reagan supporters.

Table 4-3 lists the Democratic senators defeated in the 1980 general election and their 1974 margins of victory.[23] As one examines the individual cases, explanations based on Reagan coattails, conservative trends, and any other national-level factors seem strained. Talmadge

22. Thomas E. Mann and Norman Ornstein, "The Republican Surge in Congress," in Ranney, *The American Elections of 1980*, p. 293.
23. Three other Democratic incumbents were defeated in bitter primaries (Mike Gravel of Alaska, Richard Stone of Florida, and Donald Stewart of Alabama). The Republicans captured all three seats, but the internecine struggles of the Democrats appear to be a sufficient explanation for their defeats in these cases.

Table 4-3. *Democratic Senate Incumbents Defeated in 1980,*
with Votes Received, 1974 and 1980
Percent

Senator	1974	1980
Birch E. Bayh, Jr. (Indiana)	51	46
Frank Church (Idaho)	56	49
John C. Culver (Iowa)	52	46
John A. Durkin (New Hampshire)	54[a]	48
George McGovern (South Dakota)	53	39
Warren G. Magnuson (Washington)	61	46
Robert Morgan (North Carolina)	62	49
Gaylord A. Nelson (Wisconsin)	62	49
Herman E. Talmadge (Georgia)	72	49

Source: *Congressional Quarterly Almanac,* vol. 30 (1974), vol. 31 (1975), and vol. 36 (1980).
a. Special 1975 election called after 1974 general election resulted in a virtual tie.

was tainted with scandal, and inasmuch as Carter carried Georgia, an idiosyncratic explanation appears appropriate. Magnuson was attacked as old and tired, a charge that nearly defeated Barry Goldwater on the opposite end of the political spectrum. Of the remaining losers, six are liberals; their defeats gave the overall outcome an ideological interpretation. But with the exception of Gaylord Nelson, whose previous margins were impressive, the liberal senators appear to be a group of vulnerable candidates whose luck finally ran out. Note that in 1974, a dreadful year for Republicans, the Senate liberals turned in exceedingly unimpressive showings. One cannot prove a counterfactual, but if 1974 had been anything like a normal midterm election, four or five of the Senate liberals would have lost at that time and the 1980 results would have appeared far less dramatic. Given the past weaknesses already shown by these senators, any number of factors could have made the small differences necessary to defeat them—Reagan coattails, conservative trends, and the National Conservative Political Action Committee on the one hand, or poor organization, carelessness, or local issues on the other. Their defeats hardly offer grounds for pronouncing the advent of a new electoral era.

By this point Republicans may dismiss this analysis as no more than sour grapes. Our discussion may seem to have downplayed the extent to which the 1980 elections departed from earlier ones, but only because the purported departures have been so overemphasized in much of the popular and partisan commentary. Now we will discuss some ways in which the 1980 elections were different; for indeed, where there is so much smoke, one generally finds at least some fire.

Explaining the Republican Showing

As noted previously, the 1980 elections revealed an enhanced pattern of competition in House races (figure 4-1). Given that Reagan coattails do not provide a sufficient explanation for the impressive Republican showing (table 4-1), other explanations must be sought. The organizational buildup of the national Republican party provides one plausible possibility. The Republicans are taking an increasingly active role in the recruitment, training, and campaigning of their congressional challengers. If their efforts are effective, and many observers regard them as such, there should be fewer races in which Democratic incumbents face perfunctory challenges. Hard-fought races produce closer margins and fill in the middle trough shown in figure 4-1.

Recall the situation in 1980: in the view of many voters, all was not well with America.[24] Inflation raged, unchecked by Carter's numerous inflation plans. Simultaneously, unemployment was high and growth low. On the international scene, Iran was a constant, humiliating reminder of the apparent inability of the Carter administration to manage world events. Amid it all, the administration exuded a sense of helplessness. The country seemed adrift.

Such conditions should have provided fertile ground for Republican campaign efforts, and the evidence suggests they did. The Republican campaign tried to put Democratic incumbents on the defensive and overcome the overwhelmingly individual nature of House elections by injecting national issues into the elections. Particularly vulnerable in this respect were congressmen occupying leadership positions, especially those in the Democratic party leadership. As leaders, they found it difficult to deny responsibility for national conditions. Who can forget the commercial showing a Tip O'Neill look-alike foolhardily driving a car until the last drop of gas was used? Such commercials were part of a $9 million Republican TV budget in 1980.[25] Speaker O'Neill was unbeatable, but others were not and drew strong challenges. The Democratic whip, John Brademas; the majority leader, James C. Wright; and the caucus chairman, Thomas S. Foley, faced experienced, well-financed opponents (and in Brademas's case, the opponent won).

Statistical analyses (shown in tables 4-4 and 4-5) suggest that Republican efforts may have had some of the effects they desired. But those

24. *Public Opinion*, vol. 3 (June–July 1980), pp. 30–31.
25. Mann and Ornstein, "The Republican Surge," p. 266.

Table 4-4. *Correlates of Republican Challengers' Expenditures in Districts with Democratic Incumbents, 1980 and 1984*

	Coefficient	
Variable	1980	1984
Incumbent vote[a]	-4.5**	-4.5**
Leadership position[b]	156.2*	-167.2
Presidential support[c]	-1.5	-0.6
Challenger experience[d]	41.3	123.2**
Democratic presidential vote[e]	-1.9**	-2.4*
Constant	609.3**	549.2**
Adjusted R^2	0.23	0.32
N	210	199

Sources: Michael Barone and Grant Ujifusa, *Almanac of American Politics, 1982* (Washington, D.C.: Barone and Co., 1981); *Congressional Quarterly Almanac*, vol. 36 (1980) and vol. 39 (1983); *Congressional Quarterly Weekly Report*, selected issues; *National Journal*, vol. 17 (April 20, 1985), p. 854; *National Journal*, vol. 17 (May 4, 1985), p. 972; and Federal Election Commission, Candidate 409 Index data tape.
* Significant at less than 5 percent.
** Significant at less than 1 percent.
a. Incumbent's percentage of two-party vote in the previous election.
b. 1 = Democratic incumbent is Speaker, majority leader, whip, chief deputy whip, deputy whip, or caucus chair; 0 = otherwise.
c. *Congressional Quarterly* presidential support score of incumbent in 1980 and 1984.
d. 1 = challenger has held elective office; 0 = otherwise.
e. Democratic presidential candidate's percentage of district vote.

same analyses also suggest the limitations of those efforts. We first estimated the factors associated with the levels of challengers' expenditures in 1980. Controlling for the previous showing of the incumbent and for Carter's showing in the district, we found that candidates opposing Democratic leaders (but not committee chairmen) were better able to raise funds than other Republican challengers. We estimate that opponents of leaders raised $156,000 more in campaign funds than opponents of nonleaders.[26] Of course, the large amounts of campaign funds raised by opponents of leaders generated an equivalent response by the challenged incumbents. Our analysis estimates that the Democratic leaders raised over $300,000 more than the Democratic rank and file. Thus races involving the leadership attracted more money all around. However, it is well known that challenger money is more productive than incumbent money, so perhaps the challengers profited more from their lesser amounts than leaders did with more. What is the net effect? Our analysis suggests that the small electoral advantage from holding a

26. Mann and Ornstein suggest that Republican party involvement followed rather than preceded the appearance of strong challenges to several Democratic leaders. If so, our discussion would overstate the case for Republican party targeting. See ibid., p. 285.

Table 4-5. *Correlates of Vote for Democratic Incumbents, 1980 and 1984*

	Coefficient	
Variable	1980	1984
Incumbent vote[a]	0.2**	0.2**
Leadership position[b]	2.2	4.2
Presidential support[c]	0.1	0.1*
Challenger experience[d]	−1.3	−0.02
Challenger expenditures[e]	−0.03**	−0.02**
Democratic presidential vote[f]	0.4**	0.4**
Constant	33.3**	31.4**
Adjusted R^2	0.68	0.73
N	210	199

Sources: Barone and Ujifusa, *Almanac of American Politics, 1982; Congressional Quarterly Almanac,* vols. 36 and 39; *Congressional Quarterly Weekly Report; National Journal,* vol. 17 (April 20, 1985), p. 854; *National Journal,* vol. 17 (May 4, 1985), p. 972; and Federal Election Commission, Candidate 409 Index data tape.
** Significant at less than 1 percent.
a. Incumbent's percentage of two-party vote in the previous election.
b. 1 = Democratic incumbent is Speaker, majority leader, whip, chief deputy whip, deputy whip, or caucus chair; 0 = otherwise.
c. *Congressional Quarterly* presidential support score of incumbent in 1980 and 1984.
d. 1 = challenger has held elective office; 0 = otherwise.
e. Hundreds of thousands of dollars.
f. Democratic presidential candidate's percentage of district vote.

leadership position in 1980 was slightly less than the advantage leaders' challengers enjoyed from being able to raise additional campaign funds.[27]

As for factors other than challenger spending, we found that incumbents in 1980 were affected only marginally by such variables as their presidential support score or the presence of an experienced challenger. Overall, our statistical analysis suggests that the 1980 congressional elections were not greatly different from those of the 1970s.

Another way to look at the 1980 elections is to return to our earlier examination of the pattern of competition shown in figure 4-1. While a comparison of the 1980 pattern with the 1972 pattern made 1980 appear to be a major departure, a comparison of the 1980 pattern with those for 1982 and 1984 reveals that 1980 was only a slight deviation, rather than the harbinger of a new era. In 1982 there is the hint of a return to the familiar trough around the 50 percent margin, and in 1984 the trough becomes clearly reestablished. The 1980 elections present the strongest case for a transformation in the shape of congressional voting, but in retrospect they appear to be only a small departure from familiar patterns.

27. Gary Jacobson, *Money in Congressional Elections* (Yale University Press, 1980).

The 1982 Elections

Early in 1981 the Republicans looked forward with anticipation to 1982. For a time even a House majority seemed within reach.[28] The party apparatus set about to make full use of loopholes in the campaign finance laws so as to guarantee prospective Republican challengers that ample funds would be available for the 1982 campaigns.[29] As it turned out, the ambitious Republican efforts were most useful in minimizing damage, rather than increasing the party's numbers in the House. In 1982 the country suffered the deepest recession since the Great Depression, and, according to several models of seat losses in congressional elections, the Republicans should have paid the price with losses on the order of forty to fifty seats.[30] Their actual losses of twenty-six seats, though large by 1978 standards, were smaller than projections from historical experience. Moreover, between five and ten of those seats were probably lost through reapportionment rather than Reaganomics.[31] At least two explanations for the Republicans' better than expected showing have some plausibility. First, the Republicans recruited and financed an excellent class of challengers in 1981, when Reagan was still riding the crest of his landslide victory and well before the unfavorable economic conditions of 1982 developed.[32] Second, the effects of national conditions do not carry over into congressional elections of today to the same extent they did in earlier periods, as argued above. The seat loss models were also inaccurate in 1978, in part because Democratic incumbents did not suffer from perceptions of Carter's performance and the state of the

28. Irwin Arieff, "House Democrats, GOP Elect Leaders, Draw Battle Lines," *Congressional Quarterly Weekly Report*, vol. 38 (December 13, 1980), p. 3549; and Alan Murray, "Utah Lawyer Richards Named GOP Chairman," *Congressional Quarterly Weekly Report*, vol. 39 (January 24, 1981), p. 201.

29. Gary Jacobson and Samuel Kernell, "Party Organization and the Efficient Distribution of Congressional Campaign Resources," paper prepared for the Weingart-Caltech Conference on Institutional Context of Elections, California Institute of Technology, February 16–18, 1984.

30. See Douglas A. Hibbs, Jr., "President Reagan's Mandate from the 1980 Elections: A Shift to the Right?" *American Politics Quarterly*, vol. 10 (October 1982), pp. 387–420.

31. Thomas Mann and Norman Ornstein, "The 1982 Election: What Will It Mean?" *Public Opinion*, vol. 4 (June–July 1981), p. 49.

32. This is the explanation offered by Jacobson and Kernell in *Strategy and Choice*, pp. 94–109.

economy.[33] The 1982 Republican losses were less than those that occurred under comparably bad conditions, just as were the 1974 losses.[34] Again, the 1982 outcome is at least as remarkable for its consistency with past elections as for its departures.

The 1984 Elections

And what of 1984, the election that serves as the occasion for this essay? In contrast to 1980 and 1982, the Republican party had not assembled a particularly attractive list of challengers. Much of the recruiting took place in the fall of 1983, when prospects for 1984 did not appear especially auspicious. The economic recovery was young and its future uncertain. The Lebanon reverse was fresh and the news from Central America not promising. NATO allies were grumbling about the administration's uncompromising attitude toward the Soviets. Republican incumbents in the House and Senate continued to display the independence that marked the 1982 campaigns, perhaps hedging their bets against additional trouble before 1984. And if strong challengers for incumbents were hard to find, there were only twenty-seven open seats, and just thirteen of them were held by Democrats.

Given these conditions, Republican fund-raising and campaigning capabilities could not be used as effectively as the markedly improved political situation in 1984 would seem to have allowed. Coordinators of party committees and conservative PACs complained that there were not enough good races to justify spending the sums they were capable of raising. Additionally, some Democratic officials reportedly warned business PACs that contributions to Republican challengers would be remembered in the next Congress.[35]

33. Lyn Ragsdale, "The Fiction of Congressional Elections as Presidential Events," *American Politics Quarterly,* vol. 8 (October 1980), pp. 375–98.

34. Burnham estimates that 1974 Republican losses would have been at least a dozen greater than they were if national conditions had affected congressional races as much that year as in pre-1960 elections. See Walter Dean Burnham, "Insulation and Responsiveness in Congressional Elections," *Political Science Quarterly,* vol. 90 (Fall 1975), p. 426.

35. See, for example, the comments of Bernadette Budde and the remarks about Tony Coehlo quoted in Alan Ehrenhalt, "GOP Challengers Find PACs Wary This Year," *Congressional Quarterly Weekly Report,* vol. 42 (October 20, 1984), p. 2763.

With the White House and Senate in Republican hands, it was not easy to place responsibility for national conditions on Democratic congressional leaders. Thus targeting them for special opposition had much less to recommend it than in 1980. This difference between 1984 and 1980 shows up clearly in our statistical analyses (see tables 4-4 and 4-5). Republican candidates who challenged Democratic leaders in 1984 raised significantly less money than those who challenged Democratic rank and file. The total difference from 1980 to 1984 was over $300,000 in races involving the Democratic leadership. Democratic leaders again ran better than the rank and file, taking challenger experience and spending and previous election results into account. The difference in challenger spending between 1980 and 1984 indicates that Republican strategies did have a measurable impact, but as noted earlier, the electoral consequences of such strategies simply were not major.

The estimates in table 4-5 permit us to make some observations about coattail voting in 1980 and 1984. Evidently, the marginal effect of a Democratic presidential vote on the vote for a Democratic House incumbent was 0.4. While these estimates are not fully comparable with the estimates in table 4-1, they are similar in magnitude and suggest no change between the 1980 and 1984 elections. Of more interest is the finding that support for Reagan's legislative program was positively related to electoral margin. This suggests the Democrats might have been right to worry about the electoral consequences of opposing the president's program.

At this time the data are not yet available to extend the coattail estimates of table 4-1 through 1984. Other than the small bit of evidence just presented, the best one can do is attempt to utilize exit polls, such as those conducted by CBS News/*New York Times*. Such data are not at all comparable to the data used in earlier tables, but they permit us to make a rough and ready estimate of the level of coattail voting in 1984. Unfortunately, the exit poll data do not contain information on incumbency, so we are not able to replicate the analyses underlying table 4-1, which differentiates between open seats and incumbent-contested races. Consequently, our figures represent the average coattail effect across both incumbent-contested and open seats. These calculations also overestimate the coattail vote because the CBS poll asks respondents the party of the congressional candidate they supported rather than have the respondent indicate the name of the candidate. This procedure inflates the extent to which individuals report voting for candidates of the same party.

Caveats and cautions aside, the resulting calculations yield a coattail effect of 4 percent in 1984. When we applied the same techniques to the 1980 National Election Studies data as a check, the resulting figure was 2.7 percent, compared with the 1.7 percent estimate from the more accurate analysis in table 4-1. If the 1984 CBS calculation overestimates the actual coattail effect by the same ratio as it did in 1980, the actual coattail effect in 1984 was in the neighborhood of 2.5 percent. Thus Reagan's coattails *in votes* may have been more pronounced in 1984 than in 1980—even though they yielded fewer seats in the House. The lesser effect in terms of seats is a function of the decline in closely competitive elections (see figure 4-1). Had it not been for this decline in competitive seats, Reagan might have carried more Republicans into office in 1984 than in 1980.

But even though Reagan seems to have had a slightly longer coattail with the voters in 1984, the overall pattern of congressional elections suggests a return to the norm established during the late 1960s and early 1970s, rather than a continuation of the modest deviation of 1980. As more data enable scholars to analyze the 1984 election in detail, this picture will become more refined. But the broad outlines of what happened make us doubt that such detailed analyses will find change more noteworthy than continuity. Inasmuch as genuine change may be taking place at other levels of the system, the insulated stability of the congressional arena raises interesting questions about the condition of American national government.

Congressional Stability and Presidential Change

At present we believe that the Reagan tides have washed over Congress without fundamentally altering the underlying terrain. There will continue to be a very high probability that congressmen who value reelection sufficiently to perform the activities useful in achieving it will continue to win reelection. Recessions, international setbacks, and notably popular and unpopular presidents will come and go, but most congressmen will stay. Though the Republicans still control the Senate, in 1986 two-thirds of the seats at stake will be Republican seats, including the same seats where a few thousand votes made the difference in 1980. Even a 1 or 2 percent Republican loss stemming from reactions to a new recession or Central American conflict could make the difference and return the Senate to the Democrats. All in all, it would not be surprising if by 1990 analysts look back at the congressional elections of the 1980s and judge them not so very different from those of the 1970s—one rather dramatic election in each decade (1974 and 1980)—and the rest pretty much congressional politics as usual.

Various possibilities could upset this prediction of continuity in congressional elections. A national or international crisis could produce the kind of party realignment set in motion by the depression of the 1930s—if one of the parties dealt effectively with such a crisis. On a more mundane level, the kinds of targeting efforts pioneered by the Republican party could increase in both magnitude and effectiveness, especially if the campaign finance laws were changed so as to restrict direct PAC spending in campaigns as much as constitutionally possible while simultaneously encouraging direct party spending as much as possible. Party efforts so far might best be regarded as experimental; perhaps they have more potential than our statistical estimates suggest. Additionally, channeling party expenditures to promising challengers or against opposition leaders may have a cumulative effect not as yet discernible. Under the steady hammering of a superior party organization, will Democratic incumbents eventually succumb?

Of course, organization begets counterorganization. The Democrats are behind but not standing still. If imitation is the sincerest form of flattery, Democrats are flattering the Republicans.[36] Conceivably, in the next few years the Democrats could gradually offset Republican organizational efforts with their own.

Still another possibility is that effects are occurring, but with lags so great that they are not yet apparent. If Republicans increasingly gain the loyalties of new voters, Democratic incumbents' hold on office could weaken—but only if voters choose members of Congress on the basis of party identification. However, as we noted earlier, the impact of party identification on voting for Congress has steadily declined over the course of two decades.

In chapter 2 Cavanagh and Sundquist analyze 1984 poll data on party identification. Their analyses convince them "that something historic is

36. Jacobson and Kernell, "Party Organization and Efficient Distribution," p. 9.

indeed happening to the party system. The Republicans have approached parity with the Democrats, finally establishing a genuine two-party system." Given that their conclusion appears as well based on their data as our conclusions on our data, there appears to be some basis for agreeing with Kevin Phillips that the United States has undergone a split-level realignment.[37] Of course, that is only to name the present condition of our national politics, not to explain it.

The most straightforward explanation of the apparent split-level realignment involves the following simple merger of the partial explanations offered by us and by Cavanagh and Sundquist. Beginning with Johnson's reelection in 1964, the American people saw four presidencies as disappointing at best. Against that background, the perceived success of the first Reagan administration has convinced a significant portion of the citizenry that the contemporary Republican party has the ideas and the capacity to govern competently.[38] Meanwhile, the Democratic party remains in such disarray that the electorate considers it a nonviable governing alternative. The deep divisions opened by racial and social issues two decades ago persist, and the economic troubles of the 1970s have opened new divisions over traditional interventionist economic policies. No Democrat can now win the support (let alone the enthusiasm) of all the tribes and clans of the party. Blue-collar workers, the issue groups, minorities, and the new South and West simply have too little in common. Any candidate with strong appeal to a few of the major elements in the party inevitably drives others into the arms of the Republicans. These contemporary realities have begun to make their impression on reported party identification.

At the congressional level, however, national Democrats do not contend with national Republicans. Instead, candidates adopt the appropriate local coloration. In the old industrial cities Democratic candidates ally with labor and the ethnics. In the cosmopolitan cities and suburbs they ally with the issue groups. Minorities often are concentrated and can elect their own representatives. In the South and West Democratic candidates adapt themselves to the prevailing ethos of their region. Below the presidential level, geographical segregation of the elements

37. Kevin Phillips's biweekly newsletter, *The American Political Report,* vol. 14 (January 11, 1985). See also William Schneider, "Half a Realignment," *The New Republic,* December 3, 1984, pp. 19–22.

38. This is the theory of party identification advanced by Fiorina in *Retrospective Voting,* chaps. 4, 5.

of the erstwhile Democratic coalition offsets the aggregate heterogeneity of the party.

The preceding explanation does no violence to known facts, but it fails to account for one significant feature of the contemporary political scene. Although the Democrats should be able to compete more evenly with the Republicans at the subnational level, why should they enjoy a decided edge? Some believe that this lead reflects little more than inertia: as Democratic congressional incumbents retire they will gradually be replaced by Republicans. Perhaps, but that ignores the 2-to-1 edge among Democratic governors and nearly as great a margin in the state legislatures. When one considers the superior Republican party organizations, the Democratic subnational edge becomes all the more puzzling.

This puzzling Democratic subnational advantage makes us doubt that a simple merging of the Cavanagh-Sundquist argument with ours probes deeply enough into citizen preferences. Consider the cross-pressures affecting key voting blocs that must remain in the Republican column if a permanent Republican majority is to emerge. Blue-collar workers who take pride in Reagan's economic recovery and strong presidential leadership may still feel that Democrats care more about their economic interests than Republicans do. And whatever their deeply felt patriotism, they may doubt the wisdom of a policy that could eventually send their sons to fight in Central America. It is true that many yuppies have been attracted to Republican economic policies, but do they wish to keep company with Jesse Helms? And even if they have come to believe in the need for a strong American presence in world affairs, will they go so far as to support a party given to foreign adventures of the kind that led to Vietnam? Are the southerners and westerners who have embraced the growth-oriented policies of the Reagan administration also prepared to give up their historic positions as recipients of the federal largesse that Democrats have steadfastly supported? Or does that involve a bit too much of a cutback in the role of government for even the more enthusiastic supporters of a market economy?

In order for a realignment to occur, voters must have a party to which they can move with some enthusiasm. But given the present multi-dimensional state of public opinion, few voters find that either party embodies a combination of policies they strongly prefer.[39] Thus a large

39. Though we have focused on the conflicting preferences of Democrats, Kevin Phillips makes a similar argument for the lack of internal harmony among today's Republicans in *Post-Conservative America* (Vintage, 1983), especially chap. 7.

majority feels hesitant to trust either party with full control over the government. The Republican edge in citizen perceptions of who can best handle the economy and manage foreign relations need not reflect any high degree of approval of the Republicans, only a sense that they are better than the alternative.

If the preceding line of thought has merit, then the absence of a national realignment may reflect voter design or purpose, rather than a lack of them.[40] The underlying basis of a split-level realignment may be the cross-pressures felt by independents and weak partisans. Rather than swing between the parties at different elections, some voters swing between parties at different levels of government. A majority of the electorate may prefer a Republican to a Democrat in the presidency. But some of those who feel this way may be ambivalent enough about the prospect that they lean toward the Democrats at lower positions on the ballot. Thus, consciously or unconsciously, some portion of the citizenry may vote so as to check Republican presidents with Democrats at other levels, especially Congress. There may be a split-level realignment with its accompanying divided government because that is what a critical minority of voters want, not because it reflects their notion of the ideal situation, but because they have decided it is the best they can hope for given the present configuration of the two parties. It would not be the first time that the collective common sense of the electorate has eluded the understanding of the pundits.

40. After the recent elections the pollster Louis Harris reported that Americans opposed giving Reagan a Republican Congress by a margin of 54 to 39 percent. Unfortunately, the wording of the question is sufficiently extreme as to cast doubt on these numbers. See Louis Harris, "Reagan Wins Reelection, Loses Bid for Republican Congress," *The Harris Survey,* November 8, 1984, p. 1. For a general discussion of ticket splitting see the rational choice analysis developed by Kenneth McCue in "The Structure of Individual Decisions in American Elections: The Influence of Relevant Alternatives" (Ph.D. dissertation, California Institute of Technology, 1983).

CHAPTER FIVE

Campaigning, Governing, and the Contemporary Presidency

SAMUEL KERNELL

ON THE MORNING of November 7, 1984, the winning and losing presidential candidates appeared briefly before the press—Ronald Reagan in Los Angeles, Walter Mondale in St. Paul. Each expressed his gratitude to supporters and family, praised his adversary, offered a few observations about the events of the preceding months, and fielded reporters' questions. It was a traditional "morning after" public exercise designed to display the humility of the victor and graciousness of the loser.

But despite the blandness of the comments and the differing perspectives of the two men, their observations were strikingly complementary and constituted a statement about the future of American politics. Reagan briefly thanked the American people for their support and then turned to reporters' questions about taxes, budgets, and U.S. relations with Nicaragua, issues that would be significant at the opening of his second term. Anticipating a possible replay of 1981, some reporters asked the president if he considered the election a mandate and what he might do if Congress resisted his requests. Reagan responded that "the people made it very plain they approve what we've been doing, and we're going to continue." If necessary, he added, he would take his case "to the people" to force support from Congress.[1] As the president departed, a reporter got in a last question: now that the election was won, would he hold formal news conferences more often? (He had held fewer news

1. Jack Nelson, "Reagan Vows to Extend Conservative Agenda," *Los Angeles Times,* November 8, 1984.

117

conferences on average than any modern president and none since late July.)[2] He grinned, shrugged, and replied, "Look, I won. . . . Why should I subject myself?" With that his voice trailed off, his point made.

In St. Paul, Mondale thanked his running mate, supporters, and voters, then also quickly turned to the reporters. Their questions mostly concerned what went wrong. Mondale began by conceding that a popular president, peace, and a strong economy offered long odds against victory. He also mentioned the bloodletting of the Democratic primaries and noted his failure to appeal to young voters. In his estimate, however, the campaign's most serious failure was his inability to master television: "Modern politics requires television. I've never really warmed up to television. And, in fairness to television, it never warmed up to me." Pointing to the array of microphones in front of him, he quipped, "I never liked these things either," and then slapped one, sending out a clap over the sound system. Mondale closed the subject by observing, "I don't believe it's possible anymore to run for president without the capacity to build confidence and communications every night. It's got to be done that way."[3]

As one reporter noted, Mondale's remarks saddened many of his advisers because he was only now learning this lesson of contemporary politics. After serving for four years with a president who self-consciously, if ineffectively, used televised appeals to the country in his efforts to influence Washington decisionmaking, after watching Reagan master Congress in 1981 with repeated appeals to responsive national audiences, and after watching Gary Hart campaign with techniques directed toward gaining favorable television coverage, Mondale was only now coming to appreciate this verity of modern politics. Juxtaposed with President Reagan's announcement that he would turn to the people, Mondale's remarks are inescapably poignant.

At first glance, Mondale's comments appear to belie prominent aspects of the campaign. Although early estimates indicate that Reagan probably spent more money on television, both campaigns used commercials heavily, and Mondale's media budget has been conservatively estimated at $30 million. Moreover, in the first debate, one of the most-

2. On the subject of Reagan's 1984 press conferences, see Lou Cannon, "Phantom of the White House," *Washington Post,* December 24, 1984.

3. Dudley Clendinen, "The Medium and Mondale," *New York Times,* November 9, 1984; and Sara Fritz, "Mondale Wonders If He's a Victim of the Electronic Age?" *Los Angeles Times,* November 8, 1984.

watched television events of the campaign, Mondale had scored well with all audiences. Yet when he volunteered the remarks in St. Paul, the reporters understood his reasons and agreed with his assessment. They had been saying as much for months.

The quality of the candidates' performances on television and the relative quality of the campaigns' media strategies may or may not have contributed significantly to the outcome of the election, but from what is known about voting in past presidential elections, Mondale's claims that television style was decisive must be treated seriously. Assessments of the candidates' personalities, independent of their party affiliation or their positions on issues, have always influenced voters' choices. In recent years these assessments appear to have assumed an even greater role as they have come to fill a partial void left by voters' weakening party loyalties.[4] To this development we should add another. Television seems increasingly the medium of choice by which citizens evaluate candidates.[5] With such developments shaping modern elections, television campaigning is obviously important.

Although many journalists gave the respective candidates' use of television special significance in 1984, other observers did not. When a candidate wins by a margin of 18 percentage points, multiple forces must have helped shape the victory, with none of them decisive. Economic conditions, the absence of war, and the president's popular standing in the early summer allowed one careful observer to predict the actual vote before the election.[6] Consistent with the view that the outcome was predetermined were the public opinion surveys that found Reagan

4. See Samuel L. Popkin and others, "What Have You Done For Me Lately? Toward An Investment Theory of Voting," *American Political Science Review,* vol. 70 (September 1976), pp. 779–805; Donald E. Stokes, Angus Campbell, and Warren E. Miller, "Components of Electoral Decision," *American Political Science Review,* vol. 52 (June 1958), pp. 367–87; and Samuel A. Kirkpatrick, William Lyons, and Michael R. Fitzgerald, "Candidates, Parties and Issues in the American Electorate: Two Decades of Change," *American Politics Quarterly,* vol. 3 (July 1975), pp. 247–83.

5. Austin Ranney, *Channels of Power* (Basic Books, 1983), p. 14 and throughout.

6. Steven J. Rosenstone, *Forecasting Presidential Elections* (Yale University Press, 1983). Among the seven elections since 1948 in which the incumbent president sought reelection, Reagan's 1984 vote departed from the final vote predicted in the June Gallup popularity rating more than any of the others. Predicting the full vote as a function of the president's June approval rating yields a Reagan victory with 52 percent of the votes cast. See Samuel Kernell, *Going Public: New Strategies of Presidential Leadership* (Washington, D.C.: CQ Press, forthcoming). Also see Michael S. Lewis-Beck, "Election Forecasts in 1984: How Accurate Were They?" *PS,* vol. 18 (Winter 1985), pp. 53–62.

comfortably ahead throughout the year.[7] According to this view, the false starts and mistakes that plagued the Mondale campaign, which close observers have considered important, are themselves concomitant with a campaign seemingly destined to lose.[8] As one election analyst concluded, "In 1984, the lesson may be that sometimes campaigns may not matter at all."[9]

Lessons from the 1984 Election

To disregard the campaign events of 1984 as immaterial would, however, be a mistake. Even if their ultimate effect on election results is unclear, they can be instructive for potential presidential contenders if these politicians believe that one of the campaigns was better conceived and managed than the other and that this difference could have affected the outcome if underlying political forces had been more balanced. When looked at from this perspective, the 1984 campaign has a significance that transcends any impact it may have had on the November 6 vote. It becomes a lesson for future campaigns.

Rarely has an election brought together two candidates who by virtue of experience, temperament, and ideology have held such contrasting conceptions of politics. If one adds that the glaring deficiencies of the losing campaign appeared to reflect Mondale's approach to politics, one has in the 1984 election a highly instructive demonstration case.

The presidential selection system—the delegate primaries and caucuses, the convention, campaign finance laws and subsidies, and techniques of campaigning such as the use of television and polls—constitutes a strategic environment that enhances certain skills and resources while it penalizes others. As Senator Estes Kefauver demonstrated in his

7. "See How They Ran," *Public Opinion*, vol. 7 (October–November, 1984), pp. 38–39.

8. A deficit of 15 percentage points in the polls will embolden even candidates as cautious as Walter Mondale to accept risks. By definition, high-risk strategies more often than not turn out to be mistakes. We may so judge Mondale's unprecedented campaign pledge to the American people to raise their taxes, his surprise selection of the relatively unknown Geraldine Ferraro to be his running mate without adequately checking out her husband's financial activities, and his quickly aborted selection of Bert Lance to be chairman of the Democratic National Committee. Desperate men take chances.

9. Kathleen A. Frankovic, "The 1984 Election: The Irrelevance of the Campaign," *PS*, vol. 18 (Winter 1985), p. 39.

frustrated attempt for the Democratic nomination in a different era, once upon a time insiders who had the support of party leaders were favored. Today it appears to be the outsider who can appeal effectively to a broad public through effective performance before the television cameras. Savvy politicians will, of course, recognize the changes that have occurred. Those who see in Mondale their own vulnerabilities may already have privately discounted their future prospects. Others who consider themselves more effective media personalities may have been heartened. As Lemarck wished his frogs would do, some politicians have probably already begun adapting their styles and careers to what they recognize as the requirements of the new environment for survival.[10]

A candidate's adaptability is, of course, limited. By the time a politician's career has reached the stage at which contemplating the presidency is not fantasy, he will already have an established public persona, skills and talents honed in previous campaigns, a public record that cannot be altered without obvious dissimulation, commitments that cannot easily be broken, and experience from past successes that will help him navigate an uncertain political sea. Media consultants and makeup artists may burnish the rough edges, but in the words of a frustrated Walter Mondale after his defeat in the Massachusetts primary, "I am what I am." Because they are expressions of the candidates, campaigns are not clay in the hands of image-makers.

The educational impact of a campaign, then, is not so much that it changes the style of individuals but that it determines which candidates decide to run. As they calculate the costs and risks of a presidential campaign against the potential gain from holding office, the probability that they can win by using the style with which they are most comfortable will be a significant consideration. Politicians will, of course, also be influenced by other factors—personal ambition, family preferences, conflicts between running and other aspects of their careers. Nevertheless, when heavily invested careers are at risk, the requirements of that campaign environment can be expected to weigh heavily upon the decisions of acute politicians to run for president.

It is thus primarily in the way that the processes of self-selection shape the presidential candidates that the lessons of one election carry over to the next. Eugene J. McCarthy's "victory" over President

10. After the 1980 elections, two Democrats who displayed such urges were Walter Mondale, who announced a monastic retreat to contemplate America's future, and Senator Joseph Biden, who took instruction at the American Enterprise Institute.

Johnson in the New Hampshire primary in 1968 instructed George S. McGovern and numerous other Democratic aspirants in the new opportunities provided by the expanding primary system. If McGovern proved in 1972 that a virtual unknown six months before the convention could capture the nomination, Jimmy Carter demonstrated in 1976 that such a candidate could also win the election. Similarly, Ronald Reagan demonstrated in 1976 that an incumbent president could be almost a sitting duck for a challenger from his own party, a lesson not lost on Edward M. Kennedy in 1980.

The lessons politicians learn should also not be lost on those who study politicians, because these lessons are the way the present provides insight into the future. By examining how the distinctive candidacies of 1984 fared in this rarefied environment, analysts may identify its biases and anticipate the leadership styles of our future presidents.

The lessons of 1984 for campaigning and ultimately for governing are to be found in answers to the following question: how are the success of Walter Mondale in capturing the nomination, his near catastrophe en route to doing so, and his thorough defeat in November likely to inform the strategic judgments of politicians who contemplate reaching for the White House? To answer this compound question requires reexamining these significant events from which the education of future candidates will proceed.

The Candidates

If, as I have argued, a presidential campaign is founded upon the candidate's conception of politics, then the degree to which one campaign strategy masters another says nothing less than that one kind of politician is favored over another. Future presidential aspirants watching from the sidelines recognize this. Through these politicians' subsequent self-selection, the biases of the selection system are extended and made more pronounced. In that a politician's conception of politics directs his behavior in office as much as in how he seeks office, we may expect to find the biases of the selection system showing up in the character of presidential leadership. Reviewing the campaigns of 1984 gives us an opportunity both to test the claimed consonance between candidate and campaign and to speculate upon its implications for future candidates and presidents.

Ronald Reagan

Ronald Reagan's career in movies, television, and public affairs groomed him well for his style of leadership. Movies brought him fame, a considerable asset for those seeking to transform a private into a public career. During these years in Hollywood he also served as president of the Screen Actors Guild, an office that gave him occasion to wage ideological war with liberals and which contributed to his political maturation.[11] Later, a decade in television as spokesman for 20 Mule Team Borax and then for General Electric allowed him to master the requisite techniques of the medium and of public speaking. In his autobiography he commented, "I know statistics are boring, but reducing eight years of tours, in which I reached all the 135 [General Electric] plants and personally met with 250,000 employees, down to numbers, it turns out something like this: two of the eight years were spent traveling, and with speeches sometimes running at 14 a day, I was on my feet in front of a 'mike' for about 250,000 minutes."[12] Long before the presidential selection process had been reformed, Reagan's public relations activities were unwittingly preparing him for the thirty-two-round primary campaign of 1980.

In 1966 Ronald Reagan embarked on a career in politics when he defeated Pat Brown for governor of California. Entering the public arena at the age of fifty-five and high on the rung of public offices contributed to the style of political leadership that he was later to employ so effectively. If a political career is a learning or developmental process in which lower office not only promotes a politician to higher office but also prepares him for it, Reagan's career was clearly deficient. He skipped the formative experiences that take place in city councils, state assemblies, and Congress and that expose a politician to bargaining and compromise. Instead, as governor of California, his political tutelage occurred in the Sacramento fishbowl. His tenure during years of campus unrest and Democratic legislatures gave him ample opportunity to hone his considerable rhetorical talents. After eight years of castigating liberals, he retired from office "to speak out on the issues," which meant to campaign full time for the presidency. A nationally syndicated columnist and radio commentator and one of the most sought after

11. Lou Cannon, *Reagan* (Putnam, 1982), chap. 7.
12. Ronald Reagan with Richard G. Hubler, *Where's the Rest of Me* (Duell, Sloan and Pearce, 1965), p. 257.

speakers on the Republican circuit, Reagan was better positioned than anyone else to do so.

Finally, Reagan's formative experiences included the many campaigns any candidate for the presidency invariably accumulates. He may have begun a public career late and held only one office before the presidency, but he managed to contest sixty-two primary and general elections, amassing a record of forty-four victories against eighteen defeats. All of them were in the national limelight.[13]

Such experience prepared Reagan to be a president who prefers to appeal to the public rather than bargain with Congress. Other twentieth-century presidents have won the office with the thinnest of claims of insight into the ways of Washington, much less of the presidency, but with the exception of President Carter, none was so bereft of such experience as Reagan. Even the avowedly apolitical Eisenhower occasionally pointed to his "invaluable," albeit brief, service in the War Department under George Marshall and his subsequent experience as army chief of staff.[14] Converting his deprived political upbringing into a campaign asset, Reagan sought to go to Washington by running against it.

His political ideology further distanced him from Washington. Since his early and ardent alienation from the New Deal, Reagan has been an aggressive exponent of a traditional strain of Republican conservatism.[15] A favorite rhetorical device over the years has been to decorate his attack on whatever Democratic policies were emanating from Washington with a simple, often folksy statement of his own values and a caricatured depiction of Washingtonians as bureaucrats and spendthrift politicians. His insistent rhetoric helps to explain why he had accumulated an unusually large number of both intense followers and detractors

13. Reagan contested four gubernatorial primary and general elections and fifty-seven presidential primaries in the 1976 and 1980 presidential elections. See Richard M. Scammon and Alice V. McGillivray, *America Votes 14* (CQ Press, 1980).

14. Fred I. Greenstein attaches great significance to Eisenhower's Washington experience in arguing that his style in office, including his image among Washingtonians as a bumbler, was actually an adroit strategic device to disarm potential adversaries and deflect responsibility. See *The Hidden-Hand Presidency* (Basic Books, 1982), chaps. 2 and 3.

15. Reagan's rhetoric over the years portrays such consistency as well as conviction. His record refutes the "selling of the president" myth, which holds that television packaging requires plastic candidates whose position on issues can be molded by advertising executives who are guided by marketing surveys. A best-selling representative of this genre is Joe McGinnis, *The Selling of the Presidency, 1968* (Trident Press, 1969).

when he entered the White House.[16] As a conservative outsider moving to a city he regarded as dominated by liberal insiders, Reagan was unsuited to be a president like Franklin D. Roosevelt, who relished the give and take of political bargaining. Lou Cannon, a White House reporter and long-time Reagan watcher, attributes to him a concept of his role that was congenial to his outsider status: "Reagan is a modest man, but he did not object to the frequent descriptions of him as 'the Great Communicator.' He approvingly cited Theodore Roosevelt's description of the presidency as a 'bully pulpit.' With the forum of national television available to the President, Reagan was certain that his own communicative skills were sufficient to persuade Congress and the country to do whatever it was that was asked of them."[17] As he entered his reelection campaign after nearly four years of White House residency, reporters were still writing such articles as "Reagan Projects Self-Confidence and Image as Washington Outsider."[18]

Walter Mondale

In the early summer of 1976 Water Mondale traveled to Plains, Georgia, to be interviewed for the vice-presidential nomination. He must have known that Jimmy Carter would want to have him explain once again why he had pulled out of the race a year earlier when he was the clear frontrunner. Although he had been disappointed in the failure of a groundswell of support to materialize after Edward Kennedy withdrew, Mondale had undoubtedly been far ahead of the man who now had the Democratic nomination in hand. When asked to reiterate his earlier statement that he had gained insufficient support to justify continuing, both he and Carter would recall the early straw vote in Iowa that showed Mondale ahead of Carter (the state's eventual winner) by a margin of 39 percent to 0. Mondale's false start in 1976 was fully consistent with the past behavior of this cautious politician.

Another distinguishing feature of Walter Mondale's career was luck. While every politican must be cautious in climbing up the career ladder, those few who do become senators and who come to be regarded as presidential timber take more chances than their less ambitious col-

---

16. "Reagan Popularity below Predecessors'," *Gallup Report*, no. 186 (March, 1981), pp. 2–9.

17. Cannon, *Reagan*, p. 319.

18. Francis X. Clines, *New York Times*, August 20, 1984.

leagues. Mondale's career is exceptional in defying political gravity. Despite refusing to assume risk at any juncture, he accelerated up the office ladder. His is an improbable success story.[19]

Unlike Reagan, Walter Mondale entered politics early, becoming actively involved during his college days in St. Paul. One of his first prominent roles came when he helped the forces of Hubert Humphrey wrest control of the virtually moribund Democratic Farmer-Labor party from its left-leaning Olson wing. By the age of thirty, he had built an effective campaign organization for Senate candidate Humphrey in the heavily Republican southern counties of the state; he had organized campus charters of the Students for Democratic Action, first in Minnesota and subsequently, as a paid staffer, throughout the country; he had managed Orville Freeman's unsuccessful statewide campaign for attorney general; and under the employ of the DFL he had recruited state legislative candidates throughout Minnesota.

No sooner had Mondale graduated from law school than friends asked when he was going to come out as his own candidate. "After I make a few hundred dollars," he would reply, he might try for a state legislative seat. He never got a chance to fulfill his modest aspiration. Within two years he was the state's attorney general, appointed by his friend Governor Orville Freeman to fill a vacancy. Only thirty-two years old and four years out of law school, Mondale faced the prospect of a strong Republican challenge in the next election. The appointment looked to some to have the makings of a brief political career. But his predecessor had handed him a nearly complete investigation of a major financial scandal within the Kenney Foundation, a well-known local philanthropy. As a series of announcements by the state attorney general's office revealed the shady dealings, Mondale gained abundant favorable publicity, and by the time of the election he was considered virtually unbeatable. But although he won easily, he surprised his supporters and himself with his stiffness in the electoral arena.[20]

In 1960 Freeman was upset in his reelection bid for governor and shortly thereafter joined Humphrey in Washington as John F. Kennedy's secretary of agriculture. This suddenly left a void in the ranks of the DFL, and Mondale, with only three years as an officeholder, found himself the most popular statewide DFL member. Many party and

19. This section draws heavily on Finlay Lewis, *Mondale: Portrait of an American Politician* (Harper and Row, 1984).
20. Ibid., p. 71.

personal associates encouraged him to run for governor, but after flirting coyly with the notion for months, he finally dropped out in deference to Karl Rolvaag, a long-standing DFL heavyweight who had the backing of organized labor in Minneapolis. Politically ambitious, but a loyal party man who was unwilling to risk a split in the party or damage to his prospects, Mondale was heard to remark forlornly, "I just heard the train pass by."[21]

A chain of vacancies next pulled Mondale up another notch when Kennedy was assassinated on November 22, 1963. As one of Mondale's legal staff in the attorney general's office predicted in his diary that day, Lyndon Johnson would want Hubert Humphrey to be his vice-president, which would make Mondale the next junior senator from Minnesota. The process by which Mondale advanced was by no means automatic, however. Instead it testified to his skill at negotiation and bargaining. Governor Rolvaag had to be persuaded that appointing himself would guarantee his defeat two years later. Mondale's age, statewide reputation, and ability to work with various party factions commended him to Humphrey and eventually to Rolvaag, who was now called upon to show the forbearance Mondale had demonstrated two years earlier.

Humphrey had his own groundwork to prepare, and for this he enlisted Mondale's aid in a complex bargaining situation that constituted the young Minnesotan's first national exposure. A delegation of the Mississippi Freedom Democratic party was coming to the Democratic convention insisting that it be seated in place of the regular Democratic delegation. That delegate selection had proceeded from a highly discriminatory system was obvious, but no current national party rules had been violated. When Johnson asked Humphrey to resolve the matter with minimal bloodletting, Mondale was made chairman of the convention's credentials committee to carry out the charge. Although in the end neither the regulars nor the petitioners were happy, Mondale's compromise was well received on the convention floor as the most equitable solution possible. Days later Humphrey got the nod, and after the election so too did Mondale.[22]

As Mondale sought election to the Senate in 1966 he had only one victory to his credit. And in both the 1966 campaign and the one that preceded it, he had the advantage of an incumbency gained by appointment from party leaders who recognized his loyalty and ability as a

21. Ibid., p. 79.
22. Ibid., pp. 85–98.

political insider. Mondale's prepresidential career was an extraordinary combination of caution, party loyalty, and luck. Dropping out of the presidential race before the 1976 primaries and receiving the nod for the vice-presidency was for him a standard operating procedure.

Unlike Reagan, Mondale had had an almost uninterrupted sequence of elective offices but a dearth of campaign experience. Even as late as 1976, journalists noted his unusual awkwardness in front of people and his overly intense attention to organizational activity within the campaign. One reporter described him in 1976 as "a planner in rigid control of himself who yet had a campaign without strategy or a basic idea,"[23] which was also not a bad characterization of Mondale in 1984.

The Campaigns

Walter Mondale confronted what proved to be a high-hurdles race for the nomination in 1984, while Ronald Reagan, unlike his two predecessors in the presidency, had a clear track. Reflecting on the year's events after the election, Reagan pollster Richard Wirthlin joined those who found the beginning of Mondale's autumn defeat in his first primary contest. Even as he narrowly cleared most of the other primary (and caucus) hurdles to the nomination, he fell behind his Republican opponent in public opinion polls. By the finish line, the race was not even close. While some factors were beyond his control—among others, the state of the economy and the success of the Grenada invasion—Mondale himself constructed the most formidable hurdles. Many of his travails and some cause for his defeat rested on a conception of politics at odds with the new political environment.

The Mondale Campaign

Walter Mondale had never run for office as a challenger before, but this did not deter him from adopting the campaign strategy that had served him well when he was helping to build the Democratic Farmer-Labor party and attaining his first political offices. By early 1983 he had settled upon a plan to stitch together the disparate elements of the Democratic party. He vigorously sought and received the endorsements

23. Arthur T. Hadley, *The Invisible Primary* (Prentice-Hall, 1976), pp. 29–30.

of old and new constituency groups—most prominently the AFL-CIO, the National Education Association, and the National Organization of Women. Later he solicited the support of other less well organized and more specifically Democratic constituencies as he encountered them in various states' primaries. He also lined up support among the official delegates selected by members of Congress and others among the party's elite. With a big lead over the field of Democratic aspirants in name recognition and support, this seemed all Mondale had to do. The nomination appeared his for the asking. During 1983 the closest he came to a campaign slogan was his frequently repeated comment, "I am ready."

Looking back on the folly of what came to be called the juggernaut strategy, one campaign aide remarked, "We did politics for a year; our message was straw poll winner, endorsee—not crusader for tax reform or what have you."[24] Another added, "We fed our own perceived weaknesses. Mondale's caution is a perceived weakness. . . . And yet we played everything so cautiously that we did nothing to dispel the weakness."[25]

To be fair, caution and consensus (read issueless) politics made some sense for the front-runner who had an advantage to conserve. The strategy looked promising in the fall of 1983 before Reagan's popularity began its sustained ascent and when it seemed that a united Democratic party could win the election. The juggernaut approach could be expected to mesmerize the press and even opponents in the primaries who could be criticized for undermining party unity. Nonetheless, going into the New Hampshire primary, there were signs that the risks of such a strategy were enormous.

To run as a winner and to fail at any point to fully live up to that appeal makes a candidate disposable. The Mondale campaign had seen this threat materialize the previous spring when, on the basis of his simple announcement of candidacy, Senator John Glenn had soared briefly ahead of Mondale in Democratic voters' candidate preference polls.[26]

Then in New Hampshire, Gary Hart came from nowhere in the polls

24. Elizabeth Drew, "A Political Journal," *New Yorker,* October 29, 1984, p. 132.

25. Bernard Weinraub reports another adviser pointing out that "the candidate's natural reserve and caution [led] to his selection of staff members who largely [mirrored] his own personal caution." "How Mondale Faltered," *New York Times,* March 8, 1984.

26. Robert Shogan, "Doubts Persist about Mondale Campaign," *Los Angeles Times,* August 21, 1983.

to score a sizable upset victory (39 percent to Mondale's 29 percent).[27] The juggernaut came to a screeching halt. Support for Mondale crumbled throughout New England, and Hart won Vermont, Maine, and Massachusetts in short order. A Mondale effort to get out the vote for the Maine caucuses found that 44 percent of his recently safe supporters had switched to Hart.

More damaging in the long run, however, was Mondale's image as a politician who curried the favor of special interests. The coalitional approach requires promises to the organized, and these expressed or implied commitments provided a target for primary opponents. When Gary Hart quipped, "It's between two types of candidates—the more beholden versus the less beholden," Mondale had no effective counter. After all, he had been trotting out his growing list of endorsements. When Hart challenged Mondale in a nationally televised debate to name a single issue on which he had disagreed with the leaders of the AFL-CIO, Mondale demurred, not because he could not have named any but because he felt it unseemly to criticize friends and coalition supporters publicly.

The campaign knew early on, or should have, that whatever tangible assets union endorsements offered, they also imposed significant if more diffuse costs. The campaign must have had poll results comparable to the one produced in a mid-1983 Gallup survey that found twice as many respondents saying that a union endorsement would make them less likely rather than more likely to vote for the candidate. Among independents, to whom Mondale would eventually need to appeal, the percentages ran 37 and 14 with the rest saying it would not matter. The best result a union endorsement offered was a wash and this among Democratic partisans with whom an endorsed candidate would break even.[28] As Mondale traveled from state to state openly appealing to old and new Democratic constituencies and gaining their endorsements, he

27. One of Senator Hart's favorite techniques was to fly into a local media market and conduct a fifteen-minute airport press conference in which he would state his campaign themes and answer a few questions from the press. According to some media consultants, this gave him greater control over his exposure on the local and network news than Mondale's stump speeches and lengthy news conferences. See Clendinen, "The Medium and Mondale."

28. The item administered to a national sample in mid-May 1983 read, "Labor unions are going to announce their choice of a presidential candidate before next year's presidential primaries. Would the endorsement by labor unions of a presidential candidate make you more likely or less likely to vote for that candidate?" *Gallup Report,* June 1983, p. 26.

did so in full view of the national television audience. If anyone were missing the point, John Glenn and Gary Hart were also on television educating him.

The coalitional strategy also failed the candidate by leaving him without a message, a "theme with a capital T" in the words of one media professional, with which to appeal to voters beyond the core of the Democratic constituency. For the swollen ranks of independents, for young voters, for recent immigrants to the fast-growing Sun Belt, and for white southerners, the Mondale campaign offered little. One late-arriving adviser recruited to come up with a theme for the campaign warned advisers that putting Humpty-Dumpty (the New Deal coalition) together again would not suffice.

Once again the problem was not lack of information or absence of foresight. Early in 1983 the campaign had "staffed out" the creation of an overarching theme, "the speech," with a concise message that, repeated often enough, might catch the imagination of voters. No such message or speech appeared. When asked why not by journalist Elizabeth Drew in June 1984, Mondale responded, "I'm still working on it." He then offered the following excuse: "You see, what I tried to do was campaign for the Democratic Party against Mr. Reagan. . . . Hart spent that year campaigning against me. Nearly knocked me out. So I had to then back up and start debating Gary Hart, and that's what I've done."[29] After Hart was out of the way, however, a message still failed to materialize.

The underlying reason Walter Mondale failed to run a thematic campaign with a broad national appeal lay with the candidate and the way he viewed campaigning. Mondale never cared for inspirational rhetoric or slogans. He ridiculed them as "dawnisms," as in "a new age is dawning." The concept of "the speech" violated his sensibilities about what an audience should be told. Seemingly impervious to the network cameras and the need to project a coherent message, he insisted upon telling his local audiences, frequently a convention of like-minded individuals, why his positions on the issues and not Reagan's were in their best interest. Different local audiences received different messages, while the national television audience viewed them all. Addressing this matter, one campaign aide declared him to be "the last of the great stump orators," a backhanded compliment implying more than anything else

29. Elizabeth Drew, "A Political Journal," *New Yorker,* June 25, 1984, p. 91.

that his approach was unsuited for television.[30] A telltale sign of Mondale's proclivities is that he did not bother to monitor the networks' coverage until several weeks before the election. Gary Hart's media consultant, Raymond Strother, concluded that Mondale "hit the transition between two different styles of campaigning."[31]

The coalitional strategy worked to the extent that Mondale did manage to win the nomination. Arguably, without strong organizational backing, particularly in caucus states, he might never have survived the New Hampshire disaster. But the costs were enormous. Throughout the spring and summer, national opinion surveys and studies of focus groups pointed to his growing image as a politican catering to special interests and harboring old ideas. Just as McGovern's primary campaign had complicated his general election strategy twelve years earlier, so Mondale's campaign for the nomination generated so many "negatives"—to use the vernacular of consultants—that it was unclear what the candidate should do after the convention.

Nowhere was the lack of direction more evident than in the use the campaign made of television. Again the candidate and his strategy conspired to prevent movement in the direction the professionals of electronic campaigning wished. Early in the campaign it was decided that Mondale was too formal for television. Despite the subsequent pleadings of Governor Mario M. Cuomo of New York and Democratic media consultant David Garth, the candidate never appeared prominently in his commercials. He also intentionally stayed away from network talk shows.

Identifying a message that was at once credible, positive, and damaging to President Reagan's image proved impossible. A particular approach—such as a frontal assault on Reagan—would be tried, and when it failed to register in the polls, a new one would be trotted out—say, a portentous rendering of "the Republican future"—only to be shortly discarded as well. As the campaign vacillated, pollsters and media consultants were shuffled in and out of the inner circle according to their strategic prescriptions. This only exacerbated the problem of finding and charting a steady course, any course.

One participant in these strategy sessions summed up the result: "It's a classic example of building a horse by committee. What you end up

30. Elizabeth Drew, "A Political Journal," *New Yorker*, December 3, 1984, pp. 100–75.
31. Clendinen, "The Medium and Mondale."

with is a lame camel with four humps." In September, for instance, five commercials were created, two by one advertising firm that closed with a "Think about 1985" tag line and three from another firm that emphasized a positive message. One featured highlights of Mondale with Ferraro, who was shown talking about the American dream. Another stressed the war-and-peace issue and Reagan's failure to meet the leader of the Soviet Union. The others dealt in some fashion with the "Reagan debt."[32] Despite the expenditure of nearly $30 million on television advertisements, the media campaign failed to portray Mondale as anything other than what Glenn, Hart, and Reagan had commonly said about him. Nor did it offer the public a consistent message.

The Reagan Campaign

Just as Mondale's deficit in the polls had destabilized his campaign, Reagan's continuing surplus of support rendered his campaign a model of consistency and clarity. While Mondale was still searching for convention votes, Reagan, who had had not even a hint of a primary challenge, was settling upon his fall campaign strategy. By spring the first commercial portraying America at work and play had been produced. At one screening, the president viewed a similarly positive film that was to be broadcast on prime-time television at the Republican National Convention and would later be incorporated into commercials. *Newsweek* recorded the response:

> When he saw the Tuesday Team's masterwork, an 18-minute film used first to introduce him at the convention and later as the heart of a 30-minute, three-network telecast, tears sprang to his eyes. 'I don't think I'm supposed to cry,' he said, but he did, a bit, during a three-hankie sequence of him in Normandy eulogizing the men who fell on D-Day. Mike Deaver was weeping, and two Secret Service men turned away from the screen, hiding their emotions. The mood around Reagan then was so buoyant that some negative commercials ridiculing Mondale were dry-iced for use only if necessary. *He* could do red-telephone ads if he wanted. Reagan's would be upbeat and confident, in his own image.[33]

After the Republican convention and extensive marketing research, the campaign decided upon a slogan consistent with the positive appeal

32. Jane Mayer, "Mondale Unveils Ads, but Campaign Is Divided over Marketing Strategy," *Wall Street Journal*, September 13, 1984.
33. "Making of a Landslide," *Newsweek* special edition, November–December 1984, p. 90.

of the commercials: "Leadership That's Working." Throughout the fall, even after the setback from the first debate, the campaign stood fast to this theme.

Intent upon conserving the candidate's lead in the polls, the Reagan campaign also decided early to expose the president to television only in controlled settings. News conferences were eliminated after July, impromptu interviews with reporters were kept to one-liners, and the president's appearances were designed with an eye toward the national audience.[34] The technique left reporters grumbling, but it has been judged so successful that many observers have wondered aloud if in fact this was "the lesson of 1984." According to a former White House press secretary, "No doubt, future administrations are going to school on this."[35]

Whatever the differences in Mondale's and Reagan's political circumstances, and they were considerable, the campaigns were highly compatible with the personal styles of the two politicians. Tracts like *The Selling of the President* and "How Reagan Seduced Us" miss the point.[36] No one fabricates the public persona of such politicians. Walter Mondale and Ronald Reagan waged different campaigns because they are different kinds of politicians.

The Lesson of 1984 for Campaigning

In 1984 Gary Hart joined the fraternity of presidential contenders who succeeded beyond anyone's expectations by running as outsiders. Recent practitioners of the strategy had literally been outsiders; neither Carter nor Reagan had his reputation tarnished by ever working in Washington. Outsider status is usually a more inclusive term referring less to residency than to one's standing with the party or governmental establishment. What precisely this establishment means is left to the candidate to define. It may be as specific as Eugene McCarthy's Lyndon Johnson or as general as Reagan's "bumbling bureaucrats" and

34. Jane Mayer, "Reagan Team Is Most Successful Ever in Media Manipulation," *Wall Street Journal*, October 12, 1984.

35. Ibid.; and Jack W. Germond and Jules Witcover, "On Reagan's Second-Term Plans, The Public 'Ain't Heard Nothin' Yet,'" *National Journal*, vol. 16 (November 10, 1984), p. 2176.

36. McGinnis, *The Selling of the President 1968*; and Mark Hetsgaard, "How Reagan Seduced Us," *Village Voice*, September 18, 1984.

"spendthrift politicians" who occupy the "puzzle palaces on the Potomac." For a Democrat to succeed as an outsider, organized labor must be included in the establishment.

Generally, the strategy plays better when a politican is competing against an opponent who occupies a credible insider's position. In 1972 George McGovern took apart Edmund Muskie in the early primaries and Hubert Humphrey in the later ones. Both appeared to have labor's support. Gary Hart could not have campaigned nearly as well on the ambiguous platform of new ideas and being less beholden if his adversary had not been so conspicuously beholden to the old ideas of the Democratic establishment. When newspapers around the country proclaimed, "It's Mr. Inside against Mr. Outside," Hart knew his campaign was succeeding.[37]

The outsider's route to the White House has become commonplace since McCarthy's 1968 innovation, and Gary Hart's campaign reinforced a lesson that many, including equally anonymous colleagues in the early caucuses and primaries, had already learned well. The significant departure of 1984, and its contribution to the education of future candidates, was the full realization of how weak front-running establishment candidates might be. Before the New Hampshire primary, nothing indicated the ways in which Mondale's campaign was deficient and Hart's was not. Mondale had name recognition, organization, and money; Hart was weak in all three. Yet beginning with New Hampshire, Hart won five primaries and caucuses in quick succession. Mondale's supporters had even rigged the primary and caucus schedules to create a rush of elections, thereby minimizing an outsider's chances of developing momentum with a string of early victories. It did not appear to matter. If anything, it looked as though the heavy March schedule of primaries would give Hart the nomination before anyone could stop him.

Hart's victories shocked Washington. "There's a general sense of fear because people don't know what's going on," *New Republic* editor and former Carter speechwriter Hendrik Hertzberg was quoted as saying. "You can feel a terrible shaking of the earth as new conventional wisdom struggles to be born." After sampling other Washingtonians' assessments, *New York Times* reporter Steven R. Weisman concluded, "Mr. Hart himself is widely dismissed as a fad, like Cabbage Patch dolls,

37. William Schneider, "It's Mr. Inside against Mr. Outside," *Los Angeles Times,* March 11, 1984.

or someone who benefited by fluke from the failure of Mr. Mondale."[38] Unlike the lessons of elections past, Mondale's near defeat in the primaries and the damage this and his continued strategy created for the general election reflected the deficiency of insider status. Democratic candidates will continue to address gatherings of the party's core constituency and to solicit their support, but in the future they will be careful to preserve some distance.

Now, before the next presidential campaign begins, it is too early to detect how aspiring politicians, Democrats and Republicans, will express the lessons of 1984. Certainly, they will follow Mondale's advice and pay careful attention to television as they groom themselves and their themes for the modern strategic environment.[39] But if the candidates are not yet on stage, many of the supernumeraries are. If their pronouncements can be taken as indicative, the effects of the Mondale campaign will certainly transcend Reagan's relection. Consider some of the early evidence. Within a week after the election, Democratic state chairmen met at a Virgin Islands retreat to ponder the party's future. According to one correspondent, the delegates were "absorbing a hard lesson from the comparison of Reagan and Mondale . . . [and] talking of the need to choose a candidate [for party chairman] who is effective on television as well as substantive on the issues." Governor Bob Graham echoed the sentiments of others present when he said, "We need to select a national chairman who will be the party's spokesman on television on the issues of the day," adding that without it, "the response goes to the congressional leadership . . . [which] is going to be older, Washington-based, and Washington-oriented."[40] Equally revealing, when Paul Kirk, an associate of Ted Kennedy who had the support of organized labor, was finally elected to be the new chairman of the Democratic National Committee, he used his first news conference to dissociate himself from any "special interest."

38. "Hart Successes Leave Capital Reeling," *New York Times,* March 8, 1984.

39. The only "candidate" to come forward so far is Governor Bruce Babbitt of Arizona, who announced in mid-March 1985 that in order to explore new challenges he would not be a candidate for reelection or a Senate seat. Babbitt began his quest by chastising some of his colleagues as reflecting "the party of the past" and received coaching on his oratorical style. See Robert Lindsey, "Babbitt of Arizona Eyes 'Dark Horse' Bid for Presidency in '88," *New York Times,* March 17, 1985.

40. James R. Dickensen, "It Seems the Democrats Can Win Anything but the White House," *Washington Post* national weekly edition, November 19, 1984; and Fay S. Joyce, "Leaders Meet in Virgin Islands to Ponder Party's Future," *New York Times,* November 16, 1984.

When the unions found themselves suddenly cast as the foremost of the special interests, they were similarly responsive to the new realities of Democratic politics. At the winter meeting of the AFL-CIO in February 1985, Walter Mondale conferred with union political specialists on candidate marketing and the use of television. Lane Kirkland, president of the federation, later told reporters that Mondale stressed "mastery over the television tube," and added that the unions also planned to use television more effectively.[41]

The Lesson of 1984 for Governing

Campaigning for office and governing draw upon the same conceptions of politics. They always have. In the nineteenth century, presidential candidates were the manufactured products of political machines whose members gathered at conventions to identify an acceptable nominee. Acceptability had something to do with electability and a lot to do with potential fairness in distributing patronage. Frequently, aspiring politicians with established national reputations were ruled out because of their association with a region or some state's party organization. Conventions could thus become deadlocked, and dark horses occasionally emerged with the nomination. In office these presidents were typically weak, but they suited the needs of the state party organizations that wanted someone at the patronage levers who would follow established protocols in distributing federal largesse to the hinterland.

Twentieth-century presidents have been activist figures who were expected to lead their party to victory and to build governing coalitions. In campaigning or in governing, these presidents have been expected to bargain and negotiate their way to success. With their state delegations bound to them by unit rules, the heads of state party organizations, who were in the words of Thomas Reed "governed by the base desire to win elections," brokered candidates. As late as 1968 the leading textbook on the subject noted that "decision-making at conventions is ordinarily coordinated by a process of bargaining among party leaders. . . . Each leader represents a state party or faction within a state which is independently organized and not subject to control by outsiders. . . . In order to mobilize enough nationwide support to elect a President, party

41. William Serrin, "Labor's 'Thank You,'" *New York Times*, February 20, 1985.

leaders from a large number of consitutencies must be satisfied with the nominee.''[42] During the middle decades of the twentieth century, a highly popular mlitary hero, Dwight Eisenhower, was nominated, but presidential timber consisted mostly of those with established political careers, and increasingly, careers located in Washington.

In office, presidential leadership became synonymous with bargaining. Presidential power is the "power to bargain," Richard E. Neustadt taught a generation of presidents and those who study them.[43] Gone were the patronage-driven organizations and the continuous, intricate partisan adjustments necessitated by insatiable appetites for contracts and jobs. In their place came politicians liberated by the reforms of the Progressive Era who occupied autonomous offices and shared publics with the president. Party loyalty gave the president the chance to rebuild his national electoral coalition in Washington but not much more than that. The differing institutional perspectives, time limits of office, and constituencies guaranteed that his aspirations and authority would be checked by those of other politicians who controlled critical levers of the governmental system. Arthur Vandenberg, Sam Rayburn, Wilbur Mills, John Foster Dulles, Robert Kerr, J. Edgar Hoover, and Lyndon Johnson, among others, constituted powers with whom the president *had* to keep company. As Neustadt advised in 1960, "Their vantage points confront his own; their power tempers his."[44] It was a system in which the requirements for winning office and governing were well suited to Walter Mondale's style of politics, one in which success flowed from satisfying the legitimate but disparate interests of diverse constituencies.

As we enter the last decades of the twentieth century, these political arrangements appear to be giving way to a new order. Building coalitions through quiet diplomacy counts for less and mobilizing public opinion

42. Nelson W. Polsby and Aaron B. Wildavsky, *Presidential Elections,* 2d ed. (Scribner's, 1968), pp. 80–81.

43. *Presidential Power,* 2d ed. (Wiley, 1976), throughout. Stating the matter more generally, Robert A. Dahl and Charles E. Lindblom wrote, "The politician is, above all, the man whose career depends upon the successful negotiation of bargains. To win office he must negotiate electoral alliances. To satisfy his electoral alliance he must negotiate alliances with other legislators and with administrators, for his control depends upon negotiation. Most of his time is consumed in bargaining. This is the skill he cultivates; it is the skill that distinguishes the master politician from the political failure. . . . The politician is as much the human embodiment of a bargaining society as any single role-player can be." See *Politics, Economics and Welfare* (Harper and Row, 1953), p. 333.

44. Neustadt, *Presidential Power,* p. 28.

for more. This change is pervasive. Virtually no aspect of relations among Washington politicians and bureaucrats has remained unaffected. It is as true for the way presidential candidates seek the nomination and campaign for office as it is for the way they seek to govern.

Appropriately, the causes are manifold. Reforms have removed the presidential nomination from the convention, thereby disenfranchising party leaders. The party's choice now depends on a lengthy sequence of state primaries and caucuses. Under this system the candidates best qualified to win nomination are by temperament and experience more attuned to the moods of public opinion than to the needs of other politicians and the representatives of mediating organizations. They are more skilled in using television than in bargaining. Not only do these talents have little to do with years of Washington experience, they may be at odds with it. Recent successful participants in the reformed selection system have actively advertised themselves as outsiders. When possible they have stressed their non-Washington origins.[45] So in 1985 Senate majority leader Howard Baker retired from office to have four years free to prepare a presidential bid and perhaps to dissociate himself from the Washington community.[46]

Fresh from an extended and successful stint of campaigning, an outsider enters the White House probably as uninterested in playing by pluralist rules as he is ill prepared. For him the choice between promoting his policies in Washington through negotiating with other powerful politicians and going over their heads to enlist popular support may be an easy one. And going public is easy because it is familiar. Under the reformed nomination system, few candidates are likely to win the presidency without first prevailing in a dozen or more preliminary elections. Whatever the intent of the reforms, they give us presidents who believe they can summon popular support to a degree prereform incumbents could not have imagined. Going public represents little more than an extension of the process that placed the outsider in the White House.

Evidence available in the performances of our two most recent presidents suggests that the mythic "the people" has become a motive

45. Nelson W. Polsby describes the reforms and convincingly argues their effects on the kinds of presidents we elect in *Consequences of Party Reform* (Oxford University Press, 1983).

46. Richard E. Cohen, "As a Launching Pad for the Presidency, Congress Isn't What It Used to Be," *National Journal,* vol. 12 (March 8, 1980), pp. 400–04.

force of presidential politics. It is manifest in the modern presidents' extensive itineraries of domestic and foreign travel, in the ever growing number of speeches they deliver to special publics outside of Washington, in the amount of time they spend on prime-time television.[47] After examining the routines of the Reagan White House, journalist Sidney Blumenthal concluded,

> Once elected, candidates have to deal with shaky coalitions held together by momentary moods, not stable party structures. They then must try to govern through permanent campaigns. This is something more than the selling of the President—even of a telegenic President able to project an attractive image. It has become an inescapable necessity for Reagan, and probably for his successors.
>
> The President's strategists are at the center of the new political age. At the end of the day, they become spectators, seeing their performance tested by the contents of the television news programs. For the Reagan White House, every night is election night on television.[48]

There is also good reason to suspect that outsiders will find today's Washington more congenial than they might have in the past. It is a community governed less by leaders and more by the requirements of independent, egocentric actors. Subpresidential coalitions founded largely upon congressional subcommittees and executive agencies have given way to more casual and voluntary associations such as congressional caucuses, work groups, and networks of policy analysts. For the president who attempts via bargaining to assemble a coalition across a broad institutional landscape, these changes are unattractive. Washington has become a large city in which the number of bargains necessary to secure others' support has increased dramatically. At the same time, their very number may make coordinated resistance to a president's public initiatives more difficult. Consequently these looser coalitions may well be more susceptible to the political winds that a president steeped in the use of public opinion can stir up.

The direction recent campaigns have been taking presidential leadership is not entirely new, of course. Well before the reforms in candidate selection, presidents had begun to realize the merits of prime-time television and travel to various parts of the country in dealing with the powers in Washington. The candidate selection reforms and their products—men like Jimmy Carter and Ronald Reagan—have only accelerated

47. Kernell, *Going Public*, chap. 3.
48. "Marketing the President," *New York Times Magazine*, September 13, 1981, p. 118.

the emergence of a modern style of presidential leadership. While the campaigns of 1972 and 1976 contributed to this development by demonstrating that outsider approaches to the White House are feasible, the 1984 election contributed in its own way by demonstrating that insider approaches may no longer be.

CHAPTER SIX

The Republican Advantage in Campaign Finance

GARY C. JACOBSON

THE 1980 election initiated major changes in American national politics. It was a triumph for Republicans in general and conservatives in particular. A conservative Republican, Ronald Reagan, won the White House; Republicans took control of the Senate and gained enough House seats for the coalition of Republicans and conservative Democrats to assume working control.

The election transformed the political agenda. Issues were reframed in terms that reflected conservative Republican concerns: not whether, but how much to pare domestic social programs, how rapidly to increase defense spending, how deeply to cut personal and corporate taxes, how completely to deregulate business. The Reagan administration quickly won striking victories on some of the new agenda's central policy items. Following the 1982 election, an enlarged Democratic majority in the House limited further conservative initiatives, but the range of feasible policy alternatives continued to reflect Republican dominance.

The 1984 election confirmed that 1980 was no mere aberration. Reagan was reelected by a landslide, winning forty-nine states and making deep inroads into several groups once firmly attached to the Democrats' New Deal coalition: white southerners, Catholics, and blue-collar workers.[1]

Alan Ehrenhalt and Michael Malbin provided helpful comments on the manuscript.
1. Rhodes Cook, "Reagan's Landslide Shatters Fading Democratic Coalition," *Congressional Quarterly Weekly Report*, vol. 42 (November 17, 1984), pp. 2939–42; and David Treadwell, "Longtime Democratic Coalition Splinters," *Los Angeles Times*, November 8, 1984.

Republicans were less successful in congressional elections. They lost a net two Senate seats, though they retained majority control, and added fourteen House seats, falling ten short of their 1980 totals. But these mixed results understate Republican strength at the congressional level in 1984. Most of the vulnerable senators were Republicans. Democrats had entertained hopes of unseating as many as six incumbents and retaking the Senate; they defeated only Roger Jepson of Iowa and Charles H. Percy of Illinois and came close in but one other contest (for Jesse Helms's seat in North Carolina).

The Republican share of the national House vote in 1984 was actually about as high as it had been in 1980, and the parties split the vote almost equally across all contested races;[2] only the absence of strong challengers in many likely races limited Republican gains in the House.[3] The location of those gains is significant, however; Republicans added eight seats in the South, three of which are in North Carolina and four in Texas, and also took three seats in heavily blue-collar districts in the North.[4] Most important, polls consistently showed a sharp increase in popular identification with the Republican party; on election day, at least, Republicans were approaching parity with Democrats.[5] Despite the poorer congressional numbers, 1984 produced more signs of a realigning shift toward the Republican party than had 1980.

The 1984 election results ensure that political battles will continue to be waged along the lines laid down after 1980. They also suggest that political currents associated with the Reagan ascendancy run deep. American political life appears to be undergoing its most thorough restructuring since the New Deal was introduced fifty years ago. If not a classical party realignment, the new arrangement of political forces and policy alternatives emerging in the 1980s may represent an equally fundamental political shift. This essay examines one important source of this transformation: changes in the regulations governing campaign

2. Dan Balz, "The GOP as Majority Party?" *The Washington Post*, national weekly edition, January 28, 1985.

3. Gary C. Jacobson, "Congress: Politics after a Landslide without Coattails," in Michael Nelson, ed., *The Elections of 1984* (Washington D.C.: CQ Press, 1985), pp. 218–20.

4. Rob Gurwitt, "GOP Disappointed with Gains in the House," *Congressional Quarterly Weekly Report*, vol. 42 (November 10, 1984), pp. 2898–99.

5. William Schneider, "Incumbency Saved the Democrats This Time, but What about Next?" *Los Angeles Times*, November 11, l984; and Balz, "GOP as Majority Party."

financing instituted during the 1970s and the new electoral organizations and practices that emerged to exploit them. The essay explains how the new rules, enacted largely through the efforts of Democrats and liberals, permitted Republican party officials, New Right activists, and business corporations—major components of the Reagan alliance—to develop new ways to mobilize and deploy campaign resources. It also explores the effects of these changes on the conduct of national politics. And finally, it considers how evolving campaign finance practices affect the prospects for a Republican majority.

The Consequences of Campaign Finance Reform

The liberal Democrats and allied "public interest" groups that restructured the system of financing federal election campaigns in the 1970s inadvertently helped sow the seeds of their own eclipse. Steep increases in campaign spending during the 1960s had generated both ideological and practical problems. Because money is distributed so unequally, its growing importance as a political resource threatened the liberal ideal of democratic equality; to the degree that campaign money was supplied by people pursuing narrow "special interests," it was thought to subvert the "public interest." On the practical side, members of Congress felt increasingly menaced by the specter of lavishly funded opponents. At the very least, high-spending challengers would compel members to step up their own fund-raising, a chore most of them loathed.[6]

The solution, embodied in the Federal Election Campaign Act (FECA) of 1971 and its 1974 amendments, was to expose and restrict the flow of campaign money in all its aspects. The FECA required full disclosure of all campaign contributions and expenditures. It imposed limits on contributions by individuals, interest groups, and political parties; on candidates' contributions to their own campaigns; and on expenditures made independently of any campaign. It also placed ceilings on campaign spending in primary and general election campaigns for federal office. Provision was made for full public funding of general election campaigns for president and for partial public funding, through matching grants, of

6. Gary C. Jacobson, *Money in Congressional Elections* (Yale University Press, 1980), pp. 164–73.

presidential primary campaigns. A Federal Election Commission (FEC) was established to enforce the law.[7]

Although the FECA achieved several of its purposes (for example, adequate public disclosure of campaign finance transactions), it failed signally to control the flow of campaign money, limit campaign costs, or diminish the financial role of special interests. Adverse Supreme Court rulings, the resourcefulness of campaign finance professionals—as skilled as tax lawyers in exploiting loopholes—and unintended consequences of the law itself combined to frustrate these objectives. The Court, in *Buckley* v. *Valeo*,[8] overturned as contrary to the First Amendment the limits on campaign spending (except for presidential candidates who accept federal funds), on contributions by candidates to their own campaigns, and on money spent independently of any campaign. The Court's ruling, along with other opportunities provided under the FECA's rules, offered fertile ground for the development of new campaign finance activities. Thus a legal avenue can now be found for virtually any money anyone wants to put into electoral politics.[9]

The FECA's rules governing nonparty political action committees (PACs) and national party campaign committees have turned out to be particularly conducive to innovation. Both types of organizations have been permitted to flourish, and in both cases this has worked primarily to the advantage of Republicans. The principal reason is simply that Republican party officials, conservative ideologues, and business corporations have exploited the FECA far more imaginatively and vigorously than have the Democrats and their allies; parties and groups in opposition naturally have a greater incentive to innovate. But in addition, both the regulations and the campaign finance practices they promote are, in a variety of ways, very well suited to the character and needs of Republicans and conservative groups. The campaign finance system thus contributed to the conjunction of motive, means, and opportunity that produced the political shifts of the 1980s.

Political Action Committees

Interest groups—labor unions, corporations, trade associations—had been involved in financing election campaigns for decades, but group

7. Congressional Quarterly, *Dollar Politics*, 3d ed. (CQ Press, 1982), p. 13.
8. 424 U.S.1 (1976).
9. Thomas B. Edsall, "The Ins and Outs of the American Political Money Machine," *Washington Post*, national weekly edition, December 12, 1983.

Table 6-1. *Number of Registered Political Action Committees, 1974–84*

Type of committee	1974	1976	1978	1980	1982	1984
Corporate	89	433	784	1,204	1,467	1,682
Labor	201	224	217	297	380	394
Trade, membership, health[a]	318	489	451	574	628	698
Nonconnected	...	...	165	378	746	1,053
Cooperative	...	...	12	42	47	52
Corporation without stock	...	...	24	56	103	130
Total	608	1,146	1,653	2,551	3,371	4,009

Source: "FEC Says PAC's Top 4,000 for 1984," Federal Election Commission, press release, January 28, 1985.
a. Includes all noncorporate and nonlabor PACs through December 31, 1976.

participation was generally inhibited by its doubtful legal status and the subterfuges this necessitated. The FECA encouraged the formation of PACs by giving nonparty committees a legitimate role in financing campaigns and clear guidelines on how it was to be performed. Through rapid diffusion of innovation, PACs have proliferated. The increase in the number of registered PACs between 1974 and 1984 is shown in table 6-1. Between 1974 and 1982, the most recent election for which complete data are available, total PAC contributions grew by 240 percent in real dollars, and the share of all campaign funds supplied by PACs increased from 17 percent to 31 percent for House candidates and from 11 percent to 18 percent for Senate candidates.[10] Preliminary data indicate that PAC activities continued to expand in 1984; total PAC contributions through October 17 were 29 percent above those at the same point in the 1982 campaign, and the PAC share of all money contributed to congressional candidates was also higher.[11]

It is also evident from table 6-1 that growth has not been uniform across categories of PACs. Corporate, trade, and nonconnected PACs have multiplied far more rapidly than labor PACs. The data in table 6-2 show how changes in the distribution of PAC contributions to congressional candidates reflect these different growth rates. Labor PACs once accounted for half of all PAC contributions; they now account for less

10. Gary C. Jacobson, "Money in the 1980 and 1982 Congressional Elections," in Michael J. Malbin, ed., *Money and Politics in the United States* (Washington, D.C.: American Enterprise Institute; Chatham, N.J.: Chatham House, 1984), pp. 42, 39.

11. Computed from data in Michael J. Malbin and Thomas W. Skladony, "Campaign Finance, 1984: A Preliminary Analysis of House and Senate Campaign Receipts," paper prepared for the American Enterprise Institute Public Policy Week, December 2, 1984, table 1.

Table 6-2. *The Growth of PAC Contributions to Congressional Candidates, 1974–82*
Millions of dollars; numbers in parentheses are percents

Type of PAC contribution	1974	1976	1978	1980	1982
Labor	6.3	8.2	10.3	13.2	20.2
	(50)	(36)	(29)	(24)	(24)
Corporate	2.5	7.1	9.8	19.2	27.4
	(20)	(31)	(28)	(35)	(33)
Trade, membership, health	2.3	4.5	11.5	15.9	21.7
	(18)	(20)	(33)	(29)	(26)
Other	1.4	2.8	3.5	6.9	13.9
	(11)	(12)	(10)	(12)	(17)
Total contributions	12.5	22.6	35.1	55.2	83.2
Total adjusted for inflation (1982 = 1.00)	24.5	38.4	51.9	64.7	83.2

Source: Gary C. Jacobson, "Money in the 1980 and 1982 Congressional Elections," in Michael J. Malbin, ed., *Money and Politics in the United States* (Washington, D.C.: American Enterprise Institute; Chatham, N.J.: Chatham House, 1984), p. 42. Percentages are rounded.

than one-quarter, having been surpassed by both corporate and trade PACs.

These shifts matter because different types of PACs have different predilections for the party and incumbency status of recipients. Although the objectives and strategies of different PACs within any of the FEC's broad categories are diverse, general patterns of behavior are readily apparent from aggregate data on contributions. Labor PACs favor Democrats overwhelmingly and are the only significant source of PAC funds for nonincumbent Democrats. Corporate PACs usually prefer Republicans for ideological reasons, but often also have immediate policy objectives and so, on practical grounds, are willing to contribute to Democrats holding positions of influence in Congress.[12] Thus they contribute to incumbents of both parties, but only to Republican nonincumbents.

DISTRIBUTION OF PAC FUNDS. The extent of the generosity of PACs to Republican challengers depends on the likelihood of victory; they avoid opposing (and thus angering) Democratic incumbents when the odds on defeating them are too long but will take some risks by supporting

12. Gary C. Jacobson, "Parties and PACs in Congressional Elections," in Lawrence C. Dodd and Bruce I. Oppenheimer, eds., *Congress Reconsidered*, 3d ed. (CQ Press, 1985), pp. 141–44.

challengers when circumstances seem more promising. The same tends to be true of trade associations, though they are even more strongly biased in favor of incumbents. Only nonconnected PACs, many of which pursue ideological objectives and so care more about altering the ideological makeup of Congress than about influencing specific policies, give most of their funds to nonincumbent candidates. Up to the end of 1980, most of this money had gone to Republicans, but, galvanized by the Reagan administration, liberal groups have begun to mobilize to redress this imbalance.[13]

Because of these biases, the expansion of PAC activity in financing congressional campaigns has clearly favored Republicans at the expense of Democrats. The Democrats' initial advantage in PAC funds has nearly disappeared. In the early 1970s Democrats received about two-thirds of PAC funds; in the most recent elections their share has been little more than half;[14] they retain an edge only because they have kept their House majority and most PACs are partial to incumbents.

In addition, Republicans benefit from a more efficient distribution of PAC money. Campaign funds are far more important to congressional challengers and candidates for open seats than to incumbents, because the marginal returns on campaign spending are so much greater for nonincumbents. The challenger's spending, in particular, is strongly related to his or her share of the vote; on the average, the challenger's vote increases by about 3 percentage points for every $100,000 spent. Statistically, the amount spent by the incumbent is unrelated to the vote.[15] PAC and other campaign contributions are most likely to help a party add congressional seats when they are put into campaigns of nonincumbents in close races.

Democrats receive more than half of all PAC money, but a very large percentage of it goes to incumbents, who frequently do not need it (because they do not face a serious challenge), rather than to challengers

13. Steven Pressman, "Nuclear Freeze Groups Focus on Candidates," *Congressional Quarterly Weekly Report*, vol. 42 (May 5, 1984), pp. 1021–24; Adam Clymer, "Democrats Gain in Business PAC Funds," *New York Times*, November 6, 1984; and Steven Pressman, "Special Interests Focused on Influencing the 1984 Elections," *Congressional Quarterly Weekly Report*, vol. 42 (February 18, 1984), pp. 295–300.

14. Joseph E. Cantor, *Political Action Committees*, Report 82-92GOV (Washington, D.C.: Congressional Research Service, 1981), table 18; and *Federal Election Commission Record*, vol. 10 (March 1984), p. 11.

15. Gary C. Jacobson, "Money and Votes Reconsidered: Congressional Elections, 1972–1982," *Public Choice* (forthcoming).

or candidates for open seats, who almost always do. This problem was especially noticeable in 1982, when many well-qualified Democratic congressional challengers were unable to take full advantage of the deep recession and Reagan's low standing in the polls because their campaigns were inadequately funded.[16] Corporate and trade association PACs were, as usual, generous to Democratic incumbents, but they offered very little help to Democrats not already in office. The labor and ideological PACs that did support nonincumbent Democrats were too few and too poor to supply the resources necessary for an adequate number of full-scale challenges. In a year when few Democratic incumbents were in danger and the party had fielded an unusually large number of qualified challengers, more than two-thirds of PAC contributions to House Democrats went to incumbents.[17]

PACs supported competitive Democratic challengers much more generously in 1984, and none suffered from inadequate funding. But the number of candidates in this category was very small; only eight Democratic challengers won 45 percent or more of the vote in 1984, compared with forty-seven in 1982.[18] It remains to be seen how efficiently Democratic PAC funds will be targeted in a good Democratic year when competitive Democratic challengers abound.

Republicans have been in a better position to take advantage of favorable trends in an election year because business-oriented PACs are willing to invest in the campaigns of Republican challengers when they expect the party to have a good year. In 1980, for example, corporate and trade association PACs contributed to the Republican sweep by giving heavily to Republicans opposing Democratic incumbents in both the House and the Senate. Republican challengers were also helped by

16. John J. Fialka and Dennis Farney, "Democrats Trail GOP in Ability to Direct Cash to Closest Races," *Wall Street Journal*, November 7, 1983; Adam Clymer, "Light Wallets Weigh Heavily on Democrats," *New York Times*, October 17, 1982; Dennis Farney and Brooks Jackson, "GOP Channels Money into Those Campaigns That Need It Most," *Wall Street Journal*, October 19, 1982; Gary C. Jacobson, "Party Organization and the Efficient Distribution of Campaign Resources: Republicans and Democrats in 1982," *Political Science Quarterly* (forthcoming); and Rob Gurwitt, "Democratic Campaign Panel: New Strategy and New Friends," *Congressional Quarterly Weekly Report*, vol. 41 (July 2, 1983), p. 1348.

17. Michael J. Malbin and Thomas W. Skladony, "Appendix: Selected Campaign Finance Data, 1974–1982," in Malbin, ed., *Money and Politics in the United States*, table A8.

18. Malbin and Skladony, "Campaign Finance, 1984," table 5; and Jacobson, "Party Organization."

conservative ideological PACs bent on transforming Congress by whole-sale replacement of Democrats and liberals with Republicans and con-servatives. Thus nearly half of the funds contributed by PACs to Republican House candidates in 1980 went to nonincumbents.[19] PAC biases and strategies worked to put a greater share of Republican PAC money into the hands of nonincumbents in close contests, where it was most likely to affect the outcome.

MOTIVES AND METHODS. It is not difficult to understand why groups favoring Republican candidates have taken greater advantage of the FECA than have those favoring Democrats. Losers in the policy wars have more reason to innovate. Corporations sought to reverse the trend toward more extensive government regulation of their activities. Reli-gious conservatives organized in response to adverse government deci-sions on abortion, school prayer, pornography, and other social issues. People alarmed by post-Vietnam trends sought stronger military and more aggressive foreign policies to deal with the Soviet Union and other foreign antagonists. The FECA offered the PAC as a ready way for conservative groups hoping to change existing policies to participate in electoral politics.[20] Their alliance with Republicans was natural, not only because Republicans were more likely to share their views, but also because candidates of the minority party were hungry for issues and resources that could be used to take votes from Democrats.

Coincidentally, the new technology of fund-raising has made it easier for ideological and single-issue PACs to operate successfully. Comput-erized direct-mail solicitation can raise large sums of money through small donations from millions of people scattered throughout the coun-try. Individuals with no connection beyond shared political ideas become identifiable groups, giving political organizers access to resources pre-viously inaccessible on a large scale.

Conservative ideologues and single-issue groups have been the most active and successful direct-mail entrepreneurs, partly because direct-mail solicitation is so well suited to their message and audience. Solicitors of small contributions face a classic collective goods problem;[21] no

19. Malbin and Skladony, "Appendix: Selected Campaign Finance Data," tables A17, A20.

20. See, for example, Margaret Ann Latus, "Assessing Ideological PACs: From Outrage to Understanding," in Malbin, ed., Money and Politics in the United States, pp. 142–71.

21. Mancur Olson, Jr., The Logic of Collective Action (Harvard University Press, 1965), pp. 5–52.

individual's contribution is large enough to make any difference, so no one has any instrumental incentive to contribute. The reward must come from the act of contributing itself rather than from its (vanishingly small) political consequences. This is why the most effective appeals are those that excite emotions of fear, anger, outrage, and righteous indignation and then encourage their expression through a donation. Groups taking strong stands on polarized issues are able to do this most effectively, particularly when they oppose current policy. The conservative ideological and policy groups known collectively as the New Right thus prospered during the 1970s. Similarly, the Reagan presidency has spurred the growth of peace, environmental, civil rights, and women's organizations, though they are not yet close to matching the organization and resources of the New Right.[22]

Conservative PACs and other organizations (the PAC is by no means the only mode of group involvement in election campaigns) have not been content merely to support congenial Republican candidates. Some recruit and train candidates (partly, of course, to ensure that the right kind of Republican takes the nomination). Others supply campaign workers and organize projects to reach special categories of voters.[23] Still others, most notably the National Conservative Political Action Committee (NCPAC), have tested the possibilities of independent campaigning.

NCPAC mounted harsh negative campaigns against prominent incumbent Democratic senators in 1980 and 1982 before the Republican nominee had even been chosen. Four of the six targeted in 1980 were defeated, and NCPAC gleefully claimed a share of the credit.[24] But in 1982 NCPAC was virtually shut out. Its campaigns seem to succeed only when combined with vigorous, well-financed challenges and favorable electoral conditions, so its independent contribution to Republican advances is futile to try to pin down. But its strident attacks have at least influenced the substance of campaigns, making political life more unpleasant and difficult for its liberal victims.

22. Larry Sabato, "Parties, PACs, and Independent Groups," in Thomas E. Mann and Norman J. Ornstein, eds., *The American Election of 1982* (American Enterprise Institute, 1983), pp. 88–90.

23. Latus, "Assessing Ideological PACs," p. 151; and Marjorie Randon Hershey, *Running for Office: The Political Education of Campaigners* (Chatham House, 1984), pp. 181–86.

24. Congressional Quarterly, *Dollar Politics*, p. 86; and Bill Keller, " 'New Right' Wants Credit for Democrats' Nov. 4 Losses but GOP, Others Don't Agree," *Congressional Quarterly Weekly Report*, vol. 38 (November 15, 1980), pp. 3372–73.

Table 6-3. *Independent Expenditures in the 1979–80
and 1981–82 Campaigns*
Dollars

Campaign	For candidate	Against candidate
1979–80		
President		
Jimmy Carter	45,869	245,611
Ronald Reagan	12,246,057	47,868
Senate		
Democrats	127,381	1,282,613
Republicans	261,678	12,430
House of Representatives		
Democrats	190,615	38,023
Republicans	410,478	45,132
1981–82		
Senate		
Democrats	142,512	3,119,593
Republicans	291,325	493,326
House of Representatives		
Democrats	229,477	825,524
Republicans	492,170	97,089

Source: For 1979–80, "FEC Study Shows Independent Expenditures Top $16 Million," Federal Election Commission, press release, November 29, 1981; for 1981–82, "Independent Spending Increases," Federal Election Commission, press release, March 22, 1983.

NCPAC also spent money to support Reagan's presidential bid in 1980, part of the $10.6 million spent independently by individuals and groups on Reagan's behalf.[25] In 1984 NCPAC spent an estimated $12 million all by itself on the presidential campaign ($10 million for Reagan, $2 million against Mondale).[26] Public financing was supposed to eliminate private spending in general election campaigns for president, but the *Buckley* decision left the door wide open to independent spending in any amount by anyone in any campaign. Republican supporters have, once again, done the most to exploit this loophole, as the data in table 6-3 indicate. A large Republican advantage in independent spending is evident for all federal offices.

The political currents merging in the Reagan coalition would certainly have found some form of organized expression; ideological entrepreneurs would have discovered some way to mobilize and channel the

25. Herbert E. Alexander, "Making Sense about Dollars in the 1980 Presidential Campaigns," in Malbin, ed., *Money and Politics in the United States*, p. 20.
26. Steven Pressman, "Interest Groups Net Few Changes at the Polls," *Congressional Quarterly Weekly Report*, vol. 42 (November 17, 1984), p. 2968.

various strands of popular dissatisfaction with the status quo. The rules governing PACs simply provided a particular framework for the development of organizational activity. Still, the framework was eminently suited to the purposes of emerging groups, and this coincidence of form and function surely contributed to the political changes of the Reagan years.

Party Committees

Although significant, the advances in campaign financing and organization achieved by Republicans through the expansion of PAC activity pale in comparison with what they have accomplished through the even more explosive growth of their national party campaign committees. Republican party officials took advantage of the FECA, new technologies of communication and information management, and the political environment to build a remarkably affluent and sophisticated national party apparatus. The Republican party now commands by far the strongest national party organization in American history. One sign: in the 1981–82 election cycle, Republican party committees raised more money than all PACs combined.[27]

LEGAL STATUS AND RESOURCES. The FECA's treatment of parties reflected Congress's unsettled disposition toward these organizations. From one perspective, the law regards a party as just another interest group: national and local party organizations are subject to the same direct contribution limits as PACs ($5,000 per candidate per primary or general election campaign) in House elections, for example. But the special character of parties was recognized by a provision in the law that allowed state and national party committees to spend additional money on behalf of candidates. Ceilings were also imposed on this "coordinated spending," as it is called, but they are higher and, unlike contribution limits, rise with inflation. The original limit of $10,000 set in 1974 for House campaigns had, by 1984, grown to $20,200. The ceiling on party spending for Senate candidates varies with the state's population; in 1984 it ranged from $40,400 in the five least populous states to $752,409 in California. The Senate limit applies to House candidates in states with a single House seat.[28]

---

27. Jacobson, "Parties and PACs," p. 136.
28. *Federal Election Commission Record*, vol. 10 (March 1984), pp. 1–2.

State party committees are permitted to spend the same amount as national party committees on coordinated campaigns but rarely have the money to do so. Republicans solved this problem by making the national party committee the state party's agent for raising and spending the money. In practice, this loophole doubles the amount the national party may spend for its candidates. National party committees may thus take a major role in financing congressional campaigns. In 1984, for example, national party sources could give as much as $70,400 worth of assistance to a House candidate (direct donations of $5,000 in both the primary and general election from the party's national committee, the congressional campaign committee, and the state party committee, plus twice $20,200 in coordinated expenditures). For Senate candidates, the total varied from $108,300 to more than $1.5 million, depending on the state's voting-age population.

Of course, national party committees can only spend money for candidates after they have raised it. In the past decade Republican party committees have far outstripped their Democratic counterparts in raising funds. Between 1976 and 1982 national Republican committee receipts grew from $46 million to $191 million (and to more than $215 million if money raised by national committees as agents of state parties is included). Over the same period Democratic receipts increased only from $18 million to $32 million.[29] Nor could Democrats spend much of this on candidates; until 1982 they were still trying to retire debts incurred as far back as 1968.[30] The growing advantage in party money enjoyed by Republican congressional candidates is evident in table 6-4. Half the Republican Senate candidates in 1982 received more than $200,000 in contributions and services from national party sources; Pete Wilson of California headed the list with $1.3 million. Only one Democrat got more than $200,000 worth of help from the party.[31]

Republican presidential campaigns have also benefited from the party's affluence. The FECA was amended in 1979 to permit state and local parties to spend money for grass-roots activities in presidential campaigns (voter registration, get-out-the-vote efforts, yard signs, buttons, leaflets, bumper stickers, and so forth). Local Republican committees spent $15 million for the Reagan campaign in 1980; Democratic

29. Malbin and Skladony, "Appendix: Selected Campaign Finance Data," table A9.
30. David Adamany, "Political Parties in the 1980s," in Malbin, ed., *Money and Politics*, p. 96.
31. Jacobson, "Money in the 1980 and 1982 Congressional Elections," pp. 47–48.

Table 6-4. *Average Party Contributions and Spending in Congressional Elections, 1978–82*
Dollars, adjusted for inflation (1982 = 1.00)

Item	Democrats	Republicans
	House of Representatives	
1978		
Direct contributions	4,385	13,956
Coordinated spending	253	4,999
Total	4,638	18,955
Percent of total[a]	2.7	11.1
1980		
Direct contributions	2,792	10,157
Coordinated spending	697	6,339
Total	3,489	16,496
Percent of total[a]	2.1	8.8
1982		
Direct contributions	2,410	11,717
Coordinated spending	1,584	12,131
Total	3,994	23,848
Percent of total[a]	1.8	10.3
	Senate	
1978		
Direct contributions	18,667	31,537
Coordinated spending	9,169	122,162
Total	27,836	153,699
Percent of total[a]	2.5	9.0
1980		
Direct contributions	16,062	22,002
Coordinated spending	37,873	176,630
Total	53,935	198,632
Percent of total[a]	3.9	14.8
1982		
Direct contributions	17,556	18,189
Coordinated spending	68,509	264,114
Total	86,065	282,303
Percent of total[a]	4.4	15.6

Source: Gary C. Jacobson, "Money and Votes Reconsidered: Congressional Elections, 1972–1982," *Public Choice* (forthcoming).
a. Percent of all contributions plus spending for candidate.

committees spent only $4 million for Carter.[32] Early projections of Republican party spending of this kind for 1984 ran as high as $70 million, with the Democrats far behind at $20 million. Most of this "local" party

32. Alexander, "Making Sense about Dollars," p. 20.

money is actually raised and distributed by unregistered political committees working out of Republican National Committee headquarters.[33]

Republican committees have grown rich by perfecting direct-mail fund-raising; about 85 percent of their income arrives in small sums solicited by mail from private individuals.[34] This is, in part, an ironic footnote to Watergate; the party was forced to rebuild itself on small donors because the scandal had made it impossible (and unwise) to tap traditional "fat cats." Democratic committees, though trying to imitate their rivals, remain much more dependent on large individual and PAC donations.[35] Republicans also benefited from being in opposition while they were building up their list of willing donors; parties find it easier to make the polarizing emotional appeals that stimulate donations when not burdened with the responsibilities of governing. Representing a more affluent constituency makes fund-raising easier, too.[36] So does the party's ideological homogeneity; Republican donors need not worry about which Republican gets the money, so they are willing to let the party decide. Democratic contributors have more reason to care which Democrat ends up with their donations—and so more reason to keep that decision for themselves—because the party's candidates range all over the ideological map.

Although the FECA and political circumstances provided ample opportunities for party building, Republican officials deserve a great deal of credit for recognizing and making the most of them. The national party committees are now organized to engage in a wide range of activities on a continuing basis. The party has its own staff of about 500 and keeps an auxiliary host of campaign professionals—pollsters, media specialists, direct-mail companies, stationers, computer vendors, and advertising professionals—on contract.[37] It conducts sophisticated voter registration drives, trains party workers in campaigning and fund-raising, and channels campaign donations of cooperating PACs into the close campaigns where the money can make a difference.[38] It finances lavish

33. Michael Wines, "GOP Thrives on 'Shadow' Fund Drives," *Los Angeles Times*, August 26, 1984.

34. Adamany, "Political Parties," p. 105.

35. Ibid., p. 106.

36. Jacobson, *Money in Congressional Elections*, p. 65.

37. Thomas B. Edsall, "The GOP Money Machine," *Washington Post*, national weekly edition, July 2, 1984.

38. Adamany, "Political Parties," pp. 78–85, 97–100; and Sabato, "Parties, PACs, and Independent Groups," pp. 73–83.

national campaigns with common themes designed to boost the entire party ticket during the election period and works to improve its public image with institutional advertising between elections. It has even hired caseworkers to help important campaign contributors deal with government agencies.[39] The national party recruits, trains, and guides Republican congressional candidates through all aspects of their campaigns: "preliminary organization, training, fund-raising, polling, hiring of consultants, analysis of the opposition, manipulation of the media, computerized phone banks, advertising, direct mail, and last-minute get-out-the-vote drives."[40]

Democratic party committees have begun a serious effort to match their Republican counterparts and have made some progess, but they remain far behind in every respect. It takes years to develop a successful direct-mail fund-raising system; the Democratic effort has only recently passed the stage of ferreting out enough willing Democratic donors to make a direct-mail solicitation really profitable. Even if Republicans were to stand still, Democrats would not catch up for years; but if anything, the Republican lead may be widening. By the end of June 1984, Republican party committees had raised $208 million, an increase of $46 million over the same period in 1981–82. Democratic committees increased their take by $36 million to reach a total of $60 million. Democrats enjoyed a much higher rate of increase—150 percent compared with 28 percent for the Republicans, but this was because their base was so much lower; in total income, they dropped further behind.[41] Republicans can expect to have a considerable organizational advantage for the forseeable future.

The flourishing Republican party committees and Republican-oriented PACs are, in themselves, strong indicators of a Republican resurgence. There is also little reason to doubt that they have actively contributed to Republican electoral gains. Perhaps the most important advantage Republicans derive from superior organization is that their campaign resources are deployed more efficiently. I have already mentioned that Republican PAC money is more likely to find its way into the close campaigns of competitive challengers. This is even more true of Republican party money. The National Republican Congressional Com-

---

39. Thomas B. Edsall and Helen Dewar, "The GOP Aims to Please," *Washington Post*, national weekly edition, June 4, 1984.

40. Edsall, "GOP Money Machine."

41. *Federal Election Commission Record*, vol. 11 (January, 1985), p. 10.

mittee and the National Republican Senatorial Committee exercise central control over extensive campaign resources and conduct costly tracking polls to learn when and where party assistance is most likely to help swing a seat into the Republican column. Thus they are able to respond quickly and in force to shifting opportunities and threats that arise during the course of an election year. This capacity almost certainly added to their victories in 1980 and reduced their losses in 1982.[42] It is no coincidence that Republican candidates won a disproportionate share of the close contests in these elections.[43] Republican resources and organization have grown to the point where it would be extraordinary for a Republican congressional candidate with a plausible chance of winning to lose for lack of funds. The same cannot be said of Democratic candidates, at least on the evidence of 1982. Democrats deployed their funds more efficiently in 1984, but the tiny number of competitive challengers makes this election a poor test of the party's targeting capacity; threatened Democratic incumbents have always been adequately funded.[44]

The FECA, then, provided a suitable legal framework through which diverse political groups seeking to change policies and reverse trends dominant in the 1970s could participate effectively in electoral politics. Republican partisans were given the opportunity to work for Republican control of the White House and Congress by giving to a variety of party committees. The law encouraged large and small businesses, people in the professions, and other unhappily regulated economic groups to pursue more congenial governmental policies by rewarding friends and punishing enemies through campaign contributions. Activist entrepreneurs could offer people with strong ideological views or passionate feelings about particular issues a new mode of political expression and a way to channel their efforts to change policies by changing politicians. All these groups could contribute to a Republican resurgence while retaining separate organizational identities and purposes. The campaign finance system allowed them to participate in a Republican electoral coalition by giving money and other forms of assistance to the party's

42. Jacobson, "Party Organization"; and Gary C. Jacobson and Samuel Kernell, *Strategy and Choice in Congressional Elections*, 2d ed. (Yale University Press, 1983), pp. 72–84, 94–107.

43. Thomas E. Mann and Norman J. Ornstein, "Sending a Message: Voters and Congress in 1982," in Mann and Ornstein, eds., *American Election of 1982*, pp. 136–137.

44. Jacobson, "Party Organization"; and Malbin and Skladony, "Campaign Finance, 1984," table 5.

candidates without necessarily making any of the explicit compromises that coalition-building often demands.

DRAWBACKS. The electoral alliance between the Republican party and conservative PACs is not without problems, to be sure. In the final analysis, a party is most interested in electing its candidates regardless of policy stances, and a PAC is most interested in getting preferred policies regardless of who is elected. Thus, for example, NCPAC worked to defeat Republican Senator Charles Percy of Illinois in 1984—because it deemed his ideological moderation intolerable in a chairman of the Senate Foreign Relations Committee—even though his defeat narrowed the Republican majority and increased the chances of a Democratic takeover in 1986.[45] And Republican party officials have complained for years about the corporate PACs that give to incumbent Democrats to protect short-term interests instead of pursuing the long-term benefits of a more Republican Congress.[46] A similar conflict arises among Democrats and their interest group allies, of course; the business PACs that support safe Democratic incumbents but ignore challengers do little to improve the party's strength in Congress, for example. The difference is that the Republican party has the institutional strength to dominate its electoral coalition to a far greater extent than does the Democratic party.

Despite a growing advantage in resources, organization, and efficiency, the Republican party has yet to win full control of the federal government. The final step—a Republican majority in the House—is not yet imminent, though it seems less distant than it has been in many years. Nor is the Republican Senate majority secure, with twenty-two of thirty-four seats up in 1986 held by Republicans elected in the Republican sweep of 1980. The most formidable barriers to a complete Republican takeover are the advantages of incumbency and the solid reality underlying House Speaker Thomas P. O'Neill's hyperbolic claim that "all politics is local."[47] It is significant, therefore, that emerging campaign finance practices and institutions are beginning to chip away at both these barriers.

The electoral value of incumbency, especially in the House, is widely

45. Bill Peterson, "Strange Bedfellows in Illinois," *Washington Post*, national weekly edition, June 11, 1984.

46. Edward Handler and John R. Mulkern, *Business in Politics* (Lexington, Mass.: Lexington Books, 1982), pp. 8–9.

47. Alan Ehrenhalt, "What the Republicans Need Is a Local Election," *Congressional Quarterly Weekly Report*, vol. 40 (July 31, 1982), p. 1871.

acknowledged and abundantly documented. But it is also contingent: it depends on the skill with which members exploit the generous resources that come with office to develop the kind of strong personal support back home that discourages opposition and enables members to survive adverse political tides.[48] It also depends on the prevalence of candidate-centered electoral politics; the opportunity to base a political career on assiduous cultivation of a constituency derives, in part, from the diminished relevance to voters of party cues. Incumbents survive by maintaining an edge in resources and skills, by discouraging strong opposition, and by keeping the contest focused on local candidates and issues.[49]

Party committees and PACs threaten to neutralize the incumbents' advantage in several ways. Direct contributions help challengers overcome their financial inferiority. Even if the money available to incumbents grows as much or more than the money available to challengers, challengers still benefit because their marginal return on campaign spending (in the form of votes) is much greater than that of incumbents; any increase in money available to challengers tends to reduce the advantages of incumbency regardless of how incumbents respond.[50] In-kind services provide technical skills, information, and expertise that can offset incumbents' usual superiority in these areas. The party's national media campaigns and the activities of issue-oriented PACs inject national issues into local races, letting challengers link their campaigns to a broader effort and offering voters new reasons to abandon the incumbent.

The Republicans' main problem has been finding and recruiting candidates capable of taking full advantage of the compensating help parties and PACs can offer. Although the availability of such assistance encourages better candidates to challenge incumbents because it increases the chances of success, Republicans continue to meet some frustration and disappointment in recruiting congressional candidates. The absence of competitive challengers in many promising districts kept

---

48. Morris P. Fiorina, "The Case of the Vanishing Marginals: The Bureaucracy Did It," *American Political Science Review*, vol. 71 (March 1977), p. 180; Richard F. Fenno, Jr., *Home Style: House Members in Their Districts* (Little, Brown, 1978), p. 211; and David R. Mayhew, *Congress: The Electoral Connection* (Yale University Press, 1974), pp. 37–77.

49. Gary C. Jacobson, *The Politics of Congressional Elections* (Little, Brown, 1983), pp. 102–21.

50. Jacobson, "Money and Votes Reconsidered."

Republicans from fully exploiting Reagan's overwhelming victory in 1984.[51]

There is no reason to believe that this problem is permanent. If Republican programs continue to succeed politically, the party's prospects will continue to improve, and it should become easier to attract bright, ambitious young politicians to the party's banner. This would raise the outlook for full Republican control of the federal government considerably.

The prospects for a Republican majority depend, of course, far more on the results of domestic and foreign policies during the second Reagan administration than on the relative electoral assets of the two parties. The administration's chances for success will depend in good part on its dealings with members of Congress and other Washington politicians. Thus before discussing more fully how the emerging campaign finance system might help or hamper Republican ambitions directly, it is worth examining how the system has affected political life in Washington.

Campaign Financing and National Politics in the 1980s

National politics are shaped by what elected officials do to win and hold federal office.[52] By transforming electoral politics, new campaign finance practices and institutions have helped reshape politics in Washington.

Important changes arise simply from the continual growth in campaign spending over the past decade. Since 1974, House campaign expenditures have grown by an average of about 17 percent (in constant dollars) from one election cycle to the next. Spending on Senate campaigns has increased at least as steeply, though election-to-election changes are more variable because different sets of Senate seats are involved. Over each of the six-year periods for which data are available, Senate campaign

---

51. Bruce W. Robeck and Gary C. Jacobson, "National Party Recruitment of Congressional Candidates," *Legislative Studies Section Newsletter*, vol. 8 (November 1984), pp. 7–10; Benjamin Shore, "How Will the Race Change Congress? Not Much," *San Diego Union*, October 28, 1984; Alan Ehrenhalt, "GOP Challengers Find PACs Wary This Year," *Congressional Quarterly Weekly Report*, vol. 42 (October 20, 1984), p. 2763; and Adam Clymer, "Cost of Winning a House Seat Rose in '84, but at a Slower Rate," *New York Times*, December 4, 1984.

52. Mayhew, *Congress*, pp. 81–165.

expenditures have grown by more than 50 percent (again, adjusted for inflation).[53]

Congressional campaign spending has grown in response to changes in both supply and demand. New fund-raising techniques and institutions have expanded the supply of money available to congressional candidates; so has the public financing of presidential campaigns. At the same time, the demand for funds has grown. Most nonincumbent candidates have always needed more money than they could raise; the more money available to them, the more they raise and spend. Incumbents, in contrast, are usually able to raise as much money as they think they need to deal with the threat posed by the particular challenge they face. Their demand for funds varies with the severity of the threat. This depends in part on how much money the challengers are able to raise; it depends also on the quality and skills of challengers and on the other resources available to them.[54]

The expanding activities of PACs and party committees—especially on the Republican side—have increased the likelihood of a formidable challenge. In response, incumbents have sought to protect themselves by raising ever larger campaign kitties in order to scare off or, that failing, to cope with strong opposition. As a result, members of Congress now spend more of their time thinking about, and pursuing, campaign contributions.[55] At best, this takes time away from other pursuits; its other consequences are a matter of dispute, but there is little doubt that members have become increasingly sensitive to the campaign finance implications of their actions in Washington.

Anecdotal claims that specific campaign contributions have influenced specific congressional decisions are common enough,[56] but systematic evidence is still sparse and open to challenge. Nonetheless, at least some members, on matters arousing little interest back home, evidently cast

53. Jacobson, "Money in the 1980 and 1982 Congressional Elections," p. 40; and Adam Clymer, "'84 PACs Gave More to Senate Winners," *New York Times*, January 6, 1985.

54. Jacobson, *Money in Congressional Elections*, pp. 113–23.

55. Albert Hunt, "An Inside Look at Politicians Hustling PACs," *Wall Street Journal*, October 1, 1982; and *Campaign Finance Reform*, Hearings before the Task Force on Elections of the Committee on House Administration, 98 Cong. 1 sess. (Government Printing Office, 1984), pp. 204, 610.

56. See, for example, *Campaign Finance Reform*, Hearings, pp. 49, 533, 538–47; Elizabeth Drew, *Politics and Money: The New Road to Corruption* (Macmillan, 1983), pp. 44–45; and Brooks Jackson and John J. Fialka, "New Congressmen Get Many Offers of Money to Cut Campaign Debt," *Wall Street Journal*, April 21, 1983.

votes consistent with contributors' preferences (taking other influences—ideology, party, district characteristics—into account).[57] Members may also be influenced by the hope for future contributions; and
because the best guarantee of reelection is weak opposition, they may
be reluctant to anger groups that might recruit and finance formidable
challengers. The subtle and not-so-subtle ways in which organizations
and individuals that control campaign resources might affect congressional behavior are as varied as they are difficult to prove in any given
instance. But the potential for influence has grown enormously, and
there is no reason to think that actual influence has not grown as well.

Indeed, other changes in congressional politics have clearly multiplied
the opportunities for outsiders to influence members. Rules changes
adopted in the 1970s—recorded votes in the Committee of the Whole
House, hearings open to the public, and televised proceedings in the
House are examples—have opened the congressional process to greater
scrutiny and made it more difficult for members to disguise their
activities.[58] At the same time, the attentive audience of PACs and other
interest group organizations has expanded rapidly; witness the growing
number of groups that track and rate members' votes in specific policy
areas to determine who is to be supported or who is to be on the group's
"hit list" in the next election.

Members of Congress are more exposed; they are also, in a sense,
more vulnerable. Despite a notable increase in the average vote won by
House incumbents (from 60 percent in the 1950s to 65 percent in the
1970s), their chances of losing have not diminished, because district
electorates have become more volatile. The variability of interelection
vote swings has grown to the point where a House member who wins
reelection with 65 percent of the vote is no safer than was an incumbent
who won with 60 percent in the 1950s.[59] Senate electorates are even
more fickle.[60] The greater sense of uncertainty that spurs the demand for

57. Michael J. Malbin, "Looking Back on the Future of Campaign Finance Reform,"
in Malbin, ed., *Money and Politics*, pp. 247–49; and Jacobson, "Parties and PACs."

58. Bob Michael, "Politics in the Age of Television," *Washington Post*, national
weekly edition, June 4, 1984; and Martha M. Hamilton, "Let the Sunshine In, and
Watch the Special Interests Grow," ibid., May 28, 1984.

59. Gary C. Jacobson, "The Marginals Never Vanished: Incumbency and Competition in Elections to the U.S. House of Representatives, 1952–1982," paper prepared
for the annual meeting of the Midwest Political Science Association, Chicago, Ill., April
17-20, 1985.

60. Norman J. Ornstein and others, *Vital Statistics on Congress, 1984–1985 Edition*
(American Enterprise Institute, 1984), p. 51.

campaign funds and sharpens members' sensitivity to the electoral implications of their activities in Washington is by no means unjustified.

Greater exposure, outside scrutiny, and electoral uncertainty have helped to shift the focus of congressional politics from the inside to the outside. Members spend more of their time and energy catering to people outside Congress—constituents, organized interests, the mass media—and less on politics within the institution itself. A clear sign of this is the decay of traditional congressional norms of deference, seniority, specialization, apprenticeship, and courtesy. These norms were suited to Congress's internal institutional needs and politics; they were abandoned as successful long-term congressional careers came to depend more and more on pleasing people and groups outside Congress. The shift is also evident in changing modes of lobbying. The cozy process of friends helping friends depicted in Bauer, Pool, and Dexter's classic account of lobbying a generation ago continues, of course.[61] But traditional lobbyists have been joined by a host of new groups whose influence derives from their ability to mobilize grass-roots constituencies and resources to pursue both legislative and electoral goals. Lobbying of this kind is far more likely to be felt, and resented, as real pressure.

During the Carter administration, these secular trends seemed to promise increasing immobility and stalemate in national politics. An exposed Congress subject to intense, conflicting electoral pressures would find it impossible to make the hard decisions necessary to deal with serious national problems, because it dared not impose the necessary costs on any politically significant group.[62] Presidential initiatives would be gutted by a fragmented legislature too responsive to be responsible.

The Reagan administration quickly demonstrated that this need not be the case. The successful drive to enact budget and tax cuts in 1981 showed how electoral politics and Congress's sensitivity to external demands could be turned to the president's advantage. Its key element was the administration's skillful mobilization and direction of outside pressures, but the groundwork for this had been prepared by the new campaign finance organizations and their work in the 1980 elections.

Republican support for Reagan's programs was virtually unanimous.

61. Raymond A. Bauer, Ithiel de Sola Pool, and Lewis A. Dexter, *American Business and Public Policy* (Atherton, 1963), pp. 350–57.
62. Lester Thurow, *The Zero-Sum Society: Distribution and the Possibilities for Economic Change* (Basic Books, 1980), pp. 212–14.

Even assuming that most Republicans share the administration's ideological convictions, unanimity on such controversial issues is still extraordinary. Some credit for Republican unity clearly belongs to the national party's electoral work. Party committees had of course assisted many of the new Republican members with campaign money and services and so established some degree of obligation. But the party's provision of training, information, campaign materials, and expertise also subtly injected common themes and issue positions into dispersed campaigns. The party's national campaign for a supply-side economic program was adopted by many congressional candidates, as was the strategy of clinging to Reagan's coattails. Thus many Republicans—particularly new members—came to Congress in 1981 already committed to the president and his basic approach. Those Republicans skeptical of supply-side promises or representing constituencies likely to suffer from Reagan's economic policies were kept in line by the justified fear that defection would invite formidable primary opposition from conservative Reagan loyalists.[63]

Administration strategists used the campaign finance system in a direct way to help gather the Democratic votes they needed. A computer identified individuals and PACs that had given money to both the Reagan campaign and to a Democratic incumbent in 1980; they were then asked to lobby the member to support the administration's bills.[64] Grass-roots Reagan activists in districts represented in the House by Democrats but won decisively by Reagan were also rallied to the cause. The ensuing avalanche of letters and telephone calls from back home helped persuade some reluctant Democrats to cooperate.[65]

On the tax bill, many Democrats did not need much persuading. Indeed, they tried to outbid the Republicans in conferring tax breaks on business when the bill was before Ways and Means. Representative Tony Coelho, chairman of the Democratic Congressional Campaign Committee, has worked hard to convince the business community that Democrats understand its needs and are thus deserving of business PAC support. And business interests have seen the wisdom of supporting at least incumbent Democrats. In recent elections the average Democratic

63. Interview with Representative Barney Frank, January 10, 1985.
64. Edsall, "GOP Money Machine."
65. Elizabeth Wehr, "White House Lobbying Apparatus Produces Impressive Tax Victory," *Congressional Quarterly Weekly Report*, vol. 39 (August 1, 1981), pp. 1372–73.

House candidate has received as much money from corporate, trade, and professional PACs as from labor PACs—in sharp contrast to the early 1970s, when organized labor provided more than three times as much Democratic PAC money as business-oriented groups.[66] Business PACs were given credit for the Democrats' enthusiasm for cutting business taxes.[67] Democrats no doubt find it easier to adjust to a more conservative political climate and agenda when some of the rewards are so obvious.

President Reagan's political talents are, of course, eminently suited to an outside political game. Going public is what he does best. But his persuasiveness is greatly enhanced when general appeals to the public are reinforced by a major organizational effort to mobilize the grass roots. Ironically, the budget process adopted by Congress in the 1970s to bolster its authority against executive encroachment gave Reagan the opening he needed to apply his skills most tellingly. The new process compels members to cast a small number of highly visible votes on the whole budget package, enabling the White House to concentrate public pressures effectively in a way that the old piecemeal system of budgeting would have precluded.

Congressional responsiveness to external demands thus presents opportunities as well as problems. A president who commands broad public support and the rhetorical skills and organizational capacity to mobilize the grass roots can get Congress to do his bidding. Of course, the conditions that make going public an effective strategy do not always hold. After the striking victories of 1981, the administration was often forced to compromise on major proposals in order to make any headway at all. Further cuts in spending were rejected by Congress in 1982 as Reagan's approval ratings—and faith in his economic policies—declined in the face of deepening recession. Members of Congress remain sensitive to constituencies and groups that may strongly oppose, as well as reinforce, the president's demands. Some of the same business groups that bombarded Congress with demands for a favorable vote on Reagan's tax and budget cuts were equally capable of mobilizing effective grass-roots pressure to thwart the administration's plan to withhold 10 percent of interest on savings and investment accounts to reduce tax cheating.[68]

But even without widespread public support, party resources could,

66. Jacobson, "Money in the 1980 and 1982 Congressional Elections," p. 44.
67. Gurwitt, "Democratic Campaign Panel," p. 1347.
68. Steven Pressman, "Bankers' Massive Lobbying Effort Pays Off," *Congressional Quarterly Weekly Report*, vol. 41 (April 23, 1983), p. 771.

in the face of active interest group opposition, sometimes help the Reagan administration to round up the votes it needed in Congress. When the administration decided in 1982 that it was necessary to reverse field and raise taxes, for example, some reluctant Republicans were induced to go along by party carrots (promises of help in justifying the vote to constituents) and sticks (threats to withhold party funds for the upcoming election from defectors).[69]

The coalition of forces that put Reagan in the White House and a Republican majority in the Senate is by no means monolithic; some of its major cleavages are expressed institutionally in the campaign finance system. Parties and PACs are, in many respects, natural rivals. They may form explicit or implicit electoral alliances by backing the same candidates for Congress, but this does not necessarily lead to cooperation on policy questions, because party and PAC priorities and policies often clash. So far, the Reagan administration and Republican leaders in Congress have chosen to devote their serious politicking to the economic and defense policies, assigning lower priority to the social agenda dear to many of the Reagan coalition's New Right supporters. This has left some conservative activists frustrated and disappointed with the Republican party but having nowhere else to go. The party's financial strength makes it easier for the administration to set its own priorities and to look after the party's long-term interests rather than after its short-term need for interest group resources.

The Prospects for a Republican Majority

Political trends in the 1980s—revealed most clearly in the 1984 elections—offer Republicans their best chance in more than half a century to replace the Democrats as the majority party. The decisive event would be a Republican takeover of the House. Many aspects of the present campaign finance system unquestionably enhance Republican prospects, but other of its features give Democrats a chance to hang on despite ideological and programmatic disarray.

The Republicans' wealthy and well-organized national party apparatus is obviously an enormous asset. The party commands vast resources and the organizational capacity to deploy them efficiently. It can steer

69. Dennis Farney, Leonard M. Apcar, and Rich Jaroslovsky, "How Reaganites Push Reluctant Republicans to Back Tax-Rise Bill," *Wall Street Journal*, August 18, 1982.

the large sums of money, in-kind campaign assistance, intelligence, and expertise that are necessary, if not sufficient, to defeat a congressional incumbent to virtually any Republican challenger with a reasonable chance of victory, and it has the surplus to invest in some long shots as well.

National party committees also engage in a wide range of party-building activities—carefully targeted voter registration campaigns, recruitment and funding of Republican candidates for state legislatures, and training of local party officials are examples—that add to the party's long-run strength. Institutional advertising promotes the party and its leaders between elections. Association with a highly motivated, technically sophisticated organization raises Republican morale and engenders confidence in the party's future, helping to attract people with ambition and talent to the party's banner. In these and other ways, national party committees help directly and indirectly to create a political climate conducive to Republican success.

The national party's wealth and organization help in still another way. They allow the Reagan administration—in full control of the party apparatus—to dominate the coalition of PACs and other groups that help elect Republicans to Congress. Most of these groups have their own agendas, which may or may not contribute to long-term Republican objectives. When they do not, national party resources are available to offset what might be lost from disgruntled groups and to help members defend themselves against attacks. This makes it easier for the administration to elicit support for policies that impose concentrated or short-run costs intended to produce diffuse or long-run benefits that eventually add to the party's luster and popular allegiance. A strong national party helps to overcome the rampant particularism that PACs and other interest groups encourage and so to produce more coherent policies that have a chance of actually solving problems. The Reagan administration's harsh cure for inflation—tolerance of an extraordinarily high unemployment— is a case in point. Party discipline has worked to the collective benefit of the party (witness the 1984 elections), though at the expense of some individual Republicans in Congress. Half of the twenty-six Republican incumbents defeated in 1982 were from the staunchly loyal contingent of Republican freshmen; the Gypsy Moths—northeastern and midwestern Republican moderates—also paid a disproportionate price for supporting Reagan's programs.[70]

70. Mann and Ornstein, "Sending a Message," p. 143.

The growing financial role of PACs has also improved Republican prospects. The increase in activity has been greatest among the kinds of PACs—those representing business and trade interests—generally partial to Republican candidates, especially among nonincumbents. Not only does this allow Republican nonincumbents to take fuller advantage of favorable opportunities to take congressional seats from Democrats, but it also means that if Republicans ever *do* take the House, Democrats will find themselves in serious financial trouble, since so many PACs contribute to Democrats only because they hold majority control and hence positions of power in the House.

The growth of ideological and single-issue PACs is another factor contributing to potential Republican hegemony. Such PACs, and the interest groups that sponsor them, can act as vehicles for moving people from old political allegiances (or from independence or indifference) to new ones. The support of many traditionally Democratic working-class Catholics has been transferred to Republican candidates through the work of antiabortion groups; rural white southerners responding to a PAC's call to protect their firearms end up helping to defeat Democratic advocates of stricter gun controls; and nominal Democrats favoring tougher foreign and defense policies are brought into the Republican camp indirectly by supporting militant PACs whose standards of rectitude are most frequently met by Republican candidates. The list could go on. Single-issue and ideological PACs help to incorporate segments of the working- and lower-middle-class electorate into the Republican coalition, a development that is crucial to the Republican strategy for achieving majority status. At the same time, they leave the party free to keep some distance from the positions advocated by passionate minorities that might alienate other groups it is courting. PACs decentralize organized participation in elections and so make it easier to keep ill-sorted allies (socially conservative evangelicals and urban, college-educated professionals, for example) from clashing.

The decentralized campaign finance system also helps keep Democrats in Congress, however. It contributes to the fragmented, candidate-centered style of electoral politics that allows Democrats to hold on by adapting individually to diverse local circumstances and changes in the political climate. Nationally, the Democratic party suffers from the perception that it is subservient to the (currently unfashionable) special interests of organized labor, racial minorities, feminists, teachers, and other liberal activists. But the decentralized electoral strategies pursued by congressional Democrats enable them to assemble personal coalitions that may or may not include groups important to the party nationally. They can run as staunch friends of organized labor or nuclear freeze groups when this wins votes, and they can avoid such alliances when it does not.[71]

Many Democrats in Congress have had little trouble adjusting to the nation's conservative mood; not a few turned into born-again budget and tax cutters in 1981. One reason they are free to move rightward as electoral prudence dictates is that what they may lose in campaign resources from disgruntled liberals will be more than replaced by PACs pleased with their newfound understanding of, say, the virtues of lower taxes on corporations.[72] The adaptability of congressional Democrats means that the realignment at the level of national policy does not require a party realignment.

The decentralized electoral and campaign finance system, reinforcing the advantages of incumbency, may keep the Democrats in nominal control of the House for years to come. But it does nothing to revive the party as a collective political force, and it portends disaster if the Democrats ever do lose their majority. Hence Democratic leaders are trying to imitate the party-building activities of their rivals. Despite some significant progress, they remain well behind. A party internally fragmented, lacking coherent plans or programs, naturally finds it difficult to centralize fund-raising and other campaign activities. This does not bother incumbents, of course, but the resulting inefficiencies hurt the chances of nonincumbent Democratic candidates. The challenge for the Democratic party is to improve efficiency, which requires more centralized control of campaign resources, at a time when decentralized, district-focused campaign strategies best suit its candidates.

The party's main asset here is its status as the opposition; consensus is reached more easily on the Reagan administration's misdeeds than on Democratic alternatives; and money is raised more easily by attacking policies than by defending them. The conservative tide has also stirred various liberal interest groups to organize in self-defense, and they are

71. Gurwitt, "GOP Disappointed," p. 2898; Alan Ehrenhalt, "GOP Finds All Politics Is Local—After All," *Congressional Quarterly Weekly Report*, vol. 42 (November 17, 1984), p. 2979.

72. Gurwitt, "Democratic Campaign Panel," p. 1347. See also Dennis Farney, "A Liberal Congressman Turns Conservative; Did PAC Gifts Do It?" *Wall Street Journal*, July 29, 1982.

beginning to put more resources at the disposal of Democratic candidates. This is, however, something of a mixed blessing, because Democratic party organizations are not as well situated to dominate their party's coalition (and so to use its resources to pursue the party's collective goal of winning the maximum possible number of seats). In 1984, a year when Democrats were on the defensive and therefore mainly concerned with defending vulnerable incumbents and retaining open seats, the party was able to target its resources effectively. It remains to be seen whether it can do the same in a more favorable year when a large number of competitive challengers, rather than incumbents, merit the party's attention.

In the short run, the Democrats' best hope lies in taking advantage of a loophole in the election laws that permits a party to move large sums of money from one candidate's campaign to another's. Alarmed by the growing threat posed by Republican resources and organization, many incumbent Democrats have, in recent elections, accumulated far more campaign money than they have ended up needing or spending. If even a small proportion of these leftover funds were transferred in timely fashion to nonincumbent Democrats in tight races, the party's collective performance would improve. Attempts to persuade flush Democratic incumbents to part with some of their campaign cash have so far been almost entirely futile.[73] But it is not difficult to imagine the political value to would-be congressional leaders of having other members in their debt for crucial campaign assistance. Leaders in the California legislature, for example, win leadership positions and exercise power largely through their ability to direct campaign money to legislative candidates. Stricter federal regulations would give congressional leaders fewer such opportunities, but they are by no means absent. For instance, a safe incumbent might let a PAC know that he would be more grateful for a contribution to a struggling challenger than for one to his own campaign. Obviously, it would take a major change in habits for a system of mutual aid to develop among congressional Democrats. But if the alternative is a Republican majority, simple self-interest may induce members to pay more attention to the fates of other Democratic candidates.

Democrats and their allies are fully aware that the present campaign finance system operates to their disadvantage and so have regularly proposed further "reforms." The most recent round took place in 1983.

73. Fialka and Farney, "Democrats Trail GOP."

The main proposal pushed by House Democrats included limits on how much candidates could accept from PACs, limits on total spending in House campaigns, and partial public funding of general election campaigns through matching grants, with extra funds for targets of independent expenditure campaigns.[74] Its ostensible purpose was to reduce the influence that special interests supposedly exercise through the campaign finance system, but it would also reverse trends that have strengthened Republicans and threatened Democratic officeholders.

Republicans naturally opposed this approach on the grounds that it simply protected incumbents and thus the Democratic House majority. They proposed instead to unleash the parties, tripling the direct contribution ceiling and eliminating altogether the restrictions on coordinated expenditures by party committees.[75] This, too, was defended as a way to weaken PACs by reducing their relative financial importance to candidates. But it would also obviously give Republicans an enormous financial advantage. Republicans have so much money that their main financial problems are finding ways to spend it legally for candidates and finding candidates worth spending it on. Until Democrats enjoy the same affluence, it is extremely doubtful that they can be persuaded to unleash the parties.

None of the bills proposed in 1983 got very far, and significant change in the near future is unlikely. Campaign finance issues have become highly partisan, and as long as neither party commands solid majorities in both houses of Congress and control of the White House, either one will be able to block unwelcome changes. The campaign finance system will continue to evolve under the present rules for the forseeable future, continuing to brighten Republican prospects.

74. Tom Watson, "Soaring Campaign Spending Generates Renewed Interest in Election Finance Changes," *Congressional Quarterly Weekly Report*, vol. 41 (July 16, 1983), pp. 1451–53. See also *Campaign Finance Reform*, Hearings.
75. Ibid.

CHAPTER SEVEN

The Rise
of National Parties

A. JAMES REICHLEY

THE two major national political parties, judged all but extinct by many
commentators only a few years ago, are staging a modest but conse-
quential comeback as effective forces in American politics. This revival
is considerably more advanced among the Republicans than among the
Democrats, and even the Republican party's current appearance of
vitality may turn out over the long run to be not much more than the
extended shadow of President Reagan's personal popularity. But during
the 1983–84 election cycle (the unit by which national politicians and
political operatives measure time), the major parties channeled funds
and services to candidates bearing their labels, helped mobilize competing armies of campaign workers, and offered voters a choice between
alternative approaches to public policy—all functions that had seemed
to be slipping away from them.

The Republican National Committee, operating out of the headquarters it has maintained in Washington on Capitol Hill since 1970, is giving
hands-on direction to party organizations in 650 key counties (or towns
in New England) containing 57 percent of the national electorate.
Republicans in Congress, partly as a result of the party socialization
induced by this national political apparatus, have achieved impressive
levels of party unity since the onset of the Reagan administration. Reagan

Many members of the national political community, some of whose names appear in
the footnotes, were generous with their time and recollections during the interviews on
which much of this chapter is based. I particularly thank Judith H. Newman for research
assistance.

175

has indicated that he aims to convert his 1984 coalition into an enduring Republican majority. Senate Majority Leader Robert Dole, who has witnessed a variety of attempts at fostering political realignment during his twenty-five years in Washington and been an active participant in some of them, has said: "Nixon thought he could build a conservative majority that was above party, and Ford tried to strengthen the traditional Republican party. Reagan is trying to expand the Republican party to include the majority."[1]

The Democrats, though far behind in both national organization and money, have set out to develop their own national party structure—symbolized by the opening early in 1985 on Capitol Hill of the Democratic National Committee's first self-owned headquarters building. The ongoing revolution in Democratic party rules that began with the formation of the McGovern Commission in 1969 has provided the national party with the formal means to discipline its state and local affiliates. An immediate effect of these changes in the rules was to blast further holes in the cohesion of already-declining state and local party organizations. The gap thus created was at first filled by economic and ideological interest groups and by candidates' personal campaign networks. But certain aspects of modern campaign technology offer a strategic advantage to an aggressively conducted national party organization—an advantage that the new leadership of the Democratic National Committee is acting to seize.

Both parties are moving toward the model of tightly structured, programmatic parties common in other Western democracies. Whether this trend will continue—and if so, whether it will be a good thing—are questions that remain to be answered.

Traditional Parties

National parties in the United States have generally been weak in structure and wary of ideology. E. E. Schattschneider memorably wrote that national party organizations possess "only the transparent filaments of the ghost of a party." More recently, Austin Ranney accurately conveyed "the judgment of most political scientists that the net result of

1. Interview with Senator Robert Dole, December 19, 1984.

party development from 1824 to the 1950s was to make American parties the least centralized in the world.''[2]

The argument that the parties have not represented significant differences in their policy approaches can be pushed too far. In this century, at least, the Republicans have generally been more committed than the Democrats to a market-oriented economy, while the Democrats have been more prepared to use government to attack social inequities; the Republicans have been more tough-minded in their conduct of foreign policy; and the Republicans have been more inclined than the Democrats to give legal embodiment to the standards of the Protestant ethic (such as monogamy, sobriety, and thrift). Within both parties, there has been wide variance on issues. But, in general, at the state and local levels outside the South and at the national level, the Republicans have been the more conservative party and the Democrats the more liberal.

Both parties, however, have resisted reducing these tendencies in their social, economic, and moral belief systems to a rigid ideology. And neither, until recently, vested much authority in its national party structure. There was never anything approaching a national party machine (with the possible exception of the apparatus put together by Mark Hanna for the Republicans at the end of the nineteenth century). The quadrennial national party conventions, through which the major parties have nominated their candidates for president and vice-president since 1832, were until the 1960s composed of delegates chosen through procedures wholly dictated by state laws or state party rules. The national party committees, established by the Democrats in 1848 and the Republicans in 1854, did not until the late 1940s claim even the right to unseat state party representatives who had supported the opposition's national ticket in the last election.

At the state and local levels, on the other hand, party organizations often achieved impressive levels of solidarity and internal discipline. The strength of these state and local party machines varied in different parts of the country. In the states of the former Confederacy, where the Democrats generally maintained one-party dominance during the century after the Civil War, political activity was usually organized around rival factions or personalities within the Democratic party rather than through the official party structure; therefore in most southern states the

2. E. E. Schattschneider, *Party Government* (Holt, Rinehart and Winston, 1960), p. 163; and Austin Ranney, *Curing the Mischiefs of Faction: Party Reform in America* (University of California Press, 1975), p. 179.

party as such played only a minor role in government (Virginia being a notable exception). In the belt of northern states stretching from Wisconsin to the Pacific Coast and reaching down to include California, party organizations were deliberately weakened by Progressive reformers during the first decade of the twentieth century on the theory, long established in American social thought, that parties lead naturally to corruption. But in most of the heavily populated industrial states of the Northeast and Middle West, and in some of the rural prairie states as well, state and local parties were vigorous, cohesive, manned by highly motivated workers, and politically formidable.

The Democratic organizations in such places as New York, Jersey City, Albany, Baltimore, Chicago, and Kansas City were bywords for both political efficiency and governmental corruption. The Republicans also maintained potent local machines in cities like Philadelphia and Cincinnati, and in suburban bailiwicks like Nassau County, New York. The most effective Republican organizations encompassed entire states, such as those of Pennsylvania, New York, Connecticut, Ohio, and Illinois. Democratic state organizations tended to be dependencies of city machines, while with the Republicans it was often the other way around.

These state and local parties often sponsored political clubs, but had no formal mass membership beyond that established by registration to vote. They tended, nevertheless, toward the model that Maurice Duverger termed the "mass party," permeating the entire community, as opposed to the "cadre party," composed of an elite of political activists.[3] In many city neighborhoods and small towns, each party was equipped with a full retinue of informal support services, including churches, insurance agencies, bars, lawyers, and undertakers.

Among actual party workers, who served as conduits for favors, whipped up enthusiasm during campaigns, and turned out the vote on election day, effort and discipline were maintained through distribution of patronage—government jobs that left time for political labors. As recently as 1970 the governor of Pennsylvania had at his disposal about 40,000 state jobs that could in theory be awarded to the party faithful. In some states and cities, the machine of the party in power enjoyed a kind of government subsidy, culled as a fixed share (usually 2 percent) of the

3. Maurice Duverger, *Political Parties: Their Organization and Activity in the Modern State* (Wiley, 1954), pp. 63–71.

pay of public employees.[4] Additional funds came from the machine's beneficiaries in the private sector, such as paving contractors, publishers of school textbooks, and operators of businesses either illegal (like prostitution) or frequently enmeshed with the law (like saloons).

Whatever their merits or demerits, the traditional machines, which had survived assaults by an earlier generation of reformers around the turn of the century, went into steep decline during the 1950s and 1960s. "Good government" movements, often only loosely associated with the parties, triumphed in many cities and states. The old machines, with a few exceptions like the Democratic organization in Chicago and the Republican state organizations in New York and Ohio, lost their ability to maintain internal discipline. The share of voters regarding themselves as political independents rose.

There were several reasons for the machines' loss of political effectiveness. Development of a welfare state administered by the federal government, beginning with the New Deal, established as public rights some of the services that had formerly been dispensed by the machines as political favors. Rising levels of education freed second- and third-generation members of recent immigrant groups from dependence on party workers to help cope with public bureaucracies. The inclusion of more and more state and municipal employees under civil service protection dried up some of the old wells of patronage. Growing unionization of public employees after 1960 struck an even more serious blow at the patronage system. Television brought candidates into voters' living rooms, thereby antiquating some of the communication and education functions of party workers. Most of all, perhaps, the old tribal differences associated with the parties began to seem irrelevant and even burdensome to members of generations that sought fresh identities.

Movement Politics

The decline of the state and local party organizations had important effects on the national parties. Though the national parties had not been much more than loose confederations of state party organizations that came together every four years to nominate and campaign for national

---

4. Interviews in some of the old machine strongholds in 1984 indicated that this practice (known as "macing") has declined but is by no means extinct.

tickets, they nevertheless had provided political frameworks through which national candidates operated, offered some bond of cohesion between the president and members of his party in Congress, established the formal structure of Congress, and managed the screening process through which the finalists for national leadership were chosen. After 1960 all these functions except the structuring of Congress wilted.

To replace, or intimidate, the old kind of political professionals, national candidates turned to a new breed of political activists that had begun to enter politics in large numbers in the 1950s, at first in California, where the parties had been relatively weak since the Progressive era, and then in many of the major metropolitan areas of the Northeast and Middle West. The new activists were motivated less by desire for government employment or by partisan tribal attachments than by commitment to a variety of issue-related causes. These volunteer activists usually placed the cause they served—whether it be municipal reform, civil rights, getting government "off the backs of the people," or protecting the environment—far above the party as their primary object of political loyalty.[5]

Cause-oriented activism was not new to American politics. The Republican party had grown out of the antislavery movement in the 1850s. Advocates of Prohibition and women's suffrage promoted their causes without regard for the welfare of political parties. The union movement of the 1930s concentrated its political efforts on advancing the interests of organized labor. But most of these earlier movements had eventually been absorbed into the normal workings of the party system. Though their influence had sometimes been great, it was chiefly carried out through their impact on one or both of the major parties.[6]

The difference that confronted the issue-motivated groups of the 1960s and thereafter was that state or local party organizations in most places had become so weak that they no longer were able to function effectively as brokers between the cause-oriented movements and candidates or officeholders. Movement groups in some places *became* the political structure. Candidates were either movement people themselves or were exposed to direct pressure from the movements, with no mediating party organization to protect them.[7]

5. David S. Broder, *The Party's Over* (Harper and Row, 1972), pp. 16–26; and James Q. Wilson, *The Amateur Democrat* (University of Chicago Press, 1966).

6. James L. Sundquist, *Dynamics of the Party System: Alignment and Realignment of Political Parties in the United States* (Brookings, 1983), pp. 82–98, 173–77.

7. John H. Kessel, *Presidential Parties* (Homewood, Ill.: Dorsey, 1984), pp. 319–26.

There were the usual crosscurrents and deviations from a prevailing trend. In some places, movement people who won elective offices began to behave pretty much like traditional politicians. In California, the early source and model of movement politics, the parties actually achieved a mild revival, in part because of abolition of the system of cross-filing under which candidates could run in both party primaries. When Ronald Reagan ran for governor of California in 1966, he took the unprecedented step of persuading the entire ticket of Republican candidates for state offices to run as a team. Whether or not because of this innovation, Republicans won most of the offices at stake that year. Many state parties, as Cornelius Cotter, John Bibby, and their associates have shown, actually increased the size and complexity of their headquarters bureaucracies, providing such services as campaign seminars and news-letters.[8] But these expansions hardly made up for the continuing decay of patronage-fed grass-roots organizations in the towns and precincts. In general, the direction in most states and cities was away from political competition built primarily around parties and toward a politics driven by movement enthusiasms.

The national campaign of 1968 turned out to be a kind of last stand for national party politics as it had generally been practiced for more than a century. Richard Nixon conducted a largely traditional campaign for the Republican presidential nomination, putting together a coalition of regular Republican state organizations supplemented by support from some of the nonprofessional conservative activists on the party's right wing. In the fall, Nixon made ingenious use of new techniques of television advertising to reach the large sectors of the electorate that the regular party organizations no longer touched. But he continued to entrust campaign work at the grass roots mainly to Republican regulars.

In the Democratic party as well, the candidate of the party regulars, Hubert Humphrey, managed to win the presidential nomination. But volunteer activists opposing the Vietnam War behind the banners of Eugene McCarthy and Robert Kennedy had made the primary campaign so hot that Lyndon Johnson had felt constrained to withdraw his candidacy for reelection. At the national party convention in Chicago, antiwar activists and proadministration regulars assaulted each other with verbal, and in a few instances physical, abuse. While the convention met, protesters against the war rioted and fought with police in the streets of downtown Chicago. Had Robert Kennedy lived, some observ-

8. Cornelius P. Cotter and others, *Party Organizations in American Politics* (Praeger, 1984), pp. 13–36.

ers have surmised, his charismatic presence would have overcome even
the substantial advantages that the existing party rules afforded the
regulars, thus perhaps enabling him to win the nomination.

Reforming Party Rules

The circumstances attending Humphrey's nomination, and his subsequent defeat in the general election, produced a conviction among
many movement activists that the party bosses had put over Humphrey's
selection against the will of a majority of grass-roots Democrats. The
case for this view is very dubious. But the indignation it aroused helped
produce demand for reform of the patchwork of party rules and state
laws governing the process through which parties selected their national
tickets.

Several aspects of the selection process, the reformers claimed, made
the national conventions unrepresentative of the will of party members.
In some states, delegates were picked through a system based on
caucuses composed of party officers who had been elected several years
before the convention. Some of the states using primaries, such as New
York and Pennsylvania, gave a strong advantage to machine-endorsed
delegate slates by listing candidates for delegate on the ballot without
any indication of their presidential preferences. In states with open
primaries, like Wisconsin and Michigan, members of one party were
able to play an important part in selecting delegates to the convention of
the other. Racial discrimination, particularly in the South, still kept the
proportion of black delegates well below blacks' 11 percent share of the
national population, or, at the Democratic convention, their much larger
portion of the normal Democratic electorate. (In 1968 blacks made up 6
percent of the delegates at the Democratic convention and 2 percent at
the Republican.) The voters' will was said to be distorted by devices like
the unit rule, under which all of a state delegation's vote could be cast
for the candidate favored by the delegation's majority (permitted under
Democratic rules but not under Republican), and California's winner-
take-all primary, which awarded the state's entire delegation to the
candidate whose slate won a plurality in the primary.

The national conventions in 1968 were certainly not representative in
the sense of directly expressing the preferences of either the mass of
party members or the nation as a whole. Whether this was a bad thing is

open to question. Some political theorists have argued that the job of selecting a party's national ticket should be left largely to elected officials and other party leaders. The *democratic* part of the process, they suggest, should enter when the public chooses between competing party tickets in November. But other theorists maintain that if the public has little role in the process before the general election, democracy is only a sham, and real governmental power lies with rival party oligarchies. Under this latter view, the public must exert its will at each step of the selection process if the governmental system is to be truly representative.

Even if one accepts the second of these formulations, as probably most Americans now do, "representation" may still have two quite different general meanings. It may mean that the process should provide for the election of delegates chosen on some majoritarian principle at a time reasonably close to the convention. Or it may mean that the convention should reflect the distribution of certain categories, such as race, sex, age, and income, within the party or the electorate.

Party convention delegations in the 1960s, like most other high-status American institutions, were disproportionately composed of white, middle-aged, middle-class males. Some of these disproportions, such as those based on race, were the direct result of discrimination. But others, such as those based on age, were products of long-standing social customs, some of which may be rooted in the human condition itself. Perfectly representative elections in the first sense would still produce conventions that were substantially unrepresentative in the second. In order to make the conventions demographically representative according to the second definition, it would be necessary to establish procedures that might well thwart the preferences of a majority of those voting in completely democratic elections.

The history of the seven separate commissions set up by the Democratic party from 1969 to 1982 to reform party rules has been ably related by, among others, William Crotty, Nelson Polsby, Byron Shafer, and David Price.[9] (Yet another commission was authorized by the 1984 convention, to begin its work in the spring of 1985.) Their findings show

9. William J. Crotty, *Decision for the Democrats: Reforming the Party Structure* (Johns Hopkins University Press, 1978); Nelson W. Polsby, *Consequences of Party Reform* (Oxford University Press, 1983); Byron E. Shafer, *Quiet Revolution: The Struggle for the Democratic Party and the Shaping of Post-Reform Politics* (Sage, 1983); and David E. Price, *Bringing Back the Parties* (Washington, D.C.: CQ Press, 1984). See also Ranney, *Curing the Mischiefs of Faction*, for the early rounds of the story.

that the reforms enacted by these commissions went well beyond changes to make the Democratic convention representative in the sense of reflecting the will of a majority of Democrats and encompassed requirements intended to make the convention demographically representative of American society.

The McGovern-Fraser Commission, the first and most far-reaching of these reform bodies, ordered that each state party take "affirmative steps" before the 1972 convention to ensure that its delegation include shares of blacks, women, and young people in "reasonable relationship to the group's presence in the population of the state." The Winograd Commission, concluding its work in 1978, required that each state party adopt "specific goals and timetables" to carry out its affirmative action program, and specified women, blacks, Hispanics, and Native Americans as objects of "remedial action to overcome the effects of past discrimination." In its call for the 1980 convention, the Democratic National Committee flatly decreed (going beyond the recommendations of the Winograd Commission) that each state delegation should include equal numbers of men and women.

The Democratic reform commissions took a further step that did not necessarily follow from either theory of representation: they required that candidates for delegate be clearly identified with a particular presidential candidate, and, after 1972, that delegations be divided in proportion to the support received by presidential candidates in each state's caucuses or primaries (with a threshold, set in 1973 at 15 percent, below which a candidate obtained no delegates). The effect of this change, which was intended to bring ordinary voters more directly into the presidential selection process, was to strengthen enormously the role of presidential candidates' organizations in national politics and to further weaken the state and local parties.

Even candidates' organizations were to some extent undercut by another force operating at Democratic conventions since 1972: the interest group caucuses that developed in part as a result of the new affirmative action requirements in party rules, though also partly in response to larger social trends, already mentioned. Caucuses representing feminists, blacks, Hispanics, liberal activists, and homosexuals dealt with the candidates' organizations as virtual equals—at times more than equals, since as the Democratic party grew weaker, each group claimed that its enthusiastic support was essential for the Democratic ticket to have any chance at victory in November.

The ease with which the reformers in the Democratic party imposed the new system on their party was itself a sign of the weakness of the old party organizations. The ouster from the 1972 Democratic convention of the delegation from Cook County, Illinois, led by Mayor Richard Daley of Chicago, was symbolic of the change that had taken place. At the 1968 convention, Daley had stood on the floor directly in front of the rostrum, hurling epithets at the outnumbered antiwar activists, and had packed the galleries with loyal subalterns of the Chicago machine. In 1972, while battered Democratic machines in cities like Philadelphia and Cleveland did what they could to control delegations chosen under the new rules, Daley's Cook County organization put together its approved slate of delegates as though nothing had happened. McGovern's managers, not wholly unmindful of the general election campaign that lay before them, would have preferred to allow the Cook County delegation to go unchallenged. But the spirit of party reform, from which they had profited, was too strong for them. Out of the convention went Daley and his entire delegation—representing the most efficient Democratic city organization remaining in America. The last laugh, for that year at least, may have gone to Mayor Daley: in November, McGovern sank to the worst defeat suffered in the electoral college by any Democratic candidate for president in the twentieth century (before Walter Mondale). But the convention's banishment of the Cook County delegation, which four years before would have been unthinkable, indicated that the wave of the future in the Democratic party lay with the reformers.

While the change in party rules may have weakened the Democrats' ability to compete in national politics, it also helped shift authority within the party to the national level. The national party's enhanced status was given legal underpinning as a result of litigation that grew out of the ouster of the Cook County delegation from the 1972 Democratic convention. In a 1975 Supreme Court case brought by regularly elected Chicago delegates against the reformers whom the convention had seated in their place, the Court ruled that the national party convention is the final judge of its own membership, regardless of state law. "The convention," the Court held, "serves the pervasive national interest in the selection of candidates for national office, and this national interest is greater than any interest of any individual state."[10]

The 1984 national conventions of both major parties were far more

10. *Cousins* v. *Wigoda*, 419 U.S. 477 (1975).

representative, in both the political and demographic senses, than national party conventions in the 1960s. About half the delegates at both conventions were women—at the Democratic convention as required by the rules, and at the Republican as a result of pleas by the national party leadership to state organizations. Blacks accounted for 18 percent of the delegates at the Democratic convention, though still only 3 percent at the Republican (a higher proportion than the black share of the Republican vote in November). Virtually all delegates were chosen through actions that began in the year of the convention, and the number of people participating in the selection process was vastly enlarged. The improvement in representation to some extent reflected broad social forces and to some extent sprang from pragmatic decisions by party leaders. But in very large part, it resulted from deliberate efforts at reform, principally in the Democratic party.

The Democrats in particular paid a price for party reform in reduced efficiency of state and local parties. But erosion of the authority of these traditional party organizations had opened up a possibility that few people in the 1970s grasped: that truly national parties, such as never before had existed in the United States, might become effective bases of national political power.

The Brock Revolution

The germ of the new national parties originated among the Republicans in the 1960s. Coming out of the Goldwater disaster in 1964, the Republicans named Ray Bliss, the experienced state chairman of Ohio, as chairman of the Republican National Committee (RNC), with a mandate to overhaul and modernize the party's machinery. Bliss launched mechanisms such as candidates' schools and issues conferences that became staples of later efforts at party building. (Beginning in the 1940s, both parties had experimented intermittently with issues councils, composed of party leaders. But these had little enduring effect on the institutional life of the parties.) As he had done in Ohio, Bliss directed special efforts at winning recruits to Republicanism among college students and at helping state organizations renew their strength in major cities. "We are building from the basement up," he liked to say, "not from the roof down." Bliss copied some operational techniques from the British Conservative party, whose campaigns he closely studied.[11]

In the 1968 general election campaign, Richard Nixon relied heavily on the machinery constructed by Bliss. But after his election, Nixon, ever wary against even partially autonomous sources of power, saw to it that Bliss was dropped and direction of political operations was moved to the White House. Nixon's 1972 campaign was run mainly through his separately organized reelection committee, the subsequently infamous Committee for the Reelection of the President (CREEP). Watergate caused further deterioration of the structure that Bliss had built.

After Jimmy Carter's triumph over Gerald Ford in 1976, William Brock, just defeated for reelection to his Senate seat from Tennessee, was chosen Republican national chairman. Like Bliss, Brock came in at a nadir in Republican fortunes. Some leading conservative activists, like Richard Viguerie and Howard Phillips, were arguing that what conservatives needed was an entirely new national party. Others, less extreme, proposed that the Republican party at least change its name to escape association with such political millstones as the Depression, "country club Republicanism," and Watergate. Rejecting such pessimistic counsels, Brock set out to rejuvenate and ultimately to revolutionize the national Republican party.

Brock's most critical decision was made during his first month at the RNC in 1977. Funds not needed for current operating expenses, he determined, would be invested in a direct mail program to build a mass base of small contributors. Direct mail had been used successfully to raise money for some right-wing interest groups, particularly by Viguerie. But there was little evidence that it would work for a national party. Some Republican leaders argued that available funds should be spent to help candidates planning races in the critical 1978 midterm elections. Looking back, Brock recalls the decision as having been an easy one: "There really was no other way to build an effective national party."[12]

Brock's direct mail program was a huge success. Expenditure of $7,973,000 in the 1977-78 cycle brought a return of $25,128,000—a net of $17,155,000. In the 1979-80 cycle, expenditure of $12,100,000 brought $54,100,000—a stunning net of $42,000,000. After three years of opera-

11. A. James Reichley, "Here Come the Republicans," *Fortune*, September 1, 1967, pp. 95-97.

12. Interview with U.S. Trade Representative William Brock, January 22, 1985.

tion, the overhead of the direct mail program was, according to Xandra Kayden, "at least ten percent cheaper than all other forms of raising money." Direct mail not only brought in money, but also forged a bond between millions of small givers and the RNC. By the end of 1980, the national party's list of active contributors exceeded 2 million.[13]

With the increased funds at his disposal, Brock expanded some of the operations that had been started by Bliss and began others that carried the RNC into areas never before entered by a national party. A number of developments in national and international politics had moved a sizable portion of the intellectual community to adopt more conservative positions and even to consider association with Republicanism. In order to show the party's interest in ideas and to generate programmatic proposals that might be politically useful, Brock started publication of *Commonsense*, a moderately intellectual quarterly dealing with public policy issues. Among the authors contributing to *Commonsense* were not only traditional conservatives, like Paul McCracken, and progressive Republicans, like Richard Nathan, but also neoconservative intellectuals who still identified themselves as Democrats, like Jeane Kirkpatrick and Michael Novak.

At a more popular level, the RNC published *First Monday*, a monthly magazine devoted to exuberant attacks on the Carter administration and the Democrats. Slick television commercials, poking fun at President Carter and Speaker of the House Thomas P. O'Neill and urging viewers to "vote Republican, for a change," were run nationally under RNC sponsorship.

Brock named five advisory councils, on economic policy, foreign policy, energy and environmental policies, "human concerns," and general government, composed of more than 400 political leaders and substantive experts, to develop a comprehensive party program. The work of the councils became the basis for the 1980 Republican platform.

Perhaps most important, Brock established a separate division to revive state and local party organizations and to recruit candidates for the state legislatures, which would reapportion congressional and legislative districts after 1980. In some instances, the RNC gave support to preferred candidates in contested primaries—a degree of intervention in local politics that national parties had formerly shunned.

13. Republican National Committee, *1981 Chairman's Report* (Washington, D.C.: RNC, 1981), p. 32; and Xandra Kayden, "Parties and the 1980 Presidential Election," in Campaign Finance Study Group, *Financing Presidential Campaigns* (Harvard University, John F. Kennedy School of Government, Institute of Politics, 1982), p. 11.

A National Party Machine

With help from the Carter administration, OPEC, and the Ayatollah Khomeini, Republican fortunes soon rose. After modest gains in the 1978 midterm elections, the Republicans in 1980 recaptured the presidency, won control of the Senate, and gained thirty-three seats in the House of Representatives. At the start of the fall campaign, Ronald Reagan had posed on the steps of the national Capitol with scores of Republican candidates for Congress to symbolize his commitment to an inclusive party effort. After taking office, however, Reagan at first seemed disposed to undercut the RNC, much as Nixon had done. Brock, who narrowly escaped being purged at the Republican convention by Reaganites who resented his evenhandedness during the primary season, entered the new administration as chief foreign trade negotiator. Much of the political machinery he had put in place at the national committee was permitted to run down.

During the first two years of the Reagan administration, the other two national Republican campaign bodies, the National Republican Senatorial and Congressional (House) Committees, continued to expand their efforts to raise funds and provide services at the national level for Republican candidates. In the 1981-82 election cycle, these two committees between them raised $107 million—about double what they had gathered in the 1979-80 cycle and four times what they had raised in 1977–78. (The rival Democratic Senate and House campaign committees, in contrast, raised only $12 million during 1981–82.) Besides contributing funds to targeted candidates, the two Republican committees made available great banks of issue research and provided candidates with advice from experts on advertising, polling, fund-raising, demography, and other campaign specialties. "The Republicans," Robert Squiers, a Washington-based Democratic technician, has said, "recognized in the late 1970s that the national campaign committees have a capacity to offer their candidates the new campaign technology on a wholesale basis."[14]

A major role of the Republican congressional campaign committees was to steer sympathetic political action committees (PACs) sponsored by business and professional groups to races in which their contributions

14. Press releases, Federal Election Commission, February 21, 1982, and December 3, 1983; and interviews with Kent Cooper, January 8, 1985; Ed Goeas, Fred Asbell, and Tim Hyde, January 4, 1985; Senator Richard Lugar, January 18, 1985; and Robert Squiers, January 9, 1985.

would do the most good. Though total PAC contributions to Democratic congressional candidates in 1982 exceeded those to Republicans ($43.1 million to $37.0 million), PAC gifts to the Democrats were concentrated on incumbents almost sure of reelection, while those to Republicans were more directed to candidates in close races. It is probably not coincidental that Republicans won eight of the nine Senate contests in 1982 decided by less than 3 percent of the vote. In House elections, Republicans won only 38 percent of all contests, but 47 percent of those decided by less than 3 percent.[15]

Soon after the 1982 election, Reagan's political advisers and other members of the Republican national leadership gave thought to the structures through which they would wage the 1984 campaign. A large part of the responsibility for mobilizing campaign workers at the state and local levels, they decided, should be placed on the RNC. Frank Fahrenkopf, who had built an efficient state organization during eight years as party chairman in Nevada, was installed as chairman of the RNC.

At a meeting of Republican state chairmen in April 1983, Fahrenkopf won approval for a plan under which the national committee would intervene directly to build up local Republican organizations in key metropolitan areas.[16] The willingness of state leaders to accept such a plan was further evidence of the weakened condition of state and local parties. Even twenty years ago, it is difficult to imagine the leaders of Republican machines in such states as New York, Pennsylvania, Ohio, Indiana, and Illinois agreeing to permit the national committee to work directly with their county units.

In the fall of 1983 Fahrenkopf persuaded William Lacy, a soft-spoken Tennessean who had worked previously at both Republican congressional campaign committees and the Reagan White House, to return from a private political consulting firm to serve as director of political operations for the RNC. Building on some of the structures created by Brock, Fahrenkopf and Lacy constructed what Lacy has called a "high-tech nuts-and-bolts" national political network, concentrated on 650 target counties and towns. Lacy directed a staff of forty field operators, reporting to him through eight regional directors. Each field operator was assigned a number of counties, in which he met with local party

15. Calculations based on data in "Final Official Election Returns for 1982," *Congressional Quarterly Weekly Report*, vol. 41 (February 19, 1983), pp. 386–94.
16. Interview with Frank Fahrenkopf, January 15, 1985.

leaders to develop a plan of action for the 1984 campaign. Where local organizations were weak or nonexistent, the field operator's first task was to put together some kind of party structure. According to Lacy, local leaders in a few cases were uncooperative, but generally they welcomed the field operator's guidance, attracted in part by promises of additional campaign funds, polling and advertising expertise, and access to the national committee's research facilities.[17]

In each of the targeted counties, the field operator, after consulting with local leaders, reduced the campaign plan to a series of "action steps" (such as renting a campaign headquarters, contracting for radio and newspaper advertising, setting up phone banks, mailing campaign literature, and beginning door-to-door canvassing), each of which was to be completed by a given date. The timetable of action steps for each county was fed into the RNC's central computer. By the spring of 1984 the computer contained schedules of more than 17,000 action steps. Throughout the campaign, the field operators kept the computer up to date on how each county organization was doing on its action steps.

The campaign operations actually being carried out in the precincts and towns no doubt were a good deal messier than those being recorded in the computer. From what I observed in visits to targeted areas in Pennsylvania, North Carolina, and Illinois during the last two weeks of October, Republican drives in those places had plenty of internal feuding, wheelspinning, and duplication of effort. Some local Republican leaders said they paid little attention to directions or advice coming from the national level. Nevertheless, most Republican party people indicated they were receiving more help than ever before from the national party and that the campaign was better coordinated than any they remembered.

The Democrats Respond

Thoughtful Democrats recognized by 1980 that the Republicans were getting far ahead of them in national political structure and modern campaign technology. So long as many more voters regarded themselves as Democrats than as Republicans, the Republicans' growing advantage in organization, even when combined with their long-standing superiority

17. Interviews with William Greener, January 3, 1985; and William Lacy, January 11, 1985.

in fund-raising, did not seem particularly threatening, except in presidential elections (a pretty important exception, however). But after 1980, when the gap between the parties' popular support levels began to close, the Republican edge in organization became increasingly critical. If the numerical division between the two parties is approximately equal, but one party's organization is consistently superior, then that party as a rule will win most elections.

Charles Manatt, a successful southern California lawyer with a long record of experience in Democratic politics, became chairman of the Democratic National Committee (DNC) in 1981. His party was at a low ebb. The Democrats had lost three of the last four presidential elections, and now for the first time in more than a quarter-century had lost control of the Senate as well. But the Democrats in 1981 were probably less open to change than the Republicans had been when Bliss took over the RNC in 1965 or when Brock did so in 1977. Many Democratic leaders remained securely in control of local fiefdoms. The continued Democratic majority in the House of Representatives and the Democratic lead among the governors represented potential resources for Manatt, but they were also independent concentrations of power that he could advise but not direct. The Democrats have always been more heterogeneous than the Republicans—a quality that has been in some ways a source of strength and vitality, but also has been a generator of intraparty feuding and distrust, particularly since natural diversity has been reinforced by formal establishment of interest group caucuses.

A large amount of the new chairman's time, moreover, had to be devoted to fund-raising. The Democrats, while claiming to be the party of the people, were chronically more dependent than the Republicans on large contributors. The amount of money that could be raised from big givers was now severely limited by the federal election campaign act of 1974. Making matters worse, the DNC labored under a huge debt accumulated in the last four national campaigns, beginning with the $9 million assumed from the campaigns of Hubert Humphrey and Robert Kennedy in 1968.

Manatt set out as best he could to modernize the Democrats' national machinery, frankly copying some of the devices Brock had installed. He launched a direct mail campaign aimed at broadening the party's base for fund-raising. The debt was refinanced, freeing up most current receipts for political use. The political division, led after 1981 by Ann Lewis, a former assistant to Representative Barbara Mikulski of Baltimore, was reorganized and expanded. Consulting service was provided to the rickety Democratic organizations in major industrial states, most of which were heavily Democratic in registration, but were marginal in their electoral behavior.[18]

Looking toward 1984, Manatt and Lewis made a major decision: to devote a substantial share of their limited resources to increasing voter registration. Observing that national voter turnout had fallen to 52.6 percent in 1980 and that census statistics showed that registration was particularly low among blacks, Hispanics, the poor, and the young (all groups traditionally favoring the Democrats), Ann Lewis argued that raising voter registration would go a long way toward making the Democratic ticket a strong contender in the next national election. The DNC allocated about $5 million to helping state parties conduct registration drives and urged Democratic governors to direct that registration booths be set up in state welfare and licensing offices. To supplement its own efforts, the DNC encouraged philanthropic organizations with a liberal outlook to sponsor registration drives among minority groups and the poor. Though such organizations had to keep their operations nonpartisan to maintain their tax exemptions, it was assumed that increased registration among their constituencies would be overwhelmingly Democratic. Foundations reportedly contributed about $6 million to help finance registration drives in the 1983–84 election cycle, compared with $1.2 million in 1979–80.[19]

Fahrenkopf and Lacy, viewing the Democrats' registration offensive from the other side of the checkerboard, decided to respond with a drive of their own. The RNC in the 1983-84 cycle devoted about $4 million to registration, which was matched by $4 million from the Reagan-Bush committee and $2 million from the state parties. The Republican drive, unlike the "sweep" approach used by the Democrats, was for the most part targeted at likely Republican voters. Phone banks and teams of volunteer canvassers, set in motion by Lacy's field operators, identified unregistered persons who were firmly or leaning Republican and saw to it that most of them got on the voter rolls. In some states, calls were

18. Interviews with Ann Lewis, December 17, 1984; and Debby Miller, January 16, 1985.

19. Interview with Tony Harrison, January 4, 1985; Ann Cooper, "Voter Turnout May Be Higher on Nov. 6, but for the Parties It May Be a Wash," *National Journal*, vol. 16 (November 3, 1984), pp. 2068–73; and Thomas B. Edsall, "More Bad News for Mondale," *Washington Post*, October 21, 1984.

made by computers playing recorded messages—a technique that Lacy found maximized use of resources and caused little resentment among persons contacted. Registration drives conducted by evangelical Protestant groups, particularly in the South, supplemented Republican efforts.[20]

The battle over new registration ended in an unambiguous triumph for the Republicans. Registration rose sharply among many of the groups that were expected to support the Democrats. But in most areas these increases were offset or exceeded by rises among groups favoring the Republicans. In North Carolina, for example, registration among blacks went up by 179,373, but registration among whites, many of them evangelicals, rose by 307,852. Republicans heavily outnumbered Democrats among new registrants in California and Florida and apparently took the larger share of the 19 percent increase in registration in Texas.

A study by the nonpartisan Committee for the Study of the American Electorate found that on election day Reagan outpolled Mondale among new registrants by 2 to 1. Moreover, among new registrants voting for candidates for the House of Representatives, 54 percent favored Republicans. One thing that went wrong with the Democratic strategy was that some of the groups that had been expected to favor the Democrats voted heavily Republican. New voters between the ages of eighteen and twenty-four, for example, favored Reagan over Mondale by a margin of 67 percent to 28 percent. New voters among women favored Reagan by 57 percent to 36 percent.[21]

Overall in 1984, the Democrats continued to lag behind the Republicans in financial and personnel resources. By October 17, 1984, the DNC had raised $39.8 million, compared with $97.6 million by the RNC. The DNC employed a regular staff of about 300 and the RNC about 500. Nevertheless, the DNC managed to increase the level of services and financial contributions to Democratic candidates well above the level in earlier campaigns.[22]

The Democratic Senatorial Campaign Committee and the Democratic Congressional Campaign Committee made significant progress during the 1983-84 cycle toward catching up with their Republican counterparts. Their congressional committee in particular, under the chairmanship of

20. Interview with Lacy.
21. Curtis B. Gans, *Non-Voter Study '84–'85* (Washington, D.C.: Committee for the Study of the American Electorate, 1985).
22. *Federal Election Commission Record*, vol. 11, January 1985; staff data supplied by the Republican and Democratic National Committees.

Representative Tony Coelho of California, proved itself an effective political instrument. Both Democratic campaign committees substantially increased their levels of direct financial assistance to candidates and, more important, persuaded some senior members holding safe seats to share some of their surplus funds with fellow Democrats in close contests. Coelho steered business PACs eager to ingratiate themselves with the Democrats to races in which the need was greatest. "Tony Coelho," said a Democratic House leader after the election, "was very good at explaining the facts of life to the PACs: if you want to talk to us later, you had better help us now. He also made clear that we did not expect them to contribute to Republican challengers where Democratic incumbents were in trouble."

In 1984 the Democratic Congressional Campaign Committee opened a sophisticated television studio facility on Capitol Hill, which it made available to Democratic candidates for the Senate as well as the House. Though still outgunned by the Republicans, the two Democratic committees helped keep their candidates competitive in most races that were potentially winnable and forced the Republicans to continue devoting resources to contests in which the Democrat had only an outside chance.[23]

Improved Democratic organization seemed to pay off in November: Democrats won two of the four Senate races decided by less than 3 percent of the vote and five of the seven decided by less than 6 percent.[24] "If the real story of the 1982 election was that the Republicans in a recession year lost only twenty-six seats in the House," said Martin Franks, staff director of the Democratic Congressional Campaign Committee, "the real story of 1984 was that in a landslide Republican year at the presidential level, the Democrats lost only fourteen."[25]

A New Kind of Party

The combined effectiveness of party organizations at the national, state, and local levels remains substantially less than it was in the 1950s

23. Interviews with Brian Atwood, December 21, 1984; and Martin Franks, January 8, 1985.
24. Calculations based on data in "Election Results: Returns for Governor, Senate and House," *Congressional Quarterly Weekly Report*, vol. 42 (November 10, 1984), pp. 2923–30.
25. Interview with Franks.

or earlier periods. But effectiveness of the national parties alone, regarded as the entities built around the national and congressional campaign committees, is probably at an all-time high. It is not clear whether this increased strength of the national parties is merely a short-run deviation in a more general pattern of party decline. Centrifugal forces now at work within the Democratic party could conceivably tear the party to pieces during the next few years. The Republicans currently seem more united, but the struggle within the party over the succession to Reagan may reveal deep divisions. And the next Republican president might be as little interested as Richard Nixon was in building a strong national party. On the other hand, national parties may develop enduring institutional identities and power, on the model of the British parties and those in most other European democracies.

One characteristic that the national parties now seem to be developing is increased commitment to a clearly defined ideology. While Republicans and Democrats have generally been on opposite sides of the great ideological divide that in most democracies separates the party of order from the party of equality, their differences have been softened by crosscutting attitudes and interests. There were many conservative Democrats, particularly in the South, and some liberal Republicans, particularly in the Northeast. Even in the North, many Democrats who were liberal on economic and social policies were conservative on foreign policy, in the sense of favoring a hard line against the Soviet Union and its allies. And some Republicans who were conservative on economic and foreign policies were liberal on social issues. Such mixtures still exist, but they have become much less common. As Representative Barney Frank, Democrat of Massachusetts, has observed: "It used to be that Republicans from New England were more conservative than Democrats from New England but more liberal than Democrats from Mississippi. But that isn't true any more. Most Republicans from New England are now more conservative than northern Democrats *and* southern Democrats."[26]

The growing ideological homogeneity within the two parties in part reflects the sharp programmatic distinctions drawn by the Reagan administration—surely the most ideologically consistent administration in modern American history. But the parties were becoming more united in their commitments to distinct social philosophies even before Reagan,

26. Interview with Representative Barney Frank, January 23, 1985.

perhaps responding to social, economic, and even moral forces at work throughout the industrial West.[27]

Ideological unity has contributed to rising levels of party unity in Congress. Republican unity during the first year of the Reagan administration rose to exceptional levels of 81 percent in the Senate and 74 percent in the House (figure 7-1). Since then, Republican unity has fallen back somewhat, as members have responded to the particular interests of their constituencies or expressed personal reservations about the Reagan program. But Republican unity throughout Reagan's first term remained unusually high by historic standards: from 1981 through 1984, average Republican unity in the Senate was 22 percent higher than the average from 1972 through 1980, and in the House it was 4 percent higher. The sharp increase in Republican unity in the Senate after 1980 in part resulted from the Republicans taking on the responsibilities of the majority party. But Democratic unity also rose: average Democratic unity in both the Senate and the House from 1981 through 1984 was 11 percent higher than from 1972 through 1980. In the House, unity among the Democrats during Reagan's first term, except in 1981, was actually higher than among the Republicans.[28]

The responsible party system giving the voters a clear choice between parties representing rival ideologies, called for by the American Political Science Association in 1950, seems to be coming into being, partly in response to the political clout of ideological interest groups that have clustered within the parties, and partly because of the strengthened capacity of the national parties to maintain a party line. There is danger that the increase of ideological consistency within the two parties will deprive American politics of some of the flexibility and suppleness that have enabled the political system over two centuries to accommodate, with one tragic exception, enormous social and economic change while avoiding general violence. It may be, however, that a politics tied more closely to principles and ideals is more appropriate to the current stage of our national life.

27. Walter Dean Burnham, *The Current Crisis in American Politics* (Oxford University Press, 1982), pp. 268–313.

28. Party unity scores compiled by *Congressional Quarterly* show the percentage of roll call votes the average Democrat or Republican voted with his party majority when the majorities of the two parties voted on opposite sides. *Congressional Quarterly Almanac*, vol. 38 (1982), and earlier editions; and Janet Hook, "Party Unity: Congress' Partisanship Drops Despite Hot Electoral Rhetoric," *Congressional Quarterly Weekly Report*, vol. 42 (October 27, 1984), pp. 2809–10.

Figure 7-1. *Average Party Unity Scores in the Senate and House,*
1972–84

Party unity score (percent)[a]

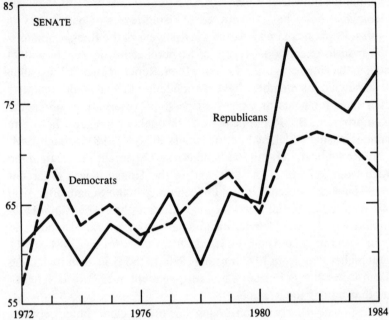

Party unity score (percent)[a]

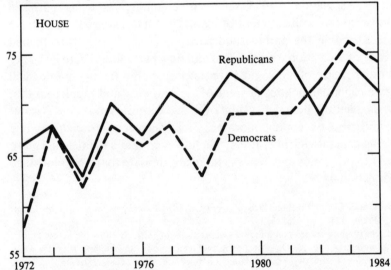

Source: *Congressional Quarterly Almanac,* vol. 38 (1982), and earlier editions; and Janet Hook, "Party Unity: Congress' Partisanship Drops Despite Hot Electoral Rhetoric," *Congressional Quarterly Weekly Report,* vol. 42 (October 27, 1984), pp. 2809–10.
a. The percentage of roll call votes the average Democrat or Republican voted with his party majority when the majorities of the two parties voted on opposite sides.

The national parties now emerging seem far removed from the mass state and local parties of earlier times. The Chicago machine managed to stage a torchlight parade for Walter Mondale in the last week of the 1984 campaign, but everybody knew it was an anachronism. Many of the large number of voters who now tell the pollsters they are independents seem anxious to free themselves from the tribal or ideological identities they associate with the Democrats or the Republicans. Even many of those who align themselves nominally with one of the major parties say they feel no strong connection with it. Most voters now appear to regard themselves as political consumers, selecting between parties as they might shop at rival department stores.

The new campaign technology contributes to the nationalization of parties. The services provided by pollsters and media specialists and the output of computerized data banks can be marketed more efficiently through national party structures than through party organizations based on statehouses, county courthouses, or city halls. The new parties resemble Duverger's model of the cadre party, in that they assign a major role to centralized national bureaucracies, but they depart from the Duverger prototype, under which the cadres are essentially pragmatic, in that they give substantial weight to ideology.[29]

If these trends continue, American politics in the future will be distinctively different from much of what we have known in the past. Some of the warmth and conviviality, some of the willingness to stop short of obliterating the opposition, and some of the knack for compromise, however unprincipled, that have usually characterized American politics may well be lost. But the new kind of parties may turn out to be more successful than the old could have been at galvanizing American society to deal with urgent and complex national and international problems.

Under the Reagan administration, the party has already helped bridge the gap between the executive and legislative branches of the federal government. If one party or the other should get simultaneous control of the presidency and both houses of Congress, the new national party structure may provide the means at last for breaking the famous "deadlock," caused by the separation of powers within the national govern-

29. Interviews with Peter Hart, January 9, 1985; and Richard Wirthlin, February 7, 1985.

ment, which many constitutional experts argue imperils American democracy.[30]

In any case, it seems very unlikely that the country is moving, as some political scientists have been predicting, to a polity essentially without parties. For the foreseeable future, parties of some kind will be important factors in national politics. Indeed, the role of the parties may soon be greater than it has ever been.

30. James MacGregor Burns, for example, has argued this view from *The Deadlock of Democracy: Four-Party Politics in America* (Prentice-Hall, 1963) to *The Power to Lead: The Crisis of the American Presidency* (Simon and Schuster, 1984).

PART TWO

Institutions and Policy

CHAPTER EIGHT

New Patterns of Decisionmaking in Congress

STEVEN S. SMITH

Is congressional decisionmaking fundamentally different in the Reagan era? Have an increased emphasis on budget politics and heightened partisanship changed the process? Have congressional party leaders been able to use the more focused agenda and demands for coherent policy to centralize policymaking and control individualism? In short, has the congressional fragmentation of the 1970s, criticized by journalists and academics alike, been overcome in the 1980s? If one looks behind the headlines, the answer to these questions is no. There are changes taking place, but they have other origins and are operating largely independent of these influences.

Two trends in congressional politics—an increase in the number of decisionmaking units and a wider access to decisionmaking processes—are having a pervasive effect on congressional policymaking. New subcommittees, select committees, and party organs have been created as rank-and-file members have sought ways to increase their role in policymaking. The term "decentralization" has been used to label this movement toward a more fragmented, disjointed, and pluralistic decisionmaking process. While this description is accurate in part, it obscures the distinction between participation structured by committees or subcommittees and more open opportunities for participation by rank-and-

The author thanks Kenneth Janda and Judy Schneider for their comments and assistance.

file members. These two patterns of decisionmaking can be labeled "decentralized" and "collegial." Because they are inconsistent with each other in a number of important ways, their coexistence creates a tension in congressional decisionmaking processes.

Party leaders are often called upon to solve the problems that are created; however, they lack the resources to do so to the satisfaction of the membership, and become the targets of repeated complaints of the rank and file. In fact, party leadership is probably the single most common target of complaints by members of Congress about their institution. In both 1976 and 1980, the House class of 1974 reported greater dissatisfaction with party leadership than with committee operations, caucus activities, or staff support. In 1975 a majority of House Democrats, junior and senior members alike, expressed dissatisfaction with Speaker Carl Albert's leadership. Many House members have been disappointed that Speaker Thomas P. O'Neill's leadership has not lived up to its original billing. Robert Byrd was roundly criticized for lack of policy direction in his first two years as Senate majority leader, and he received an unprecedented challenge to his reelection as minority leader in 1984 on the grounds that he offered weak leadership. Without exception, leaders respond that the nature of Congress now precludes the kind of leadership offered by Lyndon Johnson and Sam Rayburn in the 1950s.[1]

In the 1980s the tension between decentralized and collegial decisionmaking patterns has increased in several ways, making the job of party leadership even more difficult. This essay puts these developments into the larger context of congressional decisionmaking processes and evaluates recent developments in party and committee operations. It does so by defining the alternative decisionmaking patterns, examining the changes of the 1970s in the context of these alternatives, outlining the

1. See Burdett A. Loomis, "The 'Me Decade' and the Changing Context of House Leadership," in Frank H. Mackaman, ed., *Understanding Congressional Leadership* (Washington, D.C.: CQ Press, 1981), pp. 168–69; William Greider and Barry Sussman, *Washington Post*, June 29, 1975; Daniel Rapoport, "Congress Report: It's Not a Happy Time for House, Senate Leadership," *National Journal*, vol. 8 (February 7, 1976), p. 171; Adam Clymer, "Leadership Gap in the Senate," *New York Times*, September 28, 1977; and Robert G. Kaiser, "Majority Leader Byrd Has Made Converts in 2 Years," *Washington Post*, October 28, 1978. On various leaders' views, see Mary Russell, *Washington Post*, March 31, 1974; Steven S. Smith and Christopher J. Deering, *Committees in Congress* (CQ Press, 1984), p. 252; and Robert L. Peabody, "Senate Party Leadership: From the 1950s to the 1980s," in Mackaman, *Understanding Congressional Leadership*, pp. 71–72, 109.

consequences of the tension between decentralized and collegial patterns for congressional party leadership, and detailing recent congressional developments and likely new directions.

Participation and Structure

Most treatments of Congress characterize decisionmaking processes, usually implicitly, as a continuum running from very centralized to very decentralized. At the centralized end, a single leader, or perhaps a tightly knit group of members, makes the important policy decisions for the institution. The number of members and organizational units with an effective role in decisionmaking is very limited. At the decentralized end, members share decisionmaking responsibilities through a division of labor, with successive decisions made by separate individuals or small groups of members. There are many effective participants, all working within the limited jurisdiction of the units to which they are assigned.

The centralization-decentralization continuum has been useful in past analyses of House decisionmaking processes, but is inadequate for analyzing the Senate and many recent developments in the House. For example, the continuum does not capture collegial patterns of decision-making. In pure form, the collegial pattern involves a single unit, such as a committee of the whole, that gives all members an opportunity to participate in deliberations over all issues the chamber considers. (This would be labeled pure democracy in other settings.) Neither centralized nor decentralized patterns would allow collegial decisionmaking. Centralization limits the number of organizational units involved in effective decisionmaking, but also radically limits participation. Decentralization requires a division of labor that limits members' participation to the issues falling under the jurisdiction of their subunits.

Four Patterns of Decisionmaking

Figure 8-1 shows four pure patterns of decisionmaking, each of which has important advantages. The collegial pattern comes closest to the pattern intended by members of the first Congresses.[2] In the collegial

2. Joseph Cooper, "The Origins of the Standing Committees and the Development of the Modern House,"*Rice University Studies,* vol. 56 (Summer 1970), pp. 17–22; Ralph V. Harlow, *The History of Legislative Methods in the Period before 1825* (Yale University Press, 1917); and Lee Robinson, "The Development of the Senate Committee System" (Ph.D. dissertation, New York University, 1954).

Figure 8-1. *Four Decisionmaking Patterns*

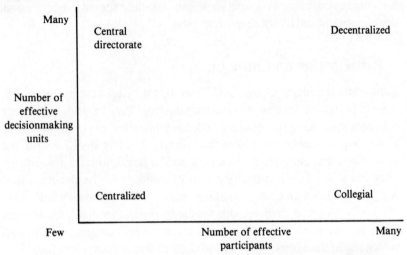

pattern, the absence of structural barriers to broad participation facilitates a free exchange of ideas and, ideally, produces a process of mutual enlightenment that takes full advantage of all members' talents and knowledge. Such a process, it is often hoped, encourages members to rise above their parochial concerns and discover the larger common good.[3] While this pattern risks atomized individualism, its egalitarianism enables members to broaden their interests and collaborate with colleagues to solve policy problems, unlike a fully decentralized pattern.

The decentralized pattern is consistent with the informal norms of apprenticeship, specialization, and committee reciprocity that governed members' behavior during most of the post–World War II period.[4] A division of labor gives Congress the means to manage a large and diverse work load, allows members to specialize in a limited number of policy areas and develop expertise, and provides specialized units (committees, subcommittees) through which the institution may interact with the executive branch and organized interests. Complex, divisive issues can be partitioned into manageable segments, and conflict can be resolved more readily by the members and outsiders most concerned about the issues. In some policy areas, the fragmentation of jurisdiction facilitates

3. The argument for this model of legislative decisionmaking was stated most recently by Arthur Maass, in *Congress and the Common Good* (Basic Books, 1984).
4. Donald R. Matthews, *U.S. Senators and Their World* (University of North Carolina Press, 1960), chap. 5.

the development of norms of universalism, in which policy benefits are distributed widely among the active participants.

The centralized pattern increases the likelihood that Congress will produce well-integrated, coherent policy. A central actor is in a position to set policy and coordinate the construction of legislation. This is especially important for complex problems because the various aspects of policy must be carefully balanced. This pattern permits central decisionmakers to focus institutional resources and makes clear who is responsible for the policy product.

The fourth pattern, with a few effective participants directing the activities of a large number of subunits, perhaps through a central directorate of committee chairmen, is difficult to imagine in Congress. The conditions that limit participation are also likely to limit the number of effective decisionmaking units. But this approach has some of the advantages of the decentralized pattern, such as multiple points of access and the partitioning of policy problems. And it has some of the advantages of the centralized pattern; indeed, rank-and-file members themselves may serve largely as staff to a few core decisionmakers. This combination puts this pattern as close to a hierarchical form as is possible in Congress. Efficiency in decisionmaking in an institution with many members, each of whom must have some organizational assignment, may be an advantage of this pattern. The Senate of the late 1800s came close to this pattern, when a few senior Republican committee chairmen ran the chamber.[5]

The Tendency toward Decentralization

It is well understood that powerful forces propel Congress toward a decentralized pattern of decisionmaking. The members' ties with geographical constituencies and the frequency of elections encourage individualism and parochialism. Constituency differences push members in a variety of directions, and the political parties do not provide substitute ties to bind legislators together for more than very short periods. Members enjoy a fragmented structure in which they can freely pursue policies meeting their individual political needs. In contrast, the centralized and central-directorate forms limit participation and impose roles on members that may not be consistent with their individually defined

5. See David J. Rothman, *Politics and Power: The United States Senate 1869–1901* (Atheneum, 1969), chaps. 1, 2.

political needs. Collegial decisionmaking may undermine the control over policy exercised by subunit members and their political clienteles by risking the interference of other members.

It is not only the reelection imperative that encourages decentralization. Rank-and-file members pursuing strongly held policy objectives or simply an interest in challenging policy problems prefer the opportunities to participate in significant policy deliberations offered by the decentralized pattern. Decentralization, with its multiplicity of effective decisionmaking units, also gives many members a piece of the institution's power. In sum, decentralization meets well the needs of members with a variety of political objectives, constituency demands, and policy concerns while providing a division of labor required for managing a massive work load.

The important differences between the chambers that continue to shape their decisionmaking processes should not be forgotten, of course. Senators' larger constituencies give them incentives to concern themselves with a broader range of policy problems; there is some breathing room at the beginning of senators' six-year terms that can be used to pursue personal policy interests; and the Senate's smaller size permits the average senator to take a more active role in chamber decisionmaking than is possible in the House. All of these factors, each a product of constitutional design, lead the Senate closer to the collegial form than the House.[6] Self-imposed rules and informal practices sometimes reinforce House-Senate differences and sometimes narrow them, but the difference in central tendency has existed since the early Congresses.[7] Consequently, the centralization-decentralization continuum has been more useful in describing change in House decisionmaking processes, where participation and structure have been related more closely.

Preferences for Decentralized or Collegial Patterns

The trade-off between decentralized and collegial patterns is a difficult one for the typical member. Decentralization constitutes a fragmen-

6. See Richard F. Fenno, Jr., *The United States Senate: A Bicameral Perspective* (Washington, D.C.: American Enterprise Institute, 1982); and Lewis A. Froman, Jr., *The Congressional Process: Strategies, Rules, and Procedures* (Little, Brown, 1967), pp. 7–8.

7. See Norman J. Ornstein, "The House and the Senate in a New Congress," in Thomas E. Mann and Norman J. Ornstein, eds., *The New Congress* (American Enterprise Institute, 1981), pp. 363–83; and Smith and Deering, *Committees in Congress*, chap. 1.

tation of legislative power, with each subunit autonomous within its jurisdiction. Collegial processes do not fragment legislative power; all power is shared equally by all members. So the trade-off is dominance over a small fragment of jurisdiction versus a little influence over the total jurisdiction of Congress. Several observers claim that members favor fragmented power, and the record for most of this century supports that view.[8] But the record of the last two decades is not so clear.

What would lead members to prefer one pattern over the other? One reasonable speculation is that members' personal political goals shape their attitudes about decisionmaking processes.[9] Those pursuing narrow interests or concentrating on reelection favor a decentralized institution with committee self-selection. Those seeking personal control over policy and staff also have to settle for decentralization. Members with broad policy interests, on the other hand, feel too constrained in a highly structured, decentralized institution. Collegial processes are much more compatible. And members seeking higher office find that the collegial pattern offers opportunities to increase their visibility to new and larger constituencies. Changing admixtures of member goals over time can be expected to produce shifts in aggregate preferences for the two patterns.

A common observation about members is that a "new breed" has arrived since the late 1950s. The first members to be so labeled were the liberals elected to the Senate between 1958 and 1964.[10] With their wide-ranging policy interests, many of them felt constrained by the decentralized system under the domination of conservative chairmen with the aid of Majority Leader Lyndon Johnson. Many also had presidential ambitions. The Senate, in fact, has since "become a veritable breeding ground for presidential candidates," recent observers comment. As a result, "more and more senators are involved in a wide spectrum of policy areas extending beyond their committee assignments and often well beyond their Senate work."[11] Many House Democrats elected since the

8. Lawrence C. Dodd, "Congress and the Quest for Power," in Lawrence C. Dodd and Bruce I. Oppenheimer, eds., *Congress Reconsidered* (Praeger, 1977), pp. 270–72; and Rochelle Jones and Peter Woll, *The Private World of Congress* (Free Press, 1979), chaps. 3, 6.

9. This is Fenno's conclusion about decisionmaking processes within congressional committees. See Richard F. Fenno, *Congressmen in Committees* (Little, Brown, 1973).

10. See Michael Foley, *The New Senate* (Yale University Press, 1980), especially chap. 4.

11. Norman J. Ornstein, Robert L. Peabody, and David W. Rohde, "The Senate through the 1980s: Cycles of Change," in Lawrence C. Dodd and Bruce I. Oppenheimer, eds., *Congress Reconsidered,* 3d ed. (CQ Press, 1985), p. 18.

early 1970s also have been identified as a new breed, described as "young, activist, nationally oriented and interested in a variety of issues."[12] Similar tendencies have been noted for House and Senate Republicans elected in 1978 and thereafter. A commentator summarized the characteristics of the "new-style" member: "His absorbing interest is governmental policy. He came to Congress with a sense of mission, even a mandate, to have an impact on the legislative process. He is impatient . . . [and] has no habit of being deferential to the established and the powerful, and he will not be so in the Congress, either in committee or on the floor."[13]

The implication is clear. Those members who can be labeled a new breed should favor collegial processes over decentralized ones. Of course, not all members, even among those elected in the last decade, are a part of the new breed and not all new-breed members have consistent views—after all, the trade-off is difficult. The result is a tension between preferences for the two patterns.

Several related aspects of Congress's environment also shape attitudes toward decisionmaking processes. Members who perceive that their institution's or party's collective image greatly affects their own political fortunes are more likely to seek influence over the relevant issues and thus seek to remove structural barriers to participation. Such a perception may be the product of an out-party's grappling with a popular president or the presence of an unusually salient issue that divides the parties or the branches of government. Members may recognize that their pet legislative causes will be better served, at least in the short term, by expanding the number of members involved and overwhelming those in positions of committee or subcommittee authority. They may find that their political interests are disadvantaged by a particular division of jurisdiction between committees. Or Congress's agenda may be so highly focused, perhaps because of a crisis or an unusual presidential effort, that participation limited to one's committees or subcommittees is meaningless. And finally, shifts in the policy agenda may produce changes in members' preferences for decisionmaking processes. For example, a shift from distributive issues to regulatory or redistributive issues is likely to expand the number of members demand-

12. Richard E. Cohen, "Strains Appear as 'New Breed' Democrats Move to Control Party in the House," *National Journal,* vol. 15 (June 25, 1983), p. 1328.
13. James L. Sundquist, *The Decline and Resurgence of Congress* (Brookings, 1981), p. 371.

ing the right to participate.[14] Such circumstances would reinforce the interest of members with broad policy or higher office concerns in collegial processes and may convince others that a more collective process is desirable. Unlike members' political motivations, however, these conditions are likely to be quite transitory.

Over the last two decades several developments have stimulated interest in overcoming the obstacles of decentralized decisionmaking. New regulatory issues in areas such as the environment, energy, consumer protection, and civil rights have attracted the interest of a wide range of members and have not fallen neatly within the division of committee jurisdictions. Sharp institutional conflicts between Congress and presidents have arisen, as have related divisions between the parties, especially between congressional Democrats and White House Republicans. And the domination of television as a medium of political communication has increased the visibility of and the interest in these issues and conflicts.

The 1970s in Perspective

Both chambers of Congress undertook major reappraisals of their decisionmaking processes during the 1970s.[15] Although the mix differed, both chambers considered structural changes and ways to improve opportunities for effective participation of rank-and-file members. The search for structural reforms was motivated by a number of concerns: poor alignment of committee jurisdictions with policy problems, unevenly distributed work loads among committees, and severe scheduling problems caused by multiple committee and subcommittee assignments. The drive to increase avenues of participation was aimed primarily at powerful committee chairmen who maintained firm control of committee agendas, staff, and policy development. Both structural and participatory concerns, then, stemmed from the manner in which the chambers had decentralized their decisionmaking processes. The resulting reforms

14. Randall B. Ripley and Grace A. Franklin, *Congress, the Bureaucracy and Public Policy,* 3d ed. (Homewood, Ill.: Dorsey, 1980), chap. 8.

15. See Roger H. Davidson, "Two Avenues of Change: House and Senate Committee Reorganization," in Lawrence C. Dodd and Bruce I. Oppenheimer, eds., *Congress Reconsidered,* 2d ed. (CQ Press, 1981), pp. 103–37; and Roger H. Davidson and Walter J. Oleszek, "Adaptation and Consolidation: Structural Innovation in the U.S. House of Representatives," *Legislative Studies Quarterly,* vol. 1 (February 1976), pp. 37–65.

do not fall neatly into categories, but in most cases their basic thrust is readily discernible.

The House of Representatives

House Democrats moved to consider wide-ranging reforms after reactivating their caucus in 1969. Between 1971 and 1974, changes in House and Democratic caucus rules limited committee chairmen to one subcommittee chairmanship, stripped chairmen of their ability to authorize and appoint subcommittees, forced the creation of subcommittees on most committees, granted subcommittees staffs and jurisdictional identities, and guaranteed the minority party significant staff assistance. This set of reforms had a decentralizing effect on House decisionmaking processes and closely tied participation to structure: more subcommittees and more members gained an effective role in decisionmaking. Despite repeated attempts, no significant jurisdictional realignment was adopted in the House, in part because strengthened subcommittee chairmen now had a greater stake in the old jurisdictional arrangement.[16] As a result, the fragmented, overlapping jurisdictions of House standing committees remain, along with the attendant problems of managing complex policy and scheduling problems.[17]

A few House reformers, led by Richard Bolling, Democrat of Missouri, sought to improve policy coordination capability and increase accountability by strengthening centralizing forces. After proposals to add to the functions of the Rules Committee were dropped, the speakership was given new political tools by House Democrats. The Speaker was made chairman of the revitalized Steering and Policy Committee (which was given committee assignment authority) and gained new powers to

16. Roger H. Davidson and Walter J. Oleszek, *Congress against Itself* (Indiana University Press, 1977), p. 263.

17. That overlapping jurisdictions continue to be a problem for the House was most evident in the House reaction to the 1983 scandals in the Environmental Protection Agency. Five separate subcommittees from four different committees stumbled over each other to investigate allegations of mismanagement and political manipulation of agency decisions, eventually forcing Speaker O'Neill to intervene. Despite appeals from the Speaker, the subcommittee chairmen refused to coordinate their activities. See Joseph A. Davis, "House Subcommittees Begin Reviewing EPA Documents: Two More Officials Are Fired," *Congressional Quarterly Weekly Report*, vol. 41 (February 26, 1983), pp. 411–13; and Howard Kurtz, "Levitas Pact on EPA Documents Faulted by Panel Chairman," *Washington Post*, February 20, 1983.

refer legislation to multiple committees or to ad hoc committees (with House approval) and the authority to make the nominations of all Democrats on the Rules Committee. The Democratic party leadership also gained additional assistant whips and staff. The clear intent was to counter decentralization by increasing the authority of the Speaker, although the focus on the "service industry" of the committee system (committee assignments, bill referral, floor scheduling, and rules) did not directly reduce the autonomy of the standing committees.[18]

Increased decentralization, qualified by limited centralizing reforms, is only part of the story in the House. The major thrust of the reforms in rules and practices was a shift toward more collegial decisionmaking processes.[19] Collegial reforms came in two forms. One was to create additional opportunities for rank-and-file participation at nearly every stage and level in the decisionmaking process. The most important was the reactivation of the Democratic caucus.[20] While the caucus was not as active as it could have been during the 1970s, it occasionally provided a forum for the expression of views that would not otherwise be heard by committee members. In addition, twelve elected members were placed on the revitalized Steering and Policy Committee to represent geographic regions in its deliberations on committee assignments and policy matters. Caucus rules were changed to require rotation of the elected and appointed members of Steering and Policy and replacement of senior members by junior members. The reform enabled the Speaker to place representatives of junior and minority members on the committee. The reforms of standing committee procedures not only guaranteed

18. Academic observers have commented that there may be an ideal mix of centralization and decentralization, labeling the mix "integrated specialization" or "channeled expressiveness." See Charles O. Jones, "House Leadership in an Age of Reform," in Mackaman, *Understanding Congressional Leadership*, p. 122; and Allen Schick, "Complex Policymaking in the United States Senate," in *Policy Analysis on Major Issues*, prepared for the Commission on the Operation of the Senate, 94 Cong. 2 sess. (Government Printing Office, 1977), p. 21.

19. Charles O. Jones comes to a similar conclusion, although Jones prefers to view the reforms as opportunities for expression rather than participation. See Jones, "House Leadership in an Age of Reform," p. 131.

20. It should also be noted that House Republicans rejuvenated their caucus in the mid-1960s. Gerald Ford promised a more active Republican conference when he became its chairman in 1963. The conference was not used as planned, however, although it established a staff and became more active after Melvin Laird took the chairmanship in 1965. See Charles O. Jones, *The Minority Party in Congress* (Little, Brown, 1970), p. 36; and Randall B. Ripley, *Party Leaders in the House of Representatives* (Brookings, 1967), p. 46.

subcommittees independence from full committee chairmen but also democratized committee operations by providing for subcommittee self-selection, giving a majority of members the power to call meetings, restricting abusive uses of proxy voting, and forcing full committee chairmen to promptly report legislation approved by their committees. And Democratic party leaders have created numerous informal opportunities for rank-and-file members to influence chamber and party decisionmaking: lengthy whip meetings, Speaker's task forces, and caucus committees.

The other type of collegial reform was to make members with special sources of influence accountable to rank-and-file members. Caucus and whip meetings created situations in which top party leaders were obliged to explain their agendas and strategies. The Democratic caucus assumed the power to require the Rules Committee to issue special orders permitting amendments in floor debate. Full committee chairmen were required to face election by the caucus every two years and subcommittee chairmen to be elected by their committee caucuses. During the 1970s, three full committee chairmen and one Appropriations subcommittee chairman were denied election by the Democratic caucus; at least six members in line for subcommittee chairmanships by virtue of seniority were denied election by their committee caucuses; and many others faced substantial opposition.[21]

House Republicans played an important role in shaping many important reforms of chamber rules in the 1970s, but were excluded in other areas where Democratic reformers sought the shelter of the majority party caucus to impose reforms on the committees. The Republicans themselves had already increased the number of opportunities for junior members to participate by the late 1960s. New and more active party committees and a more active party caucus had given rank-and-file Republicans a greater voice in party affairs by the time Democratic reformers moved their caucus to action in the 1970s. However, House Republicans lack the formal strictures limiting the power of ranking committee Republicans over the use of staff and other resources. As a result, Republican activities on several House committees remain far more centralized than those of the majority party Democrats.[22]

The net effect of the 1970s was to increase opportunities for Democratic rank-and-file members to participate actively in party and chamber

21. See Smith and Deering, *Committees in Congress*, chap. 6.
22. Ibid., chaps. 6, 7.

decisionmaking. Change took both decentralized and collegial forms, reflecting the multifaceted nature of the attack on the power of full committee chairmen. And as attacks on the same targets, the two approaches appeared consistent; together, they represented a rightward shift in the patterns shown in figure 8-1.

Most visible conflicts between the two models during the 1970s, such as committee chairmen's resistance to Democratic caucus discussion of issues under their committees' jurisdictions, could be explained away as "sour grapes" on the part of the older generation of losers in the reforms.[23] More serious conflict between decentralization and collegial patterns generally was avoided because the collegial opportunities were not fully exploited in the 1970s. While the Democratic caucus played a role in Vietnam War and tax issues for limited periods, the use of the caucus late in the decade was limited to organizational matters.[24] Very few meetings of the Steering and Policy Committee were devoted to specific legislation. Both Speakers Albert and O'Neill attempted to avoid meetings in which intraparty factionalism would surface. O'Neill flatly disliked having the caucus or Steering and Policy dictate policy or strategy to standing committees or party leaders.[25] House Democratic leaders repeatedly found themselves as the defenders of decentralized decisionmaking. In any case, there was less demand for caucus involvement than there might have been because of the policy direction offered by a president of the same party. Overall, then, the House became more decentralized, although important collegial processes were put in place as well.

The Senate

Although Senate Democratic leader Robert Byrd asserted greater control over the staff of his party's Policy and Steering committees and assumed more responsibility in managing legislation on the floor, no significant centralizing changes occurred in the Senate.[26]

The major structural change was the 1977 consolidation of committees

23. See Bruce F. Freed, "House Democrats Dispute over Caucus Role," *Congressional Quarterly Weekly Report,* vol. 33 (May 3, 1975), pp. 911–15.

24. On the use of the caucus, see Sundquist, *Decline and Resurgence of Congress,* pp. 383–87.

25. Ann Cooper, "Democrats Still Arguing Over Party Caucus Role on Legislative Issues," *Congressional Quarterly Weekly Report,* vol. 36 (April 15, 1978), pp. 875–76.

26. Smith and Deering, *Committees in Congress,* p. 196.

and subcommittees. The Senate eliminated two standing committees and several special and select committees; rearranged committee jurisdictions in areas such as energy, the environment, science and technology, and foreign commerce; and, as a by-product of new limits on senators' committee and subcommittee assignments, abolished over thirty subcommittees. These consolidating changes did not reduce opportunities for participation significantly, however, because ninety subcommittees remained and other reforms had spread subcommittee chairmanships to nearly all majority party members. In 1970 the Senate had limited senators to no more than one subcommittee chairmanship on the same committee. And at the time of the 1977 consolidation, full committee chairmen were restricted to two subcommittee chairmanships. As a result, Senate decisionmaking was slightly more decentralized by the end of the 1970s as fewer full committee chairmen held multiple subcommittee chairmanships.

The more overwhelming direction of change in the Senate, however, was toward more collegial decisionmaking. In the 1960s Democratic liberals had asserted their independence of the conservative committee chairmen, using the floor to challenge committee recommendations and raise issues blocked in committee. The liberals were tolerated and sometimes encouraged by Majority Leader Mike Mansfield, who opened more and more avenues for rank-and-file members to participate effectively, including expansion of the Democratic Policy and Steering committees and floor scheduling more in accordance with individual members' needs.[27] By the early 1970s the committee-centered norms of apprenticeship and specialization, at least in the sense that involvement in noncommittee matters was proscribed, were no longer operative in the Senate.[28] The committee and subcommittee structure retained great significance in Senate decisionmaking, but no longer posed insuperable obstacles to senators seeking to influence policy outside the jurisdiction of their own committees. As one observer noted in 1973, the Senate combined "high participation and low specialization."[29]

27. See Peabody, "Senate Party Leadership." Also see John G. Stewart, "Two Strategies of Leadership: Johnson and Mansfield," in Nelson W. Polsby, ed., *Congressional Behavior* (Random House, 1971), pp. 61–92; Randall B. Ripley, *Power in the Senate* (St. Martin's, 1969), pp. 91–96; and Andrew J. Glass, "Mansfield Reforms Spark 'Quiet Revolution' in Senate," *National Journal*, vol. 3 (March 6, 1971), p. 500.

28. David W. Rohde, Norman J. Ornstein, and Robert L. Peabody, "Political Change and Legislative Norms in the U.S. Senate, 1957–1974," in Glenn R. Parker, ed., *Studies of Congress* (CQ Press, 1985), pp. 175–79.

29. Fenno, *Congressmen in Committees*, p. 182.

In the 1970s additional changes institutionalized the power of rank-and-file members. In 1970 rules were instituted formalizing each senator's right to a seat on one of the top four committees and permitting committee majorities to call meetings.[30] A Mansfield-initiated practice of submitting Democratic committee assignments to his party's conference for approval began in 1971, and a 1972 rule required that Senate delegations to conference committees represent the Senate's majority view. In 1973 the Republicans provided for the election of ranking committee members by the committee caucuses, and in 1975 Democrats decided to permit secret ballot votes on committee chairmen at the request of one-fifth of the conference. Democratic Majority Leader Byrd began in 1977 to submit the Steering Committee's committee assignment nominations to the party conference for approval. And in 1977 rules were adopted giving each senator additional staff for committee duties and urging committees to give all senators their first subcommittee choice before any are given two subcommittee assignments. By the end of the 1970s rank-and-file senators had gained a formal voice in nearly all aspects of party, committee, and floor decisionmaking processes.

The conflict between decentralized and collegial decisionmaking was pervasive in the Senate of the 1960s and 1970s but, in contrast to the House, majority party leaders did not offer a strong defense of decentralization. Indeed, Mansfield, who served as floor leader from 1961 to 1976, has been cited frequently as having stimulated the breakdown of the apprenticeship and specialization norms and the associated increase in the willingness of senators to challenge committees on the floor. Mansfield believed that even the decision about how to make a decision was best left to the Senate as a whole.[31] "Coequal" was the codeword often used by Mansfield to describe senators' roles, a word that captures the essence of collegial decisionmaking.

The Budget Process

The new congressional budget process created by the Congressional Budget and Impoundment Control Act of 1974 offered the potential of

30. The four committees are Appropriations, Armed Services, Finance, and Foreign Relations. This rule formalized the "Johnson rule" initiated by Democratic Majority Leader Lyndon Johnson in the 1950s and adopted by the Republicans soon thereafter.
31. See Ripley, *Power in the Senate*, pp. 91–96; Rohde, Ornstein, and Peabody, "Political Change and Legislative Norms," pp. 163–65; and Stewart, "Two Strategies of Leadership," pp. 69.

radically altering the decentralized fiscal policymaking process in Congress. The process was designed to coordinate, but not undermine, the decentralized process by which Congress had made budget decisions. Budget resolutions provided a legislative vehicle through which Congress could set broad budget policy objectives and guide or direct the separate appropriations, tax, and authorizations committees to develop specific legislation consistent with the broad policy. As a result, budget resolutions provide a means for centralized decisionmakers to shape a wide range of policies. But the budget act of 1974 did not guarantee that the vehicle would or could be exploited in this manner. New House and Senate Budget committees were assigned the responsibility to write and report the budget resolutions, but they could not impose their will without the endorsement of their chambers, which were stacked with defenders of the role of the old committees. Nor did party leaders automatically acquire the power to see that coherent policy was enacted through the new process.

The record of the 1970s shows mixed results. The occasional success of both Budget committees in overcoming major challenges by other committees often has been interpreted as a victory for a newly centralized decisionmaking process over the "evil" centrifugal forces of Congress. This interpretation misses an important distinction. In the first place, the budget resolutions were constructed with an eye to what would pass the chamber. This required Budget members, and especially their chairmen, to anticipate the preferences of their colleagues. Moreover, the contests between the Budget committees and challenging tax or authorization committees were decided on the floor of the two houses, usually after lengthy debate and the active participation of a cross section of members. The membership of the two houses played a genuine, significant role in setting broad policy that had previously not received formal legislative attention.

The Consequences of Collegial Decisionmaking

In the abstract, there are several significant implications of a shift from a decentralized pattern toward a more collegial policymaking process. The most obvious is that it greatly increases the "scope of conflict" by expanding the number of members and the size of the constituency involved in a policy debate.[32] Because more interests are involved, the definition of the issue debated, the salient political divisions, and the balance of power are all likely to be different from those in committees and subcommittees. Setting the agenda is likely to be a more difficult task in the collegial pattern as members with a variety of interests seek meaningful participation. As a result, predicting which issues and political divisions will surface is more difficult.

When compared with the decentralized pattern, in which issues are often partitioned and decided in a piecemeal fashion, the collegial pattern provides opportunities for members to connect parts of policies. Such opportunities make it more difficult to suppress deeply or widely held attitudes. This may mean that underlying ideological or regional divisions will surface more frequently, increasing the intensity of divisions and, ironically, undermining norms of collegiality.

Building coalitions is difficult enough in a large institution where majorities must be re-created frequently. With a larger number of effective participants, however, coalition building is even more difficult, time consuming, and expensive. Efficient means of communication and persuasion are sought by members seeking to shape policy. In fact, coalition building may look like mass marketing. Mass mailings, such as "Dear Colleague" letters, are employed frequently. Members use the media to sell legislation to colleagues. The line between legislative assistant and press secretary becomes blurred. Indirect persuasion—through outside groups—is routine as coalition builders seek to influence members with whom they have little familiarity.

In a collegial setting, rank-and-file members recognize that their political reputations can be molded by their activity on the floor, in party caucus, in the mass media, or wherever policy debates take place. Committee and subcommittee assignments no longer constrain individuals' choices of issues on which to focus or commit staff resources. In the absence of a formal structure that effectively limits interaction between members and funnels individuals' efforts, ad hoc groups may proliferate as members coalesce in multiple combinations to pursue common interests, share resources, and create opportunities to publicize their causes and themselves.

Finally, the less structured participation of the collegial pattern poses the risk that the institution will eventually disintegrate into atomized

32. On the significance of the scope of conflict, see E. E. Schattschneider, *The Semisovereign People* (Dryden Press, 1960), chap. 1.

individualism. In contrast to the decentralized pattern, no member or group of members is in a position to enforce norms of collegiality and courtesy. Committee chairmen are not in a position to provide sanctions against violators of institutional norms, and members are reluctant to infringe upon the liberties of colleagues. The collegial pattern entails greater risks because it depends more completely on the cooperation and good will of the membership.

This description captures a great deal of the change that has accompanied the move to more collegial patterns. Other observers have noted an increased number of challenges to committee recommendations on both the House floor and Senate floor, national visibility for more House members, increased salience of ideological divisions within the Democratic party, the spread of ad hoc caucuses, and a breakdown in the observance of the norm of courtesy.[33] But the picture is even more complicated because of the continuing power of the forces of decentralization in both chambers.

An Uncomfortable Mix

The mix of decentralized and collegial patterns creates serious problems for Congress. Most concretely, the combination makes members' relative status more ambiguous. The egalitarianism of collegialism is not consistent with the special status granted to chairmen in a decentralized committee system. To take a current example, how should Republican members of Ways and Means treat Representative Jack Kemp when the committee considers tax simplification? Are they to defer to his expertise even though he has never been a member of the committee? The budget process has posed similar problems repeatedly as Budget Committee members and others shape reconciliation instructions. Chairmen and committee members believe they do not get the credit and deference

33. See, for example, Alan Ehrenhalt, "In the Senate of the '80s, Team Spirit Has Given Way to the Rule of Individuals," *Congressional Quarterly Weekly Report*, vol. 40 (September 4, 1982), pp. 2175–82; Burdett Loomis, "Congressional Caucuses and the Politics of Representation," in Dodd and Oppenheimer, *Congress Reconsidered*, 2d ed., pp. 204–20; Ornstein, "The House and Senate in a New Congress"; Norman J. Ornstein, Robert L. Peabody, and David W. Rohde, "The Contemporary Senate into the 1980s," in Dodd and Oppenheimer, *Congress Reconsidered*, 2d ed., pp. 13–30; Barbara Sinclair, *Majority Leadership in the U.S. House* (Johns Hopkins University Press, 1983), chap. 1; and Tim Cook, "Marketing the Members: The Ascent of the Congressional Press Secretary," paper prepared for the 1985 annual meeting of the Midwest Political Science Association.

they deserve, while other members are still careful not to alienate chairmen and committees responsible for acting on their pet legislation. Members complain when a chairman, such as Senator Jesse Helms, Republican of North Carolina, ignores committee duties to pursue interests on the floor, but they demand the right to participate themselves on any issue coming before the chamber.

The combination also enhances the chances that norms of collegiality and courtesy will weaken. The independence granted committee or subcommittee chairmen in a decentralized institution breeds an individualism that is not always well suited to a collegial process in which it is hoped that participants will share ideas and talents, welcome differing views, and seek common ground to resolve conflict. This problem can be expected to be especially acute when the number of chairmen is numerous, as it is in the House and Senate today.

A combination of decentralized and collegial patterns also multiplies the number of decision points at which legislation can be blocked and coalitions must be built.[34] Both committees and subcommittees retain great independence in initiative and resources, but they lack the autonomy that a truly decentralized system would provide.[35] The scope of conflict changes continually, usually expanding, as legislation passes from one stage to the next. Deals and accommodations devised at one stage cannot be adhered to later because negotiations must be reopened at each stage. Norms of mutual accommodation or logrolling, which made decisionmaking more efficient in many policy areas, are weaker as a result. Legislative outcomes are uncertain until the very end. Consequently, planning for the effective use of legislative talent and political resources is very difficult and fraught with error. The legislative process may be more exciting and challenging as a result, but it also is more frustrating and exhausting.

Problems for Leadership

These problems affect party leaders as much as other members, if not more so. James Sundquist offers this interpretation:

The headlong trend toward democracy, and dispersal of power, in the Senate and the House has changed the task of leadership. Whereas the problem of

34. Bruce I. Oppenheimer has labeled this the "new obstructionism." See his "Congress and the New Obstructionism," in Dodd and Oppenheimer, *Congress Reconsidered*, 2d ed., pp. 275–95.

35. See Smith and Deering, *Committees in Congress*, chap. 5.

Lyndon Johnson and Sam Rayburn, in the 1950s, was to wheedle and plead with committee chairmen who held the keys to legislative action, the problem of Robert Byrd and Tip O'Neill, in the 1970s, was to organize the new individualism—or new fragmentation—into some kind of working whole. And the leaders must do that without seeming to grasp for power, because the resistance of the rank and file of the new-style congressman to any hint of bossism would be instant. In their ambivalence, junior members will accept leadership only on their own terms, and subject to their continuous control. They insist on the right to decide day by day and case by case, without coercion, when they will be followers and when they will assert their right of independence.[36]

The tension is no longer one of centralization versus decentralization, leaders versus committee chairmen, sometimes a tug-of-war and sometimes cooperation. Increasingly, the tension is between decentralization and collegialism, with party leaders serving as referees, traffic cops, or fire fighters. As one sports fan in the Senate Republican leadership suggested to me, there is a sense that the party leaders are always playing away games on the home turf of the committees or of the rank and file on the floor and in caucus.

Not surprisingly, this situation yields ambiguities about leaders' roles as well. Leaders are frequently called upon to resolve conflicts between committees and other party members—that is, to resolve the disputes that arise between decentralized and collegial patterns. In a genuinely decentralized system, leaders would feel compelled to protect the prerogatives of committees; in a purely collegial setting, committee recommendations would have no special preference. In a mixed situation, there is no obvious solution. Developing a consensus about the decisionmaking process, let alone meeting the varied policy demands of members, is nearly impossible.[37]

As noted, House leaders have more frequently defended the more entrenched role of committees than have their Senate counterparts. Senate leaders have devised a more comfortable accommodation of the two sets of demands. Senate leaders of both parties have held regularly scheduled meetings with all committee chairmen, for example. These meetings give leaders opportunities to press for committee action at crucial times in a setting that does not single out particular committees. In the House, majority party leaders have felt that chairmen would

36. Sundquist, *The Decline and Resurgence of Congress*, p. 395.
37. Sinclair emphasizes this theme in *Majority Leadership in the House*.

resent regular leadership supervision. Even House leadership staff have been hesitant to organize meetings of top committee aides, and, when they have attempted to do so, senior committee aides often have been conspicuously uncooperative. But in neither chamber has the pattern been consistent as leaders have attempted to meet the inconsistent demands of their members.

Leaders often are forced to devise ad hoc mechanisms to create policy and build coalitions in this context. Formal and informal task forces of members may be created to devise policy proposals and push others; committees and their staffs may be asked to contribute to packages of party proposals; or temporary committees may be established to write legislation. All of these measures, and others, were tried in some form during the late 1970s. These innovations reflect attempts to overcome the continuing deficiencies of decentralization while being sensitive to the political egos of committee members. They also reflect a desire to accommodate the demands of those who are not members of a particular committee while recognizing that not all members can sit around the same table to write legislation and devise strategy. None is completely satisfactory and none can be applied to each major policy problem Congress faces.

Ironically, the expectations for party leadership are higher in this context than they are in the more clearly decentralized situation. Where legislative responsibilities are clearly defined, as they are in a purely decentralized institution, the role of leadership is more narrowly limited to building coalitions at the floor stage on a few major pieces of legislation. In the present context, however, leaders must regularly handle decisions about how decisions are going to be made. Deciding who is going to take the lead, write working drafts, offer alternatives, and set legislative strategy are problems party leaders frequently are called upon to solve. But leaders do not have recipes for solving these problems and they are unlikely to have them in the future. It is hardly surprising that leaders must suffer frequent criticism in this environment.

Into the 1980s

The new decade witnessed an even more rampant individualism in the Senate and further moves toward more collegial processes in the House. The changes, reflecting the trends established in the previous two decades, were colored by the dominating items on the agenda of the new Republican administration, budgets and deficits.

Budget Politics

The 1980s have been dominated by budget politics, beginning in 1980 when the reconciliation procedures of the 1974 budget act were first used successfully to package deep spending cuts. In 1981 the Reagan administration's supporters in Congress used the reconciliation procedure after the first budget resolution to prevent committees from pigeonholing administration proposals. Republican leaders in Congress served as "point men" for the president, and much of the administration's success was due to their efforts.[38] Budgetary stalemate prevailed in 1982 as President Reagan and members of Congress looked toward the midterm elections. Few appropriations bills were passed, and the major struggles were over supplemental appropriations bills and a continuing resolution. Most appropriations bills were passed in 1983 and 1984, although executive-legislative branch confrontation and stalemate ruled most of both years. By 1983 congressional budget making had again become dominated by the centrifugal forces in the committee system.

The record teaches several lessons about the evolution of congressional decisionmaking. The experience of the House in 1981 demonstrated the inherent weaknesses of party leaders in Congress when they are not reinforced by a president of their party. House Democratic leaders and weakened committee chairmen were in no position to insulate their members from the president and had no resources that could counter his. The "open" Congress was vulnerable to a popular president with a well-focused program.[39]

The subsequent years also demonstrate that 1981 was very unusual and that the centrifugal forces in Congress are still powerful. Both House and Senate committees exercised great independence from Reagan and party leaders after 1981. And many members, including Senate majority party Republicans, expressed concern that congressional decisionmak-

38. Two aides of Senate Majority Leader Howard Baker have provided an account of Baker's role. See James A. Miller and James D. Range, "Reconciling an Irreconcilable Budget: The New Politics of the Budget Process," *Harvard Journal on Legislation*, vol. 20 (Winter 1983), pp. 4–30.

39. See Norman J, Ornstein, "The Open Congress Meets the President," in Anthony King, ed., *Both Ends of the Avenue* (American Enterprise Institute, 1983), pp. 204–10.

ing processes not be "subverted" in the fashion of 1981 again.[40] In the House, the experience stimulated interest in formal reforms to ensure that the role of standing committees was not undermined again. No action was taken because House Democrats did not want reform to interfere with ongoing developments in budget politics.

The experience also stimulated other innovations. In 1981, for example, Representative Toby Moffett, Democrat of Connecticut, attempted to organize House subcommittee chairmen to write an alternative to the Republican budget plan. Few subcommittee chairmen took much interest and the effort was dropped. Before the Ninety-ninth Congress, Democrat Anthony Beilenson of California proposed that the Speaker be given the authority to appoint the Budget Committee chairman, thereby inserting the leadership more directly into the process of devising budget resolutions. The proposal was set aside by a committee of the Democratic caucus after Speaker O'Neill turned down the offer, indicating, according to a staff member, that "the caucus deserves to select its own Budget chairman."[41] In the absence of clear lines of authority and assignment of responsibility, there is a constant search for new organizational forms in the House.

The House of Representatives

The House majority party Democrats continued the movement toward more collegial decisionmaking that had begun in the 1970s but was now also entwined with the budget politics of the 1980s. The most conspicuous developments occurred in the Democratic caucus. Much of the interest in the caucus was stimulated by the desire of many Democrats to participate in constructing alternatives to Reagan administration proposals. Both new caucus chairmen—Gillis Long of Louisiana, who served as chairman in the Ninety-seventh and Ninety-eighth Congresses, and Richard Gephardt of Missouri, who was elected at the start of the Ninety-ninth—promised and delivered frequent meetings of the caucus, which had not been active in the Ninety-fifth or Ninety-sixth Congresses.

40. The term is Senator Quayle's. See Martin Tolchin, "The Changing Senate: Senators Assail Anarchy in New Chamber of Equals," *New York Times,* November 25, 25, 1984.

41. Confidential interview with the author, December 6, 1984. The proposal was considered by the Committee on Organization, Study, and Review of the Democratic caucus in November 1984.

Under Long, the caucus met about once a month while Congress was in session, and Gephardt promised meetings every other week. Long moved to close the meetings to the public so that members would feel free to participate. Among other things, this meant that party members were more willing to question party and committee leaders. In fact, Gephardt has commented that a major purpose of more frequent meetings is to "allow the leadership to talk to us and us to talk to the leadership."[42]

Gephardt's proposal for biweekly meetings faced vigorous opposition from several committee chairmen. The chairmen objected to Gephardt's suggestion that committees be barred from meeting at the same time as the caucus. And the more telling complaint concerned Gephardt's plan to use frequent caucus meetings to discuss specific policy proposals, many of which would be pending in committee. The chairmen, believing that the caucus activity would undermine their committees' roles, asked rhetorically, "Why don't we just dismantle the committees?"[43] When the strong objections were voiced in a late January caucus meeting, Gephardt's formal proposal was referred to the caucus's Committee on Organization, Study, and Review and, as of late March, no action had been taken on it. Nevertheless, Gephardt is free to call frequent caucus meetings.

The caucus has created special forums for discussion and for the creation of party policy documents. The most prominent of these is the Committee on Party Effectiveness created by Long in 1981. The committee, which had forty-three members in the Ninety-eighth Congress, has attracted the active participation of many new-breed members, most notably Richard Gephardt and Leon Panetta, Democrat of California. The committee has an explicitly collegial purpose. Its members comment that "it's one of the few places where a broad cross section of Democrats can sit down and get to know each other" and "the truth is scattered and the caucus committee is a place for an exchange of disparate views."[44] The committee produced lengthy statements on economic policy in the Ninety-seventh and Ninety-eighth Congresses that were endorsed by the caucus and helped shape the 1984 Democratic platform.

42. Diane Granat, "Junior Democrats Gain a Louder Voice; Leadership Panels Will Serve as Forum," *Congressional Quarterly Weekly Report*, vol. 42 (December 8, 1984), p. 3054.
43. Confidential interview with the author, January 31, 1985.
44. Cohen, "Strains Appear as 'New Breed' Democrats Move to Control Party," p. 1330.

The caucus was also the site of the first successful effort since 1975 to unseat an incumbent committee chairman. Les Aspin, Democrat of Wisconsin, campaigned against eighty-year-old Melvin Price of Illinois, chairman of the Armed Services Committee, on the grounds that Price's physical infirmities impaired his ability to lead the Democrats on vital defense issues and that his support of the defense establishment was out of step with the views of most House Democrats. Aspin's effort, in contrast with the rejection of three chairmen in 1975, represented a personal campaign by a challenger to unseat the incumbent. In 1975 the new chairmen played no significant role in deposing the incumbents. Aspin also was the seventh-ranking Democrat on Armed Services, leap-frogging over five other Democrats to the chairmanship; in 1975 the second-ranking Democrat was elected chairman in all three cases. And, finally, Aspin succeeded in the face of active opposition from Speaker O'Neill. Aspin appealed directly to the caucus, overcoming both the dictates of the seniority system, which insulated chairmen before the reforms of the 1970s, and the defensive maneuvers of the Speaker.

The Democrats have moved in yet other ways to increase avenues of participation for rank-and-file members and hold leaders accountable. In 1982 Democrats decided to require appointed Steering and Policy Committee members to rotate every two years instead of four, thus providing an opportunity for more members to serve on the committee that makes committee assignments and occasionally endorses legislation. At the start of the Ninety-ninth Congress, reformers succeeded in making the majority whip's position elective and convinced the Speaker to hold more frequent Steering and Policy Committee meetings to discuss policy. Democratic leaders also expanded the number of deputy whips from four to seven and the number of at-large whips from twenty-one to thirty-one. This increased the leadership's resources but also enlarged the size of whip meetings at which party strategy is discussed. Several task forces were created within the whip organization in the Ninety-eighth and early Ninety-ninth Congresses to give whips additional opportunities to shape party strategy. An innovative change was the creation of a "speaker's cabinet" composed of top party leaders, top committee chairmen, and at-large members. The group is designed to expand the range of members with regular contact with party leaders on party strategy and scheduling. These changes, Gephardt explains, are designed to "include people, to practice participatory democracy, so the actions of the leadership, Steering and Policy and the caucus come with a lot of sharing of information and consensus."[45] Democratic leaders expressed reservations about many of these developments, but they offered no significant opposition to them.

Thus the 1980s have seen even more efforts by House Democrats to broaden participation through the party caucus and to make the party leadership a more collective enterprise. The caucus is meeting more often, members have more opportunities to express themselves, there is less deference to committee chairmen, the leadership is expected to explain itself to the membership more frequently, and the caucus is seen increasingly as the vehicle for tapping the talent and stimulating the creativity of the membership. Whether these recent efforts reflect the tribulations of the out-party or represent a more permanent transformation is difficult to say. What is clear is that the gains toward more collegial processes will be difficult to reverse and that the likelihood for tension between decentralized and collegial processes is even greater.

The Senate

The recent record in the Senate is very different. Members of the new Republican majority, especially the newly elected senators, sought to take full advantage of their new status. In the view of many observers, the result was even further abuses of the committee system and floor procedures. The extreme individualism that followed in the aftermath of the 1981 budget battles stimulated a reform effort in 1984 and led to the adoption of some committee assignment reforms in February 1985. Efforts to reform floor procedures received greater opposition, indicating the determination of senators to protect their individual rights to participate actively and fully on the Senate floor.

The Senate reforms of 1977 had placed new limits on the number of committee and subcommittee assignments senators could hold. They were permitted three full committee assignments and eight subcommittee assignments, although some were granted exemptions. Because senators had to accept fewer subcommittee assignments, the total number of Senate subcommittees was cut by thirty-two. The number of exemptions has grown in each Congress since then, however, and several committees have added subcommittees since the Republicans assumed control in

---

45. Quoted in Diane Granat, "House Democrats Expand Leadership: Wright Claims Speaker's Job; Race On for Majority Leader," *Congressional Quarterly Weekly Report*, vol. 43 (February 9, 1985), p. 283.

1981. By the end of the Ninety-eighth Congress (1983–84), nearly one-third of the senators had more than three full committee assignments and well over a third had more than eight subcommittee assignments. Scheduling committee meetings and gaining a quorum became nearly impossible in many cases, and senators themselves had become weary of conflicting committee schedules and overextended commitments.

In February 1985 the Senate adopted a reform resolution reestablishing the 1977 limit of three full committee assignments per senator, thus cutting the number of slots available on "major" committees from 231 to 214.[46] However, the number of slots on minor committees was later increased by 9, in part to compensate senators for lost major committee assignments, producing a very small net decrease of 8 committee seats. Reformers failed to get the Senate or majority party caucus to impose a strict limit on the number of subcommittees that could be created by standing committees, but a number of committees complied with the Republican conference request to reduce the number of subcommittees. The Banking Committee, for example, abolished four subcommittees at the price of taking a subcommittee chairmanship away from one senator. These voluntary committee actions reflected the widespread recognition that the proliferation of subcommittees had become a major problem. Nevertheless, the Senate still lacks a formal cap on subcommittees similar to the one imposed by the House Democratic caucus in 1981.[47]

Reform of floor procedures proved more difficult to achieve. Three aspects of floor procedure had come to be especially troublesome. First, despite the 1975 reform that made it easier to invoke cloture against a filibuster, filibusters and postcloture filibusters continued to be a major obstacle to orderly floor proceedings in the late 1970s and 1980s. Filibusters and threat of filibusters stimulated cloture motions more than

46. The adopted rule reduced the number of slots on the twelve major committees and exempted eleven senators from the limit of two major committee assignments, primarily to satisfy the committee party ratios that party leaders had agreed to earlier. Jacqueline Calmes and Diane Granat, "Senate Cuts Committee Slots, Members Assigned to Panels," *Congressional Quarterly Weekly Report*, vol. 43 (February 23, 1985), pp. 348–64.

47. In 1981 the House Democratic caucus adopted a rule that provides that, except for Appropriations, standing committees are limited to eight subcommittees; committees with more than thirty-five members and fewer than six subcommittees may increase the number to six or, with the approval of the Steering and Policy Committee, may have seven. Two committees were forced to abolish subcommittees to meet the limit at that time.

five times as often in the 1970s as in the 1960s.[48] A 1979 rule limiting consideration of amendments after cloture to one hundred hours has been invoked, but has not been effective, as senators have devised means to circumvent it.[49] Second, the Senate never has had a broad germaneness rule for amendments to legislation offered on the floor. As a result, committees have been bypassed on the floor through amendments to unrelated legislation, and a great deal of floor debate is devoted to issues extraneous to the legislation on the table. Finally, the informal practice of permitting senators to place "holds" on legislation they object to blocked committee access to the floor and made floor scheduling very difficult for the majority leader. Majority Leader Howard Baker's 1982 announcement that he would no longer honor holds has not yielded a significant change in practice.[50]

These problems have created great frustration for nearly all senators at one time or another as they have sought to pass legislation from their committees—and party leaders have become increasingly frustrated in their efforts to correct the problems by informal means. Senator Sam Nunn, Democrat of Georgia, argued that the Senate was "choking on its own processes," and the chairman of the Senate reform committee, Senator Dan Quayle, Republican of Indiana, stated that there was a "growing consensus that we ought to do something."[51] Senator John Stennis, Democrat of Mississippi and the dean of the Senate, complained that the Senate "has lost much in the way of ability to debate and be heard, transmit ideas to other leaders and thereby produce conclusions."[52] The collegial processes simply have been abused by the strong individualists of the Senate. As of mid-March, the outcome of the reform effort on floor procedures was uncertain, although some action seemed likely on a limit on debate over motions to proceed with the consideration of legislation and on germaneness.

The continuing weakness of Senate party leaders in their collegial yet

48. Bruce I. Oppenheimer, "Changing Time Constraints on Congress: Historical Perspectives on the Use of Cloture," in Dodd and Oppenheimer, eds., *Congress Reconsidered,* 3d ed., p. 398.

49. See Walter J. Oleszek, *Congressional Procedures and the Policy Process,* 2d ed. (CQ Press, 1984), pp. 186–93.

50. For Baker's announcement, see *Congressional Record,* daily edition (December 6, 1982), p. S13901.

51. Quoted in Steven V. Roberts, "Panel Proposes Sweeping Changes in Senate Rules," *New York Times,* November 30, 1984.

52. Quoted in "How Senators View the Senate: What Has Changed and What It Means," *New York Times,* November 25, 1984.

decentralized chamber was evident in Majority Leader Robert Dole's effort to create a Republican budget package at the start of the Ninety-ninth Congress. On January 4, 1985, Dole announced that, with the help of committee chairmen and their staff, he would produce a Republican budget plan by February 1. Dole failed to do so, as some committee chairmen refused to support deep cuts in programs under their jurisdiction and a few simply did not recommend anything to Dole. Most chairmen did report to Dole, however, although several indicated that they felt that cuts in programs under their jurisdiction were contingent on the willingness of other committees to cut spending for other programs. Dole failed to attract a quorum of Republicans to a party caucus meeting to discuss the package just before the self-imposed deadline arrived. Dole seemed helpless in the face of delay and outright obstructionism from committee members and staff.

Prospects for the Near Future

The defense of collegial decisionmaking in the Senate and the search for more ways to improve participation for rank-and-file members in the House are unlikely to weaken in the forseeable future. There is no sign that a membership with a substantially different mix of personal political objectives will be elected to Congress. Weak local parties and independent campaigns will continue to produce a Congress whose members have weak ties to one another. And there is no reason to believe that members of Congress will become any more tolerant of organizational structures that limit their ability to participate in debates over major issues. No reversion to insulated committees or dominating party leaders can be expected. As a result, the near future offers a continuation of a mix of decentralized and collegial decisionmaking processes. Committees and their subcommittees will continue to have the dominant role in shaping policy, but their relation to party leaders, caucuses, ad hoc groups, and the floor will vary greatly. Because the two patterns are not fully consistent, party leaders will continue to be called upon to mold different decisionmaking processes for each major issue before Congress. Rank-and-file members will have very inconsistent views over time about the best combination of decisionmaking processes as their political interests vary. To the public, Congress will appear even more chaotic and confusing.

In this context, leadership in Congress will come from even more numerous and less predictable sources. Nonelected leaders will lead partisan efforts and noncommittee members will author major policy innovations. Successful party leaders will be those who recognize these new conditions, adapt to them, and take advantage of them. Party leaders will have to take advantage of collegial processes to direct their parties and of the mass media as an element of legislative coalition-building strategies.

Much of the change has made Congress appear more party-oriented and will continue to do so, but this is misleading. Many of the new opportunities for collegial activity have been created within the parties, especially in the House. To a limited degree, the collegial opportunities offered by party caucuses and committees will stimulate more party-centered policy debate and encourage standing committee members to think about policy questions in party terms. Yet much of the use of party mechanisms will continue to derive from the nonpartisan motivations of individuals or groups to influence policy through any process that works to their advantage. Because party mechanisms provide more flexible procedural settings, members seeking ways to participate in debate over important policy questions will use them frequently.

A reasonable question is whether the Republicans would retain the same mixture of decentralized and collegial practices if they should gain control of the House. Many of the reforms took the form of changes in the rules of the House, but others were the product of actions by the majority party caucus. Key rules guaranteeing independence of subcommittees—bill referral to subcommittees, management of legislation on the floor by subcommittee chairmen, written subcommittee jurisdictions—are a part of Democratic caucus rules. And many of the new avenues of participation for junior members have been created within organs of the House Democratic party.

While the political circumstances under which Republicans might organize the House cannot be foreseen, a few reasonable speculations can be made. The Senate's experience after the 1980 elections suggests that a new House Republican majority would temporarily bypass normal decentralized processes to respond to the perceived mandate that carried them into office. However, it is unlikely that Republicans would permanently reverse the thrust of the Democratic reforms. New cohorts of Republicans during the last decade have been noted for their activism and independence of elected party leaders, and there is no foreseeable shift away from issues that attract the widespread interest of the membership. Republicans occasionally have complained about the inefficiencies in House decisionmaking created by the reforms of the 1970s, but it is difficult to separate the partisan from the nonpartisan in their criticism.

Will policy produced in this mixed system be less consistent or coherent than before? There is little reason to think so. It has been argued persuasively that a more complex process, one that has more stages and makes coalition building more difficult, reduces Congress's capacity to enact coherent policy and to do so expeditiously. But the more singularly decentralized system of the 1950s and 1960s, with its jurisdictional jealousies, awkward jurisdictional divisions, and autonomous committee chairmen, was hardly more capable of producing coherent policy. A more collegial process does not solve the problem as a more centralized one might, but it does offer opportunities to overcome some of the obstacles of decentralization and it does so in a manner far more consistent with congressional egalitarianism.

CHAPTER NINE

The Politicized Presidency

TERRY M. MOE

MORE THAN any other modern president, Ronald Reagan has moved with dedication and comprehensiveness to take hold of the administrative machinery of government. At the heart of his approach are the politicization of administrative arrangements and the centralization of policy-related concerns in the White House: developments in the institutional presidency with origins in past administrations, but now significantly accelerated and expanded. The Office of Management and Budget has been thoroughly politicized, both through appointments and its active involvement in distinctly political policymaking and lobbying processes. Largely via the functioning of the Office of Policy Development, the actors in the executive policy process—the cabinet, the bureaucracy, the OMB—have been integrated and coordinated from the top, and an array of problems and issues potentially dealt with in other administrative arenas has been drawn into the White House for centralized evaluation, reconciliation, and action. With heavy emphasis on ideology and loyalty, the appointment power has been put to systematic use in "infiltrating" the bureaucracy as a means of promoting political responsiveness, changing bureaucratic decision criteria from within, and facilitating the smooth operation of the OPD.

Among those who study the institutional presidency, there is substantial agreement that, policy and ideological considerations aside, the developments described here are undesirable. Reagan is accused of "deinstitutionalizing" the presidency and eroding its long-term capacity for effective leadership. Politicization is deplored for its destructive effects on institutional memory, expertise, professionalism, objectivity, communications, continuity, and other bases of organizational competence. Centralization is disparaged for its circumvention of established institutions and for its ineffective reliance on an already overburdened White House. These developments need to be turned around, it is claimed, through reforms designed to encourage a far greater presidential reliance on the OMB, the cabinet, and the bureaucracy, and a substantially enhanced presidential respect for their integrity, their distinctive areas of expertise and experience, and the value of protecting and cultivating their neutral competence.

The issues involved here are in fact quite general. They concern the determinants of presidential behavior, the requirements of presidential leadership, and the forces driving the development of the institutional presidency. Any effort to understand or criticize the Reagan administrative experience must ultimately rest on these general sorts of concerns, which are by nature theoretical, having to do with questions of cause and effect whose scope extends well beyond the confines of a single administration.

This essay offers a theoretical argument that places the Reagan experience, as well as the criticisms directed against it, in larger perspective. The foundation of the argument is an abstract framework for understanding the dynamics of institutional development regardless of the type of institution. This framework is applied to the institutional presidency and elaborated more concretely to yield a theoretical basis for explaining its historical development. The argument is then illustrated by a brief historical analysis of the institutional presidency that focuses on the emergence of politicization and centralization. As a final step, it is put to use in addressing the standard criticisms that have been leveled against these developments.

The Logic of Institutional Development

All institutions share a simple internal logic that guides their maintenance and development. This logic acquires its dynamic from a reciprocal relationship: the distinctive behavioral structures that define an institution derive from the choices of individuals, while the choices of individuals derive from incentives and resources that are shaped by the institutional context itself, as well as its surrounding environment. Individual choices create institutions, but institutions condition individual choices.[1]

1. At a minimum, institutionalization refers to regularized behavior patterns. This

This suggests that institutional development is driven by the degree of congruence between existing structures, on the one hand, and existing incentives and resources on the other. When individuals have incentives to alter existing structures and also have the resources to act with some measure of effectiveness, institutional changes are set in motion. These changes then have reciprocal effects that alter individual incentives and resources, which in turn propel the next round of institutional changes. Over time, the system comes to rest (if at all) when prevailing structures prove to be compatible with the underlying incentives and resources. Stable systems are internally compatible systems.

The logic is the same when the environment is more fully considered. Because the environment can influence all three internal components—structures, incentives, resources—its exact configuration shapes the nature of the incongruence among them, and, in so doing, encourages certain paths of institutional development and certain patterns of institutional outcomes rather than others. As the environment changes, the kinds of institutional developments and outcomes it encourages will also tend to change. But whether the environment changes or not, the directions and dynamics of institutional change are geared to the incongruence among structures, incentives, and resources.[2]

The institutional presidency is a term commonly used in reference to the White House, the Office of Management and Budget, and other elements of the Executive Office of the President—for example, the Council of Economic Advisers and the National Security Council. Less commonly (but properly), it also refers to patterned behaviors that link the presidency to other parts of the political system—policymaking routines, for example, that incorporate the cabinet and the permanent

---

is the essential property stressed in the traditional sociological work on the subject, and this is the definition I adopt here. More elaborate definitions—incorporating complexity, specialization, and other criteria—are not uncommon. See, for example, Nelson W. Polsby, "The Institutionalization of the U.S. House of Representatives,"*American Political Science Review*, vol. 62 (March 1968), pp. 144–68.

2. The perspective developed here falls under the rubric of what March and Olsen have termed the "new institutionalism" in political science. For their discussion, see James G. March and Johan P. Olsen, "The New Institutionalism: Organizational Factors in Political Life," *American Political Science Review*, vol. 78 (September 1984), pp. 734–49. Creative applications of institutional perspectives to the study of presidents and bureaucracies can be found in Stephen Skowronek, *Building a New American State* (Cambridge University Press, 1982), and Skowronek, "Presidential Leadership in Political Time," in Michael Nelson, ed., *The Presidency and the Political System* (Washington, D.C.: CQ Press, 1984).

bureaucracy. These elements vary in the extent to which they are institutionalized. The Office of Management and Budget is a complex formal organization whose behavior is governed by a high degree of regularity and continuity, while many of the structures within the White House are quite ephemeral, often with life spans shorter than a single presidential term. Collectively, however, they constitute a variegated institutional system that conforms to the simple logic just outlined.

Thus understood, the development of the institutional presidency over time should be a reflection of its underlying degree of congruence. The precise meaning of congruence in this context is of course complicated, since in principle it involves the balance that is struck among all structures, incentives, and resources within the system. But little is lost if the focus is simply on the president, who provides the institution with orientation and is clearly the driving force behind it. The question of congruence is, above all, a question about the extent to which existing structures making up the institutional presidency are congruent with the incentives and resources of the president. If presidents are dissatisfied with the institutional arrangements they inherit, then they will initiate changes to the extent they have the resources to do so. These changes subsequently have feedback effects on the president and a variety of other participants, which may then prompt further adjustments. The process will not come to rest—that is to say, presidents will continue modifying and reforming the institutional presidency—until congruence is realized. What we need to know in order to understand the dynamics of this process as it unfolds over time, then, has to do with why presidents become dissatisfied with their institutions, what resources they can put to use in seeking change, and what kinds of changes they are likely to initiate in their efforts to create more suitable institutional arrangements.

Historically, presidents have differed widely in personality, style, and agenda. Nonetheless, certain factors have structured the incentives of all modern presidents along the same basic lines. In the American separation-of-powers system, the president is the only politician with a national constituency and thus with an electoral incentive to pursue some broader notion of the public interest, even if restricted to the interests of the coalition that supports him. This is generally a powerful incentive during the first term, less so during the second, although, even then, the demonstrated value of presidential popularity and the tendency for second-term presidents to be centrally concerned with their places in history encourage them to be responsive to broad national interests. These incentives are reinforced by popular, political, and media expectations: the president has always been a convenient governmental focus, and, as government has taken a far more positive role over the years in addressing a wide range of social problems—and as Congress has shown itself quite incapable of institutional coherence and political leadership—the president has increasingly been held responsible for designing, proposing, legislating, administering, and modifying public policy, that is, for governing. His chances for reelection, his standing with opinion leaders and the public, and his historical legacy all depend on his perceived success as the generalized leader of government.[3]

Whatever his particular policy objectives, whatever his personality and style, the modern president is driven by these formidable expectations to seek control over the structures and processes of government. In view of his limited constitutional powers and the sheer complexity of modern government, the president clearly needs the kind of information, expertise, and coordinating capacity that only a large organizational apparatus can provide. Yet the precise kind of institutional presidency he needs is determined by the kinds of expectations that drive him. He is not interested in efficiency or effectiveness or coordination per se, and he does not give preeminence to the "neutral competence" these properties may seem to require.[4] He is a politician fundamentally concerned with the dynamics of political leadership and thus with political support and opposition, political strategy, and political trade-offs. What he wants is an institutional system responsive to his needs as a political leader. He values organizational competence, to be sure, but what he seeks is "responsive competence," not neutral competence.[5]

3. For a discussion of presidential incentives and the expectations surrounding the presidential role, see Theodore J. Lowi, *The Personal Presidency* (Cornell University Press, 1985); Godfrey Hodgson, *All Things to All Men* (Simon and Schuster, 1980); Richard Neustadt, *Presidential Power* (Wiley, 1980); Thomas Cronin, *The State of the Presidency* (Little, Brown, 1975); and Aaron Wildavsky, "The Past and Future Presidency," *Public Interest*, no. 41 (Fall 1975), pp. 56–76. Note that the gap between expectations and capacity is far greater for domestic than for foreign policy. See Aaron Wildavsky, "The Two Presidencies," in Aaron Wildavsky, ed., *Perspectives on the Presidency* (Little, Brown, 1975), pp. 448–61. Not surprisingly, the growth in the institutional presidency has been disproportionately due to new and larger structures for dealing with domestic policy, and trends toward politicization and centralization are properties of this growth. The analysis of this essay will therefore center around domestic concerns.

4. On the historical role of neutral competence in public administration thought, see Herbert Kaufman, "Emerging Conflicts in the Doctrines of Public Administration," *American Political Science Review*, vol. 50 (December 1956), pp. 1057–73.

5. More specifically, with neutral competence there is no mechanism to guarantee that what the organization potentially has to offer is willingly made available in an

A president who finds institutional arrangements inadequate to his needs has incentives to pursue reform, but the reforms he actually pursues are determined by the resources he can marshal and his flexibility in putting them to use. In these respects, the president is severely constrained. Many reforms may seem well designed to enhance executive leadership, but few are in fact attainable. Several types of constraints are important.

The president is embedded in a much larger network of political institutions that seriously limit what he can do. Above all the constitutional system guarantees that the president and Congress will be locked in institutional struggle, particularly over issues bearing on their relative powers. While Congress has long recognized the need for presidential leadership and been willing to grant presidents certain statutory powers and organizational resources, the institutional presidency is nonetheless intrinsically threatening to it. Ideas to expand the presidency in any significant way can count on meeting with resistance if proposed, and for that reason alone presidents must normally dispense with grand designs. Only under special circumstances will quantum leaps in the institutional presidency meet with congressional approval.[6]

Even if the focus is only on his room for maneuver within these limits, the impediments to reform are substantial. A pervasive problem is that all organizations have their own routines, their own agendas, their own norms, their own ways of coding and interpreting the world, their own bases of support, and the president cannot expect to control them easily. This is clearly true for the usual government agencies, whose interests and world views center around their own programs, and whose support (which they orchestrate) comes from congressional committees and interest groups with political muscle. But it is also true of so-called presidential agencies like the Office of Management and Budget; while they may "exist to serve the president" and have no other constituency, formal organization inevitably creates interests and beliefs that set them

---

appropriate form and timely fashion to the president. Nor is there a mechanism to guarantee that the types of competence the organization is equipped to provide are well suited to the president's needs—a problem that has less to do with willful resistance than with organizational myopia, parochialism, insularity, and other pathologies of a systemic nature. From the president's standpoint, responsive competence calls for improvements along both dimensions. Ideally, it is competence that is developed and adapted in light of his political needs and willingly made available to him.

6. See, for example, Harold Seidman, *Politics, Position, and Power*, 3d ed. (Oxford University Press, 1980).

apart from him. This is a fact of organizational life that presidents quickly learn if they do not know it already: neutral competence is not enough.[7]

More generally still, all institutionalized behaviors, whether or not they have an organization chart or formal name, generate expectations conducive to their continuation. A structure that regularly collects and disseminates useful information becomes valuable to those on the receiving end; they incorporate the information into their own decisions, they depend on it, they expect it to continue—and, if it suddenly stops, they join a chorus of demands for its renewal. The same sort of thing occurs when political resources are used in a regular fashion over time. Continued use of the president's appointment power to reward partisans and members of Congress, for instance, does more than serve immediate political ends; it also generates expectations about how presidents in general should use their appointment power, as well as penalties if those expectations are violated. A president who comes into office intent on departing from past practices, therefore, including the organizations and routines within the institutional presidency, will find it difficult to do so without upsetting a maze of supporting expectations and relationships. All things considered, there will often be no net advantage to pressing ahead and much to be lost.[8]

In addition to facing these major structural constraints, presidents and their advisers have a serious knowledge problem: even if they had the resources to impose any reforms they liked, they would not know how to design an institutional system optimally suited to presidential needs. This is not simply because they are new to the scene; in fact, largely as a rational response to the knowledge problem, the presidential team will purposely include members with extensive experience and connections. The reason for their problem, rather, is that the social science of organizations is so poorly developed. While organization

7. On presidential dissatisfaction with bureaucratic responsiveness, see Arthur M. Schlesinger, Jr., *A Thousand Days: John F. Kennedy in the White House* (Houghton Mifflin, 1965); and Lyndon B. Johnson, *The Vantage Point: Perspectives of the Presidency, 1963–1969* (Holt, Rinehart, and Winston, 1971). For theoretical treatments of bureaucratic pathologies, see Anthony Downs, *Inside Bureaucracy* (Little, Brown, 1967); Graham Allison, *The Essence of Decision: Explaining the Cuban Missile Crisis* (Little, Brown, 1971); and John D. Steinbruner, *The Cybernetic Theory of Decision: New Dimensions of Political Analysis* (Princeton University Press, 1974).

8. The relationship between institutions and expectations is a standard point in sociological theory. See, for example, the summary in Shmuel N. Eisenstadt, "Social Institutions," in *International Encyclopedia of the Social Sciences*, vol. 14 (Macmillan, 1968), pp. 409–29.

theorists have been cranking out thousands of studies for decades, the fact is that no systematic body of knowledge is available to presidents— or anyone else—for confidently linking alternative institutional designs to alternative sets of consequences. Presidents may know where they want to go, but science cannot tell them how to get there. As a result, presidents rely—often implicitly, without conscious choice—on experience and popular belief systems about organizations. Experience is a vast storehouse of information about existing and past institutional arrangements, information that derives from the institutional memory of the system as a whole and can be "worked" by presidential team members who know where to look and whom to ask. Popular belief systems about organizations have their roots in social science but are really blends of plausible theoretical notions, common sense, and normative beliefs. In their implicit reliance on both sources of ideas, presidents tend to recognize and respect the great uncertainties involved in making nonincremental changes in institutional arrangements, since these entail very real political risks.[9]

Finally, presidents are severely constrained by time. At the outside, they have eight years in which to prove themselves and achieve their policy goals; but even this—a brief period, by congressional and bureaucratic standards—vastly understates the time pressures under which a president must act. The first year of the first term is crucial. The administration must rush to take advantage of this unique opportunity by developing, evaluating, and gathering support for its program—an effort that requires from the very start an institutional system that responds quickly and with political sensitivity to the president's pressing needs for immediate action. Beyond the first year, opposition grows and there are fewer opportunities for presidential success, but events continue to move quickly and unpredictably. Fires must be put out, bargains struck, rare "windows of opportunity" acted upon, and elections— every other year is an election year—reflected in the calculus of governing. The administration must be nimble and constantly on the move or it will be overwhelmed by the increasing odds against its success. These pressures drive out grand designs and long-term plans; they also drive out thoughtful, careful analysis. But the pressures themselves arise from

9. For a sober appraisal of organization theory, see Charles Perrow, *Complex Organizations* (Scott, Foresman, 1979). For a discussion of how presidential ideas for reform emerge, see Seidman, *Politics, Position, and Power*. See also John Kessel, *The Domestic Presidency* (North Scituate, Mass.: Duxbury Press, 1975).

the realities of politics, and the president ignores them at his peril: if he wants to be successful, he usually has no choice but to think in the short term and to demand supporting institutions that respond quickly and appropriately to his political needs. As Harold Seidman notes, "Presidents operate under rigid time constraints. What they want, they want now."[10]

All of this paints a rather bleak picture. The president is burdened by expectations that far exceed his capacity for effective action, and he has strong incentives to right the imbalance by reforming and elaborating the institutional presidency. Yet his drive toward institutional change is slowed and its directions constrained by severe limits—some environmentally imposed, some internal to the presidency—on the resources he can bring to bear. The result is an institutional system that does indeed contain forces that push it toward greater congruence, but whose constraints guarantee that adjustments will be halting, highly imperfect, and nowhere near sufficient (at least for the foreseeable future) to alleviate the massive imbalance between expectations and capacity.

In general, what should this developmental process of adjustment look like? It is best to begin by emphasizing a simple but important point: institutional change is firmly rooted in the past. The president is virtually forced to accept the basic institutional framework he inherits from his predecessors. Congressional opposition, bureaucratic resistance and parochialism, and the institutional generation of self-supporting expectations work to guarantee that most changes of real consequence will be too politically painful to justify their pursuit. Moreover, the combination of knowledge problems and time pressures helps to guarantee that the president will often prefer arrangements not too different from those already in place; he does not have the time to design and fight for fundamentally new support institutions, and his reliance upon institutional memory and popular concepts of organizational design encourages the familiar rather than the experimental.

The legacy of the past discourages comprehensive reform efforts—but, precisely because it does, it magnifies the president's incentives to pour effort into minor but feasible changes by making maximum use of the structures and resources closest to him and least controlled by outsiders. This channeling of presidential effort into areas of greatest flexibility can actually be a source of real volatility, as presidents chafing

10. Seidman, *Politics, Position, and Power*, p. 87.

at the inadequacies and constraints built into the larger system compensate with flurries of incremental reforms—followed by endless adaptations to new circumstances—that aggregate to substantial change without altering the basic institutional framework. Given the knowledge problem and time pressures, these changes may prove rather ad hoc and ill-advised; but they are often correctable, and over the long haul their movement is guided by the drive toward congruence, reflected above all in the president's desire to make the system more responsive to his needs.

This pursuit of responsive competence, as expressed through the channeling of presidential effort, encourages two basic developmental thrusts. The first is the increasing centralization of the institutional presidency in the White House. Because the president can count on unequaled responsiveness from his own people, increases in White House organizational competence—for example, through greater size, division of labor, specialization, hierarchic coordination, formal linkages with outside organizations and constituencies—appear to him to have direct, undiluted payoffs for the pursuit of presidential interests. By contrast, similar increases in competence within the permanent bureaucracy, or even within the OMB, would be discounted (perhaps very heavily) in value by lower levels of responsiveness, not to mention outright resistance. Moreover, the White House affords him far more flexibility in adapting and drawing upon organizational competence as circumstances and political needs change. The actual level of White House competence may be much lower than that of other government organizations, but the combination of responsiveness, flexibility, and strong incentives to circumvent established organizations and vested interests gives the White House a built-in advantage in the development of presidential support institutions.

In the early stages, the president will be limited in the problems and issues that can successfully be pulled into the White House; he will be forced to defer both to the greater competence of external organizations and to surrounding expectations that traditional structures and processes will be relied upon. But over time the built-in advantage of the White House will prevail: presidents will incrementally enhance its competence, problems and issues will be increasingly drawn into it for centralized coordination and control, expectations surrounding previous patterns will slowly break down, new expectations will form around a White House–centered system, and the new expectations will further accelerate the flow of problems and issues to the White House—thus enhancing the need for still greater White House competence.

The second development is the increasing politicization of the institutional system. This approach to responsive competence is particularly attractive because it is anchored in a formal presidential power that, in its implications for political and bureaucratic control, is perhaps more important than any other he possesses: the power of appointment. By appointing individuals on the basis of loyalty, ideology, or programmatic support, he can take direct action to enhance responsiveness throughout the administration, from presidential agencies like the OMB to the most remote independent boards and commissions. And, by emphasizing professionalism, expertise, and administrative experience, he can take action to enhance organizational competence. In the grander scheme of things, of course, he will want to seek out some candidates primarily for their responsiveness, some primarily for their competence, and some for their mix of scores along both dimensions, depending on where in government they are to be located and what they are expected to do. In addition, by manipulating civil service rules, proposing minor reorganizations, and pressing for modifying legislation, he can take steps to increase the number and location of administrative positions that can be occupied by appointees.

There are limits, to be sure. Presidents have traditionally used many appointments as political payoffs and have been expected to do so by other politicians. Similarly, Congress tends to oppose presidential attempts to politicize the bureaucracy. But to the extent he has the freedom to move in this direction, the president will find politicization irresistible. The appointment power is simple, readily available, and enormously flexible. It assumes no sophisticated institutional designs and little ability to predict the future, and it is incremental in the extreme: in principle, each appointment is a separate action. Thus, while knowledge demands are not negligible—somehow, candidates must be recruited, evaluated, and the like—many mistakes can be corrected and adjustments can be made as the inevitably changing short-term pressures of presidential politics seem to require. By taking advantage of these attractive properties, the president is uniquely positioned to try to construct his own foundation for countering bureaucratic resistance, mobilizing bureaucratic competence, and integrating the disparate elements of his administration into a more coherent whole. Given his general lack of resources and options, these are enticing prospects indeed.

None of this suggests that any given president will be successful, whether in terms of policy, popularity, leadership, executive control, or any other dimension of evaluation. Nor does it suggest that politicization and White House centralization will always contribute to presidential success. Indeed, the enormous gap between expectations and capacity may help ensure that most modern presidents will in the end be regarded as "failures" in basic respects.[11] The suggestion here is simply that the institutional presidency is destined to develop in a particular way over time, owing to the nature and degree of the underlying incongruence, serious constraints on presidential resources, and the consequent channeling of presidential effort into areas of greatest flexibility. In an ideal world, presidents might pursue a variety of institutional reforms in righting the imbalance between expectations and capacity. In the real world, they readily embrace politicization and centralization because they have no attractive alternatives. The causes are systemic—they are rooted in the way the larger institutional system is put together.

The Development of Politicization and Centralization

There need be no pretense that this argument can be thoroughly explored and documented here. That would require, at a minimum, a lengthy and detailed historical analysis that simply is not possible in the space allotted. Instead, this section has a less ambitious aim: to illustrate certain portions of the argument a bit more concretely by outlining some of the patterns, events, and personalities involved in the historical emergence of politicization and centralization, and, in so doing, to place the Reagan years within the stream of historical developments.[12]

The institutional presidency had its real beginning with the Budget and Accounting Act of 1921, which created the Bureau of the Budget.

11. See Lowi, *Personal Presidency*; Hodgson, *All Things to All Men*; and Wildavsky, "Past and Future Presidency."

12. This section relies in part on the following works, all of which span several administrations. Stephen Wayne, *The Legislative Presidency* (Harper and Row, 1978); Larry Berman, *The Office of Management and Budget and the Presidency, 1921–1979* (Princeton University Press, 1979); Seidman, *Politics, Position, and Power*; G. Calvin Mackenzie, *The Politics of Presidential Appointments* (New York: Free Press, 1981); Stephen Hess, *Organizing the Presidency* (Brookings, 1976); Lester M. Salamon, "The Presidency and Domestic Policy Formulation," in Hugh Heclo and Lester M. Salamon, eds., *The Illusion of Presidential Government* (Boulder, Colo.: Westview Press, 1981), pp. 177–201.

The Bureau was authorized to compile, revise, and submit agency requests to Congress, and to carry out organizational studies in the interests of efficiency. While there were some fears of presidential encroachment on legislative powers, the act was neither intended nor expected to alter the balance between the two branches and was largely viewed by Congress as a means of helping rationalize its own previously chaotic budgetary process. What proved to be a truly important reform in the development of American political institutions was feasible precisely because its far-reaching political consequences were unanticipated.

The Bureau assumed its role as a presidential staff agency, and its first director, Charles G. Dawes, quickly saw that it was firmly organized around Progressive, "scientific" principles current at the time.[13] The Bureau was to be an impartial, expert, professional organization, fundamentally concerned with efficiency and economy in government, and providing the president with strictly nonpolitical advice and services toward these ends. It was to have nothing to do with politics or policymaking; its proper focus was on agency budgets and administrative organization. From the beginning, therefore, the Bureau was built to reflect the familiar theoretical and normative notions now associated with traditional public administration and classical organization theory. And, over time, these notions found institutional embodiment in the structures, processes, and supporting norms and expectations that constituted the very essence of the Bureau. Thus, neutral competence, the politics-administration dichotomy, and their conceptual relatives became more than constellations of ideas. They became institutionalized forces whose legacy would weigh heavily on the future.

Franklin D. Roosevelt came into office dedicated to significant social change but convinced that the executive branch he inherited would be largely hostile to his policy directions (aggravated by its distinctly Republican cast), and, by its nature, unsuited to the generation of innovative ideas. What he needed was an administrative mechanism for grabbing hold of government and putting its substantial resources to coordinated use toward his own ends. What he had, aside from his White House assistants, was the Bureau of the Budget. Because the Bureau had a grand total of thirty-five employees in 1933, it was not well equipped

13. At this point, the Bureau was "in but not of" the Treasury Department, and its director, like other presidential assistants, was not subject to senatorial confirmation. See Berman, *Office of Management and Budget and the Presidency*, p. 4.

for such a job—but there was more to the Bureau's incapacity than lack of resources: it lacked the will. During the first decade of its life, the Bureau had become an established bureaucratic organization in its own right. It had its own routine ways of doing and thinking about things, oriented by a neutral concern for budgets and cost-cutting. Thus, Roosevelt's New Deal, which clearly called for large expenditures and potentially large deficits, immediately produced conflict with his first budget director, Lewis Douglas, who could bring neither himself nor his agency to support such fiscal irresponsibility. Douglas resigned in 1934. But the Bureau's distinctive ethos remained, and the damage, as far as Roosevelt was concerned, had been done.

His response was to move away from the Bureau toward a White House–centered system. By bringing in selected aides and borrowing personnel from the departments, he was able through his own adroit administrative juggling to create an internal organization that was responsive to his needs, flexible, enthusiastic, innovative—although unavoidably dependent on the rest of government for information, expertise, and operational experience. Whether he was ultimately more effective for doing so is perhaps debatable, but the choice from Roosevelt's standpoint was clear: he had to act quickly and forcefully, and he had neither the time nor the means to undo the Bureau's learned incapacity for responsiveness. While the Bureau was doubtless more competent than the White House on many grounds, the short-run political incentives were to build up the White House's competence and to rely only secondarily on the Bureau for what it routinely did best, and little more.

A second term gave Roosevelt some breathing room to construct a more solid institutional foundation for presidential leadership—and at the same time, to respond publicly to political criticism of his "chaotic" methods of administration. Presented with a complicated problem of institutional design and faced with predictable resistance from a suspicious Congress, his approach was to set up the Brownlow Committee, which was led and staffed by public administrationists with impeccable credentials and "scientific" expertise in government organization. Incredible growth in the size and complexity of government had convinced these and other public administrationists of the need for executive leadership, but their ideas were deeply embedded in traditional theoretical and normative notions about governmental organization. In 1939 a package of Brownlow recommendations was finally enacted after bitter wrangling with Congress, calling most prominently for a new Executive Office of the President within which the Bureau of the Budget would now be located, a dramatic increase in the Bureau's personnel and resources, and new powers in the areas of legislative clearance, executive orders and vetoes, statistical services, reorganization plans, and various forms of managerial assistance to the agencies.[14]

These reforms significantly enhanced the organizational competence available to the president—almost overnight the Bureau grew from nearly 40 to more than 500 employees, with a budget to match—and by placing support agencies close to him in the structure of government, attempted to enhance their responsiveness. But the emphasis was characteristically on his management needs as an executive in charge of a large, complex organization, not on the larger requirements of political leadership. There was little appreciation that institutional pathologies— parochialism, insulation, inertia—could strike here as well as anywhere else. And even this marked increase in institutional capacity left the president with nowhere near the resources needed for meeting the enormous shift in public expectations generated by Roosevelt and the New Deal. In both design and capacity, then, the new institutional system was inadequate to presidential needs from the start. Once the excitement and instabilities of reform had worn off—and once the exigencies of the war were past—it remained for subsequent presidents to move the institutional system toward greater congruence.

But they could not move it very far very fast. For both Truman and Eisenhower, the structural outlines of the institutional presidency were set by the Brownlow reforms as elaborated and routinized during the latter Roosevelt years, and they had no practical choice but to work within the confines of the framework they inherited: the Executive Office for housing presidential agencies, the enlarged Bureau of the Budget as the institutional center of the Executive Office, and the White House staff as its political center. Through incremental adjustments, however, as well as selective use of "contributions" imposed by Congress, both presidents took action to improve their institutional capacity.

14. Organizational writings of its staff were collected in Luther Gulick and L. Urwick, eds., *Papers on the Science of Administration* (Columbia University, Institute of Public Administration, 1937). This was, in Wallace Sayre's words, the "high noon of orthodoxy in public administration theory." See Sayre, "Premises of Public Administration: Past and Emerging," *Public Administration Review,* vol. 18 (Spring 1958), p. 113.

The White House, suddenly dwarfed in organizational competence by the post-Brownlow Bureau, slowly grew in size, sophistication, professionalism, and reach.[15] New organizational units were created to deal with presidential concerns that in the past were handled informally. A congressional liaison unit, for example, was set up by Eisenhower to establish regular lines of communication between the White House and Congress, to encourage a more sophisticated presidential use of rewards that legislators value highly (patronage, credit-claiming), and to coordinate the efforts of liaison offices in the departments and agencies. And similarly for appointments. Truman was the first president to have an aide whose primary responsibility was to evaluate potential appointees; and Eisenhower followed up by creating an organizational unit for identifying open positions, keeping track of job-seekers and their patrons, seeking out potential candidates, and clearing appointments with the party apparatus.[16] In general, presidents sought to build White House competence by rationalizing processes of value to them, and in most cases they did so by formalizing and elaborating upon practices that had been followed in the past. Once this was done, supporting expectations quickly emerged among outsiders (in Congress, in the party organizations, in the press), the lessons and precedents of organization became part of institutional memory—and future presidents would find it both convenient and desirable to follow in their footsteps.

Another important source of change derived from congressional efforts to impose a structure on the president's Executive Office information and advisory system. The Council of Economic Advisers was created to ensure that he received the expert, objective advice of economists in carrying out his newly enlarged responsibilities for the nation's economic well-being. And the National Security Council was created to coordinate the resources and advice of the major executive actors involved in national defense and foreign policy. The hitch, of

15. For the details of White House organization from Roosevelt through Nixon, see Hess, *Organizing the Presidency*. For figures on the size of the White House, see Thomas E. Cronin, "The Swelling of the Presidency: Can Anyone Reverse the Tide?" in Peter Woll, ed., *American Government: Readings and Cases*, 8th ed. (Little, Brown, 1984), p. 347.

16. Eisenhower also created by executive order a new category of noncareer positions, Schedule C, for jobs of a "confidential" or "policy determining" character, giving him added flexibility in reshaping a bureaucracy staffed for the last twenty years by Democratic presidents. See Paul P. Van Riper, *The History of the United States Civil Service* (Evanston, Ill.: Row, Peterson, 1958); and Frederick C. Mosher, *Democracy and the Public Service* (New York: Oxford University Press, 1982).

course, was that Congress could not force presidents to make serious use of these new bodies or even listen to their advice; and their roles did in fact fluctuate a great deal, both within and across administrations, as presidents found them more or less valuable to the decision process. But the great flexibility afforded the president in staffing and organization, along with the clear importance of the functions these units were designed to perform, encouraged their continued use; and by the end of the Eisenhower years, both were well integrated—on the president's terms— into the fabric of the institutional presidency.

Probably the most important development during this period, however, was the formalization of policymaking procedures linking the institutional presidency and the permanent bureaucracy. The stimulus was a Truman innovation designed to enhance the president's capacity for control and leadership of the nation's policy process: the annual legislative program. Inherited procedures were those for legislative clearance, whereby departments and bureaus routinely submitted legislative proposals to the Bureau, which enforced presidential criteria largely by saying no. These procedures were now altered to accommodate the positive function of program development. Proposals were to be submitted annually, at appropriate times in the legislative cycle, to the Bureau, which then worked closely with White House staff in moving toward a coherent program. The result was a rationalization of bottom-up processes of policy formulation that all presidents, like it or not, were forced to rely on in great measure. Before long, expectations grew up around these routines—and Eisenhower became their first victim: when he assumed office with no intention of proposing an annual program, he was roundly castigated by members of Congress, including those in his own party. His administration wasted little time falling into step by putting the Truman-designed institutional capacity to use. From that point on, all presidents have routinely developed and presented annual programs.

In some sense, the Truman-Eisenhower years served to develop and institutionalize within the Brownlow framework a very traditional system of politics. The president was fundamentally reliant on the permanent government and the Bureau of the Budget. At the top, the president relied heavily on his cabinet in evaluating and deciding upon policy options. At lower levels, cabinet members were afforded almost total flexibility in the management of their own sectors of the bureaucracy, and processes absolutely central to governmental outcomes—budgeting,

legislative clearance, policy development—were handled largely through
organizational routines linking the permanent government and the Bureau of the Budget. In formal terms, "politics" was confined to the
fledgling White House organization, the very highest levels of the
bureaucracy, and the director of the Budget Bureau. The system was,
in great measure, an institutional embodiment of neutral competence
and the politics-administration dichotomy.

This formalization of traditional politics and processes did not represent the emergence of a stable institutional system. Rather, it was a
necessary stage in its development, a stage that, because of the continuing
imbalance between expectations and capacity, was inherently unstable.
The underlying tension was largely masked by serious constraints on
presidential resources, by the latency of White House organizational
potential, and, not least, by the relative passivity of the Eisenhower
administration in formulating and pursuing domestic policy objectives.
But the tension remained, generating incremental, ongoing development
of the institutional presidency. While the pace of change would soon
pick up, the Truman-Eisenhower years were less a baseline from which
reforms departed than an early period of growth whose trends anticipated
and presaged later developments.

With Kennedy and Johnson, the drive toward congruence came out
strongly into the open. Both were legislative activists intent on making
historic progress in social policy, and they firmly recognized that
prevailing arrangements could not be counted upon to generate or even
support innovative domestic programs. The departments and agencies,
as advocates of their own programs and defenders of their own structures
and processes, would resist change and uncertainty. But the Bureau was
not the key to an answer. Since its "Golden Era" during the early
Truman years, its routines and supporting norms had predictably settled
around budgets, efficiency, and legislative clearance, and it was neither
structured nor institutionally motivated to mobilize the government
toward innovative ends.

Kennedy and Johnson responded by seeking to centralize the policy
process more fully in the White House, with the pivotal role played by a
domestic policy staff—headed by Theodore Sorensen under Kennedy,
by Bill D. Moyers and then Joseph A. Califano, Jr., under Johnson.
Established programming routines were modified to allow selective
circumvention of both the permanent government and the Bureau. Policy
ideas now took one of two tracks: important ones were diverted to (or

originated with) the White House; more routine ones were sent along the traditional path to the Bureau, where they were operated on in the usual way. The generation of ideas was encouraged from all sources, inside and outside the White House, with an emphasis on openness and informality. Task forces, consisting largely of interested or expert outsiders, ultimately became the prime vehicles for ensuring a steady stream of innovative proposals, timed with the legislative cycle.

Johnson's Great Society played a role much like Roosevelt's New Deal in emphasizing the deficiencies of the prevailing institutional system. The pace of politics was frantic, the political and historical stakes enormous, but presidential resources quite insufficient for the kind of leadership and control the president clearly sought. By default, the Califano group was involved in virtually all aspects of the executive policymaking process, from the formulation and evaluation of ideas to the design of a legislative program to its presentation and success in Congress. It was not well equipped for so comprehensive a job—but neither was the existing system, and the president could count on this group's responsiveness, flexibility, and boundless enthusiasm in pursuit of his program. The Bureau was indispensable to the domestic staff, but it was overwhelmed by staff demands that pushed it away from standard operating procedures and traditional functions toward a faster paced, more variegated, more politically responsive role it was not well prepared to perform. As during Roosevelt's first term, the resulting system looked to some like administrative chaos, but it was vastly preferred by the president to the institutional status quo.

The Great Society also had the unintended effect of making management an important political issue. Given the administration's mad scramble to take advantage of its brief window of opportunity for legislative success, the proliferation of programs took place with little consideration for issues of organizational design, jurisdiction, coordination, and other aspects bearing directly on how policies were to be implemented. Supporters and critics alike, including vocal members of Congress, were soon calling for managerial efforts to impose administrative coherence. Although serious studies of the situation were carried out, the operational response of the Johnson administration was characteristically ad hoc: the ineffective managerial activities of the Bureau were supplemented by the Califano group, which, while already overburdened, increasingly concerned itself with implementation.

The centralization strategy clearly did not provide Johnson with a perfectly efficient mechanism for extending his capacity for leadership. On the other hand, the existing system was inherently unsuited to his programmatic goals, and, unless he was willing to admit defeat from the outset, he was forced to graft new structures onto the ones he inherited. By pulling issues, ideas, and problems into the White House and making it the "operational center" of the executive branch,[17] he was simply relying on the people he could trust best and the resources he could manipulate most easily. His prior incentives for moving in this general direction were strong and clear. That the specific administrative machinery he adopted ultimately proved less than perfect was surely to be expected, given constraints of time, knowledge, and existing practices.

Along with centralization, Kennedy and Johnson sought to enhance their leadership capacity by building and formalizing an appointments process within the White House that went far beyond the pioneering Eisenhower operation. The purpose was not simply to rationalize the traditional procedures, but rather to move toward putting appointments systematically to use as a mechanism of presidential control—an important break with the past. Here, Kennedy was the prime mover. His new system was

> a turning point in the development of a modern and rational personnel function within the White House Office. . . . The procedures of recruitment were integrated with the goals of recruitment. Planning, standards, contacts, agency relations, and clearances were coordinated and centrally organized in a way that significantly improved the President's opportunities to use his appointment powers as a more effective tool for administrative management and political leadership. For the administrations that followed, there would be no turning back from these important developments.[18]

During the Johnson years, these arrangements were aggressively expanded under the expert guidance of John Macy, a seasoned personnel professional with many years at the Civil Service Commission (and then its chairman—he wore two hats throughout).[19] The system had many

17. William D. Carey, "Presidential Staffing in the Sixties and Seventies," *Public Administration Review*, vol. 39 (September–October 1969), p. 454.

18. Mackenzie, *Politics of Presidential Appointments*, p. 31.

19. Like Eisenhower, Johnson also created by executive order a new category of positions, Noncareer Executive Assignments (NEAs), exempt from the usual civil service requirements in recognition of their direct involvement in policymaking and advocacy. "NEAs and Schedule 'C' positions typically include the very top staff positions within the agency; the two categories differ in that the supergrades must be NEAs." United States Senate Committee on Government Operations, *Study on Federal Regulations* (Government Printing Office, 1977), vol. 1, p. 194. This gave Johnson and all future presidents a stronger foothold in the agencies.

flaws, and the appointments process remained both technically unwieldy and politically constrained. Moreover, neither president really pushed its potential as a control mechanism. While Johnson did demand loyalty from his appointees, both placed great emphasis on intelligence, substantive knowledge, experience, and other criteria more directly related to neutral organizational competence. Patronage, however, was less important than it had ever been. The declining strength of party organizations, the rise of primaries and candidate-centered organizations, candidate reliance on media and consultants, and the forging of direct links between the president and the electorate all contributed to the increasing weakness of patronage demands and freed presidents to use appointments for other ends. In this new era, party claims "were just one more competing presence in the political whirlpool surrounding the selection process. When parties lost their stranglehold on the gateways to the White House, they also lost their proprietary right to dominate selection decisions."[20]

When Nixon assumed office, he inherited an institutional presidency that was clearly in an accelerated state of transition. He also inherited many of the same incentives that drove Kennedy and Johnson to reject traditional patterns in favor of a substantially enhanced White House role. Nixon too was an activist president intent on achieving his own social goals and legislative agenda. He too was deeply distrustful of the bureaucracy. He too would be held responsible for administrative disarray in the implementation of social programs. He too would find that presidential institutions and their routine processes for policymaking and management were inadequate for his needs.[21]

Like his predecessors, Nixon had no coherent strategy for reform. Instead, he quickly set up the Ash Council, a group of business executives without governmental experience, and charged it with an all-too-familiar task: apply methods of business organization to government and come up with recommendations for a more rational structure. Once again, the classical orthodoxy was to have a crack at major institutional reform. In the meantime, Nixon muddled through. He went with a rather traditional approach to administration, relying heavily on his cabinet and allowing its members to make lower-level appointments; but he sought to en-

20. Mackenzie, *Politics of Presidential Appointments*, p. 85.

21. On the Nixon years, see especially Richard Nathan, *The Plot That Failed: Nixon and the Administrative Presidency* (Wiley, 1975), and Nathan, *The Administrative Presidency* (Wiley, 1983).

courage policy innovation by setting up special White House groups—
notably, one under Daniel Moynihan, another under Arthur Burns—for
that purpose. When these policy groups failed to work to his satisfaction,
they gave way to a central domestic policy staff controlled by John
Ehrlichman and effectively competing for influence with the cabinet.
Thus the Nixon presidency soon developed, without any plan for doing
so, an analogue to the Califano group (and before it, the Sorensen group).
As it had for Kennedy and Johnson, this more centralized arrangement
proved better suited to the president's needs.

The Ash Council operated in an unusually friendly environment. The
Bureau was highly unpopular with Congress, perceived as having
mismanaged Great Society programs and being overly insulated from
external realities and executive direction. Even the Bureau's own self-
studies, from 1959 onward, had stressed its institutional need for greater
political sensitivity and responsiveness. Thus the council's basic recommendations for the institutional presidency found a receptive audience and were passed into law in 1970.[22] The Bureau was enlarged and
more adequately funded, reorganized to accommodate broader managerial responsibilities, and renamed the Office of Management and
Budget to emphasize its new mission. A new layer of political appointees
was introduced to counter the Bureau's insular tendencies and enhance
responsiveness. In addition, a Domestic Council was established by
statute in the Executive Office, structured around cabinet participation
and designed as a domestic counterpart to the National Security Council.
Their respective functions followed traditional public administrationist
notions: policymaking was political and belonged in the Domestic
Council, management was nonpolitical and belonged in the OMB—
which was to be responsive to executive leadership but not in any sense
politicized. Again, the separation of politics and administration was
formalized in the structure of government.

Nixon, frustrated in achieving his social goals through legislative
action, put this structure to distinctly presidential use in a dedicated
attempt to achieve programmatic ends through bureaucratic control.
The Office of Management and Budget was indeed shocked out of its
bureaucratic insularity, but it was also politicized. Budget Director
George Shultz was drawn into the inner circles of White House politics

22. By contrast, its recommendations for reorganizing the departments and agencies
met with opposition and failure. See the discussion in Seidman, *Politics, Position, and
Power.*

and policymaking. Nixon appointees at the OMB now occupied strategically important positions atop the examining divisions, long the foundation of Bureau information and power in dealing with the departments and agencies, giving presidential criteria a deep anchoring in the institution.

These developments within the OMB placed the departments and agencies at a disadvantage. . . . [The political appointees] tended to be less amenable to negotiations and compromises pushed up by civil servants within the departments and more insistent on bringing the bureaucracy into line with the administration's position. Instead of ideas welling up, initiatives were sent down, especially during the first term of the Nixon presidency. This accelerated the centripetal tendencies that had been at work in the executive branch since the early 1960s.[23]

The Domestic Council, now the organizational home of Ehrlichman's domestic policy staff, was in effect an attempt to formalize developments that had taken place spontaneously, as direct expressions of presidential need, in each of the Kennedy, Johnson, and Nixon administrations. But formalization was in itself no cure for complexities that had overwhelmed policy staffs in the past, and the council quickly was awash in difficulties. Ehrlichman's tight control and abrasive style earned him the abiding hostility of cabinet members, while, operationally, he gave little attention to general policy issues and became deeply involved in day-to-day implementation matters that the council was poorly equipped to handle. A reorganization during the second term, giving hierarchic superiority to three cabinet members over the others, caused further friction and organizational problems. With the turbulence surrounding Watergate and the departure of Ehrlichman, the Domestic Council never had another chance to settle down and find an acceptable mode of operation.

Another dimension of Nixon's administrative strategy was more controversial. After a disorganized first round of appointments lacking any clear sense of presidential direction, a reexamination in 1970 led to an enhanced appointments organization within the White House that was "more specialized, more centralized, and more professional than any of its predecessors"[24]—which, given the dramatic developments during the Kennedy and Johnson administrations (whose procedures the Nixon people largely maintained), was saying a great deal. This capacity was then put to systematic use toward presidential control of

23. Wayne, *The Legislative Presidency*, p. 89.
24. Mackenzie, *Politics of Presidential Appointments*, p. 49.

the bureaucracy. It was also put to use, not coincidentally, in buffering the president from patronage demands; for he could claim, with some credibility, that appointments had been formalized and removed from the sphere of personal presidential decision.

Stressing loyalty and ideology above all else, the appointments unit moved vigorously to place White House partisans in key positions in the departments and agencies. This was something every president has a right to do, but it had never before been attempted on so grand a scale. Nixon had both opportunity and motive. He had opportunity because of the declining constraint of patronage demands and the secular growth in White House appointments capacity since the 1950s. He had motive because his legislative assault on a Congress controlled by Democrats had failed, leaving him with only one significant avenue of influence—policymaking through the bureaucracy—and, unlike Johnson, he could not fill the bureaucracy with supporters by creating new agencies and programs. Yet the political context was not quite ready for such an aggressive move toward politicization. Nixon's approach blatantly contradicted traditional expectations about presidential use of the appointment power and was widely characterized by members of Congress, the bureaucracy, and the press as an illegitimate infiltration of the bureaucracy. This only enhanced his reputation as an imperial president, an insatiable power grabber who would stop at nothing to get his way.

As the Watergate scandal revealed, there was some truth to this characterization. But it would be a mistake to view the general thrust toward centralization and politicization during the Nixon years as some sort of aberration, anchored perhaps in the deepest recesses of Nixon's personality. In fact, these trends had begun much earlier, and they were driven by a fundamental incongruence whose presence and driving force had nothing to do with Nixon. His move to increase the size and sophistication of the White House organization, his reliance on a domestic policy staff to control and coordinate from the center, his effort to enhance the responsiveness of the Budget Bureau and draw it into the politics of policymaking, his increased use of appointments for control purposes—all fit into a larger pattern of institutional development; and they extended that pattern in ways that, while sometimes excessive and politically unwise, were consistent with both its historical trajectory and the institutional forces behind it.

During the Ford-Carter period, the presidency was engaged in a holding action against a hostile environment. In the aftermath of Watergate, a resurgent Congress took action to redress the increasing imbalance of power between the two branches, most significantly by restructuring its own budgetary process and creating the Congressional Budget Office. The public, the press, and academics were all wary of strong presidential leadership and quick to emphasize its potential dangers for democracy. This was not a time for expanding the institutional presidency. Instead, Ford and Carter did their best to conform to this downturn in expectations about how good presidents conduct their affairs. Both stressed cabinet government, bureaucratic participation in decisionmaking, traditional criteria and decentralization in appointments, and openness and pluralism in policymaking.

In the meantime, however, the institutional presidency was hardly crumbling. The White House–Executive Office complex maintained its size, its high degree of specialization, and its capacity—now underutilized—for centralizing presidential resources. The Office of Management and Budget, through its layer of political appointees in key positions, maintained its enhanced capacity for responsiveness to the president; indeed, Carter actually increased the number of appointees. The Carter White House did away with the blacklisted Domestic Council but continued the historical pattern by relying instead on a newly created White House domestic staff unit that performed—like all its predecessors, not particularly well—the same basic functions.[25]

The Ford-Carter period was but a pause in the development of the modern presidency, lasting only until the unusual environmental turbulence died down. The turnaround came with the 1980 presidential election, which was more a thunderous rejection of the "weak" Carter administration and its perceived failings in both foreign and domestic policy than a mandate for Reagan's conservative program. What the public wanted, once again, was a strong, effective president who would take charge of the nation. Post-Watergate fears about presidential leadership had all but disappeared.

Reagan assumed the presidency with a clear agenda, a clear ideology,

25. Carter also took the lead in promoting a thorough study and evaluation of the public personnel system, resulting in the Civil Service Reform Act of 1978. Its salient innovation (proposed in the 1950s by the second Hoover Commission) was the Senior Executive Service, a pool of executives holding rank in person rather than position and transferable from job to job without restriction by the usual civil service requirements. While Carter's emphasis in selling and subsequently using the reform was on its contributions to flexible, effective management, its great potential as a mechanism of political control was rather obvious—and readily available to future presidents.

and a strong determination to control and coordinate the resources of government toward those ends. In the months before gaining office, his team (like those before it) went about designing and implementing an organizational strategy for governing. This strategy was by past standards innovative and comprehensive, but it was also heavily rooted in institutional memory and existing arrangements.[26]

Like Kennedy, Johnson, and Nixon, Reagan relied on task forces during the transition period. But he filled them with ideological partisans, and their task was to gain inside information on the operation and organization of specific agencies, to which they had virtually unfettered access granted by the Carter administration. Their reports and recommendations were centrally coordinated and provided the team with a crucial foundation on which to formulate their plans.

Perhaps the key part of this plan, the element that would later bind all the others together, was the use of the president's appointment and removal powers. The Reagan team spent months interviewing enormous numbers of people for jobs throughout government, placing almost exclusive emphasis on loyalty and ideology. Their concern was not simply with filling the obviously important positions; they wanted partisans located deep within the established bureaucracy, even if expertise was lacking. And they did not stop here. Cabinet appointees met frequently with the president-elect to establish a bond that Reagan hoped would prevent them from "going native" later on. Lower-level appointees were thoroughly socialized about agency programs and operations before assuming their positions; and they were socialized by Reagan aides and the conservative task forces, not by the career agency personnel whose corrupting influences were to be minimized.

In addition, Reagan ultimately went ahead to make explicitly political use of the Senior Executive Service, usually by removing career officials from important slots and filling them with partisans. He also used reductions in force as a legal means of eliminating whole bureaucratic

26. On the Reagan years, see especially Chester A. Newland, "Executive Office Policy Apparatus: Enforcing the Reagan Agenda," in Lester M. Salamon and Michael S. Lund, eds., *The Reagan Presidency and the Governing of America* (Washington, D.C.: Urban Institute Press, 1984); Chester A. Newland, "A Mid-Term Appraisal— The Reagan Presidency: Limited Government and Political Administration," *Public Administration Review*, vol. 43 (January–February 1983), pp. 1–21; Nathan, *Administrative Presidency*; and Lester M. Salamon and Alan J. Abramson, "Governance: The Politics of Retrenchment," in John L. Palmer and Isabel V. Sawhill, eds., *The Reagan Record* (Ballinger, 1984), pp. 31–68.

units staffed by careerists. This was done systematically, in the interests of presidential control and successful pursuit of the Reagan agenda. As a strategy for infiltrating the bureaucracy, it went way beyond anything Nixon had attempted. Yet it met with no serious opposition.

The sphere of politicization naturally included the Office of Management and Budget. In part because so many of the Reagan policy initiatives during the crucial first year were purposely intertwined with its budgetary strategy, the OMB quickly became a central participant in policymaking and political action. From Reagan's standpoint, its critical role on the team only underlined the absolute need for responsiveness. Budget Director David Stockman and his principal subordinates were everywhere: at high-level White House policy meetings, at lower level meetings with agency representatives, at congressional hearings, at press conferences. Stockman became a nationally recognized political figure. Yet he was also a true budgetary expert, having amassed considerable knowledge during an earlier stint in the House, and he dazzled careerists at the OMB with his mastery of their own highly technical subject matter. Thus while politicization may have exacted a trade-off price in terms of the bureaucratic foundations of OMB competence— that remains to be seen—the agency was not in the hands of novices, and Reagan got essentially what he wanted: the mobilization of OMB resources toward presidential ends.

There was no question that all the basic issues and problems related to policy had to be centrally processed and directed from the White House. The only real question was one of organization: how to do it? Here, as usual, institutional memory played a guiding role. Every effort, in particular, was made to avoid the overcentralization and lack of meaningful cabinet participation that caused difficulties for Nixon, but also to avoid the administrative chaos and lack of direction that prevailed under Carter's more open arrangements. The heart of the new system was the Office of Policy Development, which was the functional equivalent of the domestic policy staffs that all presidents since Kennedy had relied upon. The OPD did its work through cabinet councils, each with jurisdiction over specific aspects of the president's agenda, and each composed of appropriate cabinet members and subcabinet representatives from the bureaucracy, the OMB, and the White House.

The OPD system did not become the central force behind policymaking. The agenda, after all, was already set, and much of the driving force was of necessity the OMB, particularly during the first year. A few of the councils did play active, important roles, but the real contribution of the OPD system was its integration of diverse, potentially conflicting actors. It gave cabinet members and bureaucratic officials a sense of meaningful participation and a means of direct, continuing input, while it also gave the administration a regularized means of reemphasizing the president's agenda and the coordinated actions required throughout government for its pursuit. All of this was substantially facilitated, moreover, by the appointments strategy, which had produced a set of participants who, relative to those in prior administrations, were generally in philosophical agreement, presidentially oriented, and receptive to the obligations of team play.

Finally, the Reagan administration did not concern itself only with policy and the budgetary process. It also made a concerted effort to change bureaucratic decisionmaking at all levels, recognizing as Nixon had that important policy goals can be achieved administratively. In part, this was handled through a more smoothly managed version of the infiltration strategy. But it was also handled by means of a new OMB unit, staffed by presidential partisans, that reviewed proposals funneled through it by the various regulatory agencies. This process of regulatory review allowed the OMB to venture into territory long regarded as the rightful domain of the established bureaucracy and to act as the president's agent in screening and shaping decisions that would otherwise be lost to the permanent government.

There is no reason to think Reagan's administrative approach has been spectacularly efficient or successful in any absolute sense. The White House has hardly been free of in-fighting or administrative confusion; the design of the OPD system has left much to be desired, with many cabinet councils falling into disuse; the appointments strategy has sometimes backfired to generate serious political costs (the James Watt and Anne Burford cases are the obvious ones), frictions with some cabinet members, and unfilled positions; and the regulatory review process has lacked coherence, and has yet to have broad effects on the direction of regulatory policy. These sorts of observations, however, tend to miss the point. The history of the institutional presidency is a history of failures when judged by absolute standards, and, given the constraints on presidential action, there is little basis for expecting anything else.

The point to stress is that the Reagan years have seen a continuation and acceleration of the developmental logic apparent in the Kennedy,

Johnson, and Nixon years. The problem from the beginning was that the traditional institutional framework was perceived by activist presidents as inconsistent with their needs. While each had a unique personality and style, each had his own set of social goals, and each faced a somewhat different political environment, they all nonetheless responded in the same basic way: by attempting to direct the various dimensions of policymaking and political activity from the White House, by creating their own organizational units and staffing them with their own people, and by politicizing established units in the bureaucracy and the institutional presidency. Along the way there was much confusion and many missteps, and the flow of events was seriously disrupted by Watergate. But during the Reagan years the several threads seem to have come together nicely into a whole that, compared with arrangements under past administrations, is coherent, workable, and successful. In this sense, the Reagan presidency is a consummate expression of the historical drive toward congruence.[27]

Evaluating Politicization and Centralization

Students of the institutional presidency are virtually unanimous in denouncing these trends, claiming that they undermine and circumvent the competence of established institutions, inhibit the development of new sources of institutional support, and shift decisionmaking responsibilities to those least capable of handling them. Their recommendations, variously expressed, involve administrative arrangements that

27. Assessments here and in the concluding section are based on Reagan's first term. At this writing, several months into the second term, the Reagan White House is undergoing personnel changes and reorganization. Former Treasury Secretary Donald Regan has become chief of staff in what appears to be a more hierarchical, more centralized set of administrative arrangements. This has included a streamlining of the system of cabinet councils, with Edwin Meese (formerly of the White House, now attorney general) heading a Council on Domestic Policy and James Baker III (formerly of the White House, now secretary of the treasury) heading an Economic Policy Council. In effect, Meese and Baker now occupy positions hierarchically superior to those of other cabinet members in the domestic sphere—a centralizing strategy pioneered (unsuccessfully at the time) by Nixon. It remains to be seen whether these and other organizational reforms are in fact of much consequence, whether they add to or subtract from Reagan's administrative capacity, and whether they are well suited to the new, less favorable political context of the second term. Whatever happens, the administrative experience of Reagan's first term stands as a significant development in the modern presidency.

would respect and nurture neutral competence and organizational integrity—particularly in the OMB, since it is so obviously threatened, but also throughout the bureaucracy—and encourage more extensive, more systematic reliance on the cabinet and permanent government.[28]

Why are these sorts of beliefs so popular? The obvious answer is that they are overwhelmingly supported by our accumulated knowledge about governmental organization. But this is simply not the case. After more than fifty years of research on public and private organizations— the bulk of which happens to be on private organizations—we still know very little about even the most basic questions motivating the earliest work: the relationship between structure and efficiency, say, or between leadership and productivity. Actually, the uniformity of opinion has less to do with scientific knowledge than with the ideas and perspectives that have shaped the study of public administration. While the critics of politicization and centralization are a heterogeneous lot, and few would regard their own work as anchored in the academic traditions of public administration, its theoretical and normative background is nevertheless readily apparent in their approaches to government organization and their evaluations of it.

The most pervasive, long-term influences on the study of government organization derive from notions associated with classical organization theory and the politics-administration dichotomy. They entail a distinctive point of view about organizations and government that is intricately woven into the fabric of public administration thought. Dwight Waldo's remarks in 1961 were right on target:

> Not only is the classical theory still today the formal working theory of large numbers of persons technically concerned with administrative-organizational matters, both in the public and private spheres, but I expect it will be around

28. See, for example, Hugh Heclo, "OMB and the Presidency—the Problem of 'Neutral Competence,' " *Public Interest,* no. 38 (Winter 1975), pp. 80–98; Berman, *Office of Management and Budget and the Presidency*; Seidman, *Politics, Position, and Power*; Hess, *Organizing the Presidency*; and Frederick Mosher and others, *Watergate: Its Implications for Responsible Government* (Basic Books, 1974). As this list suggests, I am largely concerned here with academic studies of the presidency that focus specifically on questions of government organization. The analysis to follow is not intended to apply to the more popular treatises on the subject by various journalists and insiders—George E. Reedy's *The Twilight of the Presidency* (New York: Mentor Books, 1970), for example. Nor does it apply to those works, increasingly common after Vietnam and Watergate, that seek to argue much more generally that presidents have become too powerful. Arthur M. Schlesinger, Jr.'s *The Imperial Presidency* (Houghton, Mifflin, 1973) is perhaps the best known of these.

a long, long time. This is not necessarily because it is "true" . . . (A) social theory widely held by the actors has a self-confirming tendency and the classical theory is now deeply ingrained in our culture.[29]

The really interesting thing about the continuing influence of these ideas is that public administrationists are the first to denounce them. Since the 1950s, as most any beginning textbook will illustrate, classical organization theory has served as little more than a straw man for more advanced theoretical perspectives, and the politics-administration dichotomy has been firmly rejected as a naive misunderstanding of the inherently political context and nature of the administrative process. Nonetheless, much of the analysis, evaluation, and reform proposals concerning government organization, even in this age of enlightment, bears the unmistakable imprint of public administration's formative years, in values as well as theoretical beliefs.

Generally speaking, the ethos of public administration has always looked favorably on the bureaucracy. While the various pathologies and unintended consequences associated with formal organization have long been recognized, the overarching emphasis is on the great advantages of organization and the feasibility of reforms for correcting potential problems. The flip side is a jaundiced view of politics. While it is inevitably bound up with administrative behavior and a necessary component of democratic accountability, politics tends to be seen as a corrupting influence on the integrity and competence of formal organization—an influence that, if not kept to a minimum, can be expected to have destructive effects that far outweigh any democratic payoffs.

Since the Roosevelt years, there has been a continuing tension between the competing values of neutral competence and executive leadership, the latter gaining in importance with modern growth in the complexity of social problems, the size and fragmentation of government, and expectations surrounding presidential performance.[30] This tension has never been resolved, but it has maintained a characteristic balance in favor of neutral competence, which is clearly the core value.[31]

29. Dwight Waldo, "Organization Theory: An Elephantine Problem," *Public Administration Review,* vol. 21 (Winter 1961), p. 220.

30. On the competing values of neutral competence and executive leadership, see Kaufman, "Emerging Conflicts in the Doctrines of Public Administration."

31. Although the value of executive leadership has suffered from the backlash to Vietnam and Watergate, it was less fundamental than neutral competence even during the post-Roosevelt infatuation (especially apparent during the Kennedy and early Johnson years) with the strong presidency.

The problem for the executive is to mobilize the neutral competence of the government but without compromising it through politicizing attempts to ensure responsiveness. The notion is not only that politicization is dangerous but that there is no need to carry it very far in pursuit of responsiveness; for the problem, to the extent it really exists, is basically organizational rather than political. What we need for executive leadership is not political mechanisms to ensure responsiveness but rather a presidential version of neutral competence: a managerial capacity. Hence, the requirements of presidential leadership become, through translation, the requirements of good management. Fundamentally political problems emerge with fundamentally nonpolitical solutions.

Some of the best works on the presidency—Neustadt's *Presidential Power,* for example—are grounded in political analyses of incentives, resources, and behavior. They are essentially attempts to explain why governmental actors behave as they do, and their prescriptions derive from such behavioral foundations. This has never really been the analytical thrust of public administration. Its primary concern has been the pursuit of efficient, effective government through discovery and evaluation of appropriate organizational designs, where "appropriate" derives meaning from strongly held values and beliefs that circumscribe the role of politics and distract attention from its effects and behavioral determinants. It is fitting, then, that presidents are now exhorted to respect the neutral competence of bureaucratic agencies, to rely more heavily on the cabinet, to use appointments in pursuit of professionalism and expertise—and, in short, to move in directions that are consistent with long-standing academic beliefs about how presidents ought to behave, but entirely inconsistent with the way presidents have viewed their own incentives, resources, and constraints. Thus, presidents continue to do what they are not supposed to do, and academics continue to complain that, if only presidents would understand and see things their way, these unfortunate developments could be turned around.

There is an important parallel here with the early political science concern for "responsible" parties. About thirty years ago, many political scientists advocated reforms intended to encourage the development of parties resembling those we have come to expect in parliamentary systems—parties whose candidates run on programmatic platforms and, if in the majority, put their platforms into effect through cohesive legislative action. Since then it has come to be recognized that, however admirable the sentiments behind this position, we are not free to choose the kind of party system we want.[32] Parties develop over time within a much larger institutional system, structured in the United States by separation of powers, federalism, and a distinctive electoral system—and, for the most part, the United States has weak, decentralized, fragmented parties because of the way in which the larger institutional system shapes the incentives and resources of social actors, especially politicians. Thus, we cannot reform the party system in any dramatic way by focusing on the parties, because the parties are not really the cause of their own irresponsibility. While positive steps might be taken at the margins, only much more fundamental reforms in the institutional system can render the goal of responsible parties anything more than an impractical dream.

Reforms directed at the presidency tend to suffer from just this sort of impracticality. They often assume that presidents are the problem, that presidents continually misunderstand the great value of neutral competence, cabinet government, and all the rest. In fact, even if we grant that there is a problem, presidents are not the cause of it. Their incentives and resources are largely determined by an institutional system in which they have no choice but to operate—and the historical drive toward politicization and centralization has its roots here, not in the pathological designs of individual presidents and not in their consistent misunderstanding of administrative organization. In this respect—and it is hard to think of one that could be more fundamental—standard evaluations tend to be quite off the mark, and their proposed reforms, as a result, fail to address the basic causes of the problem.

The auxiliary issue, however, is not so easily answered: is there actually a problem? That is, are politicization and centralization undesirable, whether from the standpoint of efficient, effective government or the president's ability to pursue his own objectives? Students of the institutional presidency tend to give enthusiastically affirmative answers to both aspects of the question. And, to the extent that these issues are amenable to resolution through factual analysis—the value components resist this, of course—they could be quite correct. But their answers arise all too easily from traditionally held beliefs and values. That politicization and centralization might actually be highly positive developments is, for the most part, not seriously entertained.

Given the current state of knowledge, there is no way these questions

32. See, for example, Leon Epstein, *Political Parties in Western Democracies* (Praeger, 1967).

can be evaluated adequately. There is evidence to suggest that politicization and centralization do indeed have some of the disadvantages claimed. There is also good reason to believe that the president's short-term time perspective discourages investment in competence-building institutional arrangements, to his own disadvantage.[33] But this is less than half the story. It ignores the potential contributions of politicization and centralization to responsiveness, innovation, and other components of presidential leadership. It ignores their demonstrated compatibility with presidential incentives—a crucial property that is the Achilles' heel of standard reform proposals. It ignores the role of institutional memory in transmitting "ephemeral, politicized" structures— for example, for appointments and congressional liaison—from one administration to the next.[34] It ignores the necessary trade-offs that presidents are forced to make in seeking a working balance between responsiveness and organizational competence. And it ignores the very real threats to presidential leadership capacity that entrenched interests and established organizational routines represent.

In general, the standard arguments against politicization and centralization have something valid to say, but they do not tell us what we need to know. Over the long haul, we need to have a full, balanced accounting of both the positive and negative effects, we need to be able to compare them with those associated with alternative institutional arrangements, and we need to assess the extent to which these alternatives are in fact compatible with presidential incentives—for if they are not, they will

33. See especially Heclo, "OMB and the Presidency." This is the most thorough and persuasive statement of the negative side of the issue, but there is no real attempt at a balanced examination of both sides.

34. I should take this opportunity to question the tendency among critics to couple politicization with deinstitutionalization. It is true that the introduction of new layers of political appointees into a bureau previously run by careerists may well upset its established routines and memory processes, with destabilizing effects (at least in the short run). Yet these sorts of effects tend to be emphasized to the exclusion of all else. It is important to recognize, in particular, that thoroughly politicized behaviors can also be institutionalized. Indeed, the critics themselves commonly point to the extent to which appointments or congressional liaison—or the National Security Council, for that matter—have become institutionalized over time, without dwelling on the fact that all of these are newly reconstituted with every president and are thoroughly politicized as well as institutionalized. Although bureaucratic structures of all types might be "more" institutionalized if staffed by careerists, this in itself says little about the value or consequences of politicization—which may often promote responsiveness and flexibility while still affording sufficient institutionalization. More institutionalization is not valuable in itself anyway.

never survive intact, and indeed cannot properly be regarded as serious alternatives. At this point we simply have very little to go on. Certainly we do not know enough to justify the kind of confident criticism that now seems to prevail.[35]

Conclusion

This essay views the presidency as an institution whose development, like that of any other, is driven by incongruence among structures, incentives, and resources. The fundamental basis for the incongruence is deeply rooted in modern American politics: the expectations surrounding presidential performance far outstrip the institutional capacity of presidents to perform. This gives presidents a strong incentive to enhance their capacity by initiating reforms and making adjustments in the administrative apparatus surrounding them—but here too there is a fundamental imbalance: the resources for acting upon this strong incentive are wholly inadequate, constrained by political and bureaucratic opposition, institutional inertia, inadequate knowledge, and time pressures. It is this imbalance that channels presidential effort into areas of greatest flexibility and generates the major institutional developments we observe, politicization and centralization.

The details of presidential organization—the actual administrative arrangements adopted, the rates and types of change—vary considerably from one administration to another in response to differences in the personality, style, political objectives, and partisanship of individual presidents. Essential as these details may be to our understanding of the presidency, they represent fluctuation within a long-term historical process whose general path and underlying logic are the fundamental components of institutional development. For the most part, politicization and centralization have grown over time not because of who presidents are or what they stand for, but because of the nature of our institutions and the role and location of presidents within them. The basic causes are systemic.

This cannot tell us whether politicization and centralization are good or bad. It does tell us something about our criteria of evaluation: that

35. For a useful step toward a more comprehensive appraisal of the issues, see Salamon, "Presidency and Domestic Policy Formulation."

they must take account of the systemic forces on presidential choice. It is not enough to point to absolute standards against which politicization and centralization may seem to fare poorly—"seem" because most of the evidence is not yet in. However we appraise them in absolute terms, the practical issue is inevitably one of feasible alternatives. Do there exist reforms that are preferable (on whatever grounds), that presidents and other decisionmakers would actually adopt, and that are sufficiently compatible with the structure of presidential incentives and resources to ensure their continuity? These are the alternatives with which politicization and centralization are properly compared—and it is questionable whether many of the usual reform proposals would pass this test.

There is no reason to think that the near future will be much different from the near past. Barring some fundamental and unforeseen change in American institutions, the gap between expectations and capacity will continue to characterize the presidency, as will the serious constraints on presidential resources and the consequent attractiveness of politicization and centralization. There will likely be no turning back from the general path of historical development thus far.[36]

The heightening of politicization and centralization during the Reagan years is the most recent expression of this historical process. It is the continuation of a trend, the same basic response to roughly the same set of institutional forces—but a response that, by sequential ordering, had the advantage of being able to learn from and build upon the achievements, failures, and organizational experiences of preceding administrations. Moreover, some portion of the accelerated push in these directions is doubtless due to special features of the Reagan years: a highly ideological president, a clear agenda, a permanent government openly

36. Obviously, these trends will not continue unabated until "total" politicization and centralization are reached. Presumably well before such an extreme outcome is even remotely approached, diminishing returns—due, for instance, to organizational pathologies inevitably arising within an increasingly large, complex, bureaucratized presidency—will become readily apparent to presidents and nonpresidents alike, even if our scientific knowledge of cause and effect in government organization remains minimal. Also, members of Congress, bureaucrats, and other outsiders can be expected to place greater limits on the president's flexibility for moving in these directions as levels of politicization and centralization increasingly strike them as threatening or excessive. Such eventualities would prompt presidents to seek other means of enhancing their leadership capacity, thus defusing the historical trends we now observe and initiating new ones. But however likely in the long run, and despite the current misgivings of many academics and some political participants, there is no evidence that these kinds of reactive developments will play roles of any real consequence in the near future.

hostile to the president's program. Assuming a more normal confluence of factors during subsequent presidencies, it would seem that a period of institutional pause and consolidation is more likely than continued rapid change. From this vantage point, then, the Reagan years hardly seem to represent a dramatic new direction in American politics.

On the other hand, Reagan did much more than continue a historical trend. In moving ambitiously down the paths of politicization and centralization, he built a set of administrative arrangements that by past standards proved coherent, well integrated, and eminently workable. Given the sobering experiences of recent activist presidents, particularly Johnson and Nixon, in their attempts—against great odds—to fashion a workable administrative framework, the Reagan effort emerges as a striking success. As such, it is a lesson that will not be lost on future presidents—who will have every reason to learn from and build upon the Reagan example in seeking to enhance their own institutional capacities for leadership. This places Reagan in a pivotal historical position, and could well establish him as the most administratively influential president of the modern period.

CHAPTER TEN

Federalism and the Bias for Centralization

JOHN E. CHUBB

FROM THE NEW DEAL through the late 1970s the American federal system moved decisively in a single direction: it became centralized. The government in Washington went from spending the least, for domestic purposes, of the three levels—national, state, and local—to spending nearly twice as much as the lower levels combined. In addition, the lower levels were drawn under Washington's influence through more than 500 federal grant programs comprising more than one-fourth of state and local budgets, and a host of regulations associated with the grants as well as with national policies concerning civil rights, pollution, health, and safety.[1] Since 1979, however, a new direction has been taken. At a pace that accelerated with the first inauguration of Ronald Reagan, the federal government has decentralized, slowing the growth of assistance to state and local governments, reducing regulatory burdens, loosening the strings attached to federal grants, and generally curtailing its role in subnational affairs.[2] Only a lead over the lower levels in domestic spending has been maintained.

These developments are important because they could change domestic policy dramatically. The policy priorities of the myriad state,

Paul Wright and Steven Levine provided research assistance.

1. Advisory Commission on Intergovernmental Relations, *Significant Features of Fiscal Federalism, 1982–83 Edition* (Washington, D.C.: ACIR, 1984), p. 120; the major statutes of intergovernmental regulation can be found in ACIR, *Regulatory Federalism: Policy, Process, Impact and Reform* (ACIR, 1984), p. 6.

2. ACIR, *A Catalog of Federal Grant-in-Aid Programs to State and Local Governments: Grants Funded Fiscal Year 1984* (ACIR, 1984), p. 1.

municipal, and county governments that are acquiring more responsibilities are different from the priorities of the government in Washington that is relinquishing them. The lower governments, because they must compete with one another for businesses and taxpayers, are less inclined than the national government to tax progressively or spend for social welfare.[3] Because they have less competitive political systems than the national government, the lower governments are also less likely to represent the full spectrum of domestic political interests. To be sure, today's state and local governments are more economically sound and politically representative than those that led the national government to assume so many domestic responsibilities in the first place. Yet the prospects for significant policy change, should decentralization continue, are real.

Whether decentralization will continue, however, is an open question. Thus far decentralization has occurred without dismantling the basic structures upon which the federal system has come to rest. The pressures being placed upon those structures by President Reagan, his domestic policy agenda, and the federal budget deficit are strong indeed. But the obstacles to structural change are at least as formidable. The form of centralization that has been established in the United States is not founded on a partisan principle that might be superseded in a pro-Republican realignment; it is supported by bipartisan congressional interests—in serving local constituencies and increasing electoral safety. In that connection, the recent movement toward decentralization reflects a bipartisan concession to the federal budget deficit rather than a partisan repudiation of the value of centralization. The centralized structure is also firmly entrenched in an intergovernmental bureaucracy, nurtured by Washington, that pressures state and local governments to support and cooperate with a centralized federal system. And the dynamics of state elections seriously complicate Republican efforts to control the lower levels of government and thereby facilitate decentralization. Together, these obstacles constitute a bias for centralization, rooted in contemporary American elections, that shows little sign of changing.

3. Economists have long argued that interstate competition, to attract business and discourage indigent migration, makes the central government the more logical location for the redistribution function of government. See, for example, George Stigler, "Tenable Range of Functions of Local Government," in Joint Economic Committee, *Federal Expenditure Policy for Growth and Stability*, 85 Cong. 1 sess. (Government Printing Office, 1957), pp. 213–19. See also Wallace E. Oates, *Fiscal Federalism* (Harcourt, Brace, Jovanovich, 1972).

The Politics of Centralization

It is customary to point out that the roots of today's centralized federal system run deep.[4] The precedent for federal grants was established in 1862 when the Morrill Act provided state governments with parcels of land to sell in support of land grant colleges. The concept that the national government enjoys a superior fiscal base took hold in 1913 when the Sixteenth Amendment legalized the comprehensive income tax. And the idea that the central government could shoulder considerably more responsibility for social welfare than the lower governments was driven home by the Great Depression. In a short burst of legislation that included most importantly the Social Security Act, the national government during the 1930s increased domestic expenditures from 1.7 percent of GNP to 8.5 percent (figure 10-1). By the end of the decade the national government was spending nearly as much as the lower levels combined; it had moved from a position of clear inferiority on domestic matters to a position of rough equality; and it had established the political and statutory basis for the spending growth that has made the national government twice the size of the state and local governments today.

It is tempting to see the post-Depression process of continued centralization as an incremental extension of the political principles in place at the end of the New Deal. Notwithstanding a certain amount of conservative uneasiness about the trend, a consensus was emerging in favor of principles that encouraged centralization. The national government, benefiting from an income tax that generally yields greater income over time than sales and property taxes instituted by subnational governments, was regarded as a more efficient revenue source. Functions with benefits extending beyond the borders of states and localities, for example, interstate highways, waste water treatment facilities, and higher education, came to be viewed as justifiable areas of federal participation, if not domination. The increasing integration of the national economy and the escalating residential mobility of the population homogenized political demands and created pressure for uniformity in highways, regulation, health care, and other benefits that only the federal

4. For a recent example, see David B. Walker, *Toward a Functioning Federalism* (Winthrop, 1981).

Figure 10-1. *Government Spending from Own Funds as Percent of the Gross National Product, Fiscal Years 1929–85*[a]

Percent of GNP

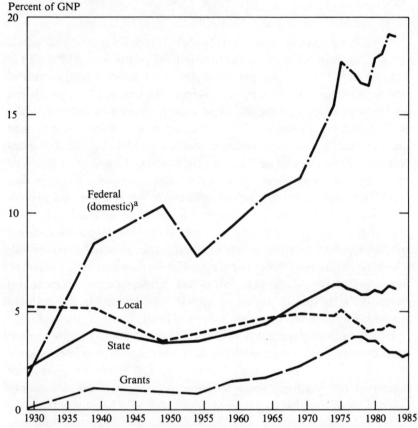

Source: Advisory Commission on Intergovernmental Relations, *Significant Features of Fiscal Federalism*, 1982–83 edition (Washington, D.C.: ACIR, 1984), tables 1, 2, 75.

a. Total federal expenditures minus national defense.

government could handle.[5] And the responsibility for insuring the social welfare against potential hardships such as old age, unemployment, medical indigence, and impoverished child rearing gravitated to the top of the federal structure, as the lower levels failed to insure adequately.

To be sure, these principles continued to spark political debate. But each of the post-World War II decades brought sizable new federal

5. This thesis is developed in Paul E. Peterson, "Introduction: Technology, Race, and Urban Policy," in Paul E. Peterson, ed., *The New Urban Reality* (Brookings, 1985), chap. 1.

grants—interstate highway assistance in the 1950s, Great Society grants in the 1960s, and various block grants in the 1970s—and steady increases in both the federal share of total domestic spending and federal grants to state and local governments. The lengthy transformation of the federal system from decentralized to centralized can reasonably be interpreted, then, as a gradual building of political consensus on basic principles governing the appropriate roles of the central and the subnational governments.

It would be wrong, however, to regard this explanation, even in more elaborate form, as sufficient. It would also be a mistake to give in to the logical temptation to regard the recent erosion of centralization as essentially a breakdown in what might be called the New Deal consensus on the appropriate organization of the federal system. Part of the system's centralization is certainly due to the growing acceptance of New Deal principles, to the conviction among Democrats as well as many Republicans that the central government is a more efficient, effective, and equitable provider of many public services than the lower levels. Part of the system's decentralization since 1980 is due to the weakening of that conviction and the leadership in that direction by President Reagan. But a closer look at the course and politics of centralization (especially since the early 1960s), and at decentralization more recently, suggests that a partisan or ideological explanation of these developments overlooks an important reality: the nature of contemporary American political institutions sustains centralization and is relatively unresponsive to the Democratic and Republican electoral swings that alternately support and oppose it.

The Federal Grant Explosion

The federal system did not become centralized in a smooth and linear fashion. It grew in bursts, one during the Depression and the other during the 1960s and early 1970s. During the 1930s domestic federal spending jumped from less than 2 percent of GNP to 8.5 percent, and federal grants rocketed from 0.1 percent of GNP to 1.1 percent. While federal spending rose during the ensuing two decades, its share of GNP remained fairly stable until the late 1950s. Then sizable growth occurred rapidly. By 1975 federal domestic spending had doubled its mid-1950s share of GNP, and by 1978, federal grants had more than tripled their share (figure 10-1). Federal grants, in other words, were expanding more than 50 percent faster than the explosive domestic budget of which they were a part.

The grant system's growth is the most important element of the federal system's centralization because grant expenditures pay a dividend in political control that the mere expansion of national governmental functions does not. The preponderance of intergovernmental assistance is provided by categorical grants (limited-purpose assistance governed by rules, sanctions, and incentives) that impose national interests on grant recipients. True, the recipients of federal grants often embrace national interests enthusiastically and sometimes succeed in untying the strings that bind them to less agreeable federal objectives. But the general effect of categorical grants is to distort the decisionmaking of governments that receive them. Regulations such as those requiring local "maintenance of effort" and "matching" requirements that make certain local expenditures a prerequisite for federal aid prohibit recipients from using federal funds for nonfederal purposes, including tax relief. Applicants for funds must stipulate how grants will be used; reports must account for how they were used; and state and local accounting and service delivery systems must pass federal audits and inspections. Lower governments can avoid the distortions and burdens of categorical assistance by choosing not to receive grants, but few ever do. Whether the price of receiving aid is matching federal dollars, or bearing administrative burdens, state and local governments seem to think it is cheaper than the political cost of raising revenue through taxation. But their thinking ignores the political cost to the system as a whole. Federal aid leads state and local governments to respond less to internal demands and more to Washington. The federal system loses much of its definitive character; it becomes centralized.

From this perspective the crucial transformation of the federal system, shifting it decisively toward central control, occurred during the 1960s and 1970s. Federal grants veritably exploded in worth and number, not only increasing the financial dependence of the bottom on the top, but connecting the levels with a network of administrative and bureaucratic relationships unknown before that time. The explosion occurred, moreover, throughout the grant system. It was not confined to grants for the poor that were promoted by the liberal Congresses of the period. Indeed, grants that were not earmarked for the poor grew at a faster rate and over a longer period of time. This point is demonstrated in table 10-1, which reports the growth rates of federal grants, in current dollars, for

Table 10-1. *Average Annual Percentage Growth Rates of Federal Outlays, Fiscal Years 1955–85*[a]

Spending category	1955–60	1960–70	1970–78	1978–81	1981–85
Grants to state and local governments	17.0	13.1	15.8	6.8	3.1
Individuals	(8.8)	(13.3)	(13.8)	(15.2)	(6.7)
Institutions	(23.6)	(13.0)	(16.9)	(2.5)	(0.6)
Direct payments to individuals	11.3	10.0	16.2	15.3	7.3
National defense	2.4	5.4	3.1	14.7	12.7
Net interest	7.5	7.5	11.9	24.7	17.4
Total outlays	6.1	7.8	11.2	13.9	9.0

Source: *Historical Tables: Budget of the United States Government, Fiscal Year 1986*, table 6-1.
a. Based on current dollars.

two categories of assistance approximating the distinction between grants for the poor and for other purposes: grants for individuals, and grants for institutions. Those in the first category (for example, aid to families with dependent children and medicaid) are for lower governments to use on behalf of needy individuals while those in the second category are for broader governmental functions such as education, transportation, and community development.

The figures are compared with other components of the federal budget. Once again the unusual growth rates of federal grants are apparent; in each of the three periods from 1955 to 1978 federal grants grew at a faster rate than national defense, net interest, and direct payments to individuals (except for a virtual tie in the 1970s). But the two types of grants did not grow in lockstep. Grants to institutions, which must be appropriated each year by Congress, grew faster than grants to individuals, which change along with changes in economic and demographic forces that are beyond annual congressional control. Grants to institutions took off, moreover, not during the heyday of the Great Society and the liberal Eighty-ninth Congress but during the late 1950s. The large increase in the rate of growth during the 1960s of grants to individuals shows the effect of Great Society legislation; but even then, grants to institutions kept pace and regained the lead during the 1970s.

These points are reinforced by the growth pattern of the number of grants (table 10-2). By 1963, 160 grant programs were in place, dwarfing the 30 extant at the end of the Depression. Two-thirds of these were "project" grants, given exclusively to institutions submitting satisfactory plans for their use. The remainder was "formula" grants allocated to lower governments—for their own use or for transmission to individ-

Table 10-2. *Federal Grants to State and Local Governments,*
Selected Fiscal Years, 1929–85

Year	Billions of current dollars	Percent of GNP	Percent of state and local expenditures	Number[a]
1929	0.1	0.1	1.5	15
1939	1.0	1.1	10.3	30
1949	2.2	0.9	11.0	n.a.
1954	2.9	0.8	9.7	n.a.
1959	6.5	1.4	13.9	132
1964	10.1	1.6	14.7	212
1969	20.3	2.2	17.1	387
1974	43.4	3.1	21.2	n.a.
1975	49.8	3.3	21.4	448
1976	59.1	3.5	23.5	n.a.
1977	68.4	3.7	25.4	n.a.
1978	77.9	3.7	26.2	n.a.
1979	82.9	3.5	25.8	n.a.
1980	91.5	3.5	25.7	539
1981	94.8	3.2	24.8	n.a.
1982	88.2	2.9	21.6	441
1983	92.5	2.9	21.6	n.a.
1984	97.6	2.7	21.2	404
1985 (est.)	107.0	2.8	n.a.	n.a.

Sources: Data for 1929–82 are from the Advisory Commission on Intergovernmental Relations, *Significant Features of Fiscal Federalism,* 1982–83 edition (Washington, D.C.: ACIR, 1984), tables 1, 2, 75; and ACIR, *Categorical Grants: Their Role and Design* (ACIR, 1978), tables I-7, I-9. Data for 1983–85 are from *Special Analyses, Budget of the United States Government, Fiscal Year 1986;* and ACIR, *A Catalog of Federal Grant-in-Aid Programs to State and Local Governments: Grants Funded Fiscal Year 1984* (ACIR, 1984).

n.a. Not available.

a. For 1963 and earlier, the number in existence is based on those grants still in existence in 1968; however, the only grants known to have been terminated were fourteen associated with the Depression and temporary emergencies of World War II; for 1975 and earlier, the number is for the nearest available year.

uals—on a noncompetitive basis, according to rules established by Congress.[6] Yet remarkable as this postwar proliferation of grants was, it was swiftly eclipsed from 1963 to 1968 when another 227 grants were established. These grants too were predominantly (80 percent) for institutions for certain projects and not formula-based inducements for local payments to individuals. The functions the grants supported, moreover, were not strictly the services for the poor that are usually associated with the Great Society; they were primarily for broad-based needs. And growth hardly slackened once President Lyndon B. Johnson left office. From 1968 to 1980 another 150 grant programs were added,

6. The exact numbers of project and formula grants in the years 1962–66 are given in ACIR, *Categorical Grants: Their Role and Design* (ACIR, 1978), p. 25.

again primarily for specific projects. Although formula grants allocate the majority of grant funds (67 percent in fiscal 1975),[7] most of that money is not for transfer to the poor, but rather is regulated to ensure use by subnational governments for popular activities such as highway construction and elementary and secondary education. In fiscal 1975 no more than 70 of more than 500 grant programs were allocated for the poor or unemployed.[8]

In sum, two-thirds of all grants extant in 1980 were created during the preceding sixteen years, and most of the grant money was not allocated to redistributive programs (those programs thought to transfer income to lower-income groups). The post-New Deal expansion of the demand for uniform national services and the scope of generally accepted national responsibilities certainly fueled the explosion of grants. And the brief triumph of liberal Democracy during the mid-1960s surely stimulated a surge in redistributive assistance. Nevertheless, those events cannot wholly account for the growth of federal aid. The character and duration of the grant explosion can be understood only by understanding the institution that designed and propagated the categorical grant.

Congress and the Institutionalization of Central Control

Congress legislated categorical grants with virtual abandon during precisely the period that it was transforming itself from an institution controlled by autocratic, and often conservative, committee chairmen, and in which the widely recommended behavior for representatives was "to get along, go along," to a more democratic institution in which power was decentralized in roughly 150 subcommittees in each house of Congress.[9] Beginning in 1961 with the enlargement of the House Rules Committee, and culminating in 1973–74 with the "subcommittee bill of rights" and the demise of the strict seniority system, representatives as well as senators were emerging as independent political actors. They were demanding and acquiring control of policy benefits and jurisdiction over program implementation to protect themselves against the uncer-

7. Ibid., p. 92.
8. Based on analysis of grants listed in ACIR, *A Catalog of Federal Grant-in-Aid Programs to State and Local Governments: Grants Funded Fiscal Year 1975* (ACIR, 1977).
9. Norman J. Ornstein and others, *Vital Statistics of Congress* (Washington, D.C.: American Enterprise Institute, 1982), pp. 98–99.

Figure 10-2. *House Roll Call Votes on Distributive Issues, Eighty-second through Ninety-sixth Congresses*

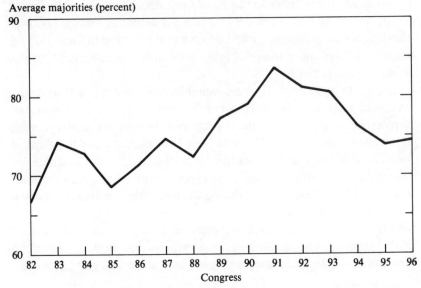

Average majorities (percent)

Congress

tainties of electoral politics. In the process, the percentage of majority members of the House who chaired commmittees or subcommittees doubled (52.2 percent in 1979); the number of House subcommittees increased nearly 100 percent; and the number of southern committee chairs in the House and the Senate was cut by two-thirds. Personal staff grew 300 percent in both chambers; the proportions of House and Senate personal staff based in the districts jumped sharply; the number of pieces of mail sent by representatives and senators to their districts grew by 500 percent, and most important, the proportion of incumbent representatives winning reelection by safe margins of 60 percent or better (now consistently over three-fourths) increased steadily.[10]

Categorical grants mushroomed in numbers and dollars during the 1960s and 1970s because they fit the political needs of representatives and senators. By their sheer number such grants provide abundant opportunities for legislators to claim credit for producing discrete benefits for their districts. Because most of the money is appropriated annually—increasing from 50 percent in 1955 to 66.6 percent in 1978—the chances

10. In their order of citation, these statistics are found ibid., pp. 101, 98, 103, 110, 112, 140, 50.

Table 10-3. *Coefficients of Variation and Means for Selected Federal Expenditures, by State per Capita, 1979*

Type of expenditure	Mean	Coefficients of variation
Defense contracts	246	87.5
Defense salaries	215	136.0
Highway and sewer grants	68	52.3
Federal grants	391	27.4

Source: Coefficients are calculated from state per capita allocations reported in Joel Havemann and Rochelle L. Stanfield, "Neutral Federal Policies Are Reducing Frostbelt–Sunbelt Spending Imbalances," *National Journal* vol. 13 (February 1981), pp. 233–36.

to claim credit are frequent.[11] Through their wide distribution, they also gain fairly easy passage in Congress. Figure 10-2, for example, depicts the average majorities of roughly 2,000 House roll call votes on distributive issues (those allocating funds for nonredistributive purposes to individuals or lower governments) for the Eighty-second through Ninety-sixth Congresses, 1951–1980.[12] While always popular, these bills increased their majorities steadily from the early 1960s to a plateau above 80 percent by the early 1970s. Most of these votes, enjoying obvious bipartisan support, authorize or appropriate funds for categorical grants.

These grants are, in fact, widely distributed to encourage universal support. In table 10-3 the allocation of federal grants among the states is compared with defense contracts and defense salaries, which are also politically popular areas of congressional spending. The coefficients of variation are much smaller for federal grants as a whole, and for highway and sewer grants individually, than for defense expenditures. In other words, individual federal grants tend to be distributed evenly among political jurisdictions, despite jurisdictional differences in the need for services such as highways, while the class of all federal grant spending

11. The importance of "credit claiming" as a reelection strategy is developed in David R. Mayhew, *Congress: The Electoral Connection* (Yale University Press, 1974). The proportion of grant expenditures appropriated annually is indicated by the proportion of total grant expenditures not for passthrough to individuals. Annual figures are provided in ACIR, *Significant Features*, p. 120.

12. Distributive programs allocate federal funds to beneficiaries who are not sufficiently numerous to be considered an economic class of American society and in a manner that is not perceived as a general transfer of income from taxpayers to nontaxpayers. Redistributive programs are those thought to shift income from the upper and middle classes to the lower. Similar definitions were introduced by Theodore J. Lowi, "American Business, Public Policy, Case Studies, and Political Theory," *World Politics,* vol. 16 (July 1964), pp. 676–715. The specific programs included in each category are far too numerous to list here, but they are available from the author.

Table 10-4. *Direct Federal Aid to Local Governments,*
Selected Fiscal Years, 1955–82

Year	As percentage of total federal grants	As percentage of locally raised revenue
1955	11.5	2.5
1960	8.5	2.6
1965	10.6	3.6
1970	10.9	5.1
1971	12.1	5.9
1972	13.2	7.1
1973	18.9	11.2
1974	23.5	13.3
1975	21.9	12.9
1976	23.0	14.6
1977	24.3	16.3
1978	24.9	17.5
1979	24.9	17.6
1980	24.0	16.3
1981	23.7	15.4
1982	23.7	12.8

Source: ACIR, *Significant Features,* tables 75, 76.

is more equitably distributed still. By distributing money universally within programs, Congress avoids conflicts within committees, and by doing the same thing across programs, Congress minimizes floor fights among competing claimants for grant funds.[13] With the decentralized congressional machinery thus oiled, categorical grants can expand quickly in number and value.

As categorical grants proliferate, they provide an additional benefit to Congress. The strings attached to categorical aid invariably generate complaints from state and local governments burdened by inflexible regulations and onerous application and reporting procedures, and from beneficiaries convinced that services have not been provided properly. The image and visibility of legislators are enhanced to the extent that they, and their burgeoning district or Washington staffs, can alleviate their constituents' problems with a little intervention in the federal bureaucracy.[14] This role as ombudsman may provide even greater electoral rewards than the traditional political benefits associated with

13. This political virture of distributive policy was first underlined in ibid.
14. This thesis was first developed by Morris P. Fiorina, *Congress: Keystone of the Washington Establishment* (Yale University Press, 1977).

Table 10-5. *Matching Ratios of Federal Grants, Selected Fiscal Years, 1932–80*

Year	Percent requiring no nonfederal match	Percent with federal share of 50 percent or less
1932	33.3	60.0
1938	23.3	46.7
1963	40.4	29.2
1968	38.2	24.0
1975	38.5	13.5
1980	46.6	9.2

Sources: ACIR, *Categorical Grants*, tables I-9, V-8; ACIR, *Catalog of Federal Grant-in-Aid Programs to State and Local Governments: Grants Funded Fiscal Year 1981* (ACIR, 1982), table 3, pp. 15–65; and ACIR, *Significant Features*, table 75.

assuring liberals that federal funds are not diverted to state and local priorities, and conservatives that they are not spent without demonstrated need and strict accountability.

Congress has done all it can, moreover, to ensure that grant expenditures are controlled directly by Washington and, in turn, that complaints are directed to congressional members. Besides relying on an exploding number of programs, Congress has also moved steadily to increase the number of institutional recipients. From 1960 to 1978 the proportion of federal grant programs going directly to local governments, municipalities, school districts, counties, and special districts, tripled (table 10-4). By the late 1970s one-fourth of all federal grant money was delivered, without state intervention, to thousands of small governments, whose dependence on Washington had increased about 700 percent. To gain not only more ombudsman opportunities but also more legislative credit, the increasingly independent members of Congress supported local governments directly rather than through middlemen in state capitals.

These rewards were also enhanced by shifting the incentive structure of federal grants. In the early days of categorical grants (table 10-5), the majority of grants had matching requirements of 50 percent or better while only a small minority required no matching at all. Generally, grants with matching incentives require less federal administrative supervision than grants without them, because compliance with matching regulations provides a reasonable assurance of appropriate state and local effort. Grants without matching rules rely more on regulations and monitoring to ensure that funds are properly used. Since the Depression era, there has been an accelerating drop in the proportion of grants requiring large

(50 percent or greater) state or local matches. The drop reached a low of 9.2 percent in 1980. At the same time, grants requiring no match at all have increased to nearly half the total. Economic logic cannot explain these changes, but political logic can.[15] The reduction in matching rates decreases the probability that eligible grant recipients will choose not to receive federal funds and increases the probability that legislators will be able to take political credit for benefits that their constituents find cheap enough to accept. The increase in administrative complexity that nonmatching grants entails creates burdens for state and local governments. But representatives and senators benefit. They gladly share those burdens in exchange for the rewards of playing the nonpartisan ombudsman.

In many respects, the growth of categorical grants stems from the nature of modern Congress as an institution and is not a product of the New Deal or its last hurrah in the liberal surge of the 1960s. Categorical grants are important elements in the electoral successes of incumbent legislators of both parties, and they are quintessential products of the decentralized congressional structure that legislators have created to facilitate their reelection. Unless the electoral fortunes of legislators come to depend on factors other than the delivery of benefits and services for constituents, the categorical grant will remain the preferred instrument of the national government for assisting state and local government.

The Politics of Decentralization

Immediately, this conclusion raises the question: how, if categorical grants are the lifeblood of the modern Congress, did Congress adopt block grants in the early 1970s; permit a turnabout in grant expenditure growth in the late 1970s; and accept extensive consolidations and cancellations of categorical grants during the Reagan administration? The simple answer is that, in important respects, these exceptions prove the rule.

Categorical grants have long been criticized for distorting state and local policymaking and imposing excessive administrative costs on Washington as well as on grant recipients. Just as long, block grants have been held up as a promising reform. Yet, notwithstanding impartial

15. On the lack of a coherent economic justification for matching rates see ACIR, *Categorical Grants*, pp. 147–73.

Table 10-6. *Percentage of Federal Grant Outlays by Different Methods, Selected Fiscal Years, 1968–86*

Year	Categorical grants	Block grants	General revenue sharing
1968	98.0	2.0	0.0
1972	90.2	8.3	1.5
1976	77.5	10.4	12.1
1980	79.3	11.3	9.4
1984	79.7	13.3	7.0
1985 (est.)	81.0	12.7	6.3
1986 (est.)	84.0	13.1	3.0

Sources: Data for 1968 are from ACIR, *Categorical Grants*, table I-11; and data for 1972–85 are from *Special Analyses, Fiscal Year 1986*, table H-9.

support for that view by the first Hoover Commission in 1949, the Kestenbaum Commission in 1955, and the Advisory Commission on Intergovernmental Relations in the mid-1960s, and despite political support from Harry S. Truman, Dwight D. Eisenhower, and to some degree Lyndon B. Johnson, Congress refused to consolidate its categoricals into blocks. In 1968, 98 percent of all federal aid was provided in categorical grants (table 10-6). When Congress finally did agree to create the comprehensive employment and training (CETA) block grant in 1973 and the community development block grant (CDBG) in 1974, it did so under exceptional circumstances: criticism of the existing categoricals was severe and bipartisan; both state and local governments agreed on the merits of consolidation; beneficiaries barely raised an objection; and perhaps most important, President Richard M. Nixon, anxious to weaken the federal bureaucracy, agreed to sweeten the pot with increased federal funding.[16] Other consolidation initiatives by the Nixon administration— for law enforcement, education, rural development, and transportation—were soundly rejected. The chairman of the House Education Committee, Carl Perkins, complained that the block proposal was like "throwing money down ratholes" while James Beggs, under secretary of transportation, explained, "Our categorical programs are nearer and dearer to Congressmen's hearts than any other; they are the porkiest of

16. This explanation of block grant legislation in the early 1970s is developed in Lawrence D. Brown, "The Politics of Devolution in Nixon's New Federalism," in Lawrence D. Brown, James W. Fossett, and Kenneth T. Palmer, *The Changing Politics of Federal Grants* (Brookings, 1984), pp. 54–107.

the pork." [17] The only other exception to this pattern, general revenue sharing, was enacted during a state-local fiscal crisis in 1972 and did not cost Congress a single categorical grant. Opposition to consolidation was the rule for the remainder of the 1970s; no new block grants were authorized, and equally pertinent, congressional strings were gradually reattached to CETÅ and the CDBG.[18] In 1976, the peak for broad-based funding as a percentage of all federal grants, categorical grants still commanded 77.5 percent of the budget for aid to state and local governments.

₀ The creation of several block grants and revenue sharing during the 1970s should not be interpreted, therefore, as a product of widespread dissatisfaction with the categorical form of assistance, or with federal centralization. The block grants were created in response to limited problems; there was no direct cost to categoricals. Far more costly was the slowdown in funding for all federal grants that began in 1979. During the final three fiscal years of the Carter administration federal grant expenditures grew at an annual rate of only 6.8 percent in current dollars—less than 50 percent of its annual growth rate over the preceding two decades (table 10-1). The inflation of the period made the slowdown worse yet, causing federal grants to fall from 3.7 to 3.2 percent of GNP (table 10-2). Most of the slowdown, moreover, came in grants to institutions, which had long been the more politically popular form of assistance. While grants to individuals continued to grow 15.2 percent annually, grants to institutions plunged to a growth rate of only 2.5 percent (table 10-1).

Dramatic as these changes are, they do not confirm a substantial weakening of congressional support for centralized assistance for state and local governments. Rather the changes illustrate the effects of two important new variables, greater concern about federal budget deficits and a "taxpayer revolt" feared to be sweeping the nation. Those variables combined to place downward pressure on discretionary federal spending. Federal grants were vulnerable because much of their spending is appropriated annually and is therefore fairly easy to control. Grants to institutions, nearly 67 percent of all federal aid in 1978, are appropriated annually while grants to individuals, for example, aid to families with

17. Quoted in Timothy J. Conlan, "The Politics of Federal Block Grants: From Nixon to Reagan," *Political Science Quarterly,* vol. 99 (Summer 1984), pp. 256–57.
18. U.S. General Accounting Office, *Lessons Learned from Past Block Grants: Implications for Congressional Oversight* (GAO, 1982), chap. 3.

dependent children and unemployment compensation, are entitlement programs that are more difficult to control.[19] Moreover, in the late 1970s discretionary grant spending constituted roughly 35 percent of all controllable spending in the federal budget.[20]

Congress's political strategy had caught up with it. Given the process of congressional decisionmaking, the programs that representatives and senators had funded annually, so they could control and take credit for them, were the easiest to trim. Congress was caught between the electoral punishment it might receive for reining in federal grants and the punishment it might receive for raising taxes or permitting deficits to grow. In the late 1970s Congress most feared the second prospect. The public seemed to have grown openly hostile to taxation, and President Jimmy Carter had launched a crusade to balance the budget. Congress put a brake on the growth of grants to institutions.

But Congress never abandoned the categorical system. It tempered proposed reductions, prevented consolidations, and added 42 new categoricals. In fiscal 1980 and 1981, Congress appropriated average annual increases of 10.5 percent for the 25 largest grant programs while Carter requested increases of only 5.8 percent.[21] Similarly, in the annual budget battles for those grants Congress appropriated more than the president requested sixteen times. Most of the reduction in grant expenditures was accomplished by allowing the countercyclical employment titles of CETA to expire, which Congress had enacted to combat the 1974 recession. Although Congress aquiesced to perceived pressures to restrict federal funding, by limiting increases for those discretionary programs easiest to adjust, it slowed spending less than it might have and continued to add new programs.

The first Reagan years, though more restrictive to grants in numbers and dollars, only reinforced the trends begun in the final Carter years. The differences in financial costs are that the growth rates for grants to individuals as well as institutions slowed to 6.7 and 0.6 percent, respectively, for fiscal 1981–85 (table 10-1). And in one year, 1982, current grant spending dropped. A structural cost was also incurred: 77 categorical grants were consolidated into nine block grants in 1981; another 10

19. ACIR, *Significant Features*, p. 120.

20. The estimate of controllable expenditures is based on *Budget of the United States Government, Fiscal Year 1986*, table 18, pp. 9–44.

21. Compiled from individual program authorization figures in *Budget of the United States Government, Fiscal Years 1980, 1981, Special Analysis H*.

were consolidated in 1982-83; and roughly 50 were allowed to die when they came up for reauthorization.[22] But these costs were exacted without Congress paying the ultimate price—substantially decentralizing the politically valuable system of centralized federal aid.

The proximate cause of most of the financial and structural change was the Reagan administration's strategic use of the budget reconciliation process in 1981: Congress was persuaded to vote on an omnibus package of spending reductions that would be binding on authorization and appropriation decisions, rather than vote on a budget resolution that would merely set targets for those decisions.[23] Through a combination of factors, including the reconciliation strategy, a perceived electoral mandate to cut federal spending, complete allegiance from congressional Republicans, and presidential persuasion of conservative Democrats, among other things, categorical grant reductions and block consolidations were approved in an omnibus bill written by the administration. The reductions were opposed by beneficiary groups, denounced by Democrats on the committees that authorize categorical grants, and supported only grudgingly by the National Governors' Association, which welcomed the increase in discretion. Yet the traditional support networks for categorical grants were insufficient to block the president's remarkable initiative.

All the same, a close look reveals that President Reagan's victory was more a triumph in his war against overall federal domestic spending than a successful strike against centralized federalism and the congressional structure that supports it. President Reagan's initial fiscal 1982 budget proposal to Congress asked for the consolidation of not only minor programs but many larger ones, such as compensatory education and educational aid for the handicapped, into seven block grants. Congress's reaction was swift and negative. On the education proposal, for example, Representative William Ford, Democrat of Michigan, argued, "We cannot send a check to Michigan addressed to: 'To whom it may concern' and hope somebody will cash it and divvy it up properly."[24] The blocks were stalled or transformed in their respective House committees. The Senate Labor Committee, with the cooperation of several Republicans,

22. Compiled from ACIR, *A Catalog of Federal Grant-in-Aid Programs to State and Local Governments: Grants Funded Fiscal Year 1981* (ACIR, 1982); and ACIR, *Catalog: Fiscal Year 1984.*

23. The impact of the reconciliation process is examined in Conlan, *Changing Politics of Federal Block Grants,* pp. 259–66.

24. Quoted in ibid., p. 262.

also rejected the more radical proposals. So chastened was the administration by this experience that it proposed much less in the omnibus bill that Congress ultimately approved. Three of the so-called block grants consolidate nothing; they provide somewhat more flexibility in existing categoricals and, in one case, shift responsibility for implementation from the local level to the state, but the money is required to be spent on single purposes specified by Congress. Most of the categoricals that were consolidated were minor educational programs, for example, metric education, that were of only peripheral interest in their authorizing committees. In the remaining five new block grants, Congress devoted part of the summer of 1981 to legislating requirements that set aside fixed portions of each block grant for services that were previously provided categorically.[25]

Congressional supporters of the categoricals acceded to the spending reductions as required by the rules of reconciliation. They also recognized that categoricals appropriated annually are vulnerable to spending cuts when fiscal concerns become strong. Indeed, half the controllable expenditures in the 1981 budget were grants-in-aid. But what congressional supporters of categoricals opposed resolutely was the dismantling of the categorical structure of aid. Indeed, the essence of the congressional strategy for bargaining with the president might well be characterized as protecting the categorical delivery system for financial recovery in better times ahead.

In 1982, and thereafter, the strategy paid off. While the total number of categorical grants dropped to approximately 400 by 1984, much of this occurred through attrition in energy and environment grants, in place only since the mid-1970s.[26] More important, a presidential proposal to create an additional four block grants in 1982 was rejected by Congress, and the president's New Federalism initiative, which would have returned 61 substantial categoricals to state control, never reached Capitol Hill. In the meantime, federal aid to state and local governments resumed its growth, increasing by 5.5 percent and 9.7 percent in 1983 and 1984, respectively.[27] Significantly, those ever-popular grants to institutions led the way, increasing by 11 percent in 1984.[28] Categorical grants also

25. Discussed in Rochelle Stanfield, "For the States It's Time to Put Up or Shut Up on Federal Block Grants," *National Journal*, vol. 13 (October 1981), pp. 1800–09.
26. Ascertained by comparing ACIR, *Catalog: Fiscal Year 1981* and ACIR, *Catalog: Fiscal Year 1984*.
27. Calculated from *Budget of the United States Government, Fiscal Year 1986, Special Analysis H*.
28. Ibid.

increased their share of all direct aid to state and local government, reaching 80 percent in 1984, and projected to go higher, as revenue sharing is permitted to expire (table 10-6). If Congress measures its satisfaction with the extant system by its electoral performance, its members must be happy indeed. In 1984 the second smallest number of representatives since World War II retired; the third largest percentage (95.1 percent) was reelected; the percentage of safe majorities of 60 percent or better set a record of 82.6 percent; and the percentage of senators winning safe majorities also set a record at 67.9 percent.[29] In short, the congressional institution, otherwise known as the categorical grant, bent, but it did not break.

The Forces from Below

The system of categorical assistance, and the centralization it entails, became institutionalized, to a significant degree, because it enabled Congress to satisfy a panoply of demands for federal assistance in a manner that was most advantageous to the electoral security of its members. Today the institutional foundation of categorical assistance is even more substantial. A vast intergovernmental bureaucracy nurtured by federal funds supports centralization. This particular bureaucracy, representing the interests of federal grant beneficiaries—many of whom had been powerless in state and local politics—presents subnational politicians with a serious dilemma. Those politicians can support a centralized federalism, or they can mediate the political conflicts among subnational program beneficiaries and taxpayers if Washington's role is reduced. Until now, those politicians have usually supported centralized federalism. This could change. Federal support for the intergovernmental bureaucracy could weaken. Subnational governments could develop the power to control the intergovernmental bureaucracy. State or local governments could come under the rule of politicians more sympathetic to a program of decentralization such as that advocated by President Reagan. But none of these developments is likely.

29. Calculated from the election returns in Richard E. Cohen, "Deadlock on Capitol Hill," *National Journal,* vol. 16 (November 1984), pp. 2134–50.

The Intergovernmental Bureaucracy

The roots of the intergovernmental bureaucracy, like those of the categorical grants it implements, can be traced to Congress. The bureaucracy took hold because it, better than any alternative, made the categorical method of assistance work. To be sure, the system does not work perfectly. But without the intergovernmental bureaucracy, categorical grants would be much less effective in serving the constituencies that Congress intends to serve. And therein is the key to that bureaucracy's development and enduring strength.

The intergovernmental bureaucracy emerged, in essence, as a solution to the implementation problems that categorical grants pose for Congress.[30] The bureaucracy helps Congress overcome the conflicts of interest and informational handicaps that would otherwise enable state and local governments to shirk the responsibilities that Congress attaches to federal aid. Congress is assiduous in directing funds to specific constituencies for specific purposes, but it fears that without supervision, grant recipients may employ federal funds for purposes not intended by the federal government. Congress cannot depend wholly on the cooperation of federal grant agencies to prevent this: the agencies have a notorious proclivity for cooperating instead with their best organized clientele—often state and local governments.[31] Yet with 400 categorical grant programs concentrated in a few congressional committees—for example, the House Education and Labor Committee has jurisdiction over 40 percent of them—Congress cannot supervise federal grant agencies directly, let alone monitor grant recipients.[32] Even with greater resources, Congress would find the performance of grant agencies difficult to measure: the readily available indicators, such as the frequency with which agencies audit or inspect their grant recipients, address only indirectly the question whether federal grants are effective. The reliable information on grant performance is distributed about the

30. The economic literature on principal-agent problems, on which this analysis of implementation problems is based, is discussed in Terry M. Moe, "The New Economics of Organization," *American Journal of Political Science*, vol. 28 (November 1984), pp. 739–77.

31. The literature on capture theory is extensive. Compare George Stigler "The Theory of Economic Regulation," *Bell Journal of Economics*, vol. 2 (Spring 1971), pp. 3–21; and James Q. Wilson, ed., *The Politics of Regulation* (Basic Books, 1980).

32. Committee jursidictions are summarized in ACIR, *Categorical Grants*, pp. 120–21.

country in fifty state capitols and thousands of city halls, township buildings, county seats, and superintendents' offices. Because the federal grant agency knows these details far better than Congress, on its own, can hope to, congressional control over grant implementation is weakened.

Similar conditions plague the relationship between the federal agency and the state and local governments that receive its funds. The agency must satisfy Congress that funds are being properly used—but without prompting bitter complaints by providers. Subnational governments, however, would prefer, all things being equal, to receive federal funds without restrictions on their use. Thus an agency's concern is much the same as Congress's: only by observing subnational bureaucracies closely can the federal agency be sure that federal funds are not supplanting local funds, and that the funds are reaching appropriate beneficiaries. This task, of course, is expensive and time-consuming to perform directly. It is also guaranteed to generate complaints if done too frequently. Requiring subnational governments to file financial reports is more practical, but only through subnational inadvertence will reports reveal funds misallocation. Individual beneficiaries, a final monitoring option, make poor signalers: they tend to be uninformed and poorly organized.

The intergovernmental bureaucracy developed as a remedy for these problems. By nurturing state and local bureaucracies with allegiances at least as much to the federal programs they administer as to the subnational governments that provide them with tenure, Congress established reliable monitors and effective enforcers in state and local government. Subnational bureaucrats concerned with survival have strong incentives to see that their programs receive full federal funding; that they maintain prior levels, if any, of state or local funding; and that they become important to some private clientele. Subnational officials can also serve as effective monitors. They know, better than any outside auditor, when funds are being diverted or when unintended beneficiaries are being served. In addition, they face few obstacles in communicating with Washington. They are in direct contact with federal agencies and represent perhaps the least biased source of information available to Congress. And finally, such officials bring considerable resources to their positions in political bargaining with the subnational governments. Besides the usual advantages of information and clientele support, they

Figure 10-3. *Full-Time-Equivalent Public Employment, 1952–82*

Millions of employees

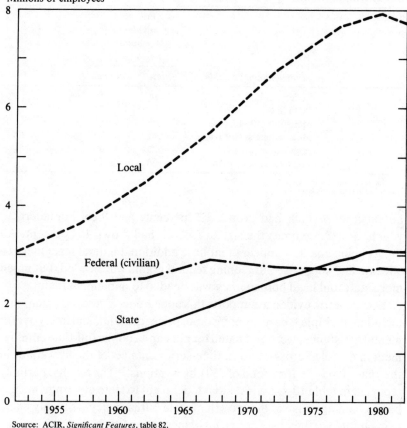

Source: ACIR, *Significant Features*, table 82.

can threaten uncooperative behavior with the sanction of federal auditing and evaluation.

The quantitative evidence that the national government, in fact, promoted the growth of state and local bureaucracy is strong. During the very period that federal categorical grants were exploding in number and dollars, a rather surprising pattern of growth was occurring in public employment. The federal bureaucracy was not growing a bit while the state and local bureaucracies were growing enormously (figure 10-3). By 1982, after growing only 4.8 percent during the preceding three decades, the federal bureaucracy was the smallest of the three levels, behind state

Table 10-7. *Estimated Effects of Variables on per Capita State and Local Employment, by State, 1965–79*

	Full-time-equivalent per capita employment	
Independent Variable	*State*	*Local*
Federal aid	.34[a]	*
State aid	. . .	.23
Median family income	.35	*
Mean public sector wage	−.41	−.29
Population	−.22	.04
Regional cost of living	.30	.12

* Not significant at p = .10 level.
a. Standardized coefficients. All significant at p = .01 level.

bureaucracy, which had grown 222 percent, and local bureaucracy, which, now three times the size of federal, had grown 154 percent. All things being equal, it appears that little additional federal machinery to allocate and supervise burgeoning federal grants was needed, but much more state and local bureaucracy was needed to implement them.

Econometric evidence supports this appearance. Demand equations, including multiple measures of income, price, demand, and intergovernmental assistance, were estimated for per capita public full-time employment in a pooled cross-section, time-series data set of the fifty states in the years 1965–79, for a total of 750 observations.[33] The results, partially reported in table 10-7, indicate that federal aid to state governments has been a leading cause of the growth of state bureaucracy—roughly equal in magnitude to the positive impact of increasing family incomes and the negative impact of public wages. At the local level, direct federal aid has not had that effect, but state aid has. A sizable portion of state aid is

33. Two linear regression models were estimated to obtain the coefficients in table 10-7. Each was corrected for serial correlation by using a generalized differencing procedure employing a unique estimate of rho for each state, and corrected for "fixed effects" by including dummy variables for regions of the country. The models included the following regressors: median family income, median local public wage (local model only), median state public wage (state model only), state population, a regional cost of living index, the percent of the state population below the poverty level (local model only), the percent of the state population that is black, the percent of the state population over sixty-five, the percent of the state population unemployed (state model only), federal grants per capita in current dollars, and state aid per capita in current dollars (local model only). No political regressors were included in the final models because they proved nonsignificant.

composed of federal dollars passed through to local governments according to the instructions of categorical grants. Another portion of state aid is made possible by the fiscal relief that federal grants can provide to states. Political factors, such as the party in control of the state government and the competitiveness of the state party system, have no significant effect. In short, federal grants have contributed substantially to the growth of the subnational bureaucracy.

As that bureaucracy has grown, moreover, Washington has courted its support. First, it has earmarked a small portion of most formula grants for hiring new staff. Second, by limiting severely state and local allocation discretion, it has discouraged overt political participation. At the state level, governors have long been in the habit of automatically transmitting categorical funds to bureaucratic agents, and in the cities, mayors and their legislative councils have often seen little political gain in involvement either.[34] Finally, state and local bureaucrats are treated very respectfully by their Washington counterparts. The officials are brought to federally sponsored conferences, organized into associations, and made to feel part of a network of professionals extending from Washington to the level of service delivery.[35] A 1976 survey of 1,581 state administrators found that a third had monthly or more frequent contact with Washington agency heads, representatives, and senators.[36] The sum of these efforts is an intergovernmental bureaucracy with the incentives and power to represent national interests effectively in state and local politics, thereby increasing the effectiveness of federal aid and the political support for its continuation.

State and Local Politics: Forces for Change?

The development of the intergovernmental bureaucracy has long been recognized and criticized by state and local politicians. As early as 1955 mayors were complaining about the "vertical functional autocracies" that united professionals and administrators in particular programs from

34. Rochelle Stanfield, "Filling the Federal Vacuum," *National Journal,* vol. 13 (October 1981), p. 1913. See also James W. Fossett, *Federal Aid to Big Cities* (Brookings, 1983).

35. A particularly instructive example is provided in Paul T. Hill, *Enforcement and Informal Pressure in the Management of Federal Categorical Grant Programs* (Santa Monica, Calif.: Rand Corp., 1979).

36. Diel S. Wright, *Understanding Intergovernmental Relations* (Belmont, Calif.: Duxbury, 1979), p. 257.

Washington to the state and local levels.[37] By the early 1970s the accretion of federal programs at the local level led one mayor to ask, "Are we going to wake up some morning and find that only 25 percent of city employees are working on city business?"[38] Even when some federal grants were made more broad-based in the mid-1970s, local politicians complained of the specialized bureaucracies with which they had to contend. As one official said, "We're putting cities and counties in a ball game they never heard of and didn't ask to be in. What does that do to generalists? . . . These cities and counties often don't have the professional staff to counteract the influence of the line agency people."[39]

These sentiments are echoed at the state level. In 1956 an analysis of the American governorship concluded that "the governor, to a considerable extent is bypassed in the line of communication and finds that his control over both policy and management of the agencies which administer these (grant) programs at the state level is weakened considerably."[40] Twenty years later a major assessment of intergovernmental relations found governors fighting the same problem, not only in the implementation of grants but in the representation of a state's needs to the national government: "Each [state] department, independently, would tell Congress . . . what it thought about a particular legislative proposal. Nine times out of ten, the Governor didn't have the faintest idea what his commissioner was saying. If the Governor subsequently wanted to take a policy position, it was very often embarrassing to find out that his commissioner had said something very much the opposite."[41] Perhaps best summarizing the frustration of state officials, an anonymous governor in the mid-1970s lamented, "Let's stop fooling ourselves. We don't have sovereign states anymore. All we have are a bunch of provinces. . . . We are becoming conveyor belts for policies signed, sealed, and delivered in Washington."[42] It is a useful measure of the potency of the intergovernmental bureaucracy that these complaints have persisted.

37. *An Advisory Committee Report on Local Government,* submitted to the Advisory Commission on Intergovernmental Relations (Government Printing Office, 1955), p. 7.

38. Mayor Edward Zorinsky of Omaha, Nebraska, speaking in 1973, as quoted in Wright, *Understanding Intergovernmental Relations,* p. 57.

39. Ibid., p. 145.

40. Ibid., p. 216.

41. Ibid., p. 241.

42. Quoted in Larry Sabato, *Goodbye to Good-time Charlie,* 2d ed. (Washington, D.C.: CQ Press, 1983), p. 161.

Near legendary weaknesses hamper subnational executives and legislatures in their battles with these expert, clientele-supported bureaucracies. Governors have long had to contend with elected rather than appointed state agency executives whose low visibility enabled them to associate with limited clienteles without fear of public rebuke. Although the number of elected executives nationwide dropped by about 10 percent from the early 1960s to the late 1970s, only nine states currently have four or fewer elected executives besides the governor and lieutenant governor, and eleven states have more elected officials now than twenty years ago.[43] Countering these challenges to gubernatorial control, to some degree, has been a substantial consolidation of the number of independent agencies in most states and the establishment of effective cabinet government in two-thirds.[44] Additionally, the relaxation of gubernatorial succession limitations, and the nearly universal adoption of four-year terms increased the modal gubernatorial tenure from three to four years in the 1960s to five to nine years in the 1970s.[45] Structural reform has, indeed, strengthened the position of governors in comparison with their bureaucracies. But it would be terribly premature to pronounce them lords of their castles.

For instance, governors have to compete with increasingly vigorous state legislatures. Since the early 1960s state legislatures have made great strides in acquiring the prerequisites of political power. The number of states with annual (rather than biennial) legislative sessions has doubled to thirty-six (table 10-8). At the same time, the average days that legislatures are in session each year has also increased. Total legislative branch expenditures increased 500 percent (roughly 250 percent after inflation) between 1963 and 1977, enabling most standing committees to hire permanent staff. Average legislative salaries more than doubled in real terms. Considering that the nonsalary compensation of these positions also rose—median biennial cash compensation, including salary, was nearly $20,000 by 1974—the position of legislator is no longer the unattractive occupation it decidedly once was. Presumably stocked with more competent people, assisted by experts, and often making government a full-time pursuit, state legislatures have established themselves as more potent checks on state bureaucracy—and on the increasingly powerful governorships as well.

43. Ibid., p. 63.
44. Ibid., p. 62.
45. Ibid., p. 104.

Table 10-8. *Selected Statistics on State Legislatures, Selected Years, 1961–81*

Year	Number with annual sessions	Average days in session	Total legislative expenditures[a]	Average salary (dollars)
1961	18	n.a.	n.a.	2,100
1963	19	51.6	87.6	2,300
1965	20	55.1	97.7	2,700
1967	21	59.2	128.4	3,580
1969	26	53.1	166.6	4,700
1971	33	63.9	224.6	5,600
1973	35	67.0	289.2	6,100
1975	36	68.5	388.5	7,100
1977	36	72.2	411.5[b]	7,800
1979	36	64.7	n.a.	9,700
1981	36	63.0	n.a.	11,300

Sources: Council of State Governments, *The Book of the States, 1960–61* (Lexington, Ky: Council of State Governments, 1960), and all biennial volumes through 1981.
n.a. Not available.
a. Current dollars in millions.
b. This figure is for 1976; the 1977 figure is unavailable.

Yet it would be a mistake to pronounce a new era in state government, or even an era in which the prerogatives of bureaucracy, shaped from Washington, were dramatically curtailed. Legislators in most states still labor with no professional support; in 1981 the senators in only nineteen states and the representatives in only fifteen had at least one year-round personal aide on staff.[46] And legislatures can become fragmented as legislative committees are lured into close relationships with state agencies, politically influential clienteles, and federal patrons. As a spokesman for the National Governors' Association explained in 1981, "The states have their own iron triangles that exert powerful pressure to keep things going as they are."[47]

The injection of discretion in federal grants, through the block concept in the 1970s and 1980s, has increased state legislative involvement in the allocation of federal grants and precipitated conflicts between legislatures and governors. The two groups tend to represent different state interests, the legislatures more suburban and rural, and the governors more urban. But even today, barely half of all the state legislatures

46. Council of State Governments, *The Book of the States, 1982–83* (Lexington, Ky.: Council of State Governments, 1982).

47. Rochelle Stanfield, "Block Grants Look Fine to the States: It's the Money That's the Problem," *National Journal*, vol. 13 (May 1981), p. 832.

deliberate on the use of block grants, and only sixteen address the questions of allocation raised by all forms of federal aid, such as whether and how to match federal funds, and how to disperse funds among lower level claimants. In most states, the bulk of federal assistance is untouched by any general political official except the governor. This could change, of course, if federal assistance came to provide greater discretion, and if the better organized beneficiaries, such as teachers, pushed legislators for comparative advantage. But even in the rather unlikely event that discretion is substantially increased, and state politics rendered more conflictual, the intergovernmental bureaucracy will act as a powerful lobby for the status quo.

The reaction of states to the 1981 budget cuts and block grants provides evidence. The administration took a strong interest in the formulation of the block grant regulations—it assigned a senior White House official to supervise the process—and succeeded in reducing the volume of existing categorical regulations from 318 pages in the Federal Register to only 11 pages.[48] Richard Schweiker, the former secretary of health and human services, in an August letter to the state governors, made the administration's position clear, "Where the law provides this department policy discretion, I will pass it on to the states."[49] But the responses of state governments have been less than creative. A detailed comparison of prior federal categorical regulations with new block grant regulations in a diverse sample of eight states revealed, although with significant variation, a pattern of only incremental change in the quantity, complexity, and flexibility of state regulations, which promised to maintain previous services' mixtures.[50] Federal funding reductions in block grants and in categoricals were generally passed on proportionately. And, as a result of tax increases in forty-eight states in 1982 and 1983, some states replaced federal cuts with their own money.[51] The incremental pattern of the response suggests that the role of Washington's agent, the intergovernmental bureaucracy, was considerable in the state capitals.

48. Stanfield, "For the States, It's Time," p. 1802.
49. Ibid.
50. Catherine Lovell, *Intergovernmental Regulatory Changes under the Reagan Administration*, prepared for the National Science Foundation (University of California, Riverside Graduate School of Management, 1984).
51. Richard P. Nathan and Fred C. Doolittle, "Overview: Effects of the Reagan Domestic Program on States and Localities," Working Paper (Princeton University Urban and Regional Research Center, 1984).

Looking Ahead: The Prospects for Realignment

Centralization has become institutionalized in the American federal system because centralization is in the electoral interest of members of Congress of both parties. While underwriting the electoral safety of members of Congress, the centralized system has also gained solid support from a massive state and local bureaucracy that, especially at the state level, is the loyal offspring of bureaucrats in Washington. Since the late 1970s, the largesse that feeds this system has proved to be susceptible to control, but the complicated system of grants that distributes it has not. Even so, there are ample signs that political times are changing in important ways, and there is ample reason to ask if the federal structure may eventually change too. The answer, at least in the foreseeable future, is no.

The political forces in ascendance, Republicanism in general and Ronald Reagan in particular, do not constitute a unified front opposed to centralization. The president's vision of a reformed federalism is one in which all responsibilities for domestic policy—selection, financing, and administration—are devolved to state and local governments, with the central government retaining only the significant domestic entitlement programs such as social security. Republicans in state government, in contrast, are not opposed to all elements of centralization; they generally favor the centralization of finance and the centralization of all elements of social welfare policy. They are mostly interested in decentralization to gain control over the allocation of federal funds and the design of locally appropriate projects to suit national goals. In a confirmation of what economists have argued for some time, the states are insisting that they are handicapped in their efforts to tax and spend progressively. And confirming the pressures they feel from bureaucrats and beneficiaries raised on federal funds, the states do not want federal assistance cut.

Republicans in local government agree. They favor a strong central role in public finance and social welfare spending, with a strong local role in allocation and implementation. They differ from the states, however, in one important respect: they want federal assistance directly from Washington and not through the discretion of state governments. Because the Reagan administration favors precisely such a role for states, as a fallback position from radical decentralization, it has driven a wedge between Republicans at the state level and those at the local. In short, Republicans in subnational government are not of a single mind on decentralization. In important respects, they are closer to Democrats. The subnational support for centralized finance and social welfare policy is bipartisan.

President Reagan learned this lesson when, in his 1982 State of the Union address, he articulated his vision of a New Federalism that would have transferred responsibility for a large number of categorical grant programs, including aid to families with dependent children and food stamps (which is not, strictly speaking, a grant-in-aid), from the national government to the states. To make the plan financially palatable Reagan also proposed to transfer medicaid from partial to complete federal funding; establish a short-term trust fund from federal excise taxes to compensate states further; and within five years, reduce federal excise taxes to open up a revenue source for states that cared to tap it. Reaction was swift and uniformly negative. Beneficiaries feared the loss of services. Local governments objected to becoming wards of their states. State governments, although anxious to be given discretion, refused to take over aid to families with dependent children and food stamps. And Congress, including many Republican members, saw little to recommend in New Federalism, other than the overall objective of making the system more efficient. Throughout the intergovernmental system the same fear was expressed: a radical restructuring of federal aid could dramatically reallocate government benefits.

Agreement must be reached between politicians in Washington and their partisan allies in state and local government on what form of decentralization is desirable before substantial decentralization can occur. Yet another reason that any near-term restructuring of federalism is unlikely is that such an agreement is increasingly difficult to establish. One party is less and less likely to control both the national government and the majority of state governments. The outcomes of elections for state level candidates are becoming divorced from the outcomes of national elections. In 1984, for example, the Republicans won the White House by a landslide and maintained control of the Senate, but they netted only one more governorship, bringing their total to a paltry sixteen.[52] Of nearly two thousand state senate seats nationwide, Republicans gained a net of only fourteen—enough to shift one of the thirty-

52. These, and subsequent election results are taken from Ann Cooper, "Statehouse Reshuffle," *National Journal*, vol. 16 (November 1984), pp. 2151–61.

three previously Democratic senates to a tie, but not enough to increase the Republican total of sixteen. The state house results were better for Republicans, enabling them to gain four and tie one, but their total increased to a mere fifteen. Under these conditions, it is difficult for a Republican president to forge an agreement with representatives of state governments on an acceptable course of decentralization.

This is not a recent trend, nor one that is showing signs of abating. Since the late 1960s, a gap has developed between the percentage of the two-party vote going Democratic in presidential elections and the percentage of states with Democratic governors, senators, and lower houses (figure 10-4). Although the Democrats have always been strong at the state level, their support paralleled fairly closely the fate of the presidential Democrats during the 1960s. But beginning in 1970 the parallel, while still apparent, occurred at a different, and higher, level. While Democrats have lost ground in national politics (congressionally and presidentially) since 1978, they have remained strong in the states. The growth of voter independence and the breakdown of party organizations are trends that have contributed to the breakdown of unified control of national and state offices, although the current Republican party may succeed in reversing those trends. A trend not as readily affected by party resurgence is the growing power of incumbent state legislators. In many states, such legislators have considerable resources to protect themselves, thus remaining independent of national election swings. Certainly the intentional separation by states of their elections from national elections also contributes to disparate federal and state representatives.

The percentage of states casting pluralities for gubernatorial and presidential candidates of the same party declined steadily from more than 90 percent in the late 1800s to an unsteady average of 61 percent since 1960 (table 10-9). But the floor that has been reached since 1960 is misleading because it is based on a rapidly decreasing pool of gubernatorial races. Until the 1940s, 70 percent of the states elected governors during presidential election years. When Franklin D. Roosevelt led the New Deal realignment, thirty-five of the forty-eight governors stood for election when he did. But since 1960 the number has plummeted, leaving only thirteen states currently electing governors at the same time as the president. Not only does this change in electoral rules hamper a president's effort to translate his strength into support among the states; it virtually ensures that he will fail. Off-year congressional elections are

Figure 10-4. *Partisan Control of State Offices, 1960–84*

Democratic (percent)

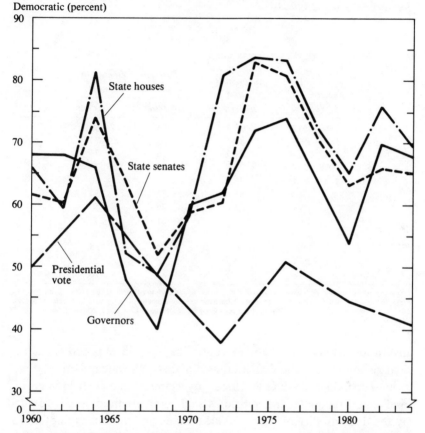

Source: Council of State Governments, 1960–61 (Lexington, Ky.: Council of State Governments, 1960), and biennial volumes through 1981; and Ann Cooper, "Statehouse Reshuffle," *National Journal* vol. 16 (November 1984), pp. 2156–2160.

notoriously hard on incumbent presidents, and off-year state elections, when most governors are elected, are no better. In the six off-year elections from 1962 to 1982, the president's party suffered net losses of governorships five times (breaking even once), senates five times (breaking even once), and houses all six times. President Reagan's losses in 1982, moreover, were exceeded only by Richard Nixon's in 1970. The system, quite simply, is stacked against unified control of the national and state governments, and unified control is a virtual prerequisite for substantial reform of the current federal system.

From Congress to the state capitals the current federal system exhibits

Table 10-9. *Presidential Coattails and Gubernatorial Elections,*
Selected Years, 1880–1984

Period or Year	Percent of states choosing same party for president and governor	Governors elected in presidential years	
		Number	Percent
1880–1892	93.1	26	68
1896–1908	89.5	33	73
1912–1924	81.2	36	75
1928–1940	77.8	35	73
1944–1956	75.5	30	62
1960	63.0	27	54
1964	64.0	25	50
1968	57.1	21	42
1972	38.9	18	36
1976	64.3	14	28
1980	69.2	13	26
1984	61.5	13	26

Sources: Data for 1880–1956 are from Larry Saboto, *Good-bye to Good-time Charlie*, 2d ed. (Washington, D.C.: CQ Press, 1983), p, 139; data for 1960–80 are from the Council of State Governments, *Book of the States*, 1960–61 to 1980–81 biennial volumes; and data for 1984 are from Ann Cooper, "Statehouse Reshuffle," *National Journal* vol. 16 (November 1984), p. 2161.

institutional biases in favor of centralization and opposed to radical change. As long as the deficit crisis remains a chronic affliction, direct federal spending for state and local governments may be held in check. And less valuable federal subsidies such as the indirect ones provided by the deductibility of state and local taxes and the tax exemption for interest on municipal bonds may be vulnerable to cuts. But the centralized system of extensive targeted subsidies will not be swept aside by a sea change in national party fortunes; it is institutionalized.

CHAPTER ELEVEN

Controlling Entitlements

R. KENT WEAVER

FEDERAL entitlement programs—programs that provide a specified set of benefits as a matter of right to all individuals who meet statutory criteria—have become an important provider of income and health care to millions of American households.[1] In 1983 more than 32 million individuals received payments under the old age and survivors insurance (OASI) component of the social security program,[2] almost 3 million received unemployment compensation in an average week, and 21.6 million received food stamps. In the health sector, 30 million people were enrolled in medicare and 21.5 million in medicaid. And many more Americans will receive entitlement benefits at some time in their lives, notably through social security and medicare.

Entitlement programs for individuals total more than 40 percent of federal expenditures. Although the Reagan administration succeeded in winning cutbacks in many of these programs during its first term, entitlements' share of the federal budget has remained fairly stable, and their percentage of GNP actually increased through fiscal year 1983 before starting a decline in 1984 with the resumption of strong economic growth. But the direction of entitlement policy choices has shifted: a

This article was written with the assistance of Alice G. Keck. Martha Derthick, Catherine Rudder, Louise Russell, and Gil Steiner made helpful comments on earlier versions.

1. In addition to entitlement programs for individuals, there are entitlement programs for state and local governments (most notably revenue sharing) and commodity price support programs, which ultimately provide benefits to individual farm households. This essay will deal solely with the first type of entitlements.

2. While OASI is in fact only one component of social security (along with disability insurance and medicare hospitalization insurance), the term "social security" will be used in this essay instead of OASI.

long-term trend toward expanded eligibility and higher benefit levels has been reversed. Indeed, this new direction in entitlement policy began before the 1980 election, but has accelerated since then. How this shift came about and what it portends for the future are the subjects of this essay.

Entitlements and Uncontrollability

What exactly are entitlements, and how do they differ from "discretionary" spending? While many entitlement programs date back to the Social Security Act of 1935, the concept of entitlement is of fairly recent origin. It is an outgrowth of the "new property" movement in legal thought that began in the 1960s.[3] Increasingly, the courts ruled that social welfare benefits are not "gratuities" that can be denied at will; rather, beneficiaries have something akin to property rights in them, and therefore have a right to due process in their distribution.[4] The term was then adopted in budgetary parlance to refer to "legislation that requires the payment of benefits . . . to any person or unit of government that meets the eligibility requirements established by such law. Authorizations for entitlements constitute a binding obligation on the part of the Federal Government, and eligible recipients have legal recourse if the obligation is not fulfilled."[5] In short, recipients can sue if payments allotted to them by statutory formula are not forthcoming. As an additional protection for recipients, most entitlement legislation includes permanent appropriations—that is, spending takes place without any

3. See Charles Reich, "The New Property," *Yale Law Journal*, vol. 73 (April 1964), pp. 733–87.

4. In *Goldberg* v. *Kelly* (397 U.S. 254 [1969]), which required that states provide recipients of aid to families with dependent children a right to hearing before terminating their benefits, Justice Brennan wrote in the majority opinion that "such benefits are a matter of statutory entitlement for persons qualified to receive them" (at 262). Brennan cited Reich's argument that "society today is built around entitlement. . . . It is only the poor whose entitlements, although recognized by public policy, have not been effectively enforced." Charles Reich, "Individual Rights and Social Welfare," *Yale Law Journal*, vol. 74 (June 1965), p. 1255.

5. U.S. General Accounting Office, *A Glossary of Terms Used in the Federal Budget Process*, 3d ed., PAD-81-27 (GAO, 1981), p. 57. For some shared-cost programs, such as AFDC, the payment obligation is at the state level, but the federal government is obligated to pay a share of those costs according to formulas established in federal statutes.

action required by the Appropriations committees. Even where such action is required, "Congress ordinarily considers itself bound to appropriate the amounts required by law."[6]

Entitlement policy choices (setting statutory eligibility standards and benefit levels) are only one of the determinants of entitlement programs' expenditure levels for a given year, however. Recessions cause unemployment insurance and public assistance expenditures to increase as more people automatically qualify for those programs, without any shift in eligibility standards or benefit levels. Thus expenditures might continue to grow during an economic downturn even if policy was becoming more restrictive. Demographic shifts, such as an aging population, may also increase spending by making a larger share of the population eligible for benefits.[7] Because entitlement policy choices most directly reflect policymakers' intentions with respect to those programs, this essay will concentrate on policy changes.

In theory, the federal government can cut entitlement spending only by changing statutory eligibility standards or benefit levels for recipients, or by lowering participation rates in the program for those legally entitled to benefits.[8] But statutory change requires action by congressional authorizing committees, which are generally seen as dominated by program proponents whose constituents have a particularly strong interest in the programs they are supervising. It is the Appropriations committees (especially in the House) that have traditionally been viewed

6. Allen Schick, *Congressional Control of Expenditures*, prepared for the House Committee on the Budget, 95 Cong. 1 sess. (Government Printing Office, 1977), p. 4. The boundaries of the entitlement spending category nevertheless remain unclear. The Office of Management and Budget, for example, does not consider the food stamp program to be an entitlement because it has had a funding cap since 1977. But Congress has always raised the cap and provided additional funding whenever a cutoff of benefits loomed; thus the General Accounting Office counts food stamps as an entitlement because Congress treats it as one de facto.

7. Interaction between programs affects spending levels as well: real expenditures for means-tested veterans' pensions have declined as more of the potential clientele for that program have become eligible for social security, which generally pays higher benefits. Expenditures for aid to families with dependent children similarly have declined in constant-dollar terms, in part as a result of complementary programs catering to the same clientele, such as food stamps and low-income energy assistance.

8. Participation rates can be lowered by decreasing "outreach" efforts to inform individuals of their eligibility for benefits and by raising administrative barriers to discourage those who know about the program from participating. Nonparticipation is particularly common in means-tested entitlement programs. Legislators can also place a funding cap on a program (as in the case of food stamps), making benefits subject to the availability of funds. But this change would eliminate its entitlement status.

as the guardians against increased spending.[9] Because entitlement spending effectively removes the Appropriations committees' spending control, authorizing committees (and subcommittees) can ostensibly protect entitlement programs simply by failing to act on reform proposals.[10] Thus legislative inertia—the difficulty of enacting any change in a system ridden with veto points—is thought to protect entitlements more than other programs in a period of fiscal stress, since they do not have to be appropriated to retain existing funding levels.

This view is in fact overly simplistic. Legislative inaction benefits only programs that are indexed to prevent erosion of benefits by inflation. Most major entitlements are indexed, but the few that are not—aid to families with dependent children (AFDC) and the earned income tax credit, for example—have suffered declines in real benefit levels in recent years. Some entitlement programs (such as social security disability insurance and trade adjustment assistance) offer administrators substantial discretion that can be used to cut program outlays. Funding requirements for some shared-cost programs (notably unemployment insurance supplemental benefits, AFDC, and medicaid) depend partially on eligibility and benefit level decisions made by the states. Moreover, the bulk of entitlement spending (over 70 percent) is under the legislative jurisdiction of the Senate Finance and House Ways and Means committees, which have traditionally had a strong concern for spending restraint. And changes in substantive law are far from impossible to enact.

The protections against cutbacks enjoyed by entitlement programs are thus by no means insurmountable. Nor are they uniform over time and across programs. But three types of potential protections do nonetheless exist. First, there are procedural protections—notably freedom from meaningful control through the appropriations mechanism and thus

9. On the role of the Appropriations committees, see Richard Fenno, *The Power of the Purse* (Little, Brown, 1966). Allen Schick has argued that changes in the Appropriations committees over the past two decades (such as self-selection of committee assignments) have weakened their performance of the "guardian of the Treasury" role. See Schick, *Congress and Money: Budgeting, Spending and Taxing* (Washington, D.C.: Urban Institute, 1980), chaps. 10–11.

10. Kenneth A. Shepsle and Barry R. Weingast, "Legislative Politics and Budget Outcomes," in Gregory B. Mills and John L. Palmer, eds., *Federal Budget Policy in the 1980s* (Urban Institute, 1984), p. 362. For a more complex formulation of legislators' preferences that differentiates programs with a substantial location-specific content from those with primarily "general" benefits, see R. Douglas Arnold, "The Local Roots of Domestic Policy," in Thomas Mann and Norman J. Ornstein, eds., *The New Congress* (Washington, D.C.: American Enterprise Institute, 1981), pp. 250–87.

disproportionate influence by authorizing committees that may be dominated by program proponents. Second, there are political protections—many entitlement programs are able to mobilize large, well-organized clienteles to protect existing claims and win expanded ones. Finally, there are ethical protections—policymakers may hold, and act upon, beliefs that certain categories of individuals are "entitled" to assistance in meeting their income and health care needs. As pressures for expenditure cuts mounted in the late 1970s, the procedural guarantees of entitlement spending became effective only if backed by political pressures from clientele groups or policymakers' convictions that current recipients were entitled to benefits at current levels. Moreover, the procedural protections have themselves been eroded.

A Decade of Expansion, 1965–74

The federal government currently funds entitlement programs of several types. Social security and related income maintenance programs (disability insurance and railroad retirement) are based on principles of "social insurance": recipients are in theory awarded benefits on the basis of past contributions when they retire or become disabled (although the link between amounts contributed and those received may be very tenuous). This is by far the largest entitlement category, with expenditures almost as large as all other entitlements combined. Federal employee retirement programs provide similar benefits for federal civilian and military employees, although civil service is only partially funded by contributions and military retirement is funded entirely from general revenues. Public assistance programs provide income support for specific categories of low-income individuals—for example, families with dependent children, veterans, and the aged, blind, and disabled. (The only program in this group that is not confined to a specific category is food stamps.) Unemployment insurance protects covered workers (those whose employers pay a payroll tax to finance the program) against involuntary loss of employment. Health entitlements pay medical expenses of the elderly on a social insurance basis (through medicare) and of the poor and "medically needy" on a means-tested basis (through medicaid). Finally, other entitlements provide benefits to a variety of specialized clienteles—including a disability program for coal miners suffering from black lung disease, a loan guarantee program for college students, and several child nutrition programs.

The period from 1965 to 1974, beginning with the "Great Society" Eighty-ninth Congress, was a decade of immense policy change in entitlement programs. Three important developments took place in this period. (1) Substantial expenditure growth occurred across all of the entitlement categories. (2) Expenditure growth resulted in large part from real policy changes as well as business cycles and demographic trends. These changes included the creation of new programs and the broadening of entitlement status, beneficiary rights, and benefit levels in existing programs. (3) The indexation of most major entitlement programs decreased their vulnerability to cutbacks.

Entitlement spending clearly grew very rapidly as a percentage of GNP between 1965 and 1976. Expenditure growth occurred in every category of entitlement spending, as figure 11-1 shows. This growth was particularly rapid between 1973 and 1976, in large measure because the post–oil embargo recession and inflation simultaneously increased the number of program recipients and boosted nominal expenditures per recipient in a stagnant economy. But most of the expansive policy changes in entitlements took place by 1974.

In the social security and related programs, for example, the number of social security beneficiaries increased more than 40 percent from 1965 to 1974, as an increasing percentage of the elderly in the population became eligible for benefits. Equally important, the average benefit (in constant dollars) for a retired worker increased by more than 20 percent in the period from 1969 to 1973.[11] These benefit changes were made through ad hoc legislative increases until 1972, when social security payments were increased 20 percent (beginning in 1974) and indexed to the consumer price index by a formula that inadvertently overcompensated for inflation.[12] Policy changes in disability insurance generally followed those in social security. Both beneficiaries and constant-dollar expenditures for this program grew at a faster rate than for social security; expenditures increased more than 180 percent from 1965 to 1974. But because disability insurance began from a much lower ex-

11. See Gary Burtless, "Social Security, Unanticipated Benefit Increases, and the Timing of Retirement," Brookings Discussion Papers in Economics, August 1984, app. A.
12. On the 1972 changes, see Martha Derthick, *Policymaking for Social Security* (Brookings, 1979), chap. 17.

Figure 11-1. *Entitlement Payments for Individuals as a Percentage of Gross National Product, Fiscal Years 1965–86*[a]

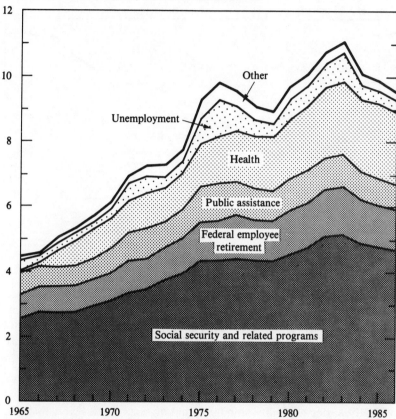

Source: *Historical Tables, Budget of the United States Government, Fiscal Year 1986,* table 8.1. Data for 1985 and 1986 are projected.

a. *Social security and related programs* includes old age and survivors insurance, social security disability insurance, and railroad retirement. *Federal employee retirement* includes military and Coast Guard retirement pay, civil service and foreign service retirement and disability, and compensation paid to veterans and their survivors as a result of service-related death or disability. *Public assistance* includes supplemental security income, grants to the states for aid to families with dependent children, food stamps, the earned income tax credit, and veterans' pensions. *Health* includes medicare hospital insurance, medicare supplementary medical insurance, and grants to the states for medicaid. *Unemployment* includes unemployment compensation, trade adjustment assistance, and federal employee unemployment benefits. *Other* includes child nutrition programs, the special milk program, guaranteed student loans, veterans' readjustment and education benefits, coal miners' (black lung) disability benefits, special workers' compensation expenses, Veterans Administration burial benefits, and the national service and U.S. government life insurance funds for veterans.

penditure base, the dollar increase in social security was much greater. (Comparative expenditure levels are shown in figure 11-2.)

Public assistance programs experienced rapid but very uneven expenditure growth in this period (figure 11-3). Comprehensive welfare reform, in the form of President Nixon's family assistance plan, failed

Figure 11-2. *Social Insurance Program Outlays, Fiscal Years 1965–86*

Billions of 1982 dollars

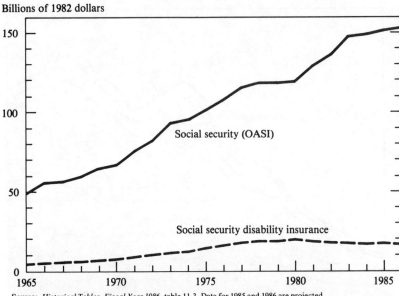

Source: *Historical Tables, Fiscal Year 1986*, table 11.3. Data for 1985 and 1986 are projected.

to win congressional enactment, but there were a number of incremental policy changes in this period that generally increased aid to the poor. In January 1974 the federal government took sole responsibility for a former shared-cost program with the states to aid the aged, blind, and disabled poor; the new supplemental security income (SSI) program provided generally easier eligibility standards and higher benefit levels than the program it replaced.[13] There was also substantial growth in aid to families with dependent children, which provides cash assistance to low-income families with children if the family head is absent, disabled, deceased, or (in some states) unemployed. The total number of AFDC recipients increased more than 150 percent between 1965 and 1972 (from 4.3 million to 10.9 million), leveling off thereafter (except during recessions). This caseload explosion resulted from higher participation rates associated with a decline in welfare stigmatization, the growth of "welfare rights" organizations, and the linkage between AFDC participation and eligibility for other public assistance programs (medicare, public housing), as well as longer-term changes in family structure (such as more divorces

13. SSI was enacted in 1972. States are allowed to supplement federal SSI payments.

Figure 11-3. *Public Assistance Program Outlays, Fiscal Years 1965–86*

Billions of 1982 dollars

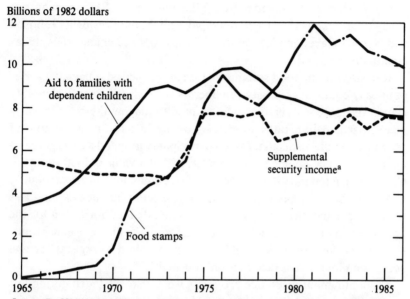

Sources: For SSI (1974–86) and food stamps, *Historical Tables, Fiscal Year 1986*, table 11.3; for AFDC (1965–69) and predecessor programs of SSI (1965–75), data provided by the Department of Health and Human Services; and for AFDC (1970–86), *Background Material and Data on Major Programs within the Jurisdiction of the Committee on Ways and Means*, Committee Print, House Committee on Ways and Means, 99 Cong. 1 sess. (Government Printing Office, 1985), p. 359. Data for SSI predecessor programs and AFDC include medical vendor payments until those were taken over by medicaid. All data are federal expenditures only. Data for 1985 and 1986 are projected.

a. Includes federal expenditures for predecessor programs to SSI: aid to the permanently and totally disabled, aid to the blind, and old age assistance.

and higher rates of illegitimacy). The courts also contributed to the growth of AFDC spending by sharply limiting administrative discretion in excluding beneficiaries through such devices as onerous residence requirements and the "man in the house" rule.[14] In addition, in an effort to increase work incentives, amendments in 1967 allowed recipients to keep part of any earnings. This change helped to boost the purchasing power of AFDC's average monthly benefit per recipient by about 22

14. The "man in the house" rule denied AFDC payments to the children of a mother who had a continuing sexual relationship with a man, whether or not he lived with the family, had a legal obligation to contribute to the child's welfare, or did so even without that obligation. This rule was overturned by the Supreme Court in an Alabama case, *King* v. *Smith*, 392 U.S. 309 (1968). See more generally Edward Sparer, "The Right to Welfare," in Norman Dorsen, ed., *The Rights of Americans* (Pantheon, 1971), pp. 65–93; and Rand E. Rosenblatt, "Legal Entitlement and Welfare Benefits," in David Kairys, ed., *The Politics of Law* (Pantheon, 1982), pp. 267–70.

percent between 1965 and 1968, and it stabilized near that level until the late 1970s.[15] AFDC expansion was by no means universally applauded: in 1967 Congress attempted to freeze the number of AFDC recipients as a way of protesting the program's rapid growth, but Presidents Johnson and Nixon delayed implementation of the proposed change, and it was eventually repealed.

Revisions in the food stamp program in this period reflected a series of uneasy compromises between liberals who wished to ease eligibility standards and conservatives who wanted to narrow them. In its early years, participation rates were low, owing in large measure to stiff purchase requirements that forced participants to spend a large percentage of their cash income to obtain a larger dollar value in food stamps.[16] Changes enacted in 1970 indexed benefits, eliminated purchase requirements for the very poorest families (four-person families earning less than $30 per month), and passed an open-ended authorization for the first time; on the other hand, able-bodied adults (with some exceptions, such as mothers of minor children) were required to register for and accept employment or face a cutoff of benefits.[17]

Unemployment insurance programs were also expanded during this period. The Federal-State Extended Unemployment Compensation Act of 1970 allowed benefits to be extended 50 percent beyond their normal duration when the rate of unemployment reached specified levels. The nearly dormant trade adjustment assistance program was liberalized in 1974 to provide additional unemployment assistance or relocation and retraining for individuals who lost their jobs because of imports.[18]

The federal government created a new area of entitlement in 1965: the contributory medicare program for the elderly and the means-tested medicaid program for poor Americans.[19] (The latter is a shared-cost

15. *Social Security Bulletin, Annual Statistical Supplement*, 1983, p. 229.

16. On the early years of the food stamp program, see Gilbert Steiner, *The State of Welfare* (Brookings, 1971), chap. 6.

17. Food Stamp Act of 1964 Amendments, 78 Stat. 703. The act also gave the secretary of agriculture authority to set national eligibility standards for food stamps (sec. 4).

18. See Charles R. Frank, *Foreign Trade and Domestic Aid* (Brookings, 1977), chap. 4. Only the cash assistance portion of the trade adjustment assistance program—which composes almost all of the outlays—is considered to be an entitlement.

19. Medicare is in fact two linked programs. Part A, hospitalization insurance, is funded by employee and employer payroll taxes as part of the social security system;

Figure 11-4. *Health Entitlement Outlays, Fiscal Years 1965–86*

Billions of 1982 dollars

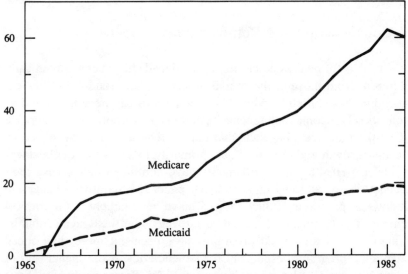

Source: *Historical Tables, Fiscal Year 1986*, table 11.3. Medicaid figures are federal share only. Data for 1985 and 1986 are projected.

program with the states.) As figures 11-1 and 11-4 show, health programs grew very rapidly in their early years to become more than 6 percent of the federal budget by 1974.

The final important change in this period was the protection of entitlement benefits against inflation through statutory indexation. Most of the major entitlement programs except AFDC were indexed by fiscal year 1975. Ironically, indexation probably was not needed to protect benefit levels in the era of growing government revenues in which it was instituted. Congress would most likely have granted those increases in any case. Real benefit increases were being granted in a number of programs (although irregularly, and often with substantial lags). Indeed, in the case of social insurance, indexation was originally seen by fiscal conservatives as a mechanism to limit legislative overcompensation for inflation. But in the era of slow economic growth and fiscal stress that has followed the 1973–74 Arab oil embargo, when pressures for spending

---

Part B, supplemental health insurance (covering physicians' bills and other, nonhospital expenses), is a voluntary program financed by premiums and general revenues.

cuts have been much greater, indexation has served as an important protective mechanism for entitlements.

Consolidation and Retrenchment, 1975–84

Entitlement policy choices in the last decade have been dramatically different from those in the previous decade. The trend in entitlement spending has shifted as well. The new pattern can be summarized as follows. (1) Income maintenance programs have continued to increase their share of GNP, but their share of the federal budget has ended its secular growth and now responds primarily to swings of the business cycle. (2) Health care entitlements have continued to increase their budget share, although at a reduced pace. (3) Statutory changes in individual programs (policy choices) have been largely in the form of cutbacks, with most of those cuts occurring under the Reagan administration. (4) Means-tested programs have been cut more than social insurance programs, especially for beneficiaries at the higher end of eligibility scales (the "working poor"). (5) Program changes have generally been marginal, rather than comprehensive reforms.

The apparent stabilization of entitlements' overall budget share is evident in table 11-1, with expenditures peaking in the 1974–76 recession and again in the 1981–83 recession and falling off after both. The actual picture is more ambiguous, however. Entitlements have continued to grow massively in constant-dollar terms, which is to be expected given continued growth in population and in the economy. But the federal budget's share of GNP has also been creeping upward as the result of a defense buildup and high interest payments on an exploding federal debt. Thus entitlements have continued to increase as a share of the federal domestic budget, the budget excluding interest payments, and (at least through 1983) GNP.

Expenditure growth has come almost exclusively as a result of past commitments, however, while policy change has been toward trimming those commitments. The trend toward cutbacks has even been felt in the largest and most popular entitlement, social security. By the mid-1970s, it was evident that this program faced serious short- and long-term funding problems. The short-term crisis stemmed from expansion and overindexation of benefits enacted in the early 1970s, combined with an economic slowdown (which lowered revenues flowing into the sys-

Table 11-1. *Entitlement Payments for Individuals, Fiscal Years 1970–86*

			Outlays			
	Amount			Percent of measure		
Year	Billions of current dollars	Billions of constant 1982 dollars	Federal budget	Federal budget net interest	Federal domestic budget	GNP
1970	60.7	150.9	31.0	33.5	61.0	6.1
1971	75.2	179.2	35.8	38.5	64.5	7.0
1972	85.8	204.9	38.5	41.3	65.3	7.2
1973	96.2	209.0	39.2	42.1	63.4	7.3
1974	111.4	218.1	41.4	44.9	66.1	7.8
1975	144.1	258.3	43.3	46.6	64.7	9.3
1976	168.5	285.7	45.3	48.8	66.0	9.8
1977	183.3	291.9	44.8	48.3	65.0	9.6
1978	196.1	290.2	42.8	46.3	61.5	9.1
1979	216.3	287.6	43.0	46.9	62.8	8.9
1980	255.7	299.5	43.3	47.5	63.2	9.7
1981	298.8	317.2	44.1	49.0	66.1	10.1
1982	331.1	331.1	44.4	50.1	69.6	10.8
1983	365.7	354.3	45.2	50.9	71.9	11.1
1984	369.0	341.7	43.3	49.8	71.9	10.1
1985	394.5	349.1	41.1	47.6	68.6	9.9
1986	414.9	348.7	42.6	49.9	76.1	9.6

Sources: *Historical Tables, Budget of the United States Government, Fiscal Year 1986*, tables 3.1, 8.1; *Economic Report of the President, February 1985*, p. 232; and Congressional Budget Office, *Economic and Budget Outlook: Fiscal Years 1986–1990*, pt. 1 (Government Printing Office, 1985), p. 46. Data for 1985 and 1986 are projected.

tem), and a faster increase in prices than in wages (which pushed indexed benefits up faster than wage-based revenues). The long-term problem results primarily from a decline in the ratio of contributors to beneficiaries in the social security system. In 1977 the Carter administration proposed injecting general revenues into the social security system during periods of high unemployment, as well as taxing employers on their total payrolls rather than the same capped wage base as employee contributions, but Congress rejected those ideas.[20] However, 1977 amendments increased

20. See James W. Singer, "Carter Is Trying to Make Social Security More Secure," *National Journal*, vol. 9 (June 11, 1977), pp. 893–95; James W. Singer, "Help Is on the Way for the Sagging Social Security System," *National Journal*, vol. 9 (October 1, 1977), pp. 1535–36; and "Congress Clears Social Security Tax Increase," *Congressional Quarterly Almanac*, vol. 33 (1977), pp. 161–72.

both social security tax rates and the taxable wage base; accelerated previously scheduled increases; corrected the overindexation of benefits beginning in 1979 (but did not make the correction retroactive for workers who retired between 1972 and 1979); and froze the minimum benefit for new recipients.[21]

The Reagan administration proposed a number of social security cuts in May 1981, but heavy opposition from congressional Democrats and advocacy groups for the elderly caused the administration to back away from its own proposals. The 1981 budget reconciliation act enacted a number of changes in the program, including elimination of the minimum benefit for both new and current recipients and phaseout of benefits for postsecondary students eighteen years of age or older.[22]

Following the recommendations of a bipartisan Commission on Social Security Reform in January 1983, Congress enacted a number of long-term and short-term reforms in the social security program. Among the changes are a requirement that new federal employees and all employees of nonprofit organizations join the social security system, taxation of social insurance benefits for high-income individuals and couples, acceleration of scheduled social security tax increases, and a gradual increase in the standard retirement age to sixty-seven beginning in the year 2000.[23]

The social security disability program was also trimmed. A 1980 statute requires that all cases except those individuals ruled permanently disabled be reviewed at least once every three years.[24] These provisions were used by the Reagan administration to remove almost 500,000 former workers from disability insurance rolls (about 160,000 were restored after appeals).[25] Congress responded to the public outcry over these cutbacks by writing new statutory guidelines making it more difficult to cut off disability insurance recipients.[26]

21. Social Security Amendments of 1977, 91 Stat. 1509.
22. The Social Security Act Amendments of 1981 restored the minimum benefit for workers who reached age sixty-two or died before 1982. 95 Stat. 1659.
23. Social Security Amendments of 1983, 97 Stat. 65. On the 1983 social security reform, see Paul Light, *Artful Work: The Politics of Social Security Reform* (Random House, 1985).
24. Social Security Disability Amendments of 1980, 94 Stat. 441, sec. 311.
25. See Pamela Fessler, "Senate Agrees to Limitations on Disabled Worker Reviews," *Congressional Quarterly Weekly Report*, vol. 42 (May 26, 1984), pp. 1253–54; and Morrow Cater, "Trimming the Disability Rolls—Changing the Rules during the Game?" *National Journal*, vol. 14 (September 4, 1982), pp. 1512–14.
26. Social Security Disability Benefits Reform Act of 1984, 98 Stat. 1794.

A number of changes also were made in the major means-tested income programs. The Omnibus Budget Reconciliation Act of 1981 limited eligibility for AFDC in a variety of ways and allowed the states to require AFDC recipients to do community service work in exchange for benefits. The food stamp program meanwhile continued to be imbedded in controversy and crosscutting legislative action. In 1975 Congress overturned a Ford administration effort to impose a higher purchase requirement through regulations.[27] Another effort by the administration in 1976 to change eligibility and benefit rules administratively was blocked in the courts.[28] Comprehensive reform of the food stamp program in 1977 tightened eligibility standards and placed a cap on expenditures (ending its entitlement status in the eyes of the Office of Management and Budget).[29] But its major impact was expansive: eliminating the purchase requirement and requiring state administering agencies to conduct "outreach" efforts increased participation rates and thus expenditures. Rapid expenditure growth (from $5.5 billion in 1978 to $9.1 billion in 1980) forced Congress to pass supplemental appropriations in 1979 and 1980 to avoid cuts or termination of food stamp benefits late in the year. It passed further benefit and eligibility restrictions in 1980, 1981 (twice), and 1982,[30] but rejected the Reagan administration's New Federalism proposal to turn food stamps over to the states.

Several restrictions have also been placed on unemployment assistance programs in recent years. Unemployment insurance benefits became subject to income taxation for high-income individuals in 1979, and the Omnibus Budget Reconciliation Act of 1981 raised the "trigger" level of unemployment at which states become eligible for payment of extended benefits.[31] The states, which administer unemployment insurance under federal guidelines, have tightened administration and eligibility requirements. Moreover, Congress did not enact a supplemental

27. 7 U.S.C. 2016. See *Suspension of Food Stamp Regulations,* H. Rept. 94-2, 94 Cong. 1 sess. (GPO, 1975).

28. *Congressional Quarterly Almanac,* vol. 32 (1976), pp. 608–09.

29. Food and Agriculture Act of 1977, 91 Stat. 913.

30. Food Stamp Act Amendments of 1980, 94 Stat. 357; Omnibus Budget Reconciliation Act of 1981; Agriculture and Food Act of 1981, 95 Stat. 1285, sec. 1311; and Omnibus Budget Reconciliation Act of 1982, 96 Stat. 763.

31. However, eligibility for unemployment insurance had been substantially expanded in 1976 (taking effect in 1978) to include most state and local government employees and some agricultural and domestic workers.

Figure 11-5. *Trade Adjustment Assistance Outlays, Fiscal Years 1970–86*

Billions of 1982 dollars

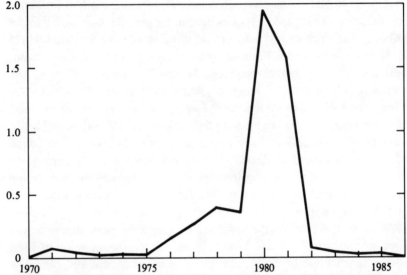

Sources: *Budget of the United States Government, Fiscal Year 1986—Appendix*, and earlier budgets. Data for 1985 and 1986 are projected.

benefits program for the long-term unemployed comparable with that in effect in the 1975 recession until the country was much deeper into the 1981–83 recession. (Legislation was finally passed two and one-half months before the 1982 election.) Thus the percentage of the unemployed receiving benefits was much lower in this recession than in the earlier one.[32]

Much greater changes were made in the trade adjustment assistance program. It grew explosively in fiscal 1980 (to $1.5 billion from $269 million the previous year), as the Carter administration sought to counter the impact of recession in an election year, but was cut drastically the following year (figure 11-5). Changes in the program made by the 1981

32. According to Gary Burtless, "In calendar year 1975, a little more than 78 percent of the unemployed were covered by regular, extended, or supplemental unemployment insurance. In calendar 1982 only 45 percent were covered by compensation." Gary Burtless, "Why Is Insured Unemployment So Low?" *Brookings Papers on Economic Activity, 1:1983*, pp. 225–53. See also the discussion in Gary Burtless and Daniel Saks, "The Decline in Insured Unemployment in the 1980s," *Brookings Discussion Papers in Economics*, March 1984.

budget reconciliation act tightened group eligibility standards, restricted and delayed the period of eligibility until after unemployment insurance benefits expired, cut benefit levels, and sought to place more emphasis on job search and relocation.[33] After the 1981 changes, trade adjustment assistance expenditures fell as quickly as they had risen, to $48 million in fiscal 1983. Administrative discretion has also been used to restrict the program. The trade adjustment assistance legislation requires a Labor Department ruling that imports "were a substantial cause" of workers' loss of employment.[34] Under the Reagan administration, the rate of denials by the Department of Labor went from 62 percent in calendar year 1980 to 84 percent in calendar year 1981.[35]

Expenditure growth for health care entitlements follows a rather different dynamic than that for income maintenance programs. While health care expenditures are driven in part by demographic trends (an aging population increases medicare enrollment) and economic cycles (which affect medicaid eligibility), they are also heavily influenced by technological change in the health care industry and by weak incentives to control costs, almost three-fourths of which are borne by third parties (notably insurance companies and governments).[36] Since 1981 both the federal government and the states (which administer and share the costs of medicaid) have responded to rising health care costs by restricting medicaid eligibility, benefits, and recipients' freedom to choose providers.[37] In the case of medicare, the federal government has attempted to

33. Omnibus Budget Reconciliation Act of 1981, 95 Stat. 357, 881, title 25. See especially secs. 2507–08. In 1982 Congress voted to delay tightening of group eligibility standards enacted in 1981. Miscellaneous Revenue Act of 1982, 96 Stat. 1733, sec. 204.

34. Trade Act of 1974, 88 Stat. 1979, sec. 222, as modified by Omnibus Budget Reconciliation Act of 1981, sec. 2501.

35. Labor Department officials interviewed by the General Accounting Office stated that the change in denial rates was due in part to "the changed atmosphere brought about by a new administration and was permitted by the flexibility in the certification process." See General Accounting Office, *Information on the 1974 Trade Act Worker Adjustment Assistance Program Certification Process,* Report HRD-82-121 (GAO, 1982), p. 7.

36. In 1983 third parties paid 72.8 percent, of which state and federal governments' share was 39.7 percent. These figures vary substantially by type of service: 92.5 percent of hospital care was paid for by third parties (53.3 percent by government), but only 71.7 percent of physician services (28 percent by government), and 43.8 percent of other health services (27.6 percent by government) such as drugs, eyeglasses, and nursing home care. Robert M. Gibson and others, "National Health Expenditures, 1983," *Health Care Financing Review,* vol. 6 (Winter 1984), pp. 1–29.

37. See Linda Demkovich, "States May Be Gaining in the Battle to Curb Medicaid

stem rising costs primarily by squeezing health care providers rather than beneficiaries. Stringent hospital cost controls were enacted in 1982, and a new prospective reimbursement system that gives hospitals strong incentives to control costs was passed as part of the 1983 social security rescue package.[38]

The general trend of entitlement policy change in recent years has clearly been toward cutbacks. Table 11-2 shows the magnitude of estimated changes in fiscal 1985 outlays for a number of entitlement programs as a result of legislative action in the first Reagan administration. Actual 1984 outlays are also shown.

For the most part, entitlement retrenchment has followed a pattern of progressivity within programs, but not across programs: programs aimed at the poor (such as AFDC, food stamps, and child nutrition) have suffered more than those with a broad clientele (social security), but within means-tested programs, recipients with higher incomes have generally had their benefits cut more than those with little or no income.[39] This pattern is consistent with the Reagan administration's efforts to avoid welfare dependency on the part of the working poor. Only supplemental security income and the special supplemental feeding program for women, infants, and children (WIC), which held entitlement status briefly in the Carter administration, have been substantially expanded in the Reagan years. Moreover, expansion of SSI is due in part to cutbacks in social security, which made more individuals eligible for the means-tested SSI program.

A close examination of the trend toward entitlement cutbacks in the first Reagan administration reveals variations not only across programs but also over time. Most of the large cutbacks were concentrated in

---

Spending Growth," *National Journal*, vol. 14 (September 12, 1982), pp. 1584–88; and Robert Pear, "Many States Limit Medicaid Program," *New York Times*, December 17, 1984.

38. Linda Demkovich, "Who Says Congress Can't Move Fast? Just Ask Hospitals about Medicare," *National Journal*, vol. 15 (April 2, 1983), pp. 704–07. Health cost inflation declined in 1984, although it is still substantially higher than the overall inflation rate. The health care inflation rate was 6.1 percent in 1984, compared with 4.0 percent overall. Robert Pear, "Medical Inflation Slackens Slightly," *New York Times*, January 28, 1985. See also Linda Demkovich, "Public and Private Pressures to Control Health Care Costs May Be Paying Off," *National Journal*, vol. 16 (December 15, 1984), pp. 2390–93.

39. See Jack Meyer, "Budget Cuts in the Reagan Administration: A Question of Fairness," in D. Lee Bawden, ed., *The Social Contract Revisited: Aims and Outcomes of President Reagan's Social Welfare Policy* (Urban Institute, 1984), pp. 33–64.

Table 11-2. *Outlays and Legislated Changes in Selected Entitlement Programs, Fiscal Years 1984 and 1985*

Program	Fiscal 1984 outlays (millions of dollars)	Estimated changes in fiscal 1985 outlays as result of 1981–84 legislative action (percent)
Social security and related programs		
Social security (including disability)	178,695	−4.5[a]
Federal employee retirement		
Veterans' compensation	9,916	−0.9
Public assistance		
Supplemental security income	8,498[b]	9.0
Aid to families with dependent children	8,346[b]	−10.5
Food stamps[c]	11,561	−13.8
Earned income tax credit	1,193	0.1
Veterans' pensions	3,874	−2.6
Special supplemental feeding program for women, infants, and children (WIC)[c]	1,367[d]	9.1
Health		
Medicare hospital insurance	41,663	−6.3
Medicare supplementary health insurance	19,475	−9.3
Medicaid	18,992[b]	−2.8
Unemployment compensation		
Unemployment insurance	23,728	2.4[e]
Trade adjustment assistance	35	−90.0
Other		
Guaranteed student loans	3,245	−39.0
Child nutrition	3,536	−28.0

Sources: *Historical Tables, Fiscal Year 1986*, table 11.3; *Budget of the United States Government, Fiscal Year 1986—Appendix; Background Material and Data on Major Programs within the Jurisdiction of the Committee on Ways and Means*, Committee Print, House Committee on Ways and Means, 99 Cong. 1 sess. (GPO, 1985), p. 500; and John L. Palmer and Isabel V. Sawhill, eds., *The Reagan Record* (Washington, D.C.: Urban Institute, 1984), pp. 185–86.

a. If taxation of benefits is included, outlays dropped 6.1 percent over law in effect at beginning of 1981.
b. Federal outlays only.
c. Not currently considered to be an entitlement by the Office of Management and Budget.
d. Budget authority.
e. If taxation of benefits is included, outlays dropped 1.2 percent over law in effect at beginning of 1981.

1981, as table 11-3 shows. The pattern of policy change in the next three years was quite mixed, as the Reagan administration lost its ability to control outcomes in Congress. Thus continued tightening of eligibility and benefits in some programs was accompanied by modest expansion in others—for example, extension of unemployment benefits in 1982 and 1983, an increase in SSI benefits in 1983, and an easing of disability

Table 11-3. *Legislative Changes in Selected Entitlement Programs, 1981–84*
Percent

Program	Changes in outlays as result of legislative action in calendar year[a]			
	1981	1982	1983	1984
Social security (old age and survivors insurance)	−2.0	0.0	−2.7[b]	*
Social security disability insurance	n.a.	n.a.		1.2
Supplemental security income	0.5	−1.2	5.7	−0.1
Aid to families with dependent children	−7.4	−0.4	n.a.	−0.1
Unemployment insurance	−11.4	−3.2[b]	11.8	0.0
Trade adjustment assistance	−88.1	0.0	0.0	*

Source: *Background Material and Data on Major Programs within the Jurisdiction of the Committee on Ways and Means,* Committee Print, House Committee on Ways and Means, 98 Cong. 1 sess. (GPO, 1983); and 99 Cong. 1 sess. (1985).
* Negligible impact on outlays.
n.a. Not available.
a. Outlay changes shown are for the two fiscal years following the calendar year in which legislative action was taken. For example, legislative action in calendar year 1981 lowered social security (old age and survivors insurance) outlays by 2.0 percent in fiscal years 1982 and 1983 over what they would have been had the statutory provisions in effect at the beginning of 1981 not been changed. The numbers in this table provide a rough estimate of long-term changes in program outlays as a result of statutory policy changes in a given calendar year. Current-year impacts of legislative change (for example, fiscal year 1981 impacts of calendar year 1981 changes) are excluded because they would give a downward bias to the data: most policy changes are not scheduled to go into effect until the next fiscal year. Moreover, three months of the fiscal year have passed by the time the calendar year even begins.
b. Includes impact of taxation of benefits.

insurance eligibility rules in 1984. This year-by-year policy change data reinforces the view that entitlement retrenchment is not likely to be a "snowballing" process resulting in a substantially smaller welfare state, but rather a limited effort to balance fiscal and social policy concerns.

The limited nature of entitlement retrenchment is also evident in the types of changes enacted. Only two of the programs shown in table 11-2—trade adjustment assistance and guaranteed student loans—have been cut by more than one-third in the Reagan years. Both of these programs had grown explosively in the last years of the Carter administration and had other widely acknowledged problems. Moreover, there have been few changes in the entitlement status of individual programs. Food stamps were "deentitled" by Congress in 1977, but legislators continued to treat the program as an entitlement. And the major initiative to alter the structure of entitlement, President Reagan's New Federalism proposal to turn over AFDC and food stamps to the states in exchange for a full federal takeover of medicaid, was never seriously considered by Congress.[40]

40. See Linda Demkovich, "Political, Budget Pressures Sidetrack Plan for Turning AFDC Over to the States," *National Journal,* vol. 13 (September 9, 1981), pp. 1671–73.

Explaining the Changes

Cuts in federal entitlement programs would seem to be a political impossibility. They impose concentrated costs on individuals and groups, while the benefits of reduced spending are widely diffused. Moreover, entitlements are accorded procedural protections denied to other programs. Then why did the budget share of most entitlement programs stabilize in the late 1970s after a decade of enormous growth? How could the federal government, and in particular legislators, agree to entitlement cutbacks? Why did they make the choices they did among possible cuts?

The forces shifting the direction of entitlement policy toward cutbacks in eligibility and benefits are complex, and their impact is by no means uniform across programs. Some of the most powerful of these influences have resulted from the Reagan administration's policy preferences. The changes can also be traced in part to underlying socioeconomic trends. The late 1960s, when entitlement expansion began, was a period of high economic growth and, in the wake of the civil rights movement, optimism concerning government's ability to solve social problems. The mid-1970s, in contrast, was a period of stagflation ushered in by the 1973 Arab oil embargo; growing taxpayer resistance (symbolized by the passage of California's Proposition 13 in 1978); and, as a consequence of Watergate and Vietnam, public skepticism about government's ability to manage its own affairs competently, let alone solve social problems. In analyzing the effects of both short- and long-term influences on entitlement policymaking, it is important to show how these forces interacted with and were filtered through the three kinds of protections (procedural, political, and ethical) potentially available to entitlement programs. The argument here is not that all aspects of these protections changed, but rather that some of them did (for example, increased pressure on legislators to limit spending), which made other attributes of the policymaking system (such as variations in ethical protections across programs) more important than they had been before.

Political Protections

Entitlements are essentially transfers of income among individuals routed through government. Thus pressures to distribute benefits are not the only forces acting on legislators. Legislators' electoral incentives can be viewed as a function of whether an additional dollar of entitlement spending will generate more votes than they will lose by voting for higher taxes or deficits to pay for that spending.[41] In addition to these competing pressures—to provide benefits or to limit taxation and appear fiscally responsible—a third pressure, to support the president's program, operates more intermittently.

Legislators' electoral calculus has changed in three important ways in recent years. First, slower revenue growth and the taxpayer revolts of the late 1970s have made legislators increasingly aware of the need to present an image of spending restraint (on public opinion toward deficits, see chapter 13). Second, the 1981 tax cut and increased military expenditures have severely squeezed the federal budget. Although legislators do not like to cut entitlements, they have decreasing room to maneuver in avoiding such cuts. Finally, President Reagan and his director of the Office of Management and Budget, David Stockman, have since 1981 exerted strong leadership in support of such cutbacks.[42] Reagan has not only proposed and pushed for specific entitlement cutbacks (although shying away from cuts in social security after getting his fingers burned in 1981); he has also attempted to make failure to support his economic program politically costly for both Republican and Democratic legislators. This strategy was most noticeable—and most effective—in the struggle over the 1981 budget reconciliation and tax reduction bills.

These changes have made entitlement cutbacks both more necessary and more palatable to Congress. But they have combined with existing electoral incentives to produce biases in the distribution of cutbacks. Policymakers obviously wish to minimize political costs to themselves. This gives clientele groups that are large (social security recipients), are well-organized to mobilize recipients (veterans), and have a wide geographic base an advantage over those that are poorly organized and have a low voter turnout (AFDC recipients). Programs with a narrow geo-

41. This trade-off is in fact a highly complex one, including such considerations as the extent to which (1) beneficiaries view the level of entitlement taxing and spending as more electorally salient than do taxpaying nonbeneficiaries, either autonomously or as a result of mobilization by others; (2) beneficiaries are more likely to turn out to support their views than nonbeneficiaries; (3) nonbeneficiaries are altruistic in favoring income transfers to others; and (4) current nonbeneficiaries may support programs because they view themselves as potential beneficiaries—for example, as part of an intergenerational transfer through social security and medicare in which their current payments increase the probability that future generations will provide similar transfers to them.

42. See Bruce E. Johnson, "From Analyst to Negotiator: The OMB's New Role," *Journal of Policy Analysis and Management*, vol. 3 (Summer 1984), pp. 501–15.

graphic base (black lung disability) are also likely to fare poorly unless thay can form logrolling coalitions with other programs, or policy control is monopolized by program supporters.

Many of the program cuts were indeed directed at groups least able to resist them. The focus of the cuts on public assistance programs has already been noted. Subtler manifestations of this tendency are evident in programs with stronger clienteles. The 1983 requirement that new federal workers hired after that year contribute to the social security system affected only a group that could not resist because it did not exist as such when the law was enacted; resistance from current federal workers was minimized by "grandfathering" them into the old system.[43] Social security recipients who had gained from overindexation of benefits in 1972 similarly did not have their benefits cut when the formula was corrected in 1977. The phaseout of social security benefits to college students who are surviving children covered by that program affects a narrow clientele, and because most people with college-age children do not expect to die in the near future, a "latent" rather than a well-organized one.

A second mechanism to weaken the political impact of cuts is to disguise or delay them. Benefit cuts were widely obscured by delaying scheduled indexation increases or by providing less than full compensation for price increases. Thus real benefits were cut, but more easily observable current-dollar benefits were not. Other cuts were deferred. The clearest case of this is the phased increase in the social security retirement age. This change will not begin until the year 2000 and will not be complete until the year 2021. Thus the bulk of today's work force (and voters) will not feel its full effects.

While variations in political protections can explain much of the difference in program retrenchment, they leave additional questions unanswered. Why were some programs cut more than others with very similar clienteles (for example, food stamps more than WIC and trade adjustment assistance more than unemployment insurance)? Why were cuts in means-tested programs concentrated at the top of income ranges (where individuals are presumably more politically active) than at the bottom? How was the alleged influence of program supporters on authorizing committees overcome? To answer these questions one must

43. On the grandfather clause, see Christopher Leman, "How to Get There from Here: The Grandfather Effect and Public Policy," *Policy Analysis,* vol. 6 (Winter 1980), pp. 99–116.

turn to developments affecting the procedural and ethical protections for entitlements.

Procedural Protections

Entitlement programs ostensibly benefit from the ability of sympathetic congressional authorizing committees to control policymaking free from outside influence. But over the past decade, this power has been relatively muted, and new procedures have been developed to control it.

In part, success in program cuts results from the peculiar jurisdictional assignment among congressional committees of most of the largest entitlement programs. Many programs (social security, social security disability, medicare hospital insurance, unemployment insurance, coal miners' disability) are financed by dedicated taxes; others were established as companions to social security (AFDC, the predecessors of supplemental security income, medicare supplemental health insurance, medicaid). Thus they are under the authorizing jurisdiction of the tax-writing committees: Senate Finance and House Ways and Means.[44] Members are likely to choose these committees primarily because of their influence on tax policy.[45] Nutrition entitlements (food stamps, WIC, school lunch, and school milk) similarly fall at least partially under the jurisdiction of the Agriculture committees, whose members are primarily producer- rather than consumer-oriented.[46] This has clear negative implications for the hypothesis of policy monopoly by program supporters: most committee members choose to serve on these commit-

44. The House Ways and Means Committee shares jurisdiction over medicare supplemental insurance (Part B) and medicaid with the Committee on Energy and Commerce. Ways and Means and Senate Finance share jurisdiction over the coal miners' disability program with the House Education and Labor and Senate Labor and Public Welfare committees, respectively.

45. In the case of House Ways and Means, committee membership had an additional incentive besides its jurisdiction over tax matters until 1974: it was the body that made Democratic committee assignments. Hence it had a strong attraction for those who sought power within the House, but not necessarily those who were interested in providing benefits. Smith and Deering argue that power and prestige within their chamber is still members' key motivation for seeking appointment to Ways and Means. This is less true of Senate Finance. Stephen S. Smith and Christopher J. Deering, *Committees in Congress* (Washington, D.C.: CQ Press, 1984), pp. 95–98, 115.

46. Food stamps are under the jurisdiction of the Agriculture committees in both houses. Child nutrition programs are under the jurisdiction of the Agriculture Committee in the Senate and the Education and Labor Committee in the House.

tees for reasons that have little to do with entitlements, and they will not necessarily be ardent supporters of the programs. Thus Senator Herman Talmadge, Democrat of Georgia, as chairman of the Senate Agriculture, Nutrition, and Forestry Committee, strongly opposed the end to a purchase requirement for food stamps precisely because it would lead to increased expenditures for the program.[47] And when Representative Andy Jacobs, Democrat of Indiana, took over leadership of the Ways and Means Subcommittee on Health in 1981, he admitted that he did so "without excitement. . . . It was what was left. I was in the pear tree of the upper echelons of the committee, but I was on the bottom limb."[48]

Developments in the House Ways and Means Committee nevertheless give credence to the program supporter hypothesis. By the mid-1970s, the House Ways and Means Committee was no longer the cohesive, relatively conservative body it had been under long-time Chairman Wilbur Mills.[49] Moreover, beginning in 1975, the House leadership forced Ways and Means to change its policy of not having subcommittees, one of the key mechanisms that had allowed Mills to control the committee agenda.[50] And the more liberal Democrats on Ways and Means have gravitated to the entitlement subcommittees.[51] But the story on Ways and Means' Senate counterpart, the Finance Committee, is quite different. While the Senate committee has a reputation as an "appeals board" for special interests on tax legislation, it entered the 1970s as a conservative entity, and it remained relatively conservative into the 1980s. Nor did subcommittees gain substantial autonomy in Senate Finance; all bills continued to be marked up in full committee. Thus even if liberal program supporters gravitated to the social spending subcommittees within Finance, they could have little effect on policy. Perhaps most important,

47. See Linda Demkovich, "The 'Odd Couple' Is Whipping Up a New Dish on Food Stamps," *National Journal,* vol. 9 (March 19, 1977), pp. 428–29.

48. Alan Murray, "Health Legislation in New Hands in 1981," *Congressional Quarterly Weekly Report,* vol. 39 (March 17, 1981), pp. 416–17.

49. On changes in the House Ways and Means Committee, see Catherine E. Rudder, "Tax Policy: Structure and Choice," in Allen Schick, ed., *Making Economic Policy in Congress* (American Enterprise Institute, 1983), pp. 196–220.

50. In addition, the leadership "stacked" the committee by overrepresenting Democrats relative to their percentage of the House membership as a whole beginning in 1979.

51. In 1983, for example, Ways and Means Committee Democrats as a whole had a mean score on the Americans for Democratic Action (ADA) index of 71.7. Democrats on the Social Security Subcommittee had a mean score of 77.9, those on Public Assistance and Unemployment Compensation 80.0, and those on Health, 85.0.

the committee through 1984 had very effective and very conservative leadership, first from Russell Long, Democrat of Louisiana, and after 1981 from Bob Dole, Republican of Kansas.[52] (Robert Packwood, Republican of Oregon, took over from Dole in 1985 when the latter was elected Senate majority leader.) Long in particular has been a persistent critic of programs that he feels give the poor and disabled an incentive to become and stay dependent on federal support. It is thus not surprising that after the expansionary lapses of the early 1970s, the Senate Finance Committee played the leading role in killing Carter administration initiatives toward welfare reform and national health insurance that would have substantially expanded entitlement spending and another Carter proposal to inject general revenues into the social security retirement trust fund.

Procedures developed to control entitlement spending have also been at least partially successful. The adoption, modification, and usage of these procedures reflect changing political forces and policy coalitions. This is nowhere more evident than in the implementation of the 1974 budget reform act. More than a decade after its passage, scholars remain divided over whether the act has been a force for spending restraint, has been neutral with respect to spending, or has even promoted increased spending.[53] But several observations can nonetheless be made. First, provisions of the 1974 budget act have made it more difficult to enact new entitlement programs.[54] These procedures have sometimes led to strange compromises: in 1978 the WIC program was granted entitlement

52. See Alan Ehrenhalt, "Senate Finance: The Fiefdom of Russell Long," *Congressional Quarterly Weekly Report*, vol. 35 (September 10, 1977), pp. 1905–15; and Dale Tate, "Senate Finance under Dole Retains Bipartisan Approach," *Congressional Quarterly Weekly Report*, vol. 39 (January 31, 1981), pp. 217–19.

53. See Louis Fisher, "The Budget Act of 1974: A Further Loss of Spending Control," in W. Thomas Wander, F. Ted Hebert, and Gary Copeland, eds., *Congressional Budgeting: Politics, Process, and Power* (Johns Hopkins University Press, 1984), pp. 170–99.

54. In general, new entitlement authority cannot be effective until the beginning of the next fiscal year. Legislation proposing new same-year entitlement authority cannot be considered until the first budget resolution is passed, and legislation that proposes such authority in excess of the most recent budget resolution is referred to the Appropriations committee of that chamber, which has an opportunity to offer amendments. Excluded from these requirements are (1) spending authority derived from one of the Social Security Act trust funds, (2) any other trust fund more than 90 percent funded by earmarked taxes, and (3) amendments to the revenue sharing act. Congressional Budget and Impoundment Control Act of 1974, 88 Stat. 297, especially secs. 303(a)(4), 401.

status for the following two years, but was required to obtain appropriations thereafter. This arrangement split the difference between the authorizing committees, which had proposed four-year entitlement status, and the Appropriations committees, which opposed it.[55]

Even more important, modifications of the budget act reconciliation procedure since 1980 have provided a new mechanism to reduce individual legislators' accountability for imposing entitlement cuts while weakening the ability of authorizing committees to resist those cuts. In its original form, reconciliation was to occur at the end of the congressional budget process in September, with authorizing or Appropriations committees being ordered to bring their spending into line with the second budget resolution, passed in the middle of that month. This proved to be a weak spending control, as the Budget committees were loath to make major challenges to decisions already passed by Congress. In 1980, however, Congress began to attach binding reconciliation instructions to its first budget resolution, passed *before* the authorizing and Appropriations committees acted. This drastically reduced the authorizing committees' freedom to maneuver. It was this vehicle that Reagan used to win major spending cuts in 1981. The revised reconciliation process converted a bundle of unpopular votes (cutting entitlement expenditures) into a single vote with substantial electoral appeal (in favor of an ostensibly more responsible spending policy and in support of a very popular president). The prohibition of floor amendments in 1981 foreclosed the tendency of legislators to respond to the demands of specific interests. While the availability of reconciliation was not sufficient to ensure total victory for the Reagan cuts, it is doubtful that he could have won as much as he did without it.

One of the most important consequences of the post-1980 budget process is its impact on logrolling—that is, the formation of coalitions between disparate groups, such as advocates of various commodity support programs and food stamps, to jointly win benefits that none of them would have been able to win independently. By placing a ceiling on spending within a committee's jurisdiction and forcing committees to allocate funds among their various clienteles within that total, the budget process splinters such coalitions. But authorizing committees may retain substantial discretion to enact their own priorities (within that externally imposed budget ceiling) free from amendment by the larger body of

55. Child Nutrition Amendments of 1978, 92 Stat. 3603. See *Congressional Quarterly Almanac*, vol. 34 (1978), pp. 625–29.

which they are a part.[56] This is particularly true in formulating omnibus reconciliation bills, where time for consideration is limited and the agenda may be very crowded.[57] In such a situation, agencies are likely to protect programs dearest to their own notion of organizational mission, and authorizing committees to attempt to shield their most important clientele from cuts. Given a choice between commodity price supports and food stamps, for example, the Agriculture committees of Congress have strong incentives to cut the latter rather than the former. The food stamp program was a victim of this committee autonomy in 1981.

The "fast track" nature of the reconciliation process and the need for compromise between the Budget committees and the authorizing committees also lessen the prospects for fundamental program reform by giving committees leeway on how to allocate cuts within their jurisdictions. Thus committees can keep programs in existence at lower funding levels, hoping to recoup lost budgets at a later time.

The social security rescue package was enacted in 1983 through a process with strong similarities to the reconciliation procedure, particularly in its limitation of individual legislators' accountability for cutbacks. Use of the commission provided an aura of both fiscal responsibility and presidential support, circumvented normal legislative procedures, and prevented potential coalition-shattering amendments on the floor. Most important, the bill was assured of such overwhelming support before its formal introduction that legislators did not need to be concerned with having their vote used against them as an election issue.

Additional procedural changes (or changes in the functioning of existing mechanisms) have also limited entitlement spending. Indexation of benefits essentially ended the growth in purchasing power of many entitlement benefits, although spending did increase in both nominal and constant-dollar terms for most programs. The trust fund mechanism, which had earlier provided an impetus for expanding benefits as young programs and a healthy economy provided automatic surpluses, now provided a catalyst for reform and retrenchment, as programs faced a maturing beneficiary base (social security), steeply rising costs (medicare), or declining revenues caused by slower economic growth (unem-

56. On reconciliation instructions, see Allen Schick, *Reconciliation and the Congressional Budget Process* (American Enterprise Institute, 1981), chap. 4.

57. See Allen Schick, "How the Budget Was Won and Lost," in Norman Ornstein, ed., *President and Congress: Assessing Reagan's First Year* (American Enterprise Institute, 1982), pp. 26–27.

ployment insurance and social security). Congress has been very reluctant to inject general revenues into entitlement trust funds on anything other than an ad hoc basis. Finally, Congress began to give increasing discretion back to program administrators. The stepped-up review of social security disability has already been noted.[58] A series of statutes since 1976 have given states discretion on funding medicaid abortions while ending federal support for those operations. And in 1981 Congress permitted states to impose mandatory "workfare" programs for AFDC recipients.

Ethical Protections

While the political and procedural constraints on Congress had a major impact on entitlement changes of the past decade, they were not completely determinative. To complete the picture, one must look at policymakers' ethical conceptions of entitlement—their views of who deserves government assistance in meeting income maintenance and health care needs and how much various categories of potential recipients should be helped. While there is never a consensus on these matters, the balance of government elite opinion has shifted dramatically over time, as a result of both electoral turnover and changes in the views of incumbent officeholders. Three components of elite opinion have been particularly important in determining entitlement policy decisions: (1) the "prevailing wisdom" on the causes of poverty and the nature of citizen rights; (2) perceptions of a program's effectiveness and efficiency; and (3) notions of a "fair share" for an agency or program that are "a convergence of expectations on roughly how much the agency [or clientele] is to receive in comparison to others."[59]

In American society, there is a widespread tendency to blame poverty on failings of the individual and hence to stigmatize recipients of government aid. The move away from means-tested (public assistance) programs in the twentieth century toward programs based on the social insurance principles of self-provision and shared risk for loss of income

58. Strictly speaking, the 1980 disability act did not increase agency discretion: it *required* periodic eligibility reviews whereas those reviews had previously been at the agency's discretion. However, it did provide a vehicle for stepped-up discretion in individual cases.

59. Aaron Wildavsky, *The Politics of the Budgetary Process,* 3d ed. (Little, Brown, 1979), p. 17.

was in large measure an effort to avoid this stigmatization. (Indeed, a program such as veterans' pensions has been able to gain politically by claiming to be based on social insurance principles, with military service constituting the contribution of the insured.)[60] Thus social insurance and public assistance programs rest on very different ethical bases. The former are supported because the vast majority of recipients are seen as "deserving" because of at least nominal contributions to the system. Even within the social insurance category, however, there are variations in moral claims, which have been reflected in the policy changes of recent years. Social security's aged retirees are the most unambiguously "deserving"—and they have been least affected by cutbacks. College student survivors over age eighteen were the most morally ambiguous social security claimants—and they have been cut off. Early retirees and those who contributed only nominally to social security have claims of middling deservingness on scarce social security funds—and have suffered middling cutbacks. Disability and unemployment insurance recipients are again more suspect than social security retirees—some may be "shirkers" from the work force, while retirees are not expected to be employed—and policy changes in the past few years have attempted to address this perceived problem.

Public assistance programs have an even more ambiguous moral status than unemployment and disability insurance. Indeed, they are supported largely because policymakers see no acceptable alternative and despite the fact that they have strong doubts about the deservingness of some of the recipients. Given the ambiguous moral status of this client base and the impossibility of drawing firm lines that can separate deserving recipients from the undeserving, these programs suffer from ethical as well as political disadvantages when cuts in eligibility and benefits are being made.

These preexisting tendencies were reinforced by the election of President Reagan. While the precise meaning and content of the "social safety net" have been disputed,[61] the Reagan administration clearly

60. See Steiner, *The State of Welfare*, chap. 7.
61. The phrase refers to the programs that were supposed to be left untouched for individuals who cannot work or who are not expected to do so (such as retirees). Martin Anderson claims that the social safety net was merely "political shorthand" for "a set of social welfare programs that would not be closely examined on the first round of budget changes because of the fierce political pressures that made it impossible to even discuss these programs without invoking a torrent of passionate, often irrational

came into office with a commitment to a reduced role for government and a belief that unleashing the private sector could make that change possible without unacceptable increases in human misery. To prevent people from becoming dependent on public assistance, government was to provide it only when individuals had no alternative source of income. This philosophy represented a sharp break from executive branch policies of the past twenty years, which had generally been moving toward an "income supplementation" philosophy to aid the working poor. These views have been reflected in particular in the Reagan administration's efforts to limit participation in public assistance programs by the working poor.

Concerns about the deservingness of entitlement recipients are closely tied to policymakers' concern for avoiding waste, fraud, and abuse and gaining good value for expenditures. Both food stamps and AFDC have suffered as a result of their reputation for—and real problems with—fraud and high error rates in state administration of the programs. Policymakers do look to policy evaluators for advice in trimming programs: many of the cutbacks that have been made followed analyses and recommendations by relatively neutral entities, notably the Congressional Budget Office and General Accounting Office. The cutbacks in the coal miners' (black lung) disability program in 1981, for example, were motivated largely by concern that the "presumptions" entitling workers to benefits had been broadened so much that workers disabled by smoking or killed in mine accidents were being awarded benefits with no evidence that they had black lung disease.[62] On the other hand, a program like WIC, which can claim that program costs are outweighed by program benefits (for example, reducing the number of low birthweight babies and hence later medicaid costs), has a strong chance of resisting cutbacks. Indeed, congressional Democrats made WIC a centerpiece of their resistance to Reagan's budget cut proposals in 1981, citing it as an example of how the administration was literally "throwing out the baby with the bathwater."

Finally, policymakers have implicit ethical notions about fair budget

---

criticism." Martin Anderson, "The Objectives of the Reagan Administration's Social Welfare Policy," in Bawden, ed., *The Social Contract Revisited*, p. 17.

62. See General Accounting Office, *Legislation Authorized Benefits without Adequate Evidence of Black Lung Disability*, Report HRD-82-26 (GAO, 1982), p. 21; and General Accounting Office, *Legislation Allows Black Lung Benefits to be Awarded without Adequate Evidence of Disability*, Report HRD-80-81 (GAO, 1980), pp. 13–14.

shares. Notions of "fair share" and "base" (the dollar level of funding for the current year) help to simplify the enormously complex process of budgeting. A program that has expanded rapidly is likely to be seen as "out of control" as well as uncontrollable, violating these implicit notions of "fair share."[63] These concerns become particularly salient in a period of fiscal stress. Trade adjustment assistance is a classic example of such a program. Health care cost increases have similarly caused a very reluctant Congress to impose cost control mechanisms on the hospital industry, after rejecting Carter administration efforts to do so.

Prospects

Rather than a continuous trend in entitlement spending, there have been two very different patterns of entitlement policy in the past twenty years: substantial expansion of individuals' entitlements between 1965 and 1974, followed by a decade of consolidation and retrenchment. Which pattern is likely to be dominant in the next few years, or is an entirely new pattern in the offing? How are the protections accorded to entitlements likely to evolve, and how will they affect the size and distribution of entitlement spending?

The future of entitlements depends in large part on the state of the economy. If the economy grows at the continuous rapid rates forecast by the Reagan administration, fiscal pressures for entitlement cutbacks will be lessened somewhat. But in the likely event that it does not, a major recession could lead to a budget crisis of unprecedented proportions. Certainly legislators' heightened concern for presenting an image of spending restraint appears likely to remain strong, weakening the political protections of entitlement programs. But Reagan is not likely to play the same leadership role in 1985 and future years that he did in 1981 in promoting cutbacks. Despite his overwhelming electoral mandate in 1984, his resistance to slowing the growth of defense spending in his fiscal 1986 budget has left the locus of budget decisionmaking in Congress. It is doubtful that his momentum can be regained in future years, as his lame-duck status becomes more salient.

63. A classic case is the social service grant amendments to the Social Security Act. After an explosion of spending in the Nixon administration, the "open-end" provisions of the act were closed in 1972. Martha Derthick, *Uncontrollable Spending for Social Services Grants* (Brookings, 1975).

Changes in procedural protections are likely to be marginal over the next few years. Indexation adjustments (for example, temporary freezes in cost-of-living adjustments) are likely to be seriously considered, but it is very unlikely that the indexation mechanism will be scrapped altogether. To do so would widen the scope of conflict over program spending levels (because of pressure for ad hoc increases by powerful clientele groups) to unacceptably high levels. The line-item veto, a procedural reform favored by Reagan, would have no effect on entitlements because it would affect only appropriations, rather than permit the substantive changes in law needed to affect entitlement outlays. Nor is there much additional room for extension of administrative discretion in entitlement programs.

The ethical protections of entitlement programs are also unlikely to weaken significantly in the near future, even if the political realignment suggested by Cavanagh and Sundquist does take place (see chapter 2). Public support for social security spending remains very strong, and despite the Reagan administration's efforts to posit a more limited role for public assistance programs, the gap by which Americans felt "too much" rather than "too little" was being spent for welfare actually narrowed substantially between 1980 and 1984.[64] Many legislators also feel that means-tested programs cannot continue to bear a disproportionate share of entitlement cutbacks.[65]

Considering these probable trends in the evolution of entitlement protections, it seems clear that another period of program expansion— even the restoration of all the cuts made in the past five years—is highly unlikely. The tax cuts of the first Reagan administration—for which Congress must share the responsibility with the president—have severely eroded the capability of Congress to fund new domestic spending initiatives. It is far easier for Congress to lower tax rates than to raise them, and any tax increases in the near term would almost certainly be devoted to reducing the deficit.

Also unlikely is adoption of an across-the-board freeze in domestic

64. In 1980 only 14 percent of Americans surveyed by the National Opinion Research Center felt that "too little" was being spent on welfare, while 59 percent felt "too much" was being spent—a gap of 45 percent. In 1984 these figures had changed to 24.6 and 41.0 percent—a narrowed gap of only 16.4 percent. Data provided by the National Opinion Research Center, January 1985.

65. See, for example, the statement of Senate Budget Committee Chairman Pete Domenici, Republican of New Mexico, in Helen Dewar, "Senate GOP Starts Work on Budget," *Washington Post*, January 10, 1985.

spending, including entitlements. Much of the appeal of this proposal rests on its "fair share" allocation of the costs of inflation.[66] But since the Reagan administration is not willing to apply the concept to defense spending as well, it will almost certainly prove to be unacceptable to congressional Democrats. Even if a freeze in entitlement benefit levels were adopted, it almost certainly would be a temporary measure, similar to earlier cost-of-living-adjustment delays. And such a measure would not necessarily freeze spending levels, for these would continue to reflect changing caseloads resulting from business cycle and demographic trends.

Even more unlikely than a budget freeze is a substantial dismantling of current entitlement programs or removal of their entitlement status. Although the political setting of entitlement policymaking has been modified during the Reagan administration, it has not been fundamentally transformed. The major social insurance programs—social security, medicare, unemployment insurance—simply have too much political momentum to be dismantled. Other suggested reforms—such as allowing individuals to opt out of social security—would probably remove many of the high-income (and therefore high-contribution) individuals who are needed to keep the trust funds in balance. The major public assistance programs, on the other hand, are unlikely to be dismantled because their critics can present no morally and politically acceptable alternative.

Indeed, cuts in entitlement programs, with the exception of cost-of-living adjustments, are unlikely to be major contributors to deficit reduction in the next few years. The reason is obvious from even a casual glance at figure 11-1: if substantial savings are to occur in entitlement programs, they will have to be in social security and health programs. These are the areas where most of the money is. But they are also the areas where each of the protections—procedural, political, and ethical—against spending cuts is greatest.

The outlook, then, is for a continuation of "tireless tinkering" with entitlement programs.[67] Social insurance programs are likely to take on increasing means-tested components (by taxation of benefits of high-income recipients). Public assistance programs are likely to suffer additional eligibility cuts at higher income ranges and a continuing

66. See the statement of outgoing House Budget Committee Chairman James Jones, Democrat of Oklahoma, in Dan Balz, "Social Security Target in Deficit-Cutting Effort," *Washington Post*, January 7, 1985.
67. The phrase is Gil Steiner's in *The State of Welfare*, p. 31.

decline in real purchasing power. Congress and the executive will continue to try to ferret out waste, fraud, and abuse in entitlements. But the overall structure of entitlement in 1995 is likely to be quite similar to that in 1985. In the area of entitlement policymaking, the new direction in American politics has taken the form of a consolidation, reevaluation, and trimming of the welfare state, rather than a fundamental rejection of welfare state commitments.

CHAPTER TWELVE

Security Policy

JOHN D. STEINBRUNER

ENDURING partisan alignments in the American electorate are largely created by divisions of opinion on matters that most directly affect people's lives. Naturally, economic interests and social values dominate these alignments, rather than the more remote matters of foreign policy. It is not that American voters consider international events insignificant but simply that their fundamental interest in these events does not divide as much as it does on domestic issues. In fact nationalist sentiment is among the strongest and most widely distributed political attitudes in the United States, highly rewarding to leaders who successfully express it and dangerous to those who seem to frustrate it. American voters have absorbed as well the unpleasant fact that they share a security threat of potentially fatal proportions, and they demand a credible stance on security as a qualification for national office.

American political leaders, recognizing the overriding significance of security and the general concern for national integrity, usually attempt to minimize their differences on these matters. In fact they compete to forge not simply a ruling partisan majority but an even more inclusive national consensus; and there is practical wisdom as well as political tradition in their efforts. With a political system that so deliberately and so effectively divides its powers, substantial internal agreement is necessary in the United States in order to yield coherent national actions. The issues of security in particular do require sustained coherence. For security policy the dominant problem of political alignment is that of establishing consensus.

Over recent decades relations with the Soviet Union have emerged

William W. Kaufmann and Lisa B. Mages contributed to the preparation of this chapter by supplying data.

Table 12-1. U.S. Force Structure, 1964–65, 1975, 1985

Strategic weapons	1964–65		1975		1985	
	Delivery systems	Warheads	Delivery systems	Warheads	Delivery systems	Warheads
Intercontinental ballistic missiles	854	854	1,054	2,154	1,000	2,100
Submarine launched ballistic missiles	496	496[a]	656	4,688	640	5,392
Bombers	807	2,652	396	2,602	297	2,152
Total	2,157	4,002	2,106	9,444	1,937	9,644

Military forces	Active[b]	Reserve[b]	Active	Reserve	Active	Reserve
Army divisions	16	23 (8)	14	8	17	9
Marine amphibious forces	3	1	3	1	3	1
Aircraft carrier battle group equivalents	14[c] (15)	…	13	…	13	…
Air force tactical air wings	21 (24)	7	26	11	26	14

Sources: Robert P. Berman and John C. Baker, *Soviet Strategic Forces: Requirements and Responses* (Brookings, 1982), table 3-2, p. 43; John M. Collins, *U.S./Soviet Military Balance: Statistical Trends, 1970–1983*, Congressional Research Service, Library of Congress, Report no. 84-163s (August 27, 1984); William W. Kaufmann, *The 1986 Defense Budget* (Brookings, 1985), table 2, p. 10, and table 7, p. 27; and *Department of Defense Annual Report to the Congress, Fiscal Year 1983*, pp. A4–A5.
a. The Polaris A-3 missile with three separate weapons is counted as a single warhead because the three weapons could only be directed to a single target.
b. These figures are for fiscal 1964. They establish the base of U.S. conventional forces before the increment that was added by the war in Vietnam. That increment was removed by 1975. Figures in parentheses show the projections made in the five-year defense plan as of 1964.
c. Because a number of World War II vintage carriers had not yet been retired in 1964, a total of twenty-four were included in the active forces as of that date. There were only enough supporting ships, however, to organize fourteen battle groups.

as the inevitable focus of American security policy and just as inevitably the central element of foreign policy in general. With the Soviet arsenal of nuclear weapons presenting the only immediate mortal danger to U.S. society as a whole and with Soviet conventional forces posing a serious threat to U.S. allies and hence to the United States' security, a nearly universal political commitment has been made to maintaining sufficient U.S. military forces to deter effective use of counterpart Soviet forces. Spirited arguments persist regarding the exact definition of sufficiency, but the number and variety of nuclear weapons that have been acquired cover the most prominently discussed requirement: the capacity to undertake proportionate retaliation for any attack even up to levels at which both societies would be annihilated. If the capacity for retaliation were alone a sufficient basis for security, effective consensus would exist in the United States, and there would be no fundamental problem of political alignment on security policy.

The raw capacity for retaliatory destruction has not been judged sufficient, however, and substantial disagreement persists regarding two supplementary requirements. First, there is an acknowledged need for direct military resistance against attacks of limited character where the full capability for retaliatory destruction could not responsibly be brought to bear. The most important instance is central Europe, where aggression by Soviet armies is feared, but other potential demands for direct defense have also been described. Should several of these imagined circumstances occur simultaneously, it is generally conceded they would require conventional military forces larger than the United States possesses. Implicitly the United States is accepting some degree of risk in order to mitigate the economic and social burden of defense preparations.

As reflected in table 12-1, the peacetime size and basic internal organization of U.S. military forces have not been altered in twenty years and thus have been ratified by five successive presidential administrations. The numbers of strategic weapons launchers, army and marine divisions, surface naval formations, and tactical air wings have remained nearly constant, though their capacities have been substantially improved by replacing older weapons with more advanced models. This consistency in the basic structure of U.S. forces does imply that the American political system has arrived at a common judgment regarding an appropriate level of military effort, but the practical result has not been accompanied by a settled political consensus. Amid sharp disputes over perceived trends in the Soviet threat, significant fluctuations in the

Table 12-2. *U.S. Force Structure Financing, Fiscal Years 1976–85*

Year	Actual budget authority	Financial requirement at invest- ment rate of 3 percent[a]	Difference
1976	187.5	200.2	− 12.7
1977	196.2	206.2	− 10.0
1978	196.4	212.4	− 16.0
1979	195.6	218.7	− 23.1
1980	198.4	225.3	− 26.9
1981	218.7	232.1	− 13.4
1982	239.9	239.0	+ 0.9
1983	257.9	246.2	+ 11.7
1984	267.9	253.6	+ 14.3
1985	284.7	261.2	+ 23.5

Source: *Historical Tables, Budget of the United States Government, Fiscal Year 1986*, table 5.1; and calculations of William W. Kaufmann.

a.   Even with a perfectly constant structure of military forces, new equipment (tanks, missiles, aircraft, and other weapons) must be produced to replace older equipment as it wears out or becomes so outmoded technically that it cannot be effectively used. Since technical advances have made new military equipment more expensive, some degree of real growth is required to maintain a technically competitive establishment of constant size. The appropriate rate is a matter of judgment—and disagreement. A 3 percent rate of real growth represents a plausible middle point in the range of opinion over the past decade. The 3 percent rate has been formally proclaimed as a guideline for the NATO alliance. The requirements of this guideline are calculated backward from 1985.

financing of the established force structure have occurred. The defense budgets of the 1970s were more strict than in the 1980s, reflecting differences in prevailing political judgment (table 12-2). It remains a question whether the most recent surge in defense spending will be sustained.

The second unsettled security requirement is the need to supplement the capacity for retaliation with some credible reassurance in order to complete a stable deterrence posture. The need arises because the forces designed and proclaimed for purposes of retaliation would in fact be much more effective if used first. As a consequence each side has a strong objective incentive to initiate attack should it judge that war has become unavoidable, and neither can fully control spontaneous crisis circumstances that might make it seem unavoidable. In seeking to prevent war under these conditions by means of deterrence, both countries must credibly convey two messages to each other: first the standard threat of retaliation and second a stable resolve not to pursue the military advantages of a preemptive attack. The second message is a form of reassurance, in effect a promise not to conclude even in severe crisis that nuclear war is unavoidable.

The inherent destructive power of nuclear weapons has made it impractical to eliminate the difference in probable outcome of an initial attack and a retaliatory one. Given the exposure of the most critical and most vulnerable targets—the respective command systems—the reductions in force deployments necessary to ensure their survival would be far in excess of any that have been seriously proposed and would raise questions about the adequacy of basic retaliatory capacity even if the reductions were proposed.[1] Efforts have been made, however, to inhibit the relative effectiveness of a preemptive attack by measures designed to restrict further evolution and highly refined optimization of offensive capabilities. As a matter of practical diplomacy these partial arms control measures have been the primary means of establishing mutual reassurance. Because of their limited character, however, they have not been accepted within the American political system. The entire enterprise of arms control has been the subject of bitter and continuing internal political dispute.

Since the United States has been able to manage security policy for several decades without encountering global disaster, it is natural to presume that the consequences of imperfect consensus can be absorbed indefinitely, just as the symptoms of a disease can sometimes be tolerated or pragmatically treated without removing or even understanding its root cause. As in the case of a chronic disease, however, long-festering symptoms might eventually accumulate or intensify to a degree that cannot be safely tolerated or adequately mitigated. The American electorate is detectably concerned that security policy is approaching such a point. In particular, the U.S. public, while disagreeing on the details of diagnosis and prescription, perceives a greater threat of disastrous war than do the professionals who manage security policy.[2]

President Reagan's Stance

Though it is an exercise in interpretive art rather than scientific inference, a central flaw in the American political consensus on security

1. Bruce G. Blair, *Strategic Command and Control: Redefining the Nuclear Threat* (Brookings, 1985); and Desmond Ball, *Can Nuclear War Be Controlled?* Adelphi Paper 169 (London: International Institute for Strategic Studies, 1981). Both document the vulnerability of strategic command systems to nuclear attack. Ball notes that the U.S. system could be disabled with fifty to one hundred weapons, approximately 1 percent of the Soviet strategic arsenal.

2. Daniel Yankelovich derives this general conclusion from a detailed review of public attitudes on security issues. *Voter Options on Nuclear Arms Policy: A Briefing Book for the 1984 Elections* (New York: Public Agenda Foundation, 1984), pp. 2–3.

policy can be detected in diverging attitudes toward the Soviet Union and in a basic conflict in political purpose that results. The clearest and most assertive position is held by a minority who believe that Soviet actions are driven by the intention to establish worldwide political domination by means of military power. They conclude that acceptable peace cannot be achieved until this fundamental intention is reversed. Proponents of this position are intensely committed not only to deny specific Soviet objectives but beyond that to force fundamental revisions in the content of Soviet policy if not indeed in the very structure of the Soviet political system. They demand that the military and economic power of the United States be marshaled in support of this cause. They reject any partial accommodation that would mitigate this pressure while leaving the imputed Soviet intention unchanged and its apparent manifestations unresolved in Eastern Europe, in Afghanistan, in Central America, in Angola, or elsewhere.

These demands are rejected by a majority who hold more diverse, more uncertain, less intense, and less coherently articulated opinions. They want primarily to prevent war and will not underwrite the risks involved in developing a degree of pressure that has any serious prospect of successfully coercing the Soviet Union. The majority share a distrust of the Soviet government and concern for the consequences of its military power but do not accept the compelling characterization of aggressive Soviet intentions. The majority will support resistance to immediate military challenge but not assertive measures to impose reform.

Proponents of each body of opinion have blocked the full program of the other, leaving an indeterminate posture for American security policy that echoes the famous Bolshevik phrase—not war but not peace either.

Throughout most of his political career, Ronald Reagan espoused the minority position, but he rose to the presidency arguing a more moderate variant presumably designed to have broader political appeal. The Soviet Union, he maintained, had achieved superior military power that must be redressed with increased investment in U.S. military forces. He rightly judged that many in the American electorate who would demur from the full enterprise of forcing revisions in Soviet behavior would nonetheless support demands to eliminate any dimension of real or apparent Soviet military advantage. The large number of Soviet land armies, the large size of Soviet intercontinental ballistic missile boosters, and the widely perceived momentum in Soviet military programs during the 1970s offered concrete instances that he effectively used to mobilize political response in the United States without confronting the more fundamental question of whether the purpose was to counter Soviet advantage or to impose reform.

In carrying out this political stance during his first term in office, President Reagan produced sharp increases in the defense budget,[3] successfully arguing that they were necessary in the face of Soviet military programs in order to restore American strength after a period of neglect. On that basis he created solid congressional majorities for the largest sustained increase in defense spending that has ever occurred in peacetime. There were significant discrepancies, however, between the rationale the president offered and the composition of the defense effort he produced. The budget increases were not used for additions to the structure of U.S. forces, as would be necessary to alter the balance of U.S. and Soviet weapons inventories.[4] The surge in spending went disproportionately to technical modernization[5]—that is, the replacement of existing weapons with more advanced models—an investment strategy that enhanced American advantage rather than directly reducing dimensions of disadvantage. The surge continued unabated, moreover, even as it became apparent that corresponding Soviet investment had stabilized after 1975 at a constant level.[6] These discrepancies between political argument and unfolding fact suggested that other influences were at work—the traditional desire of the president's core constituency to maximize military pressure on the Soviet Union and his own desire to use the defense effort to enhance his domestic priorities.

In regard to domestic priorities, the allocation of the defense effort to technical modernization has directed resources to those segments of the economy specializing in advanced technology that are widely believed to lead economic growth. Together with a large tax reduction and sharp restrictions on discretionary social programs, this allocation has produced a substantial shift in the weight and focus of government effort and reduced any likelihood of subsequent congressional revision. The

3. William W. Kaufmann, *The 1986 Defense Budget* (Brookings, 1985), table 13, p. 45.

4. Despite official requests by the Joint Chiefs of Staff for substantial force structure increases by 1991, the five-year defense plan holds U.S. force structure essentially constant through 1989. Ibid., table 7, p. 27.

5. Ibid., table 14, p. 46.

6. Richard F. Kaufman, "Causes of the Slowdown in Soviet Defense," *Soviet Economy*, vol. 1 (January–March 1985), pp. 9–32.

multiple-year financial commitments involved in defense contracting, the strong vested interests that important weapons programs rapidly create, and the large fiscal deficit produced by the tax cut combine to make significant reallocations very difficult to achieve through the cumbersome congressional process. Quite apart from its direct effects on security, the defense budget buttresses Reagan's domestic political program.

In terms of the rhetoric of strategic intention and the larger question of reassurance, President Reagan tested the limits of majority tolerance during his first term and reacted both with a series of prudent adjustments and with an unusually bold political initiative. For most of his first year in office he deprecated arms control both in principle and in practice, both in substance and in procedure. He also proclaimed the need to prepare to fight an enduring nuclear war and staffed his administration with people far more dedicated to acquiring weapons than to restricting them.[7] He displayed considerable sensitivity, however, to the negative public reactions that these political signals engendered. In response to the peace movement in Europe and the nuclear freeze movement in the United States, he intervened in his own reluctant administration to initiate formal arms control negotiations, and he issued a promise not to undercut the unratified strategic arms agreements that he had previously proclaimed to be "fatally flawed."[8] On the matter of doctrine he adopted a felicitous phrase that aptly expressed majority sentiment: "nuclear war can never be won and must never be fought."[9]

Though these adjustments were not sufficient to convince the Soviet Union, they did succeed in reducing political alarm in the United States and in Western Europe, and the president made it clear that the Western allies were the limit of his concern. He did not authorize or initiate the substantive compromise needed to bring the reinstituted negotiations to actual agreement. Indeed at the critical moment when such a compromise was expected, he indulged in particularly harsh rhetoric instead, asserting the Soviet Union to be the "focus of evil" in the world.[10] He expressly

7. The attitudes of the Reagan administration on arms control are chronicled in detail in Strobe Talbott, *Deadly Gambits: The Reagan Administration and the Stalemate in Nuclear Arms Control* (Knopf, 1984).

8. John Steinbruner, "Arms and the Art of Compromise," *Brookings Review*, vol. 1 (Summer 1983), p. 7.

9. "Address before the Japanese Diet, November 11, 1983," *Weekly Compilation of Presidential Documents*, vol. 19 (November 21, 1983), p. 1563.

10. "Remarks at the Annual Convention of the National Association of Evangelicals

altered his tone for the 1984 election, to assert an interest in arms control in principle and a strong commitment to peace in general,[11] but the timing made his motive ambiguous. Since the Soviets had suspended the negotiations in reaction to the deployment of U.S. missiles in Europe, the shift in the president's rhetorical stance was an effective means of imposing the burden of disruption on the Soviet Union. For hard-headed realists it was a characteristically adroit maneuver in the contest for public opinion. It intensified the political pressure on the Soviet Union without revealing any serious intent to compromise.

On economic matters the president campaigned for sharp restrictions on high-technology trade to Soviet bloc countries to the point of disrupting American trade relationships generally, and he imposed a variety of punitive sanctions in retaliation for the imposition of martial law in Poland. He nonetheless excluded U.S. grain trade from this general posture in obvious deference to domestic political realities, and he eventually abandoned efforts to block the Soviet gas pipeline to Europe when it became apparent he could not succeed.

Such were his sallies against Soviet iniquity and his prudent adjustments to relieve domestic and allied political displeasure with them.

The bold initiative was President Reagan's pronouncement in March of 1983 of a commitment to alter the terms of international security by developing defensive systems that would make ballistic missiles, the mainstay of modern arsenals, "impotent and obsolete."[12] That technical achievement, he asserted, would enable the basis of security to be shifted from the abhorrent threat of annihilation to the morally superior principle of mutual defense. Done without prior staff work or technical definition, the declaration rather astonished professional security bureaucracies throughout the world, but it appears to have captured public imagination and therefore the attention of practicing politicians.

The reasons are simple and powerful as far as political imagination is concerned. To anyone who reflects but for a moment on the prospects of nuclear war, effective defense is indeed a superior principle. To an

---

in Orlando, Florida, March 8, 1983," *Public Papers of the Presidents: Ronald Reagan, 1983* (Government Printing Office, 1984), bk. 1, p. 363. (Hereafter *Public Papers: Reagan, 1983.*)

11. "Soviet-American Relations: Address to the Nation, U.S. Allies, and the Soviet Union, January 16, 1984," *Weekly Compilation of Presidential Documents*, vol. 20 (January 23, 1984), pp. 40–45.

12. "Address to the Nation on Defense and National Security, March 23, 1983," *Public Papers: Reagan, 1983* (GPO, 1984), bk. 1, p. 443.

electorate attuned to the wonders of modern science, the idea, however difficult it might be, does not seem beyond plausible aspiration, since no one has determined that it violates immutable scientific laws. With its technical merit at this point a matter of faith and judgment, the strategic defense initiative, as it is officially described (or star wars as it is popularly labeled), has become at least for the moment an effective means of projecting popular desires. It promises to overcome the threat of nuclear weapons and to provide the occasion for their eventual elimination by virtue of a unilateral technical effort that, it is claimed, need not depend upon the divisive business of cooperating with the Soviet Union. A decisively better world, achieved through technical progress, with no unpleasant choices to be made—very appealing indeed.

The combination of unusual personal popularity, shrewdly allocated defense investment, prudent adjustments in political rhetoric, and a seductive vision of the future has given President Reagan a strong, even dominant domestic political position as he enters his second term. But it has not forged consensus on the underlying question of U.S. purposes toward the Soviet Union. The surge in U.S. defense investment will exert considerable pressure on the Soviet position, but it will not construct the fully developed vessel of containment that would be necessary if Soviet reactions are to be reliably channeled along the lines that the United States would prefer. The president's domestic political stance lies exposed to the will and ingenuity of a well-provoked opponent, and its ultimate viability depends a great deal on what that opponent chooses to do.

Soviet Reaction

Backed by the technical capacity and economic potential of the United States and supplemented by U.S. alliance arrangements, President Reagan's stance presents a formidable challenge to the Soviet Union both in military realities and in the separate matter of political perceptions. As has been widely noted, the challenge comes at a time of transition in the Soviet leadership from a generation of extraordinarily lengthy tenure to a better educated but less experienced group of successors. As is less frequently noted, the challenge also comes at a point of necessary transition for Soviet security planning: military programs established more than a decade ago have largely run their course and new targets stretching well into the future must be set. The posture of the United States certainly affects the fundamental assumptions of Soviet security planning and by virtue of its timing probably ensures that the process of adjusting those assumptions will be an important concern for Mikhail Gorbachev and other figures emerging into the top Soviet leadership.

The main features of the Soviet perspective are evident enough. The leading participants are likely to share a keen appreciation of the fact that the surge in U.S. defense investment is out of phase with Soviet efforts. The last time the Soviet Union initiated a comparable effort was in the 1960s, when the decisions were made providing for rapid expansion of Soviet strategic weapons and the systematic modernization and development of Soviet conventional forces. Those decisions produced the large increases in investment and eventually in available military capability that helped generate the Western perceptions of a significant Soviet buildup.[13] During the decade of the 1970s, however, and into the 1980s the Soviet leadership authorized very few major new weapons deployment initiatives, and Soviet investment after 1975 remained constant.[14] Though the world is not directly informed about internal Soviet planning assumptions, it is a reasonable inference that the constant level of Soviet military investment after 1975 was either tolerated or directly intended under the expectation that an equitable balance in military capability had been accepted in the arms control arrangements signed in 1972. The Soviets probably also believed that the mutual restrictions on U.S. and Soviet forces provided in those agreements would be gradually extended to provide more comprehensive restraints.[15] That expectation has largely been invalidated by the political eclipse of arms control and by the renewed U.S. defense effort.

Soviet leaders are also likely to maintain that their own surge in investment was a response to earlier defense efforts of the United States and to their perception that the shift in the political position of China constituted a potentially serious threat to them. They would not see their actions as a move to set standards of military capacity beyond what the Western alliance had already achieved. Except for medium-range ballis-

13. Robert P. Berman and John C. Baker, *Soviet Strategic Forces: Requirements and Responses* (Brookings, 1982).
14. Kaufman, "Causes of the Slowdown in Soviet Defense."
15. John Steinbruner, "Comments on Richard Kaufman's Article," *Soviet Economy*, vol. 1 (January–March 1985), pp. 32–37.

tic missiles for the European and Asian theaters, the initial Soviet deployment of major strategic weapons did in fact lag substantially behind that of the United States both in quantity and in quality for any year up to 1975 (figure 12-1). A crude matching of U.S. capabilities had barely been achieved when the agreement for strategic arms limitation was signed in 1972, and although the unfolding Soviet program did reduce and even reverse many of the U.S. advantages that originally existed, the United States has remained ahead in the most meaningful bottom line—the number of strategic weapons that can be independently assigned to targets (figure 12-2). Moreover, during the Berlin crisis in 1961 and the Cuban crisis in 1962, when the United States used an already extensive nuclear arsenal to support favorable political outcomes, the Soviet Union had only the most rudimentary capacity to deter the implicit threat of an American attack. The memories are undoubtedly vivid for those Soviet leaders who experienced those dramatic moments. They also remember the subsequent effort to establish a position of comparable military power and the emergence of China as a significant security problem just as overall parity was being achieved. Under these circumstances their inclination to consider the current surge in U.S. investment a justifiable reaction is undoubtedly negligible.

Finally, Soviet leaders are likely to be united in their conviction that Soviet security requirements are considerably more demanding than those of the United States. The United States is isolated from the threat of land invasion; the Soviet Union is not. The United States has spontaneously loyal allies; the Soviet Union does not. The United States alone has an economy roughly twice the size of the Soviet Union and a far more developed technical base. For the two opposing alliance systems these disparities are even greater and are not diminishing. In the West, where military balances have been the predominant political concern, NATO as a whole has invested more in military forces than the Warsaw Pact every year since 1965.[16] In the East, where economic performance is the more important measure of merit, Japan has consistently exceeded the growth rate of the Soviet Union.[17] Though these conditions are hardly publicized by the Soviet Union, they are undoubtedly perceived, and their implications, one must prudently presume, are taken seriously.

16. Richard D. DeLauer, statement on *The Fiscal Year 1984 Department of Defense Program for Research, Development, and Acquisition* (Washington, D.C.: U.S. Department of Defense, 1983), p. I-7.

17. Central Intelligence Agency, Directorate of Intelligence, *Handbook of Economic Statistics, 1984: A Reference Aid*, CPAS 84–10002 (GPO, 1984), table 13, p. 37.

Figure 12-1. *Relative Timing of U.S. and Soviet Strategic Missile
Deployment, First Year of Service to Peak Deployment*[a]

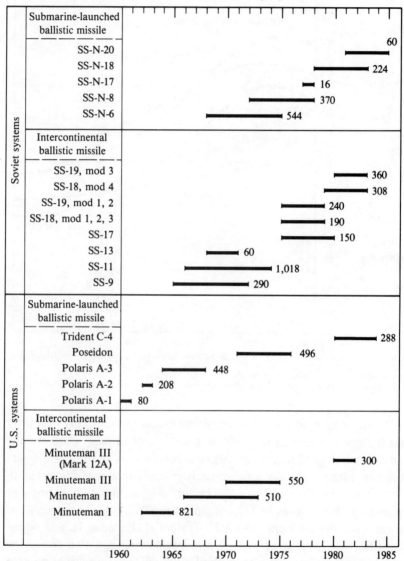

Sources: International Institute for Strategic Studies, *The Military Balance, 1970–1971* through *1984–1985* (London:
IISS, various years); Desmond J. Ball, *Politics and Force Levels: The Strategic Missile Program of the Kennedy
Administration* (University of California Press, 1980), p. 50; Norman Polmar, *The Ships and Aircraft of the U.S. Fleet,*
12th ed. (Annapolis, Md.: Naval Institute Press, 1981); Robert P. Berman and John C. Baker, *Soviet Strategic Forces:
Requirements and Responses* (Brookings, 1982), pp. 106–07; John M. Collins, *U.S./Soviet Military Balance: Statistical
Trends, 1970–1983,* Congressional Research Service, Library of Congress, Report no. 84-163 S (August 27, 1984), p. 14;
and U.S. Department of Defense, *Soviet Military Power, 1985* (Government Printing Office, 1985), p. 31.
    a. Numbers shown represent the number of weapons at peak deployment.

Figure 12-2. *Strategic Forces, Preattack Static Ratio Comparison*[a]

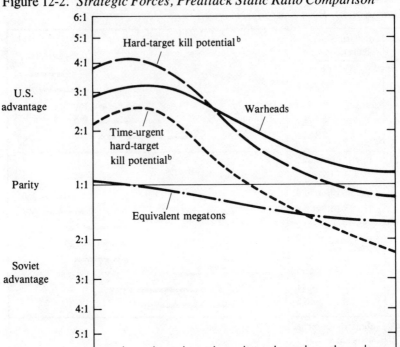

Source: Organization of the Joint Chiefs of Staff, *United States Military Posture for Fiscal Year 1985* (Washington, D.C.: U.S. Department of Defense, 1984), p. 23.
a. Total active inventory includes FB-111 and Backfire.
b. Calculations are based on potential against identical hardness targets.

Soviet commentators have explicitly declared the primary security issue they perceive in the unfolding pattern of events. They see the current surge in U.S. strategic force investment as an offensive threat representing, potentially, a significantly enhanced capacity for a preemptive attack on Soviet forces.[18] This underlying intention is imputed primarily on the basis of U.S. weapons modernization programs and force structure additions: the MX, Trident II, Pershing II, and cruise missiles with stealth technology in combination appear to create the potential for precise attacks on the Soviet military infrastructure with tactical warning that would be too short to allow protective reaction.

18. John Steinbruner, "The Security Aspect of U.S.-Soviet Relations," in Seweryn Bialer and others, *U.S.-Soviet Relations: Perspectives for the Future,* Alternatives for the 1980's, no. 14 (Washington, D.C.: Center for National Policy, 1984), pp. 41–49.

Moreover, as the Soviets view them, U.S. arms control proposals appear to have been designed to support such a preemptive strategy: if accepted, U.S. proposals would reduce deployed forces, but they would not inhibit weapons modernization, and thus they would render successful preemption easier to accomplish. The U.S. strategic defense initiative also adheres to this pattern. In Soviet estimation, the technical prospects for a successful defense against an offensive attack optimized for penetration are so unlikely that they discount it as a rational basis for security policy. The only serious aspiration is for defense against an offense severely diminished by a preemptive attack. So interpreted and fully credited, this overall pattern presents a security threat to the Soviet Union of the gravest proportions.

The extent to which the more practical-minded Soviet leaders discount this stark conception is inherently uncertain; but, even if they confidently doubt that the United States can achieve an effective capacity for strategic preemption, there are secondary implications of the U.S. effort that are also significantly threatening. At its core the U.S. strategic investment program is based on sensing and information processing technologies that represent the area of greatest U.S. advantage relative to the Soviet Union. These technologies have application across the full range of military effort—conventional as well as nuclear weapons, offensive as well as defensive missions. Despite U.S. rhetorical emphasis on defense, the most immediate and most dramatic of these effects are likely to involve offensive weapons. Beyond that the underlying technologies are also likely to have important implications for general economic productivity. In effect, the United States appears to be marshaling its strongest comparative advantage for an extended competition in military and technical position. If that process is not restrained and if equal security is not conceded, then eventually the Soviet security position is likely to be severely degraded even if the ultimate destruction of nuclear war can be prevented.

Thus far the Soviet response to this perceived pressure has been largely diplomatic in character, and that is likely to remain both the preferred means of response and important political cover if the Soviets ultimately undertake military reactions. They have sought to defend the existing framework of restrictions on strategic weapons and to supplement them first by preventing the introduction of new U.S. missile deployments in Europe and more recently by preventing the direct use of weapons in space. Both measures represent the leading edge of a more general policy to restrict the rate of weapons modernization, and that policy will probably remain a primary element in the Soviet position. The Reagan administration policy, however, makes it apparent that the Soviets are not likely to achieve their objectives solely by direct negotiations. At any rate that is the natural Soviet presumption, and one must prudently assume that Soviet leaders do consider other responses in addition to diplomacy.

There is a theoretical possibility that the Soviets would decide to forgo both agreement and material reaction and would depend upon natural economic restraints to impose eventual limits on U.S. investment. There is a case to be made for that as the most rational conclusion. Current weapons arsenals are so large and carry such enormous destructive potential that the realities of military position in fact are quite insensitive to the various improvements that technical modernization programs are currently providing. Though an indefinitely sustained and systematically programmed U.S. investment program would eventually shift the military balance in meaningful ways, a cool-headed Soviet observer might plausibly count on the American domestic political process to stop U.S. efforts well short of that point. The initial surge in U.S. strategic programs in the late 1950s and early 1960s was in fact stopped in that way. Meanwhile a restrained Soviet response would presumably minimize the danger that Soviet reactions might fuel rather than brake the U.S. surge. With a record of sustained restraint Soviet diplomacy could wrap itself in higher morality and over the longer term might in fact inspire the international respect long sought but seldom found. Truly wise advisers might well argue for such a course.

Such advisers are unlikely to be heeded or long tolerated, however. In the wake of World War II no government, least of all that of the Soviet Union, has displayed such political insouciance. There are, one may safely presume, powerful interlocutors in Moscow to argue that enduring patience would only guarantee an indefinite extension of coercive diplomacy in the United States and even more ominously that it would display dangerous weakness to the American right. The natural political dynamics within a collective leadership in transition probably ensures that what is abstractly the most rational policy is also the least likely.

Another option is a step-for-step matching of U.S. actions, a policy that relieves the burden of imagination and minimizes at least the appearance of risk. Simple matching of weapons and force levels has been a strong instinct on both sides, and in the Soviet case it has often been carried down to the details of individual weapons design. The eventual Soviet reaction will undoubtedly have some strong element of doing what the United States has done. A completely systematic reaction, however, to all dimensions of recent American investment would be quite demanding in economic and technical terms. Though a sufficient number of rubles could in principle be extracted from the Soviet economy, investment resources are so scarce and the issues of internal economic development so serious that it seems unlikely the Soviet leadership will ultimately choose that course.

The most likely responses, therefore, are those that have some strategic element enabling the Soviet Union to bring effective countervailing pressure against U.S. policy while operating with a technical and economic disadvantage. There are a variety of possible measures of this sort involving Soviet weapons programs, and it appears that three in particular are being prepared.

First, the Soviet Union is in the early phases of deploying new submarine-based cruise missiles of sufficiently advanced design that they represent in practice a new category of strategic weapons capability.[19] Though this program closely matches both in time and in technical design a similar American program, large-scale deployment of these weapons will provide a net advantage to the Soviet Union of some political significance. The reasons are inherent in geography. The United States is exposed to open ocean access with many critical targets, including the nation's capital, in immediate coastal areas. The United States does not have a significantly developed air defense system, and developing one that would offer protection against advanced cruise missiles approaching over water would be an exceedingly expensive undertaking and probably one that to be effective would also be quite intrusive in populated areas. By contrast the Soviet Union is isolated from ocean approaches, and its critical targets are well inland and protected by an elaborate air defense network, however limited its capabilities may be. Cruise missile deployment adds little to the American threat to the Soviet Union, but potentially quite a lot to the Soviet threat to the United States, particularly as the United States first perceives that threat. If accompanied by forward positioning of Soviet submarines in significantly greater numbers and advanced guidance systems capable of exerting militarily significant damage with conven-

19. U.S. Department of Defense, *Soviet Military Power, 1984*, 3d ed. (GPO, 1984), p. 31.

tional munitions, Soviet cruise missile deployment would subject the United States to a type of threat that it has not yet experienced. Even casual perusal of recent American history—the historical preoccupation with Cuba and the current concern with Nicaragua, for example— suggests that there would be enormous political sensitivity in the United States to this development.

Second, the Soviet Union is also in the early stages of deploying a new intercontinental ballistic missile system, the SS-X-25, that can be used for mobile operations on land.[20] It is one of the relatively rare cases in which the Soviet Union leads the United States in a significant weapons category. The Soviet system physically exists and has been tested several times. The U.S. counterpart is still a design idea whose future is clouded by a number of technical and political controversies. Moreover, the Soviet Union has established operational experience with mobile missile operations on land, has large, fairly open land areas in which to conduct such operations, has authoritarian political control over the use of its territory, and has an ability to restrict access effectively. The United States does not share these properties. The significance of these disparities is that the Soviet Union is immediately capable of deploying mobile missiles on land that are so highly concealed that over time they would deny both the ability to target them for retaliatory attack and the ability to count the Soviet arsenal with confidence. As a practical matter the United States is not likely to match such an enterprise but is likely to react with considerable alarm at the prospect of losing track of the exact size of Soviet nuclear forces.

Finally, and most significantly, the Soviet Union appears to have identified U.S. activities in space as a focus of leverage that is potentially very effective though inherently dangerous to use. The United States relies heavily on space assets to gather and to communicate the information necessary to manage worldwide military operations. These assets are fairly vulnerable to deliberate interference and highly vulnerable to dedicated attack. Though they can in principle be defended, the problem of defending certainly appears to be much more difficult and much more expensive than the problem of attacking. Thus far space has been used as a sanctuary for military support activities, with little operational interference and only rudimentary preparations for dedicated attacks. Both sides benefit from these arrangements that are honored in practice but not securely established in law. Should the Soviets choose to do so they can readily create severe problems for U.S. space activities that would materially affect powerful constituencies within the United States and within our alliance systems—for example, the navy, the intelligence community, the National Aeronautics and Space Administration, and all international communication companies. Even a simple verbal challenge to the legitimacy of space activities could trigger divisive political reactions in the West; actual interference would probably produce a political crisis.

Space is not "high ground" that can be seized and held, as military enthusiasts sometimes flippantly suggest, but rather an environment whose properties inherently require international cooperation to enable its effective use. Soviet leaders who want to use space for their own purposes are obviously reluctant to engage in any overt policy of disruption, and they have made a proposal to restrict the direct use of weapons in space the centerpiece of their diplomatic position. There is, however, an implicit threat in their position that the pursuit of weapons in space as envisaged by the U.S. strategic defense initiative would fundamentally alter their attitude, and Soviet representatives have suggested that assertive development of antisatellite weapons would be a feature of their response. From those basics one can project many subtle or not-so-subtle means of creating trade-offs between current space activities and the weapons development programs being pursued by the United States. That is powerful leverage at the disposal of the Soviets, and it would be foolhardy to suppose that under sustained and unrelieved pressure they would not dare to use it.

Options and Political Outcomes

Emerging from a victorious election campaign, President Reagan enjoys at the start of his second term a rare concentration of political authority and personal popularity. As he promised to do, he has provided for a general strengthening of American defenses and has displayed American resolve to the Soviet Union in a material and unmistakable fashion. He has effectively tailored his position to fit domestic political sentiment, and for the most part he can expect it to be sustained, barring serious adverse developments. The most important areas of U.S.-Soviet confrontation throughout the world are about as quiet as they have been in recent years. Apart from Central America, where initiative rests with the United States, there are no obviously building crises to unsettle the public.

If the Soviets acquiesce to his fundamental policy without substantial reaction, the president can claim diplomatic victory and vindication for his policy. In the public mind, Soviet agreement to reinstate arms control negotiations gives him a great deal of credit already. To the extent the Soviets respond with hostile reactions—particularly weapons programs—he can blame them for propelling an arms race, strengthen support for his defense program, and benefit from the predictable rallying of domestic and allied opinion. As domestic political opponents ruefully admit, he wins either way. His adversaries in the Soviet Union have probably entertained similar thoughts.

This skillful marshaling of the powers of the American presidency provides an extraordinary but probably fleeting opportunity to bring about an enduring political alignment on security policy. If President Reagan chooses to use his moment of leverage rather than simply to enjoy it, he can probably fashion an enduring political outcome. The demands upon him, however, are serious indeed—most notably, the necessity to see beyond his immediate, comfortable circumstances and the ability to adjust his own sentiments.

An enduring outcome requires, primarily, compromise of a simple but fundamental sort: restraint on weapons modernization in exchange for reductions in existing force deployments. The Soviet Union is most concerned with restraints on modernization while the United States focuses on reductions in deployments. To achieve acceptable agreements, both must be done simultaneously, probably in a series of discrete steps that feature both elements. Moreover, as a matter of practical diplomacy, the first of these steps would undoubtedly have to include restrictions on the testing and deployment of weapons in space, thereby confining the strategic defense initiative strictly to research efforts not involving weapons prototypes. With a willingness to initiate such compromise from a position of immediate strength and to offer an enduring arrangement that would set predictable limits on strategic weapons activity, President Reagan could probably achieve the dramatic reductions in deployments that the United States wants. In the process, as a popular president with his particular political orientation, President Reagan could probably forge a political alignment in the United States that would be worthy of the word consensus.

If he eschews compromise and continues to drive for what the Soviets take to be a position of unilateral advantage, President Reagan cannot be the creator of stable consensus and will ultimately inspire political reaction, first from the Soviet Union and eventually within the United States itself. A man that seems inclined to belligerence might lead a unified nation to peace, but he will eventually encounter overriding resistance if he appears to follow or to drift toward his apparent inclination.

Comments on Political Directions

Security policy imposes unique constraints on the issues of shifting political commitment that are the focus of this volume. The conditions of security do not respond to tides of opinion or redefinition of interest to the degree that is possible on other political matters. The United States is in close interaction with a potential opponent, with survival of the entire society immediately at stake. Survival is an absolute value that does not admit to redefinition; and, though there are various means of ensuring it that allow some scope for different political positions, the physical effects of past decisions impose heavy constraints even on the available means. The offensive arsenals of the United States and the Soviet Union are so large that it appears to require only small percentages of the available destructive power to reduce their respective industrial and agricultural economies to perhaps a quarter of their current capacity.[21] Full use of the arsenals would extend destruction beyond the point of probable recovery.[22] This condition has been created by thirty years of competing investment in the military applications of modern technology. It was not desired or directly intended by either political system. It emerged from technical conditions and political interactions that neither side could direct to a more constructive outcome.

In effect the United States and the Soviet Union have each taken as hostage the entire social organization of the other and have thereby

21. U.S. Congress, Office of Technology Assessment, *The Effects of Nuclear War*, OTA-NS-89 (GPO, 1979).

22. Committee on the Atmospheric Effects of Nuclear Explosions, Commission on Physical Sciences, Mathematics, and Resources, and National Research Council, *The Effects on the Atmosphere of a Major Nuclear Exchange* (Washington, D.C.: National Academy Press, 1985).

locked together the conditions of their security. This has been so thoroughly accomplished that it is no longer a matter of policy but simply a fact of life. That fact cannot be changed by moral objections, political distaste, or technical aspiration: it imposes itself in all these dimensions. The conditions might in principle be changed by mutual decision, but neither political system has yet developed either the political power or the conceptual scope to make decisions of the magnitude required.

Since the situation is truly unprecedented, it is difficult to analyze or to project its evolution. One can guess, and hope, that the two political systems are in the process of realizing the consequences of their interaction and of developing the wisdom and discipline required to manage it safely. To be able to carry such a process very far, each will have to undergo considerable internal political realignment. At best this process is in a very early stage, and the ultimate prognosis depends largely on what has yet to be done. It is an enterprise requiring a great deal of time to develop and is far larger than any single political figure, any given administration, or any political party.

CHAPTER THIRTEEN

The New Politics of Deficits

PAUL E. PETERSON

THE Reagan administration's fiscal policies represent the boldest, yet most problematic, of all its efforts to transform the domestic agenda. By tolerating deficits on a scale unprecedented in peacetime history, the administration has been able to pursue simultaneously its commitment to a stronger defense and its pledge to cut the federal income tax rate. By tolerating these deficits, it has been able to create an austere political climate in which proposed cuts, not expected increments, focus the discussions of federal domestic programs. But by tolerating deficits of great magnitude, the administration has jeopardized the Republican party's reputation for fiscal responsibility and, perhaps more important, may have created a precarious political context in which any economic recession could have disastrous electoral consequences for the government in power.

Much has been written about the possible economic consequences of current fiscal deficits. But little systematic attention has been given to the political context that has produced them. To the extent that analysts have considered the political causes of current deficits, they have depended on the cliché that politicians like to confer benefits immediately but postpone costs—at least until after the next election.[1] While this observation contains more than a grain of truth, it is a verity that applies to many times and places. It does not account for the peculiar propensity to engage in deficit financing that currently plagues American politics.

Research assistance was provided by Alice G. Keck. Barry P. Bosworth, Robert Z. Lawrence, Norman J. Ornstein, Alice M. Rivlin, Charles L. Schultze, and Robert Y. Shapiro made helpful comments on earlier versions.

1. James Buchanan has explained budget deficits in these terms. "Public Choice Theory and the Deficits," seminar at George Washington University, March 15, 1985.

To the extent that thinking about deficits has gone beyond a general suspicion of politicians' fiscal responsibility, the conventional wisdom views deficits as a gradually accelerating problem in the postwar period, a by-product of an increasingly fragmented government crisscrossed by a vast network of legislative aides, aggressive interest groups, naive policy analysts, and self-serving bureaucrats. The "keystone" of this Washington establishment is to be found in Congress, whose members are thought to be more interested in capturing benefits for their constituencies than in conceptualizing an overall framework for policy.[2] The system, it is said, is so fragmented that it is nearly out of control.

In this essay I present a quite different view of deficit politics. Deficits have not been a slowly developing political problem during the postwar period; instead they blossomed suddenly in 1981. Congress has not characteristically pursued an independent course in its tax and expenditure policies; instead, it has generally followed the presidential lead on broad fiscal policies. To account for the new politics of deficits, therefore, is to describe and explain a recent, significant shift in the policies of the executive branch.

It is too simplistic to attribute this shift just to President Reagan's own policy preferences. To say that deficits are caused by his commitment to a tax cut and a strong defense is correct but misleading—presidents have always wanted to cut taxes but spend more. To say that deficits are part of the president's plan to create an austerity climate in which he can cut domestic expenditure is also probably correct, but once again it is misleading: Republican presidents have time and again wanted to limit the size and scope of the federal government. But they did not run deficits to achieve this goal.

President Reagan's ability to persuade others—both in Congress and within his own administration—to accept and tolerate large-scale deficits has been due to changes in two factors that go well beyond the personal inclinations of the president himself. First (but definitely *not* foremost), the structure of public opinion has changed, in that people are more insistent than ever that government provide more services at less cost. Second, and more important, professional opinion on the short-term effects of deficits on economic activity has changed significantly. Whereas at one time economists thought fiscal policy was an important tool for

2. Morris Fiorina, *Congress: Keystone of the Washington Establishment* (Yale University Press, 1977).

managing the business cycle, greater stress is now placed on monetary policy. As a result, politicians now calculate the electoral consequences of deficits in quite different terms than they once did.

Changes in Deficit Politics

Budget deficits have been a pervasive feature of postwar American politics, occurring in thirty of the thirty-five years since 1950. Between 1950 and 1980 they averaged $26.7 billion annually (all deficit, expenditure, and budgetary data are reported in constant 1982 dollars, unless otherwise noted), and they made up 5.1 percent of federal outlays.[3] Presidents and Congresses regularly overestimated revenue, underestimated expenditures, or treated the current context as exceptional enough to justify deficit financing. Deficits—and the talk of deficits—became a staple of American politics. Many observers condemned them, but they nonetheless persisted.

This legacy of annual deficits was politically significant, if only because Democrats became known as the party of deficits while Republicans were regarded as fiscally more responsible. But both Democrats and Republicans contributed to the production of deficits—under Democratic presidents they averaged $19.1 billion, while Republicans until 1976 ran an average deficit of $24 billion—and both parties were generally committed to keeping deficits under control.

From 1946 to 1981 the national debt remained level in real-dollar terms and declined steadily as a percentage of GNP. But since 1981 deficits have increased rapidly, averaging about 20 percent of the federal budget and over 4 percent of GNP. The Congressional Budget Office's most recent estimate for the next four years suggests the pattern of the past four years is likely to persist unless draconian measures are taken.

Three figures (13-1, 13-2, and 13-3) illustrate how modestly the public debt of the past compares with that of the Reagan era. Figure 13-1 shows that the real value of the federal gross debt changed hardly at all over the three decades after World War II. In 1981 the debt was no larger than it had been in 1947, though it had increased moderately from the low reached in 1974. Although annual deficits were incurred throughout this

3. Author's calculations, based on *Budget of the United States Government, Fiscal Year 1950* and subsequent issues.

Figure 13-1. *Gross Federal Debt, Fiscal Years 1946–89*
Billions of 1982 dollars

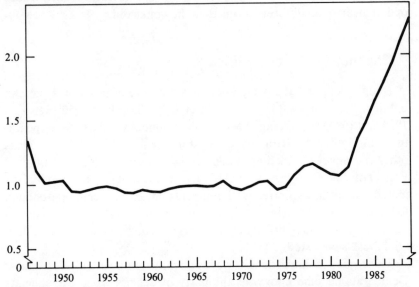

Sources: *Historical Tables, Budget of the United States Government, Fiscal Year 1986*, table 1.1; and Congressional Budget Office, *The Economic and Budget Outlook, Fiscal Years 1986–1990*, pt. 1 (CBO, 1985), p. 64. Data for 1985–89 are projected.

period, they were offset by inflation-caused declines in the real value of preexisting debt. In short, the pace of inflation was eroding the real value of the federal debt as rapidly as the government was adding to it by creating deficits in current budgets. Only after 1981 did the real value of the debt begin to increase at a remarkable rate, increasing by 54 percent between 1981 and 1985. It is expected to increase at a comparable rate in subsequent years unless current tax or expenditure policies are markedly revised.

The shift that occurred after 1981 appears even more dramatic when one examines the changes in the size of the federal debt as a percentage of GNP (see figure 13-2). Inasmuch as the economy grew steadily if unevenly throughout the postwar period, the debt, though remaining constant in real terms, declined sharply as a percentage of GNP, falling by an average of 8.8 percent a year in the decade immediately following the war. Between 1955 and 1974 it continued to fall, but at a lower rate—an average of 2 percent of GNP each year. After 1981 the debt in proportion to GNP began increasing by nearly 4 percent a year, and

Figure 13-2. *Gross Federal Debt as Percentage of Gross National Product, Fiscal Years 1946–89*

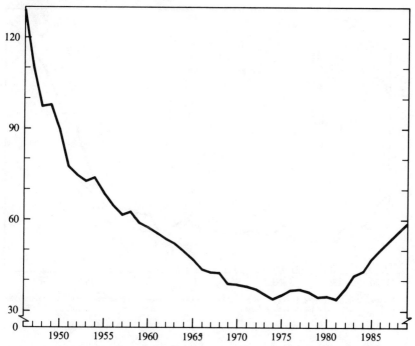

Sources: *Historical Tables, Fiscal Year 1986*, table 1.1; CBO, *Economic and Budget Outlook, Fiscal Years 1986–1990*, pt. 1, p. 40; and *Economic Report of the President, February 1985*, p. 232. Data for 1985–89 are projected.

an increase of roughly this same magnitude is expected with every passing year until the political constellation that is producing deficits at the current rate comes to an end.

Still a third measure of the magnitude of the federal debt is the percentage of GNP needed to finance the necessary interest payments (see figure 13-3). The system was more or less in equilibrium between 1950 and the mid-1970s. But after 1974 interest costs began to rise, and after 1981 they increased at a very rapid rate indeed, rising from about 2 percent of GNP in 1980 to a projected 4 percent in 1989. The rapid increases in interest charges seem to be a function of three factors: the increase in the size of the federal debt; the increase in the real rate of interest, partly caused by large deficits; and the additional increase in the nominal rate of interest, caused by higher expected inflation rates, which were also apparently affected by the size of federal deficits.

Figure 13-3. *Net Federal Interest Payments as Percentage of Gross
National Product, Fiscal Years 1946–89*

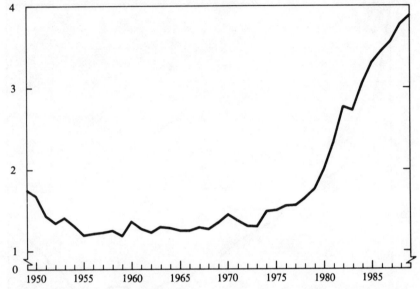

Sources: *Historical Tables, Fiscal Year 1986*, table 3.1; and CBO, *Economic and Budget Outlook, Fiscal Years 1986–
1990*, pt. 1, p. 54. Data for 1985–89 are projected.

Congress, the President, and Budget Deficits

Many believe that deficits occur because politicians seek to provide
benefits to constituents immediately, while they try to defer costs at
least until after the next election. Examples of this kind of cost post-
ponement in American politics are legion. Increases in social security
taxes are usually enacted five to ten years before they are actually
imposed. Generous but temporarily "free" retirement benefits are used
to attract people into the armed forces. Local governments also use
disproportionately high retirement benefits to compensate their workers.[4] A specialized political vocabulary has even developed to codify
and justify the political tactic of postponing costs to constituents; for

4. Temporary Commission on City Finances, *The City in Transition: Prospects and
Policies for New York* (New York: Arno Press, 1978), pp. 181–85.

example, politicians insert what are known as "grandfather" and "hold harmless" provisions when they make changes that could potentially reduce current benefits.[5]

Some have thought that Congress, more than the president, is susceptible to the temptations of postponing costs while distributing benefits as quickly as possible. Members of Congress may be particularly subject to bouts of fiscal irresponsibility, because they can blame their colleagues for undesirable outcomes, while the president is aware that for him "the buck stops here." Even if members of Congress want to be responsible, it is thought to be difficult for them to coordinate their efforts, because they are divided institutionally into two houses and hundreds of committees and subcommittees. Also, Congress has been controlled throughout most of the postwar period by the Democrats, the party that is reputed to be less fiscally conservative. As the Republican platform asserted in 1972, "Federal deficit spending beyond the balance of a full employment budget is one sure way to refuel inflation, and the prime source of such spending is the United States Congress."[6] Or, more recently, in the words of President Reagan, "Every budget that we have submitted since I've been here has been smaller than the one the Congress would finally agree to, so in fixing the blame for why we haven't done more . . . in reducing spending seems to be pretty evident."[7] Indeed, the view that congressional spending causes deficits has given currency to such proposed constitutional amendments as the one giving the president a line-item veto or another requiring a balanced budget except in emergency circumstances.

5. "Hold harmless" clauses exempt existing beneficiaries from reductions in aid for a specific period of time, even through vigorous application of the new formula for allocating aid would seem to include them. The term "grandfather" dates back to Jim Crow legislation, enacted by southern states to give voting privileges only to those whose "grandfathers" had had such rights. Since no black grandfathers could have voted, these laws (which were eventually declared unconstitutional) preserved all-white electorates. Ever since, grandfather clauses have referred to privileges that individuals or communities receive because of some previous status. On this topic, see the excellent analysis by Christopher Leman, "How to Get There from Here: The Grandfather Effect and Public Policy," *Policy Analysis*, vol. 6 (Winter 1980), pp. 99–116.

6. Donald Bruce Johnson, comp., *National Party Platforms*, vol. 2, 1960–1976 (University of Illinois Press, 1978), p. 862.

7. Helen Dewar and Margaret Shapiro, "Wright Hits Reagan, Denies Congress Culpable on Deficit," *Washington Post*, January 29, 1985.

Expenditure Politics

To examine whether Congress is to be held particularly responsible for excessive spending, I compared presidential budget requests with what Congress finally appropriated for each fiscal year in the postwar period. If Congress is more of a spendthrift than the president, its appropriations should systematically exceed the President's budget requests.[8]

DATA LIMITATIONS. Before reporting my findings, several limitations on the data need to be acknowledged. The simple comparison of presidential budget requests and congressional appropriations does not take into full account the interplay between the two institutions. Laws and appropriations are the product of continuous discussions among

8. The original presidential budget, together with all supplemental requests and rescissions, as recorded in subsequent presidential budgets, provided the basis for determining the president's expressed budgetary intentions. Eventual congressional appropriations are recorded in subsequent volumes of the president's budget. My exact procedure was as follows: I identified the total presidential budgetary request for fiscal year X (exclusive of trust fund expenditures), as given in the *Budget of the United States Government;* I then added to that figure all presidential supplemental requests and all presidential rescissions of the original request, as reported in the budget for fiscal year $(X + 1)$. I then compared the total of these figures with the increase in statutory authority provided by Congress for fiscal year X as reported in the budget for fiscal year $(X + 2)$. This procedure takes into account any changes in presidential position that took place up to twelve months after the issuance of the president's budget and four months into fiscal year X, which began the preceding October 1. (For the years before 1977, when the fiscal year ran from July 1 to June 30, the figures include information on presidential supplemental requests and rescissions seven months into fiscal year X.) Since most budgetary action for fiscal year X takes place either before the beginning of the year or in the very first months of fiscal year X, this procedure captures most of the modifications in the presidential position. However, any change in presidential requests occurring in the last eight months of fiscal year X could not be ascertained by this method. This procedure inadvertently excludes some supplemental presidential requests, and, to this extent, underestimates the size of presidential requests. I was able to refine this procedure for the fiscal years 1970 through 1980, because a study by the Congressional Budget Office compiled complete information on all supplemental requests for these years (Congressional Budget Office, *Supplemental Appropriations in the 1970s* [GPO, 1981]). By comparing the CBO's findings for these years with those that I obtained by relying solely on the figures included in the president's annual budget, I discovered that on average I underestimated the size of the supplemental request by 57 percent, or underestimated the size of the president's total request by 2.4 percent. From this one may infer that presidential requests as given in table 13-1 are underestimated by an average of about $6.5 billion for the years 1947–69. This means that had I more accurate data it would show even less propensity for Congress to spend in excess of presidential requests than my data indicate.

legislative committees, executive agencies, interested groups and organizations, and policy analysts. To state precisely what happens on Capitol Hill and in the bowels of the bureaucracy is difficult even when examining a particular program; to speak of these matters in general is all the more problematic.

Specifically, three factors generate some bias in my estimates, but it is doubtful that separately or together their impact leads to a serious underestimate of Congress's differential impact on spending. First, it may be argued that Congress might have spent more had it not been restrained by the threat and exercise of presidential vetoes. However, the veto has been used to defeat appropriations on only nineteen occasions during the postwar period. The amount of money presidents have saved by their vetoes is only $8.2 billion, 0.6 percent of the 1984 national debt. To be sure, presidential power is enhanced more by the threat of the veto than by its actual use. Had Congress not been concerned about presidential opposition, it might well have appropriated more on numerous additional occasions. The veto is a trump card that even when not played can shape the outcome of the budgetary game. Yet one should not exaggerate the influence of the veto. Like trump, it can be played more than once but it cannot be used indiscriminately. The veto is often a sign of presidential weakness, not strength. Unable to persuade Congress in other ways, the president is forced to rely directly upon the authority the Constitution ascribes to him. Thus it was Gerald Ford who used the veto most often (three times in a little more than two years) but who was also the president least able to keep expenditures close to his requests.

If the threat of veto has kept my estimates of congressional spending propensities too low, the same can be said of my estimates of presidential requests. If a president wants to spend less than he thinks Congress will appropriate, it is to his advantage to propose even less than he really wants.[9] In the bargaining process that ensues, a compromise may be struck that gives the president what he actually wants but more than he originally proposed. To the extent that this happens, my analysis exaggerates rather than underestimates the differences between the spending tendencies of the executive and those of the legislature.

Second, the president's budget may include expenditures for projects

9. D. Roderick Kiewiet and Mathew D. McCubbins, "Agenda Power in the Federal Appropriations Process: The Role of Reversionary Expenditure Levels," paper prepared for the 1984 annual meeting of the American Political Science Association.

he opposes, because he is aware of congressional commitment to certain programs and he fears a congressional override of a presidential veto or other political costs. But if on occasion the president may include items in the budget to please Congress, he has incentives to keep such inclusions to a minimum. Presidents prefer, all things being equal, to propose balanced budgets. Only in the relatively rare case when cutting an item might antagonize a particularly powerful congressional leader— for example, Howard Baker's Clinch River breeder reactor or Jesse Helms's price supports for tobacco—would a president be tempted to place specifically congressional considerations ahead of broader political and policy concerns. What is more likely is that presidential refusal to cut such dubious items as exceptionally high retirement benefits for army officers—even when his own budget officer queries them[10]—is because he fears adverse reaction from sources such as his own defense advisers, veterans' groups, and a country grateful for the sacrifice its men were once called upon to make. In such cases, Congress often takes the blame for waste and extravagance that the president finds equally inconvenient to eliminate.

Third, it may be argued that the president often becomes "locked into" proposing additional expenditures for projects Congress has already begun. Such instances certainly do happen, but once again they do not necessarily lead to an underestimate of differential congressional spending propensities. For one thing, if the president does not exercise his veto but instead includes such proposals in his own budget, he seems prepared to accept the political blame—or, more often, the political credit—for approving a popular program. Second, starting a new program with a small expenditure is as apt a device for an executive agency as for a congressional committee. For every dam begun at the initiative of a legislative committee, one can find a new weapons system conceived in the Pentagon. Indeed, President Lyndon Johnson became famous for his use of this "camel's nose" strategy—for domestic as well as for defense expenditures. There is little evidentiary basis for concluding that one end or another of Pennsylvania Avenue is particularly successful at locking the other into its set of objectives.

FINDINGS. Bearing these caveats in mind, let us consider the data presented in table 13-1, which compares the president's budgetary requests with subsequent congressional appropriations over a thirty-

10. Helen Dewar, "Stockman Attacks Military Pension System," *Washington Post,* February 6, 1985.

Table 13-1. *Differences in Appropriations Proposed by President and Passed by Congress, 1947–84*
Billions of 1982 dollars

	Average annual difference[a]		
President	Defense	Nondefense	Total[b]
Harry Truman (1947–53)	17.5	−3.1	14.5
Dwight Eisenhower (1954–57)	−4.6	−0.3	−5.3
Dwight Eisenhower (1958–61)	−1.0	0.1	−1.0
John Kennedy/Lyndon Johnson (1962–65)	−2.4	−7.4	−9.3
Lyndon Johnson (1966–69)	1.0	−10.4	−10.9
Richard Nixon (1970–73)	−16.0	2.5	−12.8
Richard Nixon/Gerald Ford (1974–77)	−9.2	25.4	15.8
Jimmy Carter (1978–81)	9.8	−32.3	−21.6
Ronald Reagan (1982–84)	8.9	5.6	16.4
Average			
Republican administrations	−5.1	6.7	1.9
Democratic administrations	7.8	−11.7	−3.4
All years	−1.4	−2.5	−0.8

Source: *Budget of the U.S. Government, Fiscal Year 1985* and earlier editions.
a. Positive numbers indicate Congress authorized more than the president requested, and negative numbers indicate the reverse.
b. Includes defense, nondefense, and interest payments.

seven-year period. As the table shows, executive-legislative differences are marginal, not fundamental. Over the postwar period Congress actually appropriated an average of $0.8 billion a year less than the president had requested. To be sure, Congress spent more than the president requested when a Republican held the presidency—appropriations exceeded requests by an average of $1.9 billion during these years, compared with $3.4 billion less than requested during Democratic administrations—but even when Republicans held office, the differences between White House and Capitol Hill were limited.

Agreement on the overall size of the federal government does not necessarily mean agreement on the size of its parts. Congress rejected some presidential initiatives (such as Nixon's family assistance plan and Carter's welfare initiative) while appropriating extra amounts to such legislative favorites as federally impacted school districts and projects to improve rivers and harbors. In this paper I do not examine these kinds of policy differences on individual programs. But in the aggregate it is the similarity of congressional and presidential judgments that is striking. This is particularly true with respect to defense policy, where Congress has enacted what the president has requested within an average of $1.4 billion. Admittedly, this average is the product of appropriations exceeding requests when a Democrat was president and the opposite when a Republican was in office, but the numbers, though large enough to provoke frequent political disputations, hardly reflect wildly differing estimates of the country's needs for national defense.

The conflict over nondefense policy was somewhat greater. Congress spent an average of $11.7 billion less than Democratic presidents requested, but $6.7 billion more than Republicans wanted. During the Watergate years (1974–77), the differences between the two ends of Pennsylvania Avenue were especially great, as Congress outspent the administration's requests by over $25 billion a year. But the dramatic struggles of this era appear as much of a disturbance from the normal budgetary pattern as presidential impeachments themselves.

A public grown used to continuous bickering between president and Congress may wonder why these figures portray a working relationship so different from what cursory observation of Washington politics might lead one to expect. But it is to be remembered that politicians—and the news media that cover their activities—necessarily focus on their differences, not on the basics to which all consent. In fact it is difficult to imagine how a government operating under a separation of powers doctrine could operate effectively if the legislative and executive branches were not in broad agreement. The president is constrained to propose budgets that are at least minimally acceptable to Congress, while Congress must appropriate amounts that will survive a presidential veto. Even more important, both the executive branch, with its far-flung set of departments, bureaus, and offices, and the legislative branch, with its array of committees and subcommittees, respond to a roughly similar set of political interests and pressures. If the emphasis varies from one party to the next, or between the executive and legislative branches of the political parties, these differences are more often one of degree than completely different concepts of government's responsibility.

Also, it is worth reemphasizing the macropolitical and macroeconomic character of the policy under discussion. The numbers in the tables measure agreement on broad policies such as maintaining national defense, not commitments to specific means of achieving it, such as the construction of the B-1 bomber or the missile experimental (MX). On the domestic side the data show a fair degree of consensus on overall expenditure levels, not identical views on the relative importance of mass transportation as opposed to highways, or veterans' benefits as opposed to aid to families with dependent children.

On spending policies Congress seems willing to concede to the president the responsibility for setting overall targets. Traditionally, it has been the responsibility of the Treasury and the Office of Management and Budget (OMB) to predict revenue flows, to anticipate the outlays required by entitlements, and to propose a budget that is in some rough equilibrium. Not until the mid-1970s did Congress even begin to acquire its own capability for assessing overall budgetary policy, and not until the Carter years did the newly formed Congressional Budget Office acquire a stature that rivaled that of the OMB. Congress questioned the details of spending, but for it to move dramatically away from the president's overall view of what was fiscally prudent took more political or institutional resources.

The data shown in table 13-1 not only put in question popular conceptions of Congress's spending predispositions but contradict recent scholarly interpretations as well. According to one school of thought, Congress as an institution is incapable of disciplining its spending proclivities.[11] Since members of Congress are primarily concerned about their own reelection, they are said to focus attention only on the consequences of policies for their own state or district. Because program expenditures are concentrated in particular districts, members of Congress readily support such expenditures in order to realize visibility and gratitude in their home districts. The costs of paying for the new projects, on the other hand, are spread over all congressional districts, and, it is argued, have little, if any, effect on any one member of Congress. In the words of the proponents of this point of view, "Because public expenditures often have a significant impact on a local economy . . . the purchase of program inputs is politically valuable wholly apart from the objectives sought by the program. Put simply, economic costs become political benefits when they are appropriately targeted."[12] In short, Congress may talk the language of fiscal integrity, but institutionally it is incapable of acting upon such talk.

This argument, however persuasive it seems at first blush, is empirically and conceptually flawed. In order to see its theoretical difficulties, imagine the case of an entirely wasteful project—say, the construction of a full-scale replica of Stonehenge in each of 218 congressional districts

11. Kenneth A. Shepsle and Barry R. Weingast, "Legislative Politics and Budget Outcomes," in Gregory B. Mills and John L. Palmer, eds., *Federal Budget Policy in the 1980s* (Washington, D.C.: Urban Institute, 1984), pp. 343–67.

12. Ibid., p. 356.

(a majority of districts). If members of Congress were insensitive to costs, there is no reason why they would not appropriate funds for such a project. Because the benefits would be concentrated and visible—construction workers would be given jobs and contractors would make money, while the costs would be diffused among all taxpayers—the Stonehenge projects, and any other projects the mind can conceive, would be enacted. The difficulty with such an understanding of how Congress works is that the total cost of such waste would be borne by taxpayers living in all districts, with no commensurate gain in benefits except to relatively few members of the construction industry. If opposition candidates for Congress held identical views with incumbents on all policies other than the elimination of the Stonehenge projects, incumbents would risk defeat.

I choose an extreme example to show that the institutional structure of Congress does not preclude political controls on spending. The data in table 13-1 demonstrate that political constraints on congressional spending not only are theoretically present but in practice are nearly as strong as those restraining the president. Moreover, discretionary spending, which Congress is supposedly so adept at promoting, has not been growing rapidly in recent years. Instead, recent growth has been greatest in entitlement programs, which do not have well-defined territorial impacts, and defense programs, whose expansion has been at the behest of a president who perceives a need for strengthened national security. Indeed, domestic programs having the well-defined territorial impacts that Congress is said to focus on have been the very ones to have suffered the greatest reductions during the period excessive deficits have developed.[13]

Members of Congress have a political interest in disciplining spending that equals their interest in the enactment and implementation of federal programs. Members of Congress represent both recipients of government services and the taxpayers who pay for these services; they can be—and have been—defeated for spending either too little or too much. If they are eager to obtain as many government programs for their district as is feasible, they are equally concerned about their constituents' money being wasted on useless projects elsewhere.

The overt behavior of individual members of Congress may make it

13. R. Douglas Arnold, "The Local Roots of Domestic Policy," in Thomas E. Mann and Norman J. Ornstein, eds., *The New Congress* (Washington, D.C.: American Enterprise Institute, 1981), pp. 250–87.

appear as if Congress is not conscious of cost constraints. If one only observes the overt activities in which individual members engage and does not examine their institutional context, one may exaggerate congressional interest in spending money. Individual members of Congress must concentrate upon the programs and activities that impinge on their own districts. They must maintain large staffs, attend to casework, obtain membership on the subcommittees whose missions are of relevance to their constituents, and proclaim loudly—through local and regional media—the benefits to the district of their untiring efforts. If the members of Congress do not fight for their districts, no one else will. If they were to meddle in the concerns of other districts by trying to cut everyone else's favorite subsidies, they would only earn the enmity of colleagues and jeopardize their own capacity to deliver the bacon. Very few representatives and senators (such as William Proxmire, Charles E. Grassley, and Wayne Morse) have found that playing "gadfly" pays political dividends.

But if few members are gadflies, many more—indeed, virtually all—recognize that undisciplined pursuit of district interests by most members of Congress would produce its own electoral havoc. The members have thus created and sustained a set of institutional arrangements that limit expenditure-prone behavior. These institutions are threefold: (1) powerful committees, to which are appointed the most senior members of Congress, that screen appropriation proposals; (2) party organizations whose elected leaders place member concerns within an overall party program; and (3) a tradition of respect for and deference to the institutionalized presidency's guidelines on fiscal policy.

The weight and significance of each of these institutions vary with time and circumstance. In the 1940s and 1950s great authority was ceded to the House Appropriations Committee, within which a bipartisan conservative coalition exercised fiscal constraints. Since the budget reforms of the early 1970s, the Budget committees in the House and Senate have gained influence. But the most stable force has been the control of the fiscal agenda by the institutionalized presidency. Throughout the postwar period Congress has operated within a budget framework initially specified by the president, who (with the help of the OMB, the Treasury, and the Council of Economic Advisers) is best able to construct an overall national fiscal policy. However much Congress may modify the details of that policy, it seems to have accepted the executive's prerogative to define the budget's general contours.

Tax Politics

Deficits are a function of both revenue and expenditure policies. If Congress did not cause deficits by approving disproportionately large expenditures, perhaps deficits have been instead the by-product of Congress's disproportionate readiness to cut taxes. Although in recent years one has heard more about Congress's propensity to spend, it is also widely believed that nothing is more popular than a tax cut or more courageous than levying an increase. In 1981, for example, House Republicans and Democrats are said to have engaged in a virtual bidding war by proposing ever-deeper tax cuts to woo fellow members and their interest group allies.[14] Is this only a specific instance of a more general phenomenon? Does Congress regularly cut taxes over the resistance of the president? Does it typically go well beyond what he initially proposes? Or is Congress often faulted for currying popular favor when it does little more than what the president requests?

Before considering the findings in table 13-2, certain qualifications on the information presented there must be acknowledged. The table shows information on the expected size of tax cuts for the first full year after their enactment and for the first full year after all of their features are to take effect. The expected size of tax cuts is notoriously inaccurate, of course. Tax incentives are turned into tax loopholes by creative accountants. As one loophole is closed, tax escapers exploit another one more assiduously. Also, the effects of marginal rate reductions are eroded by inflation-induced increases in income. These and other poorly anticipated consequences of tax changes alter the tax yield in ways that neither presidential nor congressional advisers can predict. To take these numbers as the actual consequence of tax policy would be quite misleading. But the official estimates of the expected effects are still the best available indicator of what the president and Congress intended when the law was signed. Although the revenue effects of tax changes may at times be either minimized or exaggerated for political purposes, the numbers employed are usually accepted as roughly correct by participants in the legislative process, and it is these numbers that Congress and the president typically expect the voters to praise—or blame—them for.

---

14. Norman J. Ornstein, "The Politics of the Deficit," in Phillip Cagan, ed., *Contemporary Economic Problems* (American Enterprise Institute, 1985), pp. 311–33.

Table 13-2. *Presidential Tax Proposals and Congressional Enactments, 1948–84*
Billions of 1982 dollars

Year	Presidential proposal		Congressional enactment		Difference	
	First year[a]	Fully effective[b]	First year[a]	Fully effective[b]	First year[a]	Fully effective[b]
1948	−3.2	...	−4.8	...	−1.6	...
1950	5.5	...	8.8	...	3.3	...
1951	10.0	...	5.7	...	−4.3	...
1954	−1.3	...	−1.4	...	0.1	...
1964	−6.3	−10.3	−7.7	−11.5	−1.4	−1.2
1968	7.4	...	10.9	...	3.5	...
1969	*	...	−2.5	...	−2.5	...
1971	−12.9	−9.3	−11.4	−10.0	1.5	−0.7
1975	−16.0	...	−22.8	...	−6.8	...
1976	*	...	−15.7	−6.2	−15.7	−6.2
1977	−13.8	−15.7	−17.7	−13.8	3.9	−1.9
1978	−24.5	−34.9	−18.7	−34.1	5.8	0.8
1980	*	...	3.6	...	3.6	...
1981	−56.6	−129.8	−37.7	−150.0	18.9	−20.2
1982	*	...	18.0	51.8	18.0	51.8
1984	*	...	10.6	22.5	10.6	22.5

Sources: Congressional Quarterly, *Congress and the Nation*, vols. 1–5 (Washington, D.C.: CQ, 1965–81); *Congressional Quarterly Almanac*, vol. 38 (1982) and earlier years; *President's 1963 Tax Message*, Hearings before the House Committee on Ways and Means, 88 Cong. 1 sess. (Government Printing Office, 1963), p. 57; *Legislative History of H.R. 8363*, prepared for the House Committee on Ways and Means, 89 Cong. 2 sess. (GPO, 1966), pt. 4; *President's 1967 Tax Proposals*, Hearings before the House Committee on Ways and Means, 90 Cong. 1 sess. (GPO, 1967), p. 5; *Summary of Tax and Spending Reduction Provisions (within the Jurisdiction of the Committees on Ways and Means and Finance) of H.R. 4170 as Passed by the House and the Senate*, prepared for the Joint Committee on Taxation, 98 Cong. 2 sess. (GPO, 1984), p. 118; *Revised Budget of the United States Government, Fiscal Year 1982*, p. 15; and Joseph A. Pechman, *Federal Tax Policy* (Brookings, 1983), p. 40.
* No presidential proposal.
a. Expected revenue change first full year after law is passed.
b. Expected revenue change first full year after law is fully effective, if different from first column.

On tax matters, Congress also mainly follows the presidential lead. The data in table 13-2 identify only the overall revenue effects of tax legislation, of course. Information on the incidence of taxation—that is, how it affects individuals or firms, higher- or lower-income taxpayers, broad classes or narrow groups affected by loophole closures—is not included in the table, because these features of tax policy have no direct bearing on fiscal deficits. Had these more specific aspects of the legislation been examined, significant congressional modification of presidential proposals would have been evident. But on the overall revenue effects, Congress seems to accept the president's guidelines. It is true that up until 1976 Congress tended to cut taxes a bit more than presidents suggested and to raise them somewhat less than they proposed. But after 1976 the opposite tendency occurred: Congress became more resistant to tax cuts and showed more sympathy to tax increases.

During the first Reagan administration this new trend became quite pronounced as Congress became increasingly concerned about fiscal deficits. Even in 1981, when Democrats and Republicans were said to be outdoing one another in their enthusiasm for tax cuts, the cuts that were to take effect in 1982 actually generated a smaller short-term revenue loss than the president had initially proposed. In 1982, without having received any proposal from the president at all, Congress enacted a tax increase that reduced several "Christmas tree" items it had enacted in June 1981, as well as closing other loopholes.[15] Again in 1984 Congress passed still another "revenue enhancement" bill without a presidential request. However, these tax increases were not forced upon a recalcitrant administration. Whatever doubts about a tax increase President Reagan himself may have had, his key advisers welcomed the measure and persuaded the president to sign the tax bills Congress submitted to him. In short, in the immediate postwar period Congress was nearly as fiscally responsible as the president on tax matters, and recently it has shown more "courage" than has the executive branch.

The Transformation of Deficit Politics in 1981

Because big peacetime deficits are a political innovation that began in 1981, and because presidential initiatives in overall tax and expenditure policy are usually accepted on Capitol Hill, the transformation in deficit politics is likely to be a White House phenomenon. More detailed examination of the recent politics of deficits will confirm this expectation.

The immediate causes of the upsurge in deficits after 1981 are well known. (1) Congress, at the administration's urging, passed a bill in July 1981 that cut taxes by an estimated $150 billion annually, even though cuts in outlays totaled less than $50 billion annually.[16] (2) The effect of these legislative actions was exacerbated by a recession that began in

---

15. Accelerated deduction features in the 1981 tax bill scheduled to go into effect in 1985 and again in 1988 were eliminated, and the "safe-harbor" leasing provisions of that law, which enabled firms to sell unused tax breaks, were restricted. *Congressional Quarterly Almanac*, vol. 38 (1982), pp. 29–31.

16. *Congressional Quarterly Almanac*, vol. 37 (1981), pp. 93, 259.

Table 13-3. *Deficit Projections by Office of Management and Budget and Congressional Budget Office and Actual Deficits, Fiscal Years 1981–84*
Billions of nominal dollars

	Projections				
	Office of Management and Budget		Congressional Budget Office		Actual deficit
Year	Advance[a]	Current[b]	Advance[a]	Current[b]	
1981	−1.2	−16.0	−21.0	−47.9	−57.9
1982	5.0	−45.0	−29.6	−109.0	−110.6
1983	−22.9	−91.5	−157.0	−194.0	−195.4
1984	−82.9	−188.8	−197.0	−190.0	−175.4

Sources: *Budget of the United States Government, Fiscal Year 1980*, p. 14; *Fiscal Year 1981*, p. M3; *Budget Revisions, Fiscal Year 1982*, pp. 6, 97; *Fiscal Year 1983*, p. M5; *Fiscal Year 1984*, p. 9-3; *Fiscal Year 1985*, p. 9-4; *Fiscal Year 1986*, p. 9-10; Congressional Budget Office, *Baseline Budget Projections: Fiscal Years 1981–1985*, pt. 2, p. xix; *Fiscal Years 1982–1986*, p. 10; *Fiscal Years 1983–1987*, p. 9; *Fiscal Years 1984–1988*, p. 9; and *Fiscal Years 1985–1989*, p. 7.
a. Estimate twenty months before beginning of fiscal year.
b. Estimate eight months before beginning of fiscal year.

the very month the tax bill was approved. As a result, the 1983 deficit exceeded the Congressional Budget Office's 1981 estimates by nearly $40 billion (see table 13-3). (3) The Federal Reserve Board, by pursuing a restrictive monetary policy that offset the stimulative effects of the tax cut, aggravated the recession and increased the cost of financing the public debt, which further contributed to the size of the deficit. These policies also lowered inflation rates, a development that may have been desirable in other respects but that reduced the rate at which the public debt was being devalued in real-dollar terms.[17]

The upsurge in the deficit was partly unplanned. The Reagan administration clung to a rosy forecast of the immediate economic future as late as the fall of 1981, even after the recession had begun. Even if many in the administration did not believe the supply-side calculations that were projecting extraordinarily rapid economic growth in the wake of the tax cuts, they also did not anticipate the deepest recession of the postwar period or continued high interest rates in the midst of an

17. Some Reagan administration officials have argued that the deficits were not "caused" by the tax cut of 1981. They cite as evidence the fact that revenue as a percentage of GNP did not fall between 1981 and 1983. Instead, expenditures as a percentage of GNP continued to rise. What this ignores is that the 1981 tax cut did not take full effect until 1985 (when federal revenue as a percentage of GNP was in fact falling) and that the rise in expenditures after 1981 (due to defense and entitlement increases) could be—and was—anticipated at the very time the tax cut was passed.

Figure 13-4. *Presidential Estimates of Deficits and Actual Deficits,*
1947–84[a]

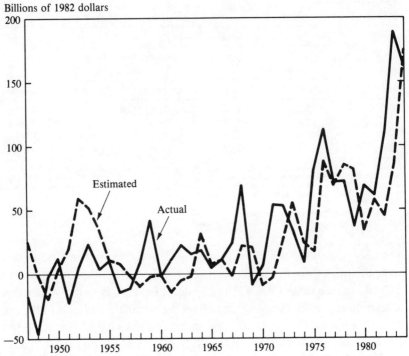

Billions of 1982 dollars

Sources: *Historical Tables, Fiscal Year 1986*, table 1.1; and *Budget of the United States Government*, various years.
a. Negative numbers indicate a surplus, and positive numbers indicate a deficit.

economic recession. The Reagan administration, to be sure, is not the
first to misperceive economic reality in making optimistic economic
projections. As can be seen from figure 13-4, presidents—and their
economic advisers—have generally been quite inaccurate in forecasting
future deficits; indeed, only 53 percent of the variance in postwar deficits
can be accounted for by presidential budget estimates made five to eight
months before the beginning of the fiscal year.[18] Yet the Reagan admin-

18. Indeed, presidential budgets seem to forecast little more than a continuation of
the trends of the moment rather than accurately anticipate future developments; over
two-thirds of the variance in presidential deficit estimates can be accounted for by
current-year deficits. Of course, this is due as much to the difficulty with which
economists predict turning points in the economy (from growth to recession or vice
versa) as to any political motivations on the part of the White House. In fact, presidents

istration's underestimates were particularly egregious. The White House 1983 deficit estimate was off by over $100 billion, by far the largest margin of error in the postwar period (see table 13-3). Furthermore, as can be seen by the much greater accuracy with which the CBO estimated the deficit at the same time, this error was not simply one of professional misjudgment.

There is additional evidence that the Reagan administration was hardly innocent of the consequences of the fiscal policies it was proposing. In May 1981, two months before the tax cut was enacted, Reagan's advisers discussed with the president a memorandum that showed that "the potential revenue loss from the tax bill was worsening the out-year deficit problem to a dangerous point."[19] Some members of Reagan's inner circle, including David Stockman, even contemplated accepting legislative defeat of the tax bill in the House. By the time the administration was using its full political muscle to push the 1981 tax cut through Congress, at least some Reagan advisers were saying to one another that the deficit would be as high as $60 billion in the next fiscal year. But to waver when victory was at hand seemed a foolish political course, whatever the long-range deficit consequences of the tax cut might be. And some advisers in the Treasury Department were drawing on supply-side theory to make the case that the government would be able to grow out of its deficits.

But if it remains uncertain whether the president himself was aware of the fiscal consequences of the 1981 tax cut at the time it was passed, it is quite clear that the administration did not modify its policies in subsequent years when large deficits were openly admitted in its own public statements. Although the administration underestimated the size of future deficits in its 1983 budget, even its own figures admitted deficits of a magnitude—$91 billion—unknown since World War II. And, working with the same information, the CBO predicted quite precisely the $195 billion deficit that eventually ensued (see table 13-3). By 1984 presidential and CBO estimates began to correspond, but accurate

---

predicted larger deficits (or smaller surpluses) than those that actually occurred seventeen times in the course of the thirty-eight-year postwar period.

19. Laurence I. Barrett, *Gambling with History* (Doubleday, 1983), pp. 166–67. Also see the analysis of these events in Paul J. Quirk, "The Economy: Economists, Electoral Politics, and Reagan Economics," in Michael Nelson, ed., *The Elections of 1984* (Washington, D.C.: CQ Press, 1985), pp. 155–87.

projections did little to cause the administration to change course on fiscal policy. In short, deficits were hardly a political accident.

Public Opinion

Politicians are criticized for deficit spending when the problem is partly rooted in the structure of public opinion. A majority of the public, even though approving the idea of a balanced budget, demands increases in spending for public services at the same time that it complains that taxes are excessively high. To explore the changing shape of public opinion, I examined available trend data on the public views toward balanced budgets, taxes, and spending over the past two decades.

Polling is an inexact science, to be sure, and no great weight should be placed on any given percentage presented in the accompanying figure and table. Much depends on the wording of the question, the particular context within which it was asked, and the polling techniques of specific organizations. Even slight adjustments in the ordering of a question in an interview or in its exact phrasing can sharply alter the apparent picture of public opinion. In interpreting the data one should thus concentrate on any changes that can be identified when similar, or preferably the same, questions are asked by the same polling firm over time.

At first glance it seems the public was as opposed to deficits in the 1980s as it was in earlier decades. Indeed, expressed concern about deficits increased in the period immediately before 1981. Table 13-4, for example, shows that throughout the 1970s the public was ostensibly becoming ever more committed to a balanced budget. Although the shifts were only moderate in size, the direction was toward more fiscal integrity. But it should be noted that a much higher percentage of those surveyed supported a balanced budget than supported cuts in social programs to achieve it. When the question was cast in terms of an amendment to the Constitution, the rhetorical support for a balanced budget was even greater. After 1981 the support for an amendment faltered somewhat, but this could well be because the amendment had now become a somewhat partisan issue. Even so, the public hardly wavered in its proclaimed commitment to the ideal of budget balancing.

But asking the public directly about budget balancing may not be the best way to ascertain the political context in which deficit decisions are made. Public opinion varies so much with the way in which the question

Table 13-4. *Support for a Balanced Budget, as Indicated by Polls, 1973–84*

Percent

Polling organization and date	Response	Polling organization and date	Response
General support for a balanced budget		*Support for a constitutional amendment requiring balanced budget*	
Gallup[a]			
February 1973	60	Gallup[e]	
March 1976	69	March 1976	78
		July 1978	81
NBC[b]		February 1979	78
February 1979	68	April 1981	65
March 1980	76	September 1981	67
Support for cutting social spending to balance budget		September 1982	75
CBS[c]		NBC[f]	
March 1976	43	November 1978	75
April 1976	44	December 1978	79
May 1976	40	February 1979	70
June 1976	42	May 1979	73
June 1978	51	May 1982	66
		August 1982	63
ABC[d]			
February 1982	45	Roper[g]	
March 1982	43	March 1979	80
January 1983	44	August 1980	79
January 1984	34		

Sources: Gallup Opinion Index, June 1976, p. 20; March 1979, p. 23; November 1981, p. 9; November 1982, p. 5; and data provided by Robert Shapiro, Department of Political Science, Columbia University, January 1985.

a. The question asked was "How important do you think it is to balance the federal budget—very important, fairly important, or not so important?" The response shown here was "very important."

b. The question asked was "Would you favor or oppose balancing the federal budget even if it meant the things you like about the federal government would have to be cut substantially?"

c. The question asked was "The federal government must have a more balanced budget even if that means spending less money on programs for such things as health and education" (agree or disagree).

d. The question asked was "Do you think the government should cut spending for social programs to reduce the budget deficit, or not?"

e. The questions asked were: "Would you favor or oppose a constitutional amendment that would require Congress to balance the federal budget each year—that is, keep taxes and expenditures in balance?" (March 1976, July 1978, and February 1979); "A proposed amendment to the Constitution would require Congress to approve a balanced Federal budget each year. Government spending would have to be limited to no more than expected revenues, unless a three-fifths majority of Congress voted to spend more than expected revenue. Would you favor or oppose this amendment to the Constitution?" (April and September 1981); "I favor a constitutional amendment to balance the federal budget" or "I oppose a constitutional amendment to balance the federal budget" (September 1982).

f. The question asked was "Would you favor or oppose a constitutional amendment which would require the Federal government to balance its budget?"

g. The question asked was if respondents would favor or oppose "an amendment to require a balanced national budget—to prevent the government from spending more money than it takes in, except in certain specified cases of crisis or emergency."

Figure 13-5. *Public Opinion on Federal Tax and Expenditure Policies,*
1955–84[a]

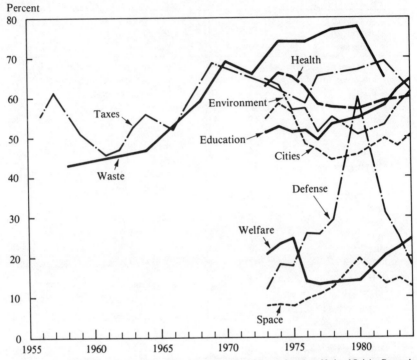

Sources: Tom W. Smith, *A Compendium of Trends on General Social Survey Questions,* National Opinion Research
Center, report 129 (NORC, 1980); survey data from the General Social Survey, NORC archives; and Kirk Brown, *Public*
Opinion on Government Spending, Taxes and the Budget Deficit, report 84.718 GOV (Congressional Research Service,
1984), p. 23.
    a. The opinions on taxes and waste indicate the percentage of respondents stating that they are "too high"; the
opinions on expenditure categories indicate the percentage of respondents stating that "too little" is being spent. Polls
were not conducted in each year for each category.

is phrased that one is tempted to conclude that opinion on this issue is
neither consistent nor entrenched. And even as the public was continuing
to insist on a balanced budget, it was also demanding a combination of
tax cuts and increased expenditures that could only have the opposite
result.

    The data presented in figure 13-5 lend support to this conclusion.
Between 1961 and 1982 the percentage who felt taxes were too high
increased from 46 to 69 percent, an unusual and significant shift in public
opinion on a major domestic issue.[20] Opinion on expenditure issues over

    20. Benjamin I. Page and Robert Y. Shapiro, "Effects of Public Opinion on Policy,"
paper prepared for the 1981 annual meeting of the American Political Science Association.

the same period of time is not available, but, as can be seen in the same figure, the trend since 1973 does not show a corresponding decrease in support for public expenditures. Although opinion varied from year to year, overall the public continued to think in the 1980s, as in the 1970s, that the government spent too little on the nation's health, education, and environment. The percentage that felt too little was being spent on national defense fluctuated widely over the period, but overall the trend was upward. Support for more money for space and for welfare was generally weak and fluctuating, but the level of support in the 1980s was still higher than it had been in the 1970s. Only with respect to aid to the cities did the public become slightly more stingy with the nation's purse and even here the changes were not great.[21]

In short, Americans increasingly came to believe that taxes should be cut, but not at the expense of national defense or broad public services. They think the savings should come from money that is "wasted," which a significantly larger percentage of Americans think is "a lot" than was the case in the early 1960s (see figure 13-5). To declare much government expenditure "a waste" is, of course, one way of rationalizing the call for lower taxes but more expenditure on specific programs. But one voter's waste may be another voter's vital public service. Unfortunately, political leaders, no matter what their ideological coloration, have not been able to find enough of what most people would agree is waste to bring budgets into balance.

Professional Opinion

If the structure of public opinion had changed, with voters more willing to demand simultaneously higher expenditures, lower taxes, and a balanced budget, opinion was not so well defined that political leaders were prevented from constructing a policy that was both fiscally responsible and politically acceptable. To understand how deficit financing on a grand scale became standard practice, one has to appreciate not only

21. It should be noted that the question asks if taxes are *currently* too high and expenditures *currently* too low. Thus it is significant that the percentage of those thinking the federal income tax is too high continues at a high level, even though tax rates were cut in 1981. Also, those calling for more defense in the 1980s do so even in the face of substantial increases in defense expenditures. The greater support for domestic expenditure in recent years may be due to increased dissatisfaction with recent and proposed reductions.

the evolution in public opinion but also the way in which professional economic opinion on deficits was changing.

THE KEYNESIANS. For two decades or more a consensus on deficit financing had existed and the system seemed to be in equilibrium. The government incurred mild deficits annually (higher in periods of recession), but these hardly constituted an immediate threat to the postwar financial system. In time political leaders came to accept these deficits as normal, and the righteous concern with budget balancing that characterized immediate postwar rhetoric gave way to vaguer commitments to a full-employment budget. The Democrats led the way, arguing as early as 1960 that a balanced budget need not be realized "in periods of recession." But even the Republicans, after having held the reins of power, declared in 1972 only their commitment to "the balance of the full employment budget."[22]

Republicans in fact had adapted to the reality of mild deficits well before 1972. As fiscally conservative as the Eisenhower administration is reputed to have been, even its economic advisers stated as early as January 1954 that "tax policy was continually reviewed by the Treasury, not only from the viewpoint of moving toward budgetary balance, but also in light of . . . the part that fiscal policy could play in contributing to economic growth and stability."[23] As Herbert Stein has observed, a "post war consensus on macroeconomic policy" had emerged.[24]

The name usually given to this consensus was Keynesianism, though in fact it was only loosely related to Keynes's own views. Among its key tenets were (1) political management of the economy was possible; (2) such management should be by means of indirect financial tools, rather than direct control of labor or capital through such devices as wage and price controls; and (3) monetary and fiscal policies were the key mechanisms by which the government could achieve short-term economic objectives.

Differences of opinion could be discerned between more liberal and more conservative Keynesians. Liberals were especially concerned about high rates of unemployment, opposed to high interest rates, and more willing to use fiscal—as distinct from monetary—policy to pursue broad economic objectives. Conservatives were more concerned about rising inflation rates, more acceptant of rising unemployment, and more

22. Johnson, *National Party Platforms*, pp. 598, 862.
23. *Economic Report of the President, January 1954*, p. 52.
24. Herbert Stein, *Presidential Economics* (Simon and Schuster, 1984), p. 75.

reluctant to use deficits as a means of providing an economic stimulus. But these differences were contained within a fundamental consensus that in retrospect can be seen to have shaped deficit politics. For one thing, the consensus placed upon the president and his advisers primary responsibility for the short-term performance of the economy. If the proper course for the postwar economy was the narrow channel between the Scyllian songs of inflation and the Charybdian rock of unemployment, then only the president could steer the ship of state on its perilous journey. With the good help of his mates in the Federal Reserve, Treasury, and the OMB, the captain needed to find the correct mix of interest rates, tax rates, and expenditure levels to maintain stability in potentially turbulent economic waters. With a certain amount of political jostling, Congress could be counted on to acquiesce in his overall judgment.

Presidents accepted with alacrity the assignment the postwar consensus gave to them. If the dustbin of history into which Herbert Hoover had been swept were not by itself sufficient incentive, presidents were also well aware that their day-to-day political influence, their monthly popularity ratings, and their success in off-year congressional elections, to say nothing of their own reelection prospects, depended heavily on economic trends (see chapter 3). It was better to believe that one could control these economic and political forces through carefully balanced policies than to regard oneself as utterly dependent upon the Goddess Fortuna.

And so it was that a delicious blend of economic consensus and political pragmatism produced decades of mild deficits that were regularly offset by inflationary trends and economic growth. It is true that in times of recession politicians were encouraged to incur deficits on the grounds that they would stimulate the economy. And the government did spend somewhat more—roughly 5 percent annually—than it collected in revenues between 1946 and 1980. For years, conservative Keynesians expressed concern that politicians would run ever-larger deficits to try to keep the economy growing at a faster rate. And in fact the federal budget ran an actual surplus in only eight of the thirty-eight postwar years. Yet the temptation to spend more was disciplined by the stern advice of even the more liberal Keynesians: big deficits will cause big inflation, which will require big jumps in interest rates, which will induce a big recession, which will mean a big defeat. In the end it was the perceived close connection between short-term fiscal policy and short-term economic trends that both induced mild deficits and kept them within a tolerable range.

The Reagan deficits of the 1980s cannot be understood apart from the breakdown of this economic consensus. To be sure, Ronald Reagan, who identifies himself with Franklin Roosevelt, is well aware that rapidly advancing deficits did nothing to harm Roosevelt's popularity—with either the public or the historians. In addition, Ronald Reagan is well aware that his program calling for decreased domestic expenditures is more likely to succeed in a world of budget deficits than one of budget surpluses.[25] And to be sure, Ronald Reagan wears a party label that has earned a reputation for fiscal integrity, thereby diffusing and confusing political opposition. Yet Reagan, like Roosevelt, needed an economic theory that would provide the intellectual basis for a dramatic departure from past political practice. No president, no matter how willful and committed, can retain the confidence of his advisers and allies, to say nothing of the public more generally, unless his policies are consistent with at least some minimally acceptable policy doctrine.

THE SUPPLY-SIDERS. Supply-side economists have received much of the credit (or, more often, the blame) for the new politics of deficits. A small band of economists led by Arthur Laffer of the University of Southern California have made the rather dubious claim that the United States could increase its revenues by cutting its taxes. While most economists called it the "laughter" curve, some political leaders—notably Jack Kemp and Ronald Reagan—seemed to give credence to the extraordinary suggestion that activity in the private sector could be so stimulated by reductions in marginal tax rates that the ensuing growth would actually produce increased tax revenues. This reasoning underpinned the figures contained in President Reagan's budget estimates in his first six months in office.

But if supply-siders were used to justify Reagan's initial budget figures, their actual influence remains a matter open to considerable dispute. It can be argued that they achieved key positions within the Treasury and persuaded Secretary Donald Regan, who became an increasingly influential adviser to the president (indeed the chief of staff in 1985), that revenue flows would be greater than those projected by critics on Capitol

25. In this regard, Reagan is, of course, little different from the Johnsonian enthusiasts who conceived new programs for spending the "fiscal dividend" that was eagerly anticipated in the mid-1960s. They, too, delighted in a budgetary climate that would facilitate their policy objectives.

Hill. Thus it is possible that the magnitude and growing size of the deficits caught the administration unaware. But it can also be argued that the Federal Reserve, the OMB, and the CEA all had more realistic assessments of the deficit picture, as apparently did James Baker, the president's chief of staff at the time. According to this view, the president and his top staff espoused a supply-side doctrine not because it was inherently persuasive, but because it was politically convenient. The president wanted to increase defense spending, cut taxes, and balance the budget. Only by accepting the supply-side argument could he propose a program that would appear to achieve all these objectives simultaneously.

The estimates of extraordinary revenue growth made by supply-side economists may have been influential in the first year of the Reagan administration. But by 1982 it was becoming increasingly apparent that the revenue growth predicted by the supply-siders was not to occur in the immediate future. For the administration to adhere to its budgetary course, it needed a much more substantial body of economic opinion than supply-siders could offer. Quite ironically, it found its answer in monetarism.

THE MONETARISTS. The most significant change in macroeconomic theory in recent decades has not been the formation of a small band of "supply-siders" whose dubious theories have remained on the edge of academic respectability. Instead, it has been the increasingly widespread acceptance of the doctrine that monetary policy—not fiscal policy—has the greatest short-term effect on the business cycle. This view was articulated by University of Chicago economist Milton Friedman, both holder of a Nobel laureate for fundamental research in economics and a newspaper commentator whose conservative views were especially persuasive to business and Republican party leaders. He emphasized the central—indeed, the almost exclusive—role of the Federal Reserve in determining swings in the business cycle. Initially treated with considerable skepticism, monetarist theory gained rapid ascendance in the 1970s and was accepted as the leading macroeconomic theory by many within the Reagan administration.

The core element in monetarist theory, as it relates to fiscal policy, is the proposition that prices, income, and economic stability are a function of growth in the money supply, not a function of the proportion of public expenditures paid for by borrowed funds. As long as the money supply grows at a constant rate commensurate with potential growth in GNP, economic activity will expand without placing upward pressure on prices and wages. In this monetarist world, fiscal policy has short-term macroeconomic consequences only when it is accommodated by monetary policy, that is, only when the cost of financing the public debt is eased by allowing the money supply to grow more rapidly than potential growth in GNP.

Most monetarists recognize long-term effects of fiscal policy on economic growth. For one thing, it is thought that deficits reduce the amount of capital available for private investment.[26] But, in the view of many monetarists, private investment would still be "crowded out" even if the deficits were eliminated by a tax increase as long as government expenditure remained the same. "Suppose that the $200 billion of borrowing [occurring in 1984] were replaced by $200 billion of additional taxes," Friedman has argued. "The extra tax payments would reduce the funds available to the public to spend and to lend. This too would crowd out private borrowers. . . . Our aggregate wealth, our 'permanent income,' is precisely the same [in either case]."[27] Given this perspective, the fiscal policy that holds the greatest promise for stimulating long-term growth is one that reduces public-sector spending. High expenditure levels—whether paid for either by taxes or by borrowing—reduce private incentives to work and invest. If deficits create a political climate in which expenditure cuts can be made more easily, it may be argued that they have a salutary, not a negative, effect on economic growth. Even Edward Gramlich, an economist with no known ties to the monetarist school, has argued that the "short-run impact of the deficits" is marginal, though the consequent "reduction in the national savings rate seems undesirable from a long-term perspective." But, he admits, "that perspective must be a very long term one indeed, from ten to twenty-five years."[28]

This does not mean that any major group of economists—Keynesians, monetarists, or supply-siders—advocates continued high deficit levels such as the United States is currently experiencing. On the contrary, most condemn continued high deficits as counterproductive and eventually dangerous. Deficit-prone policies have borne the unrelenting

26. Edward M. Gramlich, "How Bad Are the Large Deficits?" in Mills and Palmer, *Federal Budget Policy in the 1980s*, pp. 43–68.

27. Milton Friedman, "The Taxes Called Deficits," *Wall Street Journal*, April 26, 1984.

28. Gramlich, "How Bad Are the Large Deficits?" pp. 49, 64.

criticisms of such prominent economists as Martin Feldstein, former chairman of Reagan's Council of Economic Advisers, and Federal Reserve Chairman Paul Volker. But if politically influential economists are continuing to denounce deficits, their pronouncements no longer have the political bite they once had. To the extent that the business cycle is determined by monetary policy, as the monetarists say, to that extent politicians need not be concerned about the short-term (that is, the politically relevant) effects of their fiscal policies.

Some monetarists may be more concerned about negative long-term consequences of the deficit, but the presidents who listen to them have no strong incentives to share this concern. Negative effects that may take place a decade or more in the future mean little to a political leader whose influence depends on the current public mood and immediate economic prospects. Once monetarist doctrine moves the economic consequences of fiscal deficits to the long term, political leaders in the White House and on Capitol Hill are free to propose long-term reforms such as constitutional amendments instead of making hard decisions that involve major tax increases or spending cuts.

The political success of monetarism owes much to the inflation of the 1970s and to the 1979 decision of the Federal Reserve Board to use money targets as a means of bringing price increases under control. Even before 1979 the Keynesian consensus had eroded in the face of increasing unemployment levels, accelerating inflation, and slowing rates of growth in productivity. Some analysts attributed these developments to the formation of the oil cartel and the extraordinary upsurge in the price of commodities; others insisted they were due to increased government expenditures and new regulatory interventions in the economy; and still others claimed that they were caused by presidential mismanagement of the macroeconomy: Johnson's pursuit of both guns and butter during the Vietnam War; Nixon's price controls and over-stimulation of the economy in 1972; and the unwillingness of the Carter administration to tighten interest rates. But throughout these debates one set of economic analysts argued self-confidently that inflationary problems could be contained only by keeping growth of the money supply at a rate commensurate with potential growth in GNP.

When the Federal Reserve seemed to accept this argument in 1979 and when inflationary pressures began to subside shortly thereafter, monetarist theory gained the political ascendancy. The Reagan administration brought with it this new school of economic thought, which proved to have a more enduring influence than did the supply-siders who received so much publicity. Monetarists did not advocate deficits, as Keynes once had. On the other hand, neither did they identify any short-term negative consequences of deficit financing. Politicians were given a free hand to please the public in a manner unknown since the days of that master politician Franklin Roosevelt.

Conclusions

The aphorism that politicians benefit if they can spend now but pay later rings true. Yet there is little evidence that members of Congress are any more susceptible to this tendency than are members of the executive branch. Instead, Congress seems to defer to the president on fiscal policy. If the president finds a way of keeping expenditures and revenues roughly in balance, Congress does little to disturb the equilibrium. But if the president insists on major new expenditures or significant tax reductions, Congress is also willing to acquiesce, even if this may mean budget deficits. In short, on overall fiscal policy Congress is not so much responsible as deferential. It seems to have the mechanisms for keeping its own program within the framework set forth by the administration, but it does not have the resources to impose a discipline the executive itself has not achieved.

Presidents, no less than members of Congress, can benefit from postponing the costs of their programs. Roosevelt discovered that secret and founded a New Deal coalition that owed much to this political insight. His successors—whether Democrats or Republicans—continued to outspend revenues, but only to the moderate degree permitted by the Keynesian consensus. Yet the secret to the success of this consensus—modest inflation that reduced the real value of the nominal debt at roughly the same rate as annual deficits were adding to it—may also have been its undoing. The minuscule inflation rate of the Eisenhower years gave way to a moderate level during the Great Society years. And after the Vietnam War ended, inflation, rather than returning to prewar levels, continued to accelerate. Keynesian confidence that politicians could steer a middle course eroded, and a tough monetarist doctrine asserted itself instead.

Monetarism was a strict taskmaster. The Federal Reserve, by severely controlling the growth of the money supply, induced the longest and most severe postwar recession during 1979–83 in spite of the increase in deficits. Yet it succeeded—temporarily at least—at the one task it regarded as paramount: the reduction of inflationary pressures. Even though the United States economy is now launched on a recovery, it has yet to cause an upsurge in inflation despite massive deficit financing. But the Reserve's very success has had an ironic consequence no economist of the Keynesian era could have anticipated: it has provided presidents and acquiescent Congresses with a virtually unprecedented license to incur deficits. Although political leaders will denounce deficits, none want to give up their favorite policy objectives—defense, social security, domestic welfare, or tax cuts—to address a problem whose unfortunate consequences are now said to be long term.

At least, this will be the politics of deficits until the next major recession. The causes of such a recession will be as obscure and open to conflicting interpretations as any the United States has suffered in the past. But one fact will loom large: it will have occurred in the midst of a large, growing public debt. In a recession context the size of annual deficits will increase dramatically from a large number to an astounding one. Those in office will be blamed for letting this happen. The public will lose confidence in government, and the party in power will suffer a reverse. Whatever the reality, it will be widely believed that the cause of the economic and political turmoil is the growing public debt, and the era of deficit politics will come to an end.

INDEX

399